SOCIETY, MANNERS, AND POLITICS
IN THE UNITED STATES

JOHN WILLIAM WARD is an associate professor of history at Princeton University and also teaches there in the Program in American Civilization. He is the author of *Andrew Jackson: Symbol for an Age,* a study of the cultural ideals of early nineteenth-century America, and the author of numerous articles in *The American Scholar, The Virginia Quarterly Review, The Yale Review,* and other magazines. He is presently engaged in a study of the ideal of individualism in America.

Society, Manners, and Politics in the United States:

Letters on North America
BY
MICHAEL CHEVALIER

EDITED AND WITH AN INTRODUCTION BY
JOHN WILLIAM WARD

TRANSLATED AFTER
THE T. G. BRADFORD EDITION

GLOUCESTER, MASS.

PETER SMITH

1967

Copyright, 1961 by John William Ward
Reprinted, 1967 by Permission of
Doubleday and Company, Inc.

Editor's Introduction

Michael Chevalier was in the United States for two years, from the end of 1833 to the end of 1835. The occasion of his visit was a mission for the French government to inquire into the construction of canals and railroads, the need for which was being debated in France and the value of which Chevalier ardently supported. Although he fulfilled his mission by publishing in 1840 a history of the means of communication in the United States, Chevalier's purpose in coming to America was broader than the engineering fact. He wished to discover no less than the future of civilization itself.

Chevalier believed that the United States presented to Europe, and especially to France, the image of its own future. Civilization, he thought, had marched inevitably westward until it was stopped by the Atlantic Ocean. Then "Columbus showed it the way to a new world." In the new world, "new beliefs and new customs, new laws and new ways of life" were appearing as civilization sought new solutions for the perennial problems of the relation of man to man and man to society. If France was to meet the challenge of its own future, it must, thought Chevalier, study America to see how it might adapt its own traditions to the necessities of the future.

When Chevalier came to the United States in 1833, he was not quite twenty-eight years old. Later in life he was to achieve fame as the leading spokesman for the French free trade movement and to be co-author with the English leader of free trade, Richard Cobden, of the Anglo-French treaty of commerce in 1860. But in 1833 he was just emerging from his immersion in the cult of Saint-Simon in France.

Saint-Simonianism was one of the many *systèmes* which bobbed to the surface in the wake of the social destruction of the French Revolution and the Napoleonic wars. Intellectuals sought by verbal incantation to contain the incipient social chaos and to provide some new moral principle to fill the vacuum left by the shattered authority of the Christian Church. Saint-Simon's thought had many turnings but, broadly, it was an attempt to fuse the scientific positivism and belief in progress of the eighteenth-century enlightenment with the emotions and conservatism of the French religious tradition. Saint-Simon saw himself as the prophet of a new epoch in the history of civilization founded socially on the peaceful power of industry, supported emotionally by a mystical vision of fraternity—a new Christianity stripped of supernaturalism—and administered by an intellectual elite.

Chevalier had graduated with high distinction from the *École Polytechnique* and had entered on a promising career in the government as a mining engineer when his idealism and his belief in the potentiality of industrialism led him to the Saint-Simonians. In 1829, four years after Saint-Simon's death, Chevalier joined with others in the Saint-Simonian movement to revive *L'Organisateur* to propagandize the master's ideas. In 1830, when the *Globe* was founded as the official organ of the Saint-Simonians, Chevalier was put in charge as editor. The religious cult which was developing around the memory of Saint-Simon and his social and political ideas was already producing schisms in the movement, but Chevalier was still enough at its center to rebuke Auguste Comte publicly for rejecting "the name of the master." In 1832 the French government, uneasy over discussions about the institutions of marriage and private property, seized Saint-Simon's papers and arrested the leaders of the movement, among them Chevalier.

Although he argued that his politics were reformist and not revolutionary, Chevalier was sentenced to one year in prison. Before his year was up, he was pardoned and returned to a post in the Ministry of Public Works. By this time Chevalier had separated himself from the mystical side of the Saint-Simonian cult, although his formal and open break with the whole movement did not take place until 1838.

So in 1833 the intellectual attitude that Chevalier brought to his analysis of American society derived largely from the Saint-Simonian movement. His very purpose, to discern the shape of the future in the present of America, had its precedent in the master's career. As one of our French allies, Saint-Simon had fought at the Battle of Yorktown and in his later years imputed considerable significance to his participation in the American Revolution. "It was in America," wrote Saint-Simon long after the event, "it was while fighting for the cause of industrial liberty, that I first conceived the desire to see this plant of another world flower in my country . . . I realized that the revolution in America signaled the beginning of a new political era, that this revolution would necessarily bring about major progress in general civilization, and that in a short time it would cause great changes in the social order which then existed in Europe."

Saint-Simon's influence shows most clearly in Chevalier's description of the course of civilization. The progress of civilization is the result of the interaction of contrary and opposite qualities which, for Europe, Chevalier characterizes as Northern or Southern, Saxon or Latin. Progress is not a straight line development but an oscillating series of stages, each one superior to the former, each one solving its own characteristic problem. In Saint-Simonian language, Western civilization was passing through a critical period of transition to a new "organic" epoch. The new epoch would be characterized by the peaceful and philanthropic power of industrialism, which would solve the basic problem facing nineteenth-century civilization—the provision of the basic necessities of life for the mass of ordinary people. Chevalier paid such close attention to the United States because he thought that, whatever its other shortcomings, it had solved this basic problem and was, therefore, in the vanguard of the emerging, organic epoch of civilization.

The notion that history proceeds by the interaction of polar opposites also informs the particulars of Chevalier's analysis of American society. Just as the English and the French embody opposite but mutually needed qualities, in America the Yankee and the Virginian (Chapter X) stand for complementary types: the Virginian, the bold passionate leader of men; the Yankee, the practical, methodical controller of nature. So the chapters which follow are an account of John Smith's personal leadership in Virginia and a description of the careful industrial organization of the Lowell mills. Similarly, a superabundance of one quality demanded the emergence of its opposite; so Chevalier searched keenly for tendencies toward centralization in an age which seemed to be pushing separation and division to a logical extreme, for manifestations of authority in an age which spurned it, for evidences of aristocracy and hierarchy among a people who celebrated democracy and equality (see, in particular, Chapters XXX and XXXIII).

Now anyone who finds delight in ideas themselves—in this instance, the idea of civilization—may find sufficient pleasure in reading Chevalier today on this score alone. But Chevalier's participation in a stream of thought widely present in western Europe in the early nineteenth century had a considerable further advantage. It made him a superb student of the early years of the society in which we now live.

Since Chevalier came as a Frenchman to the United States in the 1830's, he inevitably invites comparison with his more famous countryman, Alexis de Tocqueville, whose shorter visit in 1831–32 resulted in the magistral analysis of democracy in America which is today so much better known than Chevalier's own account.[1] The most obvious comparison is in the matter of style. Where Tocqueville is generally philosophical and abstract, Chevalier is normally descriptive and concrete. For certain tastes the advantage will lie with Chevalier. The two authors often reach strikingly similar conclusions: for examples, the prophecy that Russia in the East and America in the West may well one day divide the world, the discovery of the tyranny of majority opinion in an equalitarian society, the fear that American emphasis on individual self-sufficiency may prove a threat to social stability, the recognition of the need for religion to provide order. One could easily extend the list. But the most striking comparison is a contrast. Chevalier saw what Tocqueville never saw, the basic importance of the communications and industrial revolutions in American society. As Chevalier put it, America's "most suitable emblem would be a locomotive engine or a steamboat." Long before most Americans, let alone foreign visitors such as Tocqueville, understood what was happening in their society, Chevalier clearly saw the transforming effect of the application of machine power to production and to movement through space.

Why Chevalier was alert to what others missed is obvious enough. He came to America fresh from Saint-Simon's "industrial doctrine," a vision of the good society founded on the machine, administered by an industrial elite, dedi-

[1] Tocqueville published the first volume of *Democracy in America* in 1835, the second in 1840. Chevalier had read the first volume by 1838 when he prepared the third edition of his own book (see "A Note on This Edition"), because in a note on the last page he recommends it to his readers. It was Tocqueville's habit, and one of his weaknesses, not to read other commentaries on American society while in the process of writing his own; we can be fairly sure he did not read Chevalier because he wrote his friend and fellow traveler in America, Gustave de Beaumont, in 1836 when the first edition of Chevalier's letters appeared that "I will not read Chevalier's work; you know that it's a principle with me."

cated to the good of the mass of mankind. Not only his general perspective but his particular purpose set the focus of his attention; he was sent by M. Thiers, the French Minister of the Interior, to report on the communications revolution in the United States. He was thus admirably equipped to discern what we, looking backward, see so easily, but what few in Jacksonian America could see at the time.

In 1815, Hezekiah Niles, the editor of *Niles' Weekly Register* in Washington, the single most important newspaper of early nineteenth-century America, remarked that the distinguishing feature of the American character was "the almost universal ambition to get forward." One of the chief moods of Jacksonian America was this entrepreneurial psychology, this high level of economic aspiration. But this almost universal ambition to get forward required auspicious social circumstances. Relatively speaking, the American economy up to 1815, the date of Niles' remark, was a static economy. America had not yet entered what today we have come to call the "take-off" period of economic growth. The relatively underdeveloped potentiality of the American economy in, say, 1815 did not provide the occasion to realize the ambition that Niles commented on; in other words, the economy sharply limited the ability of most men to realize their ambition, however powerful it may have been. But once the United States developed internal means of communication, growth and opportunity appeared where physical and economic obstacles had before stood in the way. After 1825 (the date of the completion of the Erie Canal), the boom in transportation and the incredibly rapid expansion of the economy gave substance and a tremendous impetus to American ambition. Chevalier's Chapter XXII, on "The Means of Communication," by far the longest chapter in his book, should also make us sensitive to the fact that the "take-off" period of American economic growth was made possible by social capital—that is, by governmental investment through the agencies of the states. We think so much of the nineteenth century as the heyday of laissez-faire that until only recently we have been blinded to the fact that in its early stages of growth the American economy was clearly a mixed economy in which the government willingly and enthusiastically played a major role.

Chevalier saw clearly, and is one of our best early reporters on the fact, that the building of canals and railroads in the early nineteenth century promoted "a real, positive, and practical liberty" by providing economic opportunity and a material basis for American equalitarian ideals. He also foresaw that national consolidation would be the logical consequence of improved communications. All political compromise between the sections he dismissed as secondary to the nationalizing, consolidating power of the machine. While American historians down into the twentieth century continued to name the frontier experience, the constant westering into a virgin continent, as the unique and identifying element in our national experience, Chevalier saw from the beginning that America, despite its outward thrust, was becoming increasingly a more closely knit, interdependent society, effectively smaller than France, because of the speed of communication among its parts. Hardly a spokesman of the time, native or foreign, saw so clearly the double thrust—the industrial consolidation as well as the physical expansion—of Jacksonian America.

Chevalier is such a splendid contemporary witness of the transforming effect of the industrial and communications revolution on American society that he deserves to be rescued from obscurity for this reason alone. But he has still more to offer. His next most important contribution to an understanding of American society is his clear discussion of the nature of liberty in the United States. His passages on the power of majority opinion are helpful to our comprehension of the phenomenon upon which Tocqueville spent so many pages because Chevalier links it more carefully to social conditions. On one side—the extreme political liberty of Americans—Chevalier points to the fact that such liberty presupposes a wide and tacit consensus on manners and morals in the society. Much as a contemporary sociologist might, he suggests that democratic liberty is the result of a certain type of character as well as its cause. On the other side—the tyranny of majority opinion—Chevalier observes that it is simply the obverse of the conditions of political liberty. Order must be present somewhere in society and in the United States it was present in the calm assumption that an industrious and moral life comprised the whole of the good life. "Hemmed in," writes Chevalier, "by the laborious habits of the community, by political notions, and by religion, a man must either resign himself to the same mode of life with the mass, or seek a soil less unfriendly to his tastes in the great cities of New York, Philadelphia, or New Orleans, or even in Europe." That remark looks ahead to our own social and intellectual life.

Chevalier also has some marvelous pages on the symbolic role that politics played in young America. Where today stage and screen celebrities are used so that entertainment becomes a form of politics, in those days politics was a form of entertainment. The torchlight parades, the banners, the giant hickory poles—all provided the occasion for the expression, the dramatic acting out, of personal identification with a mass democratic society. But these introductory remarks are meant only to suggest some of the reasons why Chevalier is worth rescuing from the obscurity of the scholar's long list of foreign travelers' accounts of the United States. Here is his book. For one who believed that the basic problem of an industrial society is to serve the needs of the whole society, and not just the few, there is a particular pleasure in presenting Chevalier to as wide an audience as possible in the format of a Doubleday Anchor edition.

John William Ward
Princeton University

FOR FURTHER READING

The most convenient and one of the best studies of Saint-Simon's thought is Frank E. Manuel, *The New World of Henri Saint-Simon* (Harvard University Press, 1956). F. M. H. Markham has provided a selection of Saint-Simon's writings and a succinct introduction to his thought in *Henri Comte de Saint-Simon (1760–1825): Selected Writings* (The Macmillan Company, 1952). The principal sources on Chevalier himself are in French. Arthur L. Dunham, *The Anglo-French Treaty of Commerce of 1860 and the Progress of the Industrial Revolution in France* (University of Michigan Press, 1930), has a good deal on Chevalier's later career and includes a short biographical account. The best general study of the communications revolution in Jacksonian America is George Taylor, *The Transportation Revolution, 1815–1860* (Holt, Rinehart, & Winston, Inc., 1951).

A Note on This Edition

Michael Chevalier was in the United States from 1833 to 1835. While traveling here he sent home letters to the *Journal des Débats,* for which he had formerly been a staff writer. These, with additional letters, were put into book form by the Paris publisher, C. Gosselin, in 1836 to make the first edition of *Lettres sur l'Amerique du Nord.* In 1837, Gosselin brought out a much expanded "special" edition which provided the text for the most generally known and most available edition, the third, of 1838. In a prefatory note to the third edition, Chevalier says that the letters published in the *Journal des Débats* comprise only about one third of the text.

In 1839, Weeks, Jordan and Company of Boston provided the first and only English translation of Chevalier's *Lettres* under the title, *Society, Manners and Politics in the United States; Being A Series of Letters on North America.* This edition was translated from the third Paris edition by T. G. Bradford.

The present edition keeps the title of the first American edition and follows Bradford's translation in the desire to keep some of the flavor of the period with which the book deals. But Bradford's translation was obviously done in haste to satisfy an American public always curious about what Europe thought of it. Bradford used punctuation with an abandon that is not only offensive to the modern eye but resulted often in a perversion of Chevalier's sense. He was often simply wrong in his translation and he left out words, phrases, paragraphs, whole pages, and—in one instance—a

A NOTE ON THIS EDITION

whole chapter, the one on Captain John Smith, which is important to the structure of Chevalier's book. So, although this edition is "after" Bradford's, it contains nearly five thousand corrections of Bradford's translation as well as supplying what Bradford omitted. Chevalier, in the third Paris edition, provided many footnotes for his French readers which it seems unnecessary to print for American readers today. So, except for the notes, this Doubleday Anchor edition is the first complete edition of Chevalier's *Lettres* in English.

Contents

	Editor's Introduction	v
	A Note on This Edition	xv
	Introduction	1
I.	The Railroad from London to Paris	11
II.	Liverpool and Its Railroad	21
III.	War of the President of the United States upon the Bank	30
IV.	Democracy and the Bank	38
V.	Movement of Parties and the Bank Question	47
VI.	Progress of the Struggle—New Powers	60
VII.	Railroads in America	71
VIII.	The Banks—The Preservation of the Union	77
IX.	The First People in the World	90
X.	The Yankee and the Virginian	99
XI.	Captain John Smith	114
XII.	Lowell	126
XIII.	The Factory Girls of Lowell	134
XIV.	The Bank and Slavery	144
XV.	The Elections	156
XVI.	Pittsburg	164
XVII.	General Jackson	172
XVIII.	Public Opinion	180

CONTENTS

XIX.	Cincinnati	186
XX.	Cincinnati	194
XXI.	Western Steamboats	203
XXII.	The Means of Communication	219
XXIII.	Labor	261
XXIV.	Money	278
XXV.	Speculations	295
XXVI.	Bedford Springs	304
XXVII.	Authority and Liberty	313
XXVIII.	Social Improvement	329
XXIX.	Social Reform	348
XXX.	The Empire State	357
XXXI.	Symptoms of Revolution	371
XXXII.	The Middle Classes	380
XXXIII.	Aristocracy	389
XXXIV.	Democracy	405

SOCIETY, MANNERS, AND POLITICS
IN THE UNITED STATES

Introduction

Course of Our Civilization Over the World — Oriental Civilization, European Civilization — Their Approaching Contact — The Arabians Stand Between Them — Movement of European Civilization Toward the East — Two Routes to the East — The Three European Types — Latin Europe, Teutonic Europe, Slavic Europe — Mixed Character of France and Austria — The Part to be Played by France — What France Should Borrow from the Example of the Anglo-Saxon Race in the Old and New Worlds

That form of civilization which has prevailed among the peoples of Europe has moved in its march over the globe from east to west. From its cradles in old Asia and upper Egypt, it advanced, by successive stages, to the shores of the Atlantic, along which it spread itself from the southern extremity of Spain to the northern point of the British Isles and the Scandinavian peninsula. It seemed to have reached its goal when Christopher Columbus showed it the way to a new world.

At each stage civilization has adopted new beliefs and new customs, new laws and new ways of life, a new language, new dress, new diet, a new mode of life, both public and private. Each time, the great questions touching the relation of man to God, to his fellows, and to the universe, and of domestic, social, and political order, which had all been solved at the beginning of a halt, were after a time all brought again under discussion, and then civilization starting again on her march has moved onward toward the West to give them a new solution.

This stream, setting from east to west, is formed by the junction of two others flowing from the great Biblical races of Japhet and Shem which, coming from the North and the South, meet and mingle together and are replenished from their respective sources during each period of our civilization, through all the episodes which obstruct and checker this majestic pilgrimage. By turns each of these forces, one from the North, one from the South, whose combined action constitutes the motive power that carries mankind forward, has been overborne by the other. Thence it is that our civilization, instead of advancing in a straight line from east to west, has swerved in its march, from north to south, or south to north, taking a winding course, and gathering up at each turn purer drops from the blood of Shem or Japhet. There has been, however, this difference between the North and the South; the South has most often acted on the North by sending it the germs of civilization, without overrunning it with a new race, while the North has awakened the slumbering civilization of the South by pouring into its enervated population swarms of hardy barbarians, *audax Japeti genus*. Thus is fulfilled the great prophecy concerning Japhet, "and he shall dwell in the tents of Shem."

Independent of our civilization, there is another in the farthest East, whose center is China and whose outposts are Japan and which embraces its hundreds of millions of people. It moves in a direction contrary to our own, from west to east, and its locomotive powers are slight. We might compare the respective speeds of these two civilizations to the two great revolutions of the globe, the annual revolution in its total orbit and that which produces the seasons of the year. This Oriental civilization, like that of the West, has repeatedly regenerated itself at different epochs by a new mixture of the man of the North with the man of the South. The race of Japhet, which gave us our barbarians, and before the barbarians had given us the Pelasgians, Scythians, Celts, and Thracians, and has since given us the Turks and the Slavs, has furnished the East with its Mongols and Manchoos. The family of Genghis Khan, which conquered the East, also pushed its victorious hordes to the edge of the Rhine.

Oriental civilization, less active and less easily set in motion than Western civilization, probably because it does not have enough of the blood of Shem and has too much of that of the inferior races, has not raised itself to the same degree of improvement as its sister. But we must do it the justice to confess that to it belongs the honor of many capital inventions, such as the compass, printing, and gunpowder, on which we pride ourselves. We must, moreover, recognize that it has solved the problem of keeping under one law, for an indefinite number of ages, a population greater than that of all Europe. The Roman Empire, with a population less than that of China, stood whole only three hundred years. The spiritual authority of the Pope extended over less territory than that of the Roman Empire and was absolutely acknowledged only from Charlemagne to Luther.

The two civilizations, Western and Eastern, gathered together at the two extremities of the old continent and turning their backs on each other, were separated by an immense space before the West had fixed itself in America. Now, more than half the distance between them is passed; Mexico and South America are covered with the offshoots of Western civilization, on the side which looks toward Asia as well as that which fronts us; the United States cannot long wait before they too extend themselves from sea to sea; the Islands of the South Sea are beginning to be peopled by Europeans.

From this point of view, it is clear that America, placed between two civilizations, is called to high destinies and that the progress made by the people of the New World is a matter of deepest interest to the whole human race.

The connection of two civilizations, Eastern and Western, is certainly the largest subject that can occupy the human mind; it is, in the eyes of a friend of man, an event most big with hope. It embraces:

INTRODUCTION

Politically, the association of all peoples, the balance of the world, of which the balance of Europe is only a part;

Religiously, the law of the entire human family, the true *catholicism;*

Morally, the most harmonious balance of the two opposite natures which divide each race, each sex, each people, each family, and which are typified in the Bible by Cain and Abel;

Intellectually, the complete sum of knowledge and the universal language;

Industrially, a definite plan for developing the resources of the whole globe.

In our time, this question is no longer merely speculative. Now it is something more than merely food for the dreams of philosophers; it should be the subject of the meditations of statesmen.

Since the age of Louis XIV, the merchants, who are the pioneers of state policy, have striven with a constantly increasing ardor to open relations with China, because they have felt the importance of a regular system of exchange between Europe and a mass of two hundred millions of producers and consumers. The emancipation of North America and, quite lately, the abolition of the English East India Company's monopoly have given to the efforts of commerce an irresistible force. Before this power, the laws which close up the celestial empire are nothing. China is encircled, on the south by the English in India or by their tributaries; on the north by the Cossacks, the vanguard of Russia; British and American fleets prowl along her coasts; the sleepy Spaniards of Mexico and the Philippines think of the days of the galleons and keep their half-opened eyes fixed upon her. The human race has just come into possession of new means of communication which shorten distance in an unhoped-for degree. The two civilizations will soon reach each other and mingle together. It will be the greatest event in the history of man.

Before the art of navigation was brought to perfection,

before Christopher Columbus and Vasco da Gama, Europe, apart from the caravans which traversed central Asia, had had communications with China through the medium of the Arabs. Conquerors and missionaries, the Arabs, poised between two civilizations, had spread themselves by turns toward the East and the West. That people, so active by starts, has been to the East the messenger of the West, and to the West the courier and factor of the East. Unhappily, since Western civilization has begun to shine with the greatest brilliance in our Europe, Arabia has flung out but feeble gleams of light; since Providence has filled us with a devouring activity, the Arabians are fallen into a deep lethargy; on that side, therefore, the intercourse which was never complete or speedy has almost ceased. But if, as some suppose, the Arab race is about to rouse itself from its long stupor, at the voice and by the aid of Europe, then Europe will have a powerful ally in its efforts to seize and hold Asia, or to transmit to her the means of working out her own advance; and this illustrious race will thus contribute powerfully to the marriage of the two civilizations.

Our civilization, in its march westward, has sometimes turned back toward the East. Thus it has had its Argonauts, its Agamemnons, and its Alexanders, and, more lately, its heroes of the Crusades and its Portuguese captains. These subordinate movements were but temporary interruptions of its solemn march toward the West; they were merely counter-currents, resembling the eddies which always exist in the currents of rivers. Until our own time, Europe has founded no durable and important establishment in Asia; in proportion as our civilization advanced westward, the countries which it left behind escaped from its influence and the distance between it and Oriental civilization became greater. Alexander is the only person of whom China could feel any fear, and he passed away like the lightning flash. The Parthians, the Saracens, or the Turks were the impregnable bulwarks of the Orient. The mission of Europe was, above all, to reach and settle the new hemisphere.

INTRODUCTION

At present, the incontestable superiority of the Western nations in wealth, in mechanical skill, in means of transportation, in the arts of government and war, enables them to make their way across the Old World toward the remotest recesses of Asia. The nations we are accustomed to call Oriental, but who are only inhabitants of the Near East (*Petit Orient*), have ceased to be formidable adversaries to Europe. They delivered up their swords at Heliopolis, Navarino, and Adrianople. The colonization of America is now finally completed from Hudson's Bay to Cape Horn. Europe can and ought to move toward the East as well as toward the West. The isthmus of Suez has as good a chance as the isthmus of Panama to become the route of Western civilization in its expeditions toward the Far East (*Grand Orient*).

Our European civilization has a twofold source, the Roman people and the Germanic tribes. Setting aside for a moment Russia, who is a newcomer, and who already, however, equals the most powerful of the elder states, our civilization is subdivided into two families, each of which is marked by its strong likeness to one of the two mother nations which have given birth to both. Thus there is Latin Europe and Teutonic Europe; the former comprises the South, the latter the people of the North and of England. The former is Catholic, the latter, Protestant. One speaks the Teutonic languages; the other, idioms in which Latin is predominant.

These two branches, Latin and German, reappear in the New World. South America, like southern Europe, is Catholic and Latin. North America belongs to the Protestant and Anglo-Saxon population.

In the great enterprise of bringing together European and Asiatic civilization, the Teutonic and Latin nations may both find a field of action. Both occupy in Europe and in America, by land and sea, admirable outposts and excellent positions around that imperturbable Asia into which it is their object to force their way. But during the last age, the superiority which formerly belonged to the Latin family has passed into the hands of the Teutonic race, owing partly to the energy of England in the Old World and her sons in the New, and partly to the loosening of the old religious and moral ties among the Latin nations. The Slavic race, which has lately shown itself and which now forms a third group of nations in Europe, seems ready to contest with the Latin race even the possession of the second rank. Today it is only the Russians and the Anglo-Saxons who concern themselves about distant Asia and press upon its frontiers by land and sea.

The people of Latin stock must not, however, stand idle in the coming struggle, or the case will go against them by default. An admirable opportunity offers them the chance to regain their lost rank.

In our three-headed Europe, Teutonic, Latin, and Slavic, two nations, France and Austria, present themselves under less distinct features and with less exclusive characters than the others. France shares in the Teutonic and Latin natures; in religion she is Catholic in feeling, but Protestant out of caprice; she unites the nervous understanding of the Germans with the elegant taste of the southern nations. Austria, by the education and the origin of the people of her different states, is half Slav, half Teutonic, and she is connected with the Latin family by her religion.

France and Austria are, then, natural intermediaries, one between the Germans and the Latins, the other between the Germans and the Slavs. Also, for a very long time, Austria has, and still continues, the pretense of tracing its connection to several members of the Latin family. It is because of this tendency toward the South that she has retained to this day the royal house of Lombardy and Venice. Yet certainly, Austria is mainly German; just as France, by the sum of her distinctive traits, is essentially Latin.

From this mixed character of France and Austria, we may conclude that whenever the balance of Europe, or the harmonious combination of all European nations in one common object, shall become subjects of discussion, both will exercise a decisive influence and their hearty co-operation in a common cause will make them irresistible. Austria has a more central position than France. She has a greater number of points of contact with the different types of Western civilization, but France combines the invaluable advantages of a more homogeneous constitution and a more flexible temperament; she has a racial character more strongly marked, a mission more clearly defined, and, above all, she has more of the social spirit. She is at the head of the Latin group; she is its protectress.

In the events which seem about to dawn upon us, France may, then, take a most important part. France is the depository of the destinies of all the Latin nations of both continents. She alone can save the whole family from being overwhelmed by a double flood of Germans or Saxons and Slavs. It belongs to her to rouse them from the lethargy into which they are plunged on both continents, to raise them to the level of other nations, to enable them again to take a stand in the world. She is called, perhaps more than any other power, to encourage the new spirit which seems to be re-animating the Arabs and through them to shake the East.

Thus the political theater, seen from a French point of view, shows, in a distant background, the meeting of the Oriental and Western civilizations in which we are called upon to act as mediators, and in the foreground the education by France of all the Latin nations and of many of the Arab tribes living around the Mediterranean.

There may be a difference of opinion as to the time when these revolutions which are to agitate the depths of Asia will take place. I am one of those who think it not far off. I can easily conceive, also, that some persons should wish to lessen the circle of French influence and confine it to the southern countries of Europe; although to me France seems called upon to exercise a benevolent and wholesome care over the people of South America, who are not yet fit to

INTRODUCTION

take care of themselves; and although the old traditions of the Crusades, the conquest of Algiers, and the recollection of the expedition into Egypt seem to promise us one of the first parts in the drama which will be acted on the eastern shores of the Mediterranean.

As for the European nations of the Latin family, no one, I suppose, can have any doubts concerning our supremacy over them, or concerning our duties both to them and to ourselves in relation to them. We have been notoriously the head of the family since the time of Louis XIV, and we can shrink neither from the burdens nor the privileges of our situation. Our superiority is acknowledged by all its members, our protection has been accepted by all whenever it has been offered without selfish views. Happy would it have been for France if, content with this high prerogative, her princes, and above all he who has added new luster to the name of Emperor, had not been obstinately bent on the unnatural purpose of extending their authority over the members of the Teutonic family!

Since the weight has been thrown into the Saxon scale, since the English race has overborne France and Spain in Asia, in America, and in Europe—new institutions, new rules of government, new ideas, new modes of action in social, political, and individual life have sprung up among the English and more especially among their descendants in the New World. Everything connected with labor and the condition of the greater number of working men has been carried to a degree of perfection before unheard of. It seems as if, by the aid of these improvements, the superiority of the Anglo-Saxons over the Latins must go on constantly increasing.

We French, we are of all the Latin nations most favorably placed, we are the only ones well placed, to avail ourselves of these improvements by adapting them to the exigencies of our nature. We are full of energy; never has our mind been more fairly thrown open; never were our hearts more ready to throb for noble enterprises.

INTRODUCTION

But we must set ourselves at work without delay. We must do this, setting aside all considerations of universal policy and of the contact, whether more or less remote, of the two civilizations. It is a matter of the last necessity in regard to ourselves, even supposing that we have not to transmit to the southern nations of Europe, of whom we are the eldest, and to the inhabitants of the eastern Mediterranean, those improvements which their situation demands and which they are ready to receive at our hands. Our own welfare, our own existence, is at stake.

How and under what form shall we be able to make the innovations of the English race our own? This difficult and complicated question has been the chief object of my attention during my sojourn in the New World. I do not claim the honor of having even partially solved it. But I shall feel satisfied if the thoughts suggested by the sight of an order of things so unlike our own, falling under the eyes of one wiser and more far-sighted than I, shall put him in the way of its solution.

I

The Railroad from London to Paris

Analogy Between Certain Political and Electrical Phenomena — France and England — In What We Should Imitate the English — Railroads — Object of a Journey in England — The Feudal Castle of Heidelberg and a London Brewery

London, November 1, 1833.
While railroads are talked of at Paris, they are made in London. The road from London to Birmingham is already begun; it will be 112 miles in length, and all the stock, to the amount of $12,000,000, has been taken up by subscription. This road will be continued by another of nearly the same length, from Birmingham to Liverpool. In five years, Liverpool and London will be only eight hours apart. While English capitalists are executing these great undertakings, Parisian capitalists look on, but do not stir. They do not even form projects. Not one of them seems to have seriously considered that even in the present state of things there is more than twice the number of travelers between Paris and Versailles than between Liverpool and Manchester, today, in 1833, when the Liverpool-London railroad has been operating three years. In London, therefore, they count little upon the aid of French capitalists in the construction of a railroad from London to Paris. They desire it; they would be glad to be able to go from one capital to the other in fifteen hours and at trifling expense; all classes are delighted with the idea of such a thing. But they feel that such a work is neither expedient nor feasible without the joint action of both nations, and as they dare

not hope for the co-operation of France, little is said about it as a serious affair.

Among all the acquisitions which, since the end of the last century, have enriched the domain of science, none has opened a wider field than Volta's discoveries relative to the motion of electricity and its development by contact. The phenomena resulting from the two poles of the Voltaic battery offer an inexhaustible mine to the physical philosopher. There is no fact in science more general in its nature, for if any two bodies whatsoever touch each other they form at once, by their mutual action and reaction, a Voltaic pile of greater or less energy. The consequences of this inspired work of genius are incalculable, especially after the brilliant discoveries of Davy, the admirable work of Ampère, and the ingenious experiments of Becquerel. This physical, material fact has its counterpart in the moral order of things. If you bring together two men who have hitherto been separated from each other, in however slight a degree they may have any striking quality, their friction will inevitably produce a spark. If instead of two men, the two poles of your battery are two nations, the result is greater in the proportion of a nation to an individual. If these two nations are England and France, that is to say the two most powerful and most enlightened peoples in the world, this sort of Voltaic phenomenon then acquires a prodigious intensity. It involves nothing less than the safety of an old civilization or the creation of a new civilization.

The predominant qualities, good and bad, of France and England may be arranged in a series of parallels, the corresponding terms in each of which will complement one another. England is pre-eminent in affairs and the qualities which go with them, coolness, economy, precision, method, perseverance. To France's lot have fallen the taste and genius for the fine arts, with the ardor, the enthusiasm, the prodigious waste at least in time and words, the caprice and the irregular habits which characterize the artist. On one side is reason, cautious and sober, but sure-footed, and good sense, creeping along the ground; on the other, imagination with her brilliant audacity, but also with her ignorance of things and method, her starts and stops. Here, an admirable energy in struggling against nature and metamorphosing the physical features of the globe; there, an unequaled intellectual activity and the gift of warming the heart of mankind with its fires. In England, the treasures of industry and heaps of gold; in France, treasures of thought, wells of science, torrents of inspiration. In proud Albion, staid, but cheerless, manners, reserve pushed to a chilling excess; in our fair France, easiness of manners carried to licentiousness, the old Gallic gaiety often savoring somewhat of the camp, a free and easy air bordering on the promiscuous. On both sides a large dose of pride. Among our neighbors, a calculating, ambitious pride, the pride of the statesman and the merchant, which feeds only on power and wealth; which desires conquests for the country, vast colonies, all the Gibraltars and St. Helenas, eagles' nests by which all seas and shores may be commanded; a pride for one's self which pants for riches, an aristocratic park, a seat in the House of Lords, a tomb in Westminster Abbey. Among us, a pride vainglorious but not material, a pride which savors the joys of the ideal, applause for one's self, glory for the country; a pride which, for France, would be satisfied with the admiration of the world; for oneself, with castles in Spain, a riband, an epaulet, a line of Béranger as a funeral oration; the pride of the actor on the stage, of the knight in the lists. On the north of the Channel, people who combine religion and positivism; on the south, a race at once skeptical and enthusiastic. There, a deep sentiment of order and respect for rank, combined with a haughty feeling of the dignity of man; here, a people passionate for equality, excitable, restless, turbulent, yet docile to the point of weakness, confiding to the point of credulity, easily cajoled by flatterers, letting itself during periods of lethargy be trampled under foot like a carcass and at times given over to the obsequiousness of the courtesan. Among the English, a reverence for tradition; among the French, a passion for novelty. Among them a respect for law and obedience to man on the condition that his supreme rule shall be lawful; among us, the worship of great men and submission to the laws, provided they are defended by the sword of Caesar. On one side, the ruler of the seas, on the other, the arbiter of the continent; both rousing the world at its pleasure, one by its lever of gold, the other by the sound of its voice alone. Surely from the reciprocal influence of two nations thus constituted and thus situated in the world, there will come the most important results for the general cause of civilization as well as for their mutual improvement.

Industrial development is not, indeed, all of human development, but since the beginning of the nineteenth century no people can count itself in the first rank of nations if it is not advanced in the course of industrialism, if it cannot labor and produce. No people will be powerful that is not rich, and there is no other way of growing rich but by work. In regard to production and labor, we have much to learn from England, and it is a lesson better learned by the eyes than by the ears, by observation rather than reading. If, then, there were a railroad between London and Paris, the French, who now have little knowledge of business, would in order to learn go to London, where the instinct of management is in the blood. Our entrepreneurs would go to see how simply, promptly, and plainly great enterprises are carried on; our shopkeepers and buyers have to learn from England that to overcharge and to haggle have no connection with buying or selling advantageously; our capitalists and merchants, that there can be no durable commercial prosperity nor security for capital where there is no sound system of credit; they would see the operations of the Bank of England with its branches and the private banks, and perhaps they might be incited to bring home with the needful modifications institutions and practices so profitable at once to the shareholders and to the public.

THE RAILROAD FROM LONDON TO PARIS

They would imbibe the spirit of association which, in London, is breathed in at every pore. All of us might here see what comfort consists of and how it is realized, that care of the person so essential to the peace and quiet of life; and perhaps then Paris might free itself from the filth of centuries which of old gave it its name and against which Voltaire, he whom the ancient monarchy and the faith of our fathers could not withstand, warred in vain. As we are a people full of self-love, we should return from England fully ashamed of the state of our agriculture, our roads, and our elementary schools, humbled at the insignificance of our foreign commerce, and eager to vie with our neighbors. I need not stop to point out what the English might come to seek among us: they are already converts in this matter; they swarm in Paris while it would be easy to count up the number of Frenchmen who have been in London. Without saying what the English would get in Paris, I can say that they would leave plenty of sovereigns there. To Paris, the city of pleasures, the terrestrial paradise of strangers, the railroad would be a gold mine. And the English, getting familiar with France, would find profitable investments for their capital among us which would give life to essential enterprises.

The railroad from London to Paris would be a commercial enterprise of the first importance; it would also be a political instrument, a strong bond of union between England and France. But it is more especially as a means of education that it should be most highly recommended, for there is no fear that the commercial and political considerations will be overlooked. Industry, as I said before, is learned chiefly through the eyes. This is particularly true for the workers, for in them, owing to their way of life, the world of sensation prevails over the world of ideas. Now, the advance of industry depends no less on the progress of the workers than on the foremen and superintendents of the works. It would be expedient, therefore, to send a certain number of picked workers to pass some time in England, just as now the Board of Public Works is in the habit of sending a few engineers there. The railroad, by considerably reducing the expense and trouble of the journey, would probably furnish an opportunity of sending, from France to England, groups of those workers who have been selected as worthy of the favor. According to the plan of a merchant of Lyons, a very sensible man, this might be done on a large scale and at little expense. In his project, which is at least ingenious, these travelers could be given compensation as, say, students in adult education, perhaps by the Chamber of Commerce or a Board of Arbitration in the industrial regions, or by municipal councils or general councils in the agricultural regions; also, the Minister of War could assign to such duty those soldiers who had good conduct records or who had shown special industrial skill; those sent could then be gathered together under the name of the Army of Public Works. He further proposed a system of reciprocity by which English workmen should be employed in France and French workmen in England. It is not impossible that this project may one day be made the basis of a new law, designed to further the aims of our excellent law of primary education. But first the railroad between London and Paris must be constructed.

Of the small number of Frenchmen who have visited England, very few have been led by motives of business. Most have undertaken the voyage from vague feelings of curiosity or merely for pleasure. The objects of their notice have been the picturesque, the poetical. They have visited the Gothic ruins of the monasteries and castles, the cave of Fingal, and the lakes of Scotland, admired the costume of the Highlanders, the horses and the jockeys of the great lords, and the blooming complexion of the women. They have walked through one or two parks, visited the hothouses where all the plants of the world are collected, braving, behind glass, the cloudy sky of Great Britain. They have been through the military arsenals, when they could get permission, under the escort of a sergeant; they have seen the young beauties at the balls and the old curiosities of the Tower of London. They have traveled over England, just as they would make the tour of Italy or Switzerland. If the subject of industry has occupied their attention a moment, it is as if it were some minor adornment to the whole pageant. They have, to be sure, stood amazed at the thousands of vessels whose masts stretch out of sight along the Thames or in the docks (it is estimated that twenty-five thousand vessels enter the port of London each year). They have been delighted with the immensity of the manufacturing cities, the size of the factories and the height of their chimneys, with the magic brilliance of the gaslights, with the daring bridges of stone and iron, and with the fantastical appearance of the forge-fires in the night. But they have never asked, how came England to have such a vast number of ships, how has she multiplied and extended her manufactures to such an amazing degree, and how created these towns, so simple in their architecture but so fastidiously neat in their spacious streets? They have not thought to ask the causes of all this wealth and prosperity.

In England, the monuments and the picturesque are only the accessories; those who seek that should not ask it of England. If you seek the picturesque, go to Switzerland; if you have a passion for antique buildings, look in Italy; along the banks of the Rhine, stroll among the churches of Holland and Belgium; if you are not afraid of the loathsome pests and insects which have been in Egypt since the cholera in Mosaic times, cross the Mediterranean, travel the Nile, the Orient, Greece; you shall climb the Pyramids, sit in the Parthenon at the foot of the columns where Miltiades and Pericles held forth; you shall gather up a bit of the earth where the Scipians walked and where the blood of Caesar ran. If you are seduced by monumental cities, stay on the continent and survey the capitals of Germany which their kings embellished in competition with one another. If you like museums, if you adore painting and sculpture, go to the Eternal City, or go see what we have left of

Murillo in the cathedrals of Spain. If you prefer great feasts and solemn ceremonies, take a swift carriage and find yourself in St. Petersburg the day the emperor's guard passes in review; or be in Rome during Holy Week, be there when the successor of Saint Peter gives his blessing to the world, because it is still the most imposing spectacle there is in the world.

He who expects to return satisfied from England should visit her as the queen of industry. He should see the City rather than Regent's Park, the East India House rather than Windsor Castle, visit the Bank before St. Paul's, the Clearing House rather than Somerset Palace, take more interest in the docks and Commercial House than in the armor preserved in the Tower. He should go to the warehouses, the countinghouses, the workshops, in pursuit of the genius of Great Britain. He must tear himself from the magnificent hospitality of the English country seats and give up his time to the mines and the forges which furnish industry with its daily bread, its coal and iron. He must mingle with stout and active workmen quite as much as with the more refined society in the salons of the nobility. For myself, I have found nothing in London which has struck me as more original and given me greater pleasure than a shop in the Old 'Change whose storerooms contain twenty times as many goods as the largest warehouse in Paris and whose business transactions amount to two millions sterling a year; above all there is the great brewery of Barclay, Perkins & Company near London Bridge, the order and arrangement of which are more striking than even its vast extent.

As I stood in this brewery, on a floor where there were ranged, in a series of frames, ninety-nine vats, some of them holding five or six hundred thousand bottles, I thought of the famous Heidelberg tun which I had seen some years before. It is the only object which is passably preserved in the delicious *château* of the Palatine counts, and it is faithfully visited by all travelers who come to see that fine ruin, perhaps the finest of all the medieval ruins. What a difference today between the old castle of Heidelberg with its tun and the colossal establishment of the English brewer with its regiment of vats!

The old castle is crumbling to pieces; the rich Gothic sculptures are deteriorating. In vain has a French designer (strange coincidence! that designer himself another part of the debris of feudalism, an *émigré* who, with praiseworthy zeal, has been for a long time the self-appointed guardian and cicerone of this lovely monument) urged the government of Baden, to which the castle belongs, to take some steps for its preservation. Each year some new dilapidation is caused by the frosts of winter and the storms of autumn; soon the old castle will be a shapeless mass, the very stones will perhaps be sold at auction, and nothing will remain but the drawings of M. Charles de Graimbert to show what it has been. The Knight's Hall is stripped of its roof; the arches which support the superb terrace from where the view extends in the distance along the course of the Neckar and the lovely hills which border it—those arches, battered by the cannon fire of the Louvois, will some day collapse. No, not even M. de Graimbert dreams of raising the fallen tower from the underbrush where it lies. Meanwhile, the brewery is enriched one day with a new building, the next with a new steam engine. And in case of any damage, as by a fire which recently happened, the loss is immediately repaired; in place of the building destroyed by flames rises another more splendid in which the free use of iron will offer protection against the ravages of fire.

The statues of the Palatine electors are overthrown in their niches; no son of their vassals will take the pains to set them up again. But at the brewery, everything is in perfect order. Each tool has its nail, each copper cauldron, bright and shining, its range. The stables of the noble prince are a heap of ruins; in the stables of the brewer, rivaling those of Chantilly where the great Condé entertained kings, 150 horses, fit steeds for Goliath, are objects of attention as careful, perhaps, as that which surrounded the persons of the first Electors and their knights. The old tun has been empty for a century and a half; the curious may enter it and take its measure. Once only has M. de Graimbert seen it spout wine; it was in 1813 in honor of the Emperor Alexander and his allies, the sovereigns of Austria and Prussia. But even then it was only a pious fraud: the old tun was not full, the wine flowed from a base barrel which had been stuck in it the night before. The ninety-nine vats of Barclay, Perkins & Company are always full of slowly fermenting beer. The beer which is daily drawn off and sent all over the United Kingdom and North America, which finds its way even to the East Indies, would fill the classical tun of the Palatine Casimir (fifty thousand gallons).

The secret of this contrast is easily explained: the great feudal tun could be filled only by the produce taken by feudal privilege, while the vats of the brewery are filled by the voluntary co-operation of three hundred men, sure of gathering daily the fruits of their industry. The Heidelberg tun was emptied only to administer to the pleasures of the prince or his favorites, while the vats of the brewer quench the thirst of a numerous population which works hard, receives good pay, and pays its providers well.

The silence and desolation of the old castle, contrasted with the bustle and prosperity of the English brewery, are a striking emblem of the feudal system compared with the modern power of peaceful and creative industry. All nations, in proportion as they have the power to change the warlike qualities of the feudal age into the useful qualities of the laborer, or as they want the capacity thus to recast themselves, may read their own destiny, either in the state of the flourishing manufactory, or in that of the deserted and crumbling castle. Happy the people who, like France and England, have had the strength to shake off the past and who, tranquil in their liberties, have only to concern themselves with the future! Woe to that people who will not or cannot tear themselves away from the past! Such people are worn out; they will die of consumption and leave behind nothing but ruins, poetical perhaps, but still only ruins, that is, death and desolation. Unless, indeed, new blood be fed into its veins, which is to say unless it be conquered like unhappy Poland.

II

Liverpool and Its Railroad

Impressions of the Railroad — Railroads in France — Steam Carriages Will Not Interfere with Railroads — Analogy Between the Present Condition of France and England After the Expulsion of the Stuarts — Religion in Liverpool

Liverpool, November 7, 1833. I have just come back from Manchester by the railroad. It is a fine piece of work. I know of nothing that gives a higher idea of the power of man. There are impressions which one cannot describe; such as, for example, being hurried along at the rate of half a mile a minute, or thirty miles an hour (the speed of the train as we started from Manchester), without being the least incommoded and with the most complete feeling of security, for only one accident has happened since the opening of the road and that was owing to the imprudence of the individual who perished. You pass over and under roads, rivers, and canals; you cross other railroads and a great number of other roads on the same level without any trouble or confusion. The great forethought and spirit of order, which in England they suck in with their mothers' milk, preside in every part and make it impossible that the trains should fall foul of each other, or that the cars should run down unlucky travelers or the farmers' wagons. All along the route are gates which open and shut at the precise moment and watchmen on the lookout. How many persons in France would be benefited by this short trip, did it serve only as a lesson of order and planning! And then the Mount Olive cut is as well worth seeing as Roland's Breach; the Wapping tunnel will bear a comparison with the caves of Campan; the dike across Chat Moss seems to me as full of interest as the remains of the most famous Roman roads, not excepting even the Appian Way itself. And there is a column which, though only a chimney for a steam engine, is not, perhaps, less elegant in its proportions than Pompey's Pillar. Many tourists, even persons who have not been made weary of sightseeing in Switzerland and Italy, would find Chester Bridge, which is not, indeed, on the railroad, but is nevertheless very near it, quite as worthy of a visit as the Devil's Bridge; not to mention that the burning cinders which the engine strews along the route might suggest to the traveler, without any great stretch of fancy, the idea of being transported in a fiery car, certainly the most poetical of all vehicles.

Actually, while plans are afoot to endow France with a system of railroads, and it is generally admitted that the project would be impossible without government intervention, opposition against the railroads is starting to take shape. Some will say, or have said already, that twenty, thirty, fifty millions, added every year to public expenditures, would be a crushing burden, considering the heavy budgets which circumstances have imposed on France in the past three years. One can only say that it would be a productive expenditure and that the increase alone of receipts coming from the growth of business would, in every likelihood, produce for the Treasury a sum at least equal to the interest on the capital which the government would have to pledge for its part toward the construction of the railroads; and, after all, if the railroads provide little yield to the Treasury, they provide much to the public which is the real state. Others will object that, instead of launching such grand undertakings, it would be more opportune to pay attention to the local roads, the upkeep of which is so essential to the progress of our agriculture. To them one can only say that, more and more, the local roads are the object of the effective concern of the government from top to bottom; that the railroads and the local roads comprise opposite extremes equally essential to an entire system of transportation; and that it would no more do to sacrifice the local roads to the railroads than to sacrifice the railroads to the local roads. France has enough strength to carry on simultaneously the establishment of local communications, the achievement of our system of interior navigation, and the construction of a great railroad network. These public works, as enormous as they seem, would not require two hundred thousand men in order to carry them out effectively. During winter, the rural population, which is then inactive, could lend its assistance, especially for the local roads. And two hundred thousand men is only half our army. It is apparent, moreover, that France produces enough food to support these workers and enough cloth to clothe them, which comes to the same thing as saying that France has sufficient capital to attack this great enterprise. We lack only one thing, the will.

Finally, there is that class of men, prudent to the extreme, those who, in the administrative machinery which is supposed to produce social change, play the part of sticking spokes in the wheel. They are those who will remark that one should not be too precipitate, that it would be wise to wait before attacking the subject of railroads, that it would be prudent to wait for more light from experience. They cite, among other arguments, the experiments continually being made in England to apply locomotive engines to common roads, the success of which, they think, would save the expense of rails. There is no doubt that railroads, like every other new invention, are susceptible of improvement; but they will always be expensive, and while other nations keep up such schools as the Manchester and Liverpool railroad, and we stand looking on with folded arms, we shall soon find ourselves, by excess of caution, fallen behind all Europe in manufactures and commerce.

As for the steam carriages of Gurney, Dance, or anybody else, there is no hope that they will enable us to save the expense of rails. I think it, indeed, very probable that engines may be made to take the place of horses on roads kept in such a state as the English highways. But upon any road whatsoever—and whatever motive power is employed, engines or horses—in order to reach a great speed (from twenty-five to thirty miles an hour, for instance) it is absolutely necessary to cut through hills and to fill up or bridge over the valleys, just as is done for railroads. Besides, this great speed forbids the free circulation of vehicles and makes it necessary to avoid the level of the frequented routes and to pass over or under them by means of tunnels or bridges. None of the inconveniences or liabilities of railroads would be avoided by this system; the expense would be almost the same because the most costly portion of the work in railroads is the cuts and embankments, the bridges and viaducts; the iron required for the rails forms less than one third of the expenditure. The expenses of superintending the routes would be the same. Besides, the road once graded, there would be a great gain in laying rails, that is, in making a complete railroad, however little might be the amount of transportation; for on a Macadamized road the force of friction is ten times that on iron rails, so that the use of these new locomotive carriages can never supply the place of railways.

What is happening in England proves this well. While the new steam carriages are getting ready for regular service, railroad companies are already at work or are organizing everywhere. Two works are now in progress which will connect Liverpool and Manchester with London, by way of Birmingham; the whole length will be 195 miles. Although the new steam carriage is being tested on the Birmingham-London road, shares in the railroad between that town and London are at a high premium. Another company is preparing to construct a railroad from London to Bath and Bristol, a distance of 115 miles. Companies are also formed for connecting London with Southampton (on the Havre route to Paris) and with Brighton (on the Dieppe route); there are plans to join London and Windsor and London and Greenwich. It is not that the experiments of Gurney and Dance are unknown or slighted; on the contrary, their importance is fully felt; the newspapers are full of them, and they even excite some enthusiasm. In this country, where it is a settled maxim that the laborer is worthy of his hire, I saw some days ago, at place after place along the route from London to Birmingham, casks full of water which the inhabitants brought *gratis* to replenish the machine. Unluckily, the steam carriage did not arrive when it was expected; it had got out of order, as it too often does.

The Liverpool and Manchester railroad owes its brilliant success to the substantial and permanent nature of the interest which binds the two towns together. It would be impossible to realize a more complete division of labor; Manchester, with the country twenty miles round it, is nothing but a workshop; Liverpool manufactures nothing, but merely sells what her neighbors produce. Liverpool is not, whatever the guide book may say, another Venice rising from the waves; it is a countinghouse and nothing but a countinghouse, though on a vast scale, and under the most perfect regulations of any in the world. The business is all done in a space smaller than the *Place du Carrousel*, where the handsome Exchange, the Town House, and all the offices are. At four or five o'clock in the evening, everything is closed; each one shuts up his cell (for the offices deserve this name) and retires to his house or even to his country seat, for many of the residences are on the other side of the Mersey. Liverpool and Manchester are surrounded by a double and threefold series of canals; the Duke of Bridgewater's Canal, the Leeds and Liverpool, the Sankey, Leigh, Bolton and Bury, Mersey and Irwell canals, without taking into account the rivers Irwell, Mersey, and Weaver, which, though small, form fine bays at their mouths and are more easily and regularly navigable than our great rivers, while the navigation is carried on with a promptitude and despatch wholly unknown in France. Since the peace, these two towns have enjoyed such a high degree of prosperity that ten years ago these means of communication, with the addition of a fine road, were found to be insufficient. The countinghouse and the manufactory wished to be nearer to each other; accordingly, on the twentieth of May, 1824, a memorial, signed by 150 merchants, declared the necessity of new routes and a railroad was decided on. The work was begun in June, 1826, and the road was formally opened on the fifteenth of September, 1830. A tunnel is now being built, one mile and a quarter in length, which will carry the railroad into the heart of the town and will cost about $800,000.

The chief article of English commerce, one in which it has no rival, and which opens all the ports of the world to English vessels, is cottons of all descriptions. The value of agricultural produce and manufactures annually exported from the United Kingdom, during the last ten years, has averaged 190 millions of dollars. That of cottons alone has ranged from 80 to 90 millions, and the greater part is made in Manchester and the vicinity. This fact alone would sufficiently explain the commercial importance of Liverpool; add to this that Liverpool is in the neighborhood of the foundries and forges of Staffordshire and Shropshire and the manufactories of Birmingham and Sheffield; that the diminished width of the island, in the fifty-third degree of latitude, enables her to reach out her hands at once to the eastern and western coasts; that she is the center of the business between England and Ireland; that she approaches, at the same time, Scotland and Wales; that she is the headquarters of steam navigation in England—and it will be seen at a glance that Liverpool is the seat of a prodigious commerce, inferior only to that of London.

Eleven thousand vessels measuring 1,400,000 tons enter her nine docks every year; two fifths of the whole exports of England leave through Liverpool and more than one fifth of the British customs duty, or nearly $20,000,000 (equal to the total sum of the French customs), are collected here. Since the modification of the East India Company's charter, the Liverpool merchants flatter themselves with the hope of securing a great part of the India trade, which has hitherto been monopolized by London. They aspire to rival the commerce of the capital, and it must be confessed that they are taking the right road to success.

In tracing the history of Liverpool, Manchester, or any other English town, we are struck with a fact which is full of good omen for France; it is this, that a people never engages heartily and successfully in commerce and manufactures until it feels itself safe from civil or religious despotism; but once assured on that point, it moves rapidly and right forward in its industrial career. So long as England was restrained in her franchises or her faith, she was possessed with one idea, how to throw off the yoke. Once freed from this care, she has achieved in industry what no nation has ever done before. In the beginning of the last century, after the expulsion of the Stuarts, Liverpool had only 5,000 inhabitants, with no other commerce than a feeble coasting trade, when some of her merchants conceived the idea of competing with Bristol, which then monopolized the West Indian trade. Bristol exported to America the products of the fisheries in the North Sea and some fustians and checks manufactured in Germany, and the Liverpool adventurers took cargoes of Scotch stuffs; but the attempt was unsuccessful, the Scotch goods were of inferior quality. Manchester then relieved them from this difficulty. There were already some manufacturers in that place who imitated and surpassed the German articles and, thus provided, the merchants of Liverpool were able to sustain a competition with those of Bristol. The smuggling trade with the Spanish colonies and the slave trade, undertaken in competition with Bristol, continued to enrich Liverpool and consequently Manchester. In 1764, when Bristol fitted out 32 ships for Africa and 74 for America, Liverpool ran 105 to the former and 141 to the latter. In the same year 1,589 vessels entered the port of Liverpool, while only 675 arrived at Bristol. At present Bristol is a second-rate mart compared with Liverpool; not that the former has declined; on the contrary, it is a wealthy city, with a trade tenfold what it was a hundred years ago. But in the midst of the general progress, Liverpool has advanced at high speed. It now contains 180,000 inhabitants, or, including the suburbs, 225,000, without reckoning the floating population of strangers and sailors. During the siege of Calais, when Edward III collected all the strength of England, this town found it difficult to furnish one vessel carrying 6 men; in 1829, it owned 806 vessels of 161,780 tons burthen, manned by 9,091 sailors. During the wars of the French Revolution, Liverpool was able to bear her share of the burdens of the country and to spend $170,000 annually in works of public utility and in embellishing the town. In 1797 she volunteered to raise a troop of cavalry and 8 companies of infantry at her own charge; in 1798 she raised a regiment of volunteers and the sum of $80,000, and in 1803, when Napoleon threatened England with invasion, 2 regiments of infantry and 600 artillerists. In the same period a host of useful and charitable institutions were founded by subscription, and the Exchange was built at the cost of $600,000. All this is the work of one century. Right after the revolution, hardly had James II reached Saint-Germain when the first dock in Liverpool was opened; within thirty years the Mersey and Irwell were canalled. It was the same throughout England. We must not exaggerate and abuse historical parallels, but unless we shut our eyes it is impossible not to perceive a striking analogy between the state of England after the fall of the Stuarts and that of France since 1830. With both peoples there is a feeling of profound security in regard to their liberties, a deep conviction that they have gained a decisive victory, and that they have nothing to fear from the encroachments of the civil power or of a religious corporation. The same wish to see political reforms gives rise to substantial and palpable improvement in the condition of the people and the same disposition on the part of the government to enlighten and realize the popular will.

The old dynasties of England and France fell in consequence of their efforts to give political power to the clergy —which would have been, however, the negation of Christianity—rather than from any attempt to restore the feudal system with its brutality and its rapacity; for the deposed princes themselves were neither rapacious nor violent. The English revolution, however, was far from giving birth to irreligion; Liverpool—modern Liverpool, that is, which bears the stamp, not of England as she was in the sixteenth or the fourteenth century, but of England as she was in the eighteenth century, as she is in our own time—Liverpool is a proof of this. There is no town in France which has as many churches as Liverpool, where there are thirty-seven of the Anglican religion, in addition to forty-three dissenters' chapels and meetinghouses, Presbyterian, Baptist, Methodist, Unitarian, Quaker, Jewish, and Roman Catholic; the last have here five chapels. Most of these have been built since 1750, and nearly one half since 1800; I have a list under my eye, and the dates are 1803, 1810, 1813, 1814, 1815, 1815, 1815, 1816, 1821, 1826, 1826, 1827, 1827, 1830, 1831. Are we to believe that this analogy will hold good on our own soil, and that as she grows rich by industry, France will return to the religious sentiment? I wish it, I hope it. We are already past the time when atheism was fashionable in France. It will not, however, be under the flag of the Anglican Church, or of any other Protestant sect that France will rally; she must have a more imposing and pompous worship.

III

War of the President of the United States upon the Bank

State of the Question — History of Banks in the United States — Creation of the Bank of the United States in 1816; It Restored Order in the Finances of the Country — Causes of the Antipathy of the People Against the Bank — Benefits Which All Classes Have Derived from Banks — Commercial Crisis

New York, January 1, 1834.
This country is now the victim of an industrial crisis which has assumed a political character and is of a very serious nature, for the industrial interest, in this country, is the most important. Last year, when the dispute between the Northern and Southern States relative to the tariff was settled, the wise and prudent thanked God that the danger which had threatened their country had been averted. There seemed to them nothing further to obstruct its triumphant career of conquests over nature, with an ever accelerated rapidity and increased success. A series of causes, to all appearances of slight moment, has changed these hopes into fears.

Some trifling circumstances revived the old quarrel between the Democratic party, to which the President belongs, and the Bank of the United States, and both sides grew warm. President Jackson, a brave man, zealous for the good of his country, but too hasty towards those who contradict him, declared a war to the death against the Bank and pushed it with all the energy and fury, in the same cut-and-thrust style that he had the war against the Indians and English twenty years before. He set his veto to the bill that had passed both houses of Congress, renewing the Bank charter which was about to expire in three years. Not satisfied with having struck at the future of the Bank, he dealt it an immediate blow by withdrawing from the Bank the public money which, by the provisions of its charter, had been deposited in it, and which gave it the means of very materially extending its operations; for the excess of the deposits over the exigencies of the government amount to not less than $10,000,000. The Bank, which had paid to the government a bonus of $1,500,000 for the privilege of being the depository of the public funds, cried out loudly against this measure and with good reason, for no one denies that no institution in the Union is better able to meet all its liabilities. It has reduced its discounts, first, because the removal of the public deposits has diminished the amount of specie in its vaults, and also—as it declares, whether right or wrong—because, its very existence being threatened by the President's veto, it is prudent to hold on to its reserves and at the same time to prepare in advance for its liquidation. As this institution takes the lead in the financial world, the other banks, even those to which the public deposits have been transferred, have been obliged in their turn to restrict their operations. Not only are they afraid to extend their discounts in proportion to the amount of these deposits, but they are obliged to contract them because they find themselves, as objects of the favor of government in this respect, in a state of hostility with the Bank of the United States and it is necessary to be on their guard in the presence of so formidable an adversary. Thus are the sources of credit suddenly dried up. Now credit is the lifeblood of the prosperity of the United States; it lives on credit. Without credit, the populous towns which are springing up on all sides as if by magic, the opulent States which, far away from the Atlantic and beyond the Alleghenies, stretch along the Ohio and the Mississippi would become again a solitary wilderness of savage forests or pathless swamps. The city of New York alone has twenty banks, the annual average discounts of which during the last eight years have amounted to 100 millions of dollars, or 533 millions of francs. At Paris, where the transactions are certainly more extensive than in New York, the discounts of the Bank of France in 1831 amounted to 223 million francs, and in 1832 to 151 millions. The amount of the discounts of the Philadelphia banks in 1831 was 150 millions. A general shock to credit, however transient, is here more terrible than the most frightful earthquake.

If I did not fear to lengthen out this account beyond measure, I would give some details concerning the struggle between the two parties, concerning their tactics and their measures in Congress and out of it, concerning Mr. Clay's speeches and General Jackson's home thrusts. But I think it more important at present to call your attention to the part which the Bank of the United States has played since its establishment and to the causes which stirred up against it that mass of hatred and distrust from which General Jackson derives support. For it is not merely his own dislike that he gratifies; from the last elections, which in almost all the States are based on universal suffrage, it is plain that the numerical majority of the population is, at this moment, opposed to the Bank.

The Americans had already used and abused systems of credit while under the English rule. As soon as they had achieved their independence, they became bolder in their enterprises, more sanguine, or, if you please, more rash in their speculations. They stood in great need of credit; the number of banks was multiplied and many abuses crept in. The State legislatures made no difficulty in granting bank charters to whoever asked for them and in this respect they have not changed their practice. If they imposed some restraints, they had no means of ascertaining or securing their strict observance. The banks, therefore, often issued an amount of bills wholly disproportionate to their real capital, not merely twice or thrice, but ten, twenty times the value of their specie and other assets. The originators of the bank often chose themselves directors and discounted no paper but their own, or rather they lent to themselves the whole circulation of the bank on the bare deposit of the bank shares. This was an ingenious process to enable whoever pleased to coin current money, without ingots of gold or silver. The mismanagement of these banking companies has sometimes been such that instances have occurred where the officers of the bank have, on their own authority, opened a credit for themselves and generally admitted their friends to share in the privilege. Thus it was discovered one lovely day that the cashier of the City Bank in Baltimore had lent himself $166,548, and had made loans to one of his friends to the amount of $185,382. All the other officers had taken the same liberty, with the exception of one clerk and the porter.

The banks abused the privilege of issuing bills, that is to say of making loans; individuals abused the privilege of borrowing. Hence mad speculations and consequently losses by the lender and borrower. The banks cloaked theirs by new issues of paper, individuals theirs by new loans. Each side drew back only to jump further. Many speculators failed, and a few banks. The latter excited public indignation without reforming anyone. The honest and moderate working classes, the farmers (the Americans have retained the English word *farmer*, which properly signifies one who cultivates a hired soil, *fermier*, although among them the cultivators are proprietors) and mechanics—who found that in the end they were the dupes of the speculators since by the depreciation of the paper money which they had taken as so much specie they came in for a share of the loss but had no part in the gain, that is, in the dividends—conceived a violent hatred against the banking system. To this particular cause of dislike was added that aversion which may be found in Europe and everywhere else, felt by persons of methodical habits, gaining little by hard labor, but gaining regularly, against those who are impatient to make their fortune, and to make it by all means, and who waste what they make in the most unbounded luxury and by the most foolish enterprises in less time than they have been in acquiring it. Then there was the natural jealousy of simplicity against cunning, of naïveté against shrewdness, of slow and heavy minds against the quickness of others. There was finally that suspicious distrust of all new influences, and all power that aims to strike its roots deep, a distrust which is essential to the American and which is the source, explanation, and safeguard of his republican institutions. In short, in 1811, when the old Bank of the United States, which was on a much smaller scale than the present Bank, petitioned Congress for a renewal of its charter, an appeal was made to the farmers and mechanics, and, as at the present day, the hobgoblin of a *new aristocracy and, the worst of all, an aristocracy of money,* was summoned up. The charter was not granted.

Soon after, in 1812, war broke out between England and the United States. The natural effect of war is to diminish confidence, to make merchants timid, speculators cautious. Most of the banks, having been managed with little prudence in better times, were soon unable to meet the call for specie by the public. They solicited and obtained from their respective legislatures leave to suspend specie payments. Their bills had a forced circulation.

At the peace of 1815 the banks were not able to resume specie payments, and the system of inconvertible paper money was continued. Imagine then 246 classes of paper money (the number of banks at that time), circulating side by side, having all degrees of value, according to the good or bad credit of the bank which issued them, at twenty per-cent, thirty per-cent, or fifty per-cent discount. Gold and silver had entirely disappeared. There was no longer any standard of price and value; the amount of bills in circulation had become prodigious. (There was more paper in circulation in 1816 than in 1834, when the extent and value of business were very much greater.) To the bills of the banks was added a great number of individual obligations of still less value, issued by private persons as suited their wants, and which circulated more or less freely in the neighborhood. It was a frightful scene of confusion, a Babel, where all business became impracticable from the utter impossibility of the parties understanding each other.

It was now felt that to restore order in the bosom of this chaos there was needed a regulating power, capable of commanding confidence, with ample funds to enable it to pay out specie freely, and whose presence and, in case of necessity, whose authority should serve to recall the local banks to their duty. In 1816 the present Bank of the United States was, therefore, chartered by Congress for a term of twenty years, with a capital of 35 millions, and it went into operation on the first of January, 1817. The seat of the mother bank is Philadelphia and it has twenty-five branches scattered over the Union.

By its intervention and assistance specie payments were resumed by the New York, Philadelphia, Baltimore, Richmond, Norfolk banks on the twentieth of February, 1817. Little by little, step by step, all the other banks followed the example. This resumption of specie payments was, first for the banks and then for individuals, the signal, the occasion, the rule of a general settling up of old accounts. As there had been much prodigality, unsuccessful speculations, and dead loss, accumulated through a period of twenty years, there was now a complete debacle. A great number of banks failed or suspended their operations. From 1811 to 1830, 165 banks were reduced to one or the other of these alternatives.

This liquidation lasted three years; they were three years of crisis, three years of suffering for industry, that is, for the people of the United States; for this people is identified with its commerce. The trials of this period have left a deep and lasting impression. Hatred of speculators and of the banking system has taken root in the hearts of the mass of the people and now springs up in hostility to the Bank of the United States, which, in the eyes of the multitude, is the representative of the system, although it is itself innocent of the mischief and can alone prevent its recurrence.

The antipathy of the greatest number against the banks has then a reasonable cause, but it is not, therefore, any the less blind and unjust. They see nothing but abuses, and shut their eyes against the advantages. The great extension of credit, which resulted from the great number of banks and from the absence of all restraint on their proceedings, has been beneficial to all classes, to the farmers and mechanics not less than to the merchants. The banks have served the Americans as a lever to transfer to their soil, to the profit of all classes, the agriculture and manufactures of Europe, and to cover their country with roads, canals, factories, schools, churches, and, in a word, with everything that goes to make up civilization. Without the banks, the cultivator could not have had the first advances nor the implements necessary for the cultivation of his farm, and if the credit system has given facilities for stockjobbing to speculators, it has also enabled him, although indirectly, to buy at the rate of one, two, or three dollars an acre and to cultivate lands which are now, in his hands, worth tenfold or a hundredfold their first cost. The mechanics who attack the banking system forget that they owe to it that growth of manufacturing industry which has raised their wages from one dollar to two dollars a day. They forget that it furnishes the means by which many of their number raise themselves to competence or wealth; for in this country every enterprising man of a respectable character is sure of obtaining credit and thenceforth his fortune depends upon his own exertions.

At the end of 1819, commerce revived and the financial system of the United States seemed settled on a sure basis. Since that time some shocks have been felt, as in 1822 and in 1825, the latter the reaction of the great English crisis, but in both cases the storm soon passed away. The root of the evil was struck on the day that the Bank of the

United States went into operation. This great institution, which committed some errors at first and paid the penalty, has for a long time been conducted with the most consummate prudence. Most of the leading commercial men, that is to say most of the talents of the country, are attached to it as directors. Its foreign correspondents or associates are the houses whose credit is most firmly established, such as the Barings of London, and the Hottinguers of Paris. It exercises the necessary control over all the local banks, obliges them to restrain their emissions by calling upon them for specie or by refusing to receive their bills when the issues are excessive. It was by its agency that the currency of the United States was established on so large a basis that, in 1831, the banks were able, without any effort, to discount the amount of $800,000,000 in the principal cities of the Union, or $1,100,000,000 for the whole country.

Now, suddenly, this state of prosperity seems to be coming to an end. Here, in New York, the banks have ceased to discount. On good paper, for notes of two or three months, 15, 18, and 24 per cent per annum have been paid, the usual rate of the Bank of the United States and of most of the local banks being 6 per cent. At Philadelphia, 18 per cent per annum has been given on excellent paper at short dates. At Baltimore, merchants of great wealth have been obliged to stop payment. Nobody buys; nobody can sell. Orders for foreign goods are held back. As everybody here is engaged in business, this state of things threatens all interests, menaces everyone's existence. It is the subject of all conversations, of all writing, and of all thoughts.

God grant that the sight of the impending danger may calm the passions, and that the good sense of the community may banish empty prejudices and false fears! God grant that both parties may forget their mutual animosities in their anxiety for the common welfare! This should be our prayer, not only for the sake of the destinies of this great nation, but also because our silk manufacturers and the owners of our vineyards will pay a part of the expenses of the campaign against the banks in general which the radical party is about to open, by a mortal contest, with the Bank of the United States.

IV

Democracy and the Bank

Democratic Movements in France — Less Influence Than in the United States — Errors of the Local Banks — Their Dividends — Wisdom of the Bank of the United States — Political Dangers of the Great National Bank — Services Rendered by It — The President's Accusations Against the Bank — The Multitude Applauds

New York, January 11, 1834.
The financial crisis brought on by the quarrel between the President and the Bank has not become more serious. There is a great scarcity of money, that is, a great diminution of credit, but the failures are not yet numerous or considerable. The last arrivals from Europe have brought us the news that several of the trades in Paris and at Lyons have refused to work. What is taking place here in regard to the Bank is analogous to what is passing in France among the tailors, bakers, and carpenters, and what occurs daily in England among the manufacturing operatives. In Europe, and particularly in France, it is the rising of a democracy, or rather a radicalism, which is yet in embryo and which, if it please God, will never come to maturity. In America it is the despotic humor of a full-grown democracy, passing more and more into radicalism the longer it rules without a rival and without a counterpoise. In France, up to 1830, and in England, up to the Reform Acts, the general tenor of the gov-

ernment constantly bore the mark of the aristocracy; that is to say, in the two countries government was pretty much to the exclusive benefit of the upper and middle classes, without too much worry about the laboring class. Since 1830 and since the reform movement in England, which we can say with pride followed our lead, there has been an obvious tendency on both sides of the Channel toward a more just balance. We are necessarily moving toward a state of affairs where all interests, the poor as well as the rich, the worker as well as the master, will have the same protection, not just nominally, but truly. Men who have the greatest influence on public affairs work to establish a balance which, in successive stages, is more and more favorable to the working class; and the majority of that class, especially in France, leaves the care of its future in the hands of responsible citizens who have devoted themselves to their cause. Because of that the three days of the July Revolution and the reform movement are fortunate revolutions. It is for that reason also that in France all attempts to precipitate, that is to say to compromise, the reform movement, which the wisest men inside and outside of government agree to direct with a prudent firmness, should have today no support among the people and cannot fail to be easily turned aside.

It seems to me improbable that the journeymen carpenters, tailors, and bakers of Paris, should ever give the law to their masters. Among us, the middling class (*bourgeoisie*) is beginning to feel that it is a duty and a necessity to improve the condition of the working class. It has the authority, but it is conscious that the people have the physical force. The people have counted their ranks and those of the *bourgeoisie,* but feel that it is not enough to have the number; they see that they have nothing to expect from violence and can back their friends only by improved habits of order and morality. On both sides reciprocal rights are mutually acknowledged; each fears and respects the other. Here, on the contrary, it is perfectly natural that the democracy should rule the capitalists, merchants, and manufacturers; it possesses at once the physical force and the political power. The *bourgeoisie* inspire it neither with fear nor with respect. The equilibrium is gone; there is no guarantee against the popular caprice in the United States but the good sense of a well-informed people. It must be allowed that this good sense is quite extraordinary, but it is not infallible. A popular despotism is as easily deluded by flatterers as any other despotism.

The Bank of the United States is at this time experiencing the truth of this observation. I have already alluded to some of the crying abuses which have excited a violent hatred against the banks in general, although without the aid of the banks it would have been impossible for the United States to have increased in population, wealth, and territory as they have done. These abuses were and are the acts of the local banks, and not of the Mammoth Bank. On the contrary, the latter, by the control which it exercises over the local banks for its own security, checks and limits these abuses, if it does not completely prevent them. The legislatures of the different States have been repeatedly called to deliberate on the question of abolishing all banks and breaking up the banking system, but they have generally thought, and justly, that the remedy would be worse than the disease. They have attempted to cure the disorder by restrictive provisions in the charter of new banks. The State of New York, in 1829, embraced the whole subject in the Safety Fund Act which established a mutual supervision of the banks over each other, under the direction of special Bank Commissioners, and creates at their common expense a safety fund designed to indemnify the public in case of the failure of any one of the banks. But these measures of repression or prevention have generally proved inefficacious, either from a defect in the means of coercion possessed by the government or from a reluctance to use the powers conferred by the laws.

In their report of the thirty-first of January, 1833, the

New York Bank Commissioners urgently call the attention of the legislature to the serious dangers which may result from these institutions as they are now organized, particularly in the country, and to their excessive issues in proportion to the small quantity of specie in their vaults. With two millions in specie, the banks of the State had, at that time, a circulation of about twelve millions. But this report itself proves that the commissioners did not dare to fulfill the duties imposed on them by the Safety Fund Act; they had the authority to shut up the offending banks. Their warnings have not prevented the legislature from chartering new banks by the dozen. This year it will have to act on 105 petitions for charters, that is, 18 more than the actual number of banks in the State. To be sure in the present instance, the *let alone* principle will probably be violated, for the Governor's Message of January 7, 1834, urges the two Houses to arrest the flood. This bank mania, as Jefferson called it, is created by the profits of banking, which is, and more especially was, before the institution of the Bank of the United States, the best kind of speculation, exactly in the ratio of the abuses attending it. (The dividends of the Bank of North America were, in 1792, 15 per cent; in 1793, 13½ per cent; from 1794 to 1799 inclusive, 12 per cent; from 1804 to 1810, 9 per cent. Those of the old Bank of the United States varied from 7⅝ to 10 per cent. Those of the Pennsylvania Bank, from 1792 to 1810, from 8 to 10 per cent. The Bank of the United States regularly divides 7 per cent to the shareholders. In the city of New York the average dividends of the banks in 1832 was 6.14 per cent; of the country banks 9 per cent. It must not be forgotten that the legal rate of interest is higher in the United States than in Europe; it is 6 per cent in Pennsylvania, 7 in New York, from 8 to 9 in the Southern States, and even 10 in Louisiana. In the Western States there is no regulation of interest by law, but the ordinary rate is very high.)

In the local banks, especially outside the large cities, the chief aim of the president and directors is, at all events, come what may, to make the semi-annual dividend as large as possible. By extending their operations excessively, they may, if they lose the public confidence, be driven to a failure; but in the United States the prospect of such a disaster is much less terrible to the greater number of merchants, and even to the smaller companies, than it is in Europe. When a bank fails there is, indeed, a great outcry, because the number of victims is large and the loss extends to all classes; most of the bills, being of the denomination of five dollars and under, are very generally distributed in the hands of the laborers, as well as of the wealthier classes. But just in proportion to the distribution of the loss over the greater number of persons is the quickness with which the clamor ceases. The president, the cashier, the directors, and others principally interested readily find means to recover from the blow by obtaining credit elsewhere, and the whole affair is at an end.

The Bank of the United States, on the contrary—directed by men of large fortune and established reputation, connected in business with the principal houses in Europe, charged with a vast responsibility, subject to the supervision of the Federal government, which names five of the directors out of twenty-five, and officiously watched by an army of journalists—is interested and obliged to follow another course. Not that it has not committed some errors; but it paid dear for them and has never repeated them. Neither are its rules and regulations perfect; the experience of twenty years will doubtless suggest some modifications. But even its adversaries admit that it has been admirably managed. They pretended at first that the public money was not safe in its vaults, but they are at present ashamed to insist upon this point as the investigation made by the House of Representatives proved the absurdity of the charge. The accusations now brought against it are of a political character.

Politically speaking, the existence of an institution so powerful as the Bank in a country such as the United

States can indeed present some inconveniences. The fundamental maxim of the Federal and State constitutions is that the supreme authority is null and void; there is no government here in the true sense of the word; that is, no directing power. Each one is his own master; it is self-government in all its purity. This anomalous and monstrous development of the individual principle is no evil here, it is even a great good at present; it is the present stage in the progress of the United States because self-government is the only form of government to which the American character, as it is, can accommodate itself. If individuality had not free elbowroom here, this people would fall short of its destiny, which is to extend its conquests rapidly over an immense territory for the good of the whole human race, to substitute, in the shortest time possible, civilization for the solitude of the primitive forests over a surface ten times greater than all France, of as great average fertility as that country, and capable, therefore, of accommodating 350 millions of inhabitants.

From these considerations it is clear that any power whatsoever, if possessed of great influence and exercising it over a great space, would be inconsistent with the political system of the country. For this reason the Federal and State governments are in a permanent state of eclipse. And it is furthermore evident that the Bank, which is met at every turn as an agent in all transactions, which governs credit, regulates the currency, animates or checks at will the activity of commerce by narrowing or widening the channels of circulation, the Bank, which by its numerous branches is, like the fabled polypus, everywhere present, the Bank with its funds, its centralization, its trusty creatures, is certainly an anomaly, which may become big with danger. One might, from an abstract, theoretical point of view, imagine cases in which this financial colossus, seated in the heart of a country absorbed in business, would press with a crushing weight on the liberties of the people. If it were possible that one day a new Monk should wish to restore

English rule here, or that a new Bonaparte, the savior of the republic, in another Marengo should attempt to make himself dictator, it would also be possible that a conspiracy between the Bank and this Monk or this Napoleon might overthrow the liberties of America. But such an event, possible to be sure in theory (for in theory nothing is impossible), is at present wholly impracticable in fact. Yet there are honest and enlightened men on whom this theoretical danger makes more impression than the necessity of a regulator amidst the labyrinth of five hundred banks, or of an agent which, by controlling the currency, should be in financial affairs what the vast rivers of the country are in the system of internal communication. They fear more, for this land of industry, the imperceptible chance of tyranny by the Bank than a system in which there would be no check on the cupidity of the local banks and in which they might renew, with their paper money—if not the *assignats* of France, or the Continental money of the Revolution—at least the commercial anarchy which followed the war of 1812.

Unluckily for the United States, it is not on this high ground of foresight that President Jackson and his friends take their stand in their attack on the Bank. They do not say that it is possible that it may one day, under a new state of things, become an instrument of oppression. They pretend that it is so already. According to them, it tends to nothing less than the subjugation of the country to its rule. In his last annual message, and in an official paper read to the cabinet on the eighteenth of September, 1833, the President accuses the Bank: [1.] With having intrigued to bring up the question of the renewal of its charter in Congress during the session of 1831–32 in order to reduce him to the alternative of giving his sanction to the bill, or losing the votes of the friends of the Bank in the approaching presidential election, if he refused it. He forgets that he had himself in his message at the opening of that session recommended to Congress to settle the business. [2.] Of having meddled with politics in opposing his election in 1832, and of having, with this purpose, enlarged its loans and discounts 28½ millions. The Bank replies that the statement is incorrect; that its books show that its available means having been augmented, between January, 1831, and May, 1832, by 10 millions; and, the needs of commerce having increased, it had judged it expedient to extend its credits 17½ millions, so that the actual extension of its operations was only 4½ millions. [3.] Of having attempted to corrupt the public press, either by printing a great number of pamphlets, or by winning over the newspapers to its side. The Bank answers to this charge that it has a perfect right to defend itself by the press against the continual attacks upon it to which the press gives currency; that it may certainly be allowed to reprint the speeches delivered in its favor in Congress, or essays in which questions of banking are luminously treated, such as that by the celebrated Mr. Gallatin, who was twelve years Secretary of the Treasury and afterward Minister to France. As to the vague imputation of attempting to corrupt a press, which pours forth such a number of journals as the press of the United States, it does not deserve a serious answer.

If a European government, from motives of this character, on facts thus destitute of proof, should attempt to destroy an institution essential to the prosperity of the country, the cry of despotism would be raised on all sides. If the state were itself interested in the institution to the amount of one fifth of its capital (seven millions of dollars), many persons would charge such an attempt not only with violence, but with folly. In the United States the numerical majority, which is the majority of electors, applauded General Jackson's campaign against the Bank with as much enthusiasm as his campaign at New Orleans. The military success of General Jackson, his honesty, his iron firmness, have given him an astonishing popularity. The Bank, on the contrary, in spite of its daily services, is unpopular. It is so on account of the popular hatred of the banking system, on account of that jealousy which, in a land of absolute equality and suspicious democracy, follows in the steps of wealth and pomp; it is so because its extensive privileges shock all republican feelings. In the United States, in spite of the general habits and laws of equality, there is a sort of aristocracy founded on knowledge or on commercial distinction. This aristocracy, somewhat prone to entertain a contempt for the vulgar multitude, causes a strong reaction against itself in the popular mind; and, as it supports the Bank by its influence and its writings, this is enough of itself to set the pure democracy against the institution. Add to this that the Bank, irritated by the hostile demonstrations of the Administration, has sometimes answered it by angry acts of reprisal, not grave in themselves but unfortunate in their consequences, and of which its adversaries have adroitly availed themselves to excite the popular passions. Although the Bank has the majority of the Senate in its favor, the chances are now against it. Unless the masses who today shout HURRAH FOR JACKSON! without reflection, shall be led, between this and March, 1836, when its charter expires, to reflect seriously on the matter, it will disappear, until a new experience shall again prove that it is impossible to get along without it.

Thus, at the very moment when the English Reform ministry is extending the privileges of the Bank of England with the approbation of all Europe, here a compact mass in which, indeed, the enlightened do not form the majority but in which, notwithstanding, some are included, deals the death blow to a similar institution, tried and proved by long services. Thus—while one of the greatest, perhaps in an economical point of view the very greatest, of the benefits which France could receive would be the establishment of a system of banks, connected with each other as the twenty branches of the Bank of the United States are with the mother bank—America is about to witness, if not the death, at least the suspension for some years of an institution that has been fruitful of so much good, without the slightest immediate loss of popularity by those who are doing the work of destruction. So goes the world in the United States. The history of this affair shows that the political springs are here wholly different from those that operate in Europe and that, nevertheless, intrigue and petty hate have free course here as well as elsewhere.

V

Movement of Parties and the Bank Question

Industrial Crisis — Backstairs Influences in Monarchies and Republics — Party Demonstrations — Imperfection of the Banking System — Excess of Paper Money — Modification of the Bank Charter — Good Sense of the American Democracy — How Great Questions are Settled in the United States

Philadelphia, January 5, 1834.

Of all the cities of the Union, peaceful Philadelphia is most disturbed by the Bank question because it is the seat of the mother bank. The State of Pennsylvania also, of all the States, suffers the most from the financial crisis because it is the most deeply in debt and is obliged to borrow more, either to finish its canals and railroads, or to pay the interest on its existing debt. Conceive of the situation of a State whose population amounts to only 1,500,000 souls, loaded with a debt of $20,500,000, whose ordinary expenditures are less than $600,000, but which must raise $1,000,000 to pay interest already accrued and nearly $2,500,000 by the next summer, under penalty of seeing her great works, executed at an enormous expense, go to ruin, and who knows not whither to turn. This is not all; some old loans must be reimbursed next May, or in three months; and, to crown the whole, the capitalists who contracted last year for a loan of $3,000,000 to be employed on the public works are, in consequence of the present crisis, unable to fulfill their contracts. The local banks, which are bound by their charters to lend to the State at the rate of five per cent, rather stand in need of assistance themselves. To these public embarrassments is added private distress. Thus this country, which Cobbett, who always shows talent and occasionally gleams of good sense, dubs the *Anti-Malthusian,* exhibits for the present the spectacle of a superabundance of laborers. In the manufacturing districts of Pennsylvania many of the operatives are without work.

The condition of the rest of the country is not, in general, any more favorable. I am very ready to believe that the Anti-Jackson newspapers, for so they call themselves, exaggerate the distress; but, making all due allowance for rhetorical flourishes, it is still undeniable that there is much distress, especially among the commercial class. Bare figures are more eloquent than the best advocates of the Bank. It is a notorious fact that excellent paper has been discounted at the rate of 18 per cent per annum, and at even higher rates, in New York, Philadelphia, and Baltimore. The price currents and the state of the stock market show a general fall in prices of 15, 20, 30, and even 40 per cent. Thus far the efforts of the President to fell the hydra of the moneyed aristocracy, the Mammoth, the Monster, have had no other effect than to blast credit and the commercial prosperity of the country; for the Bank has been administered with so much ability, especially since the presidency of Mr. Biddle, one of the most distinguished men in the country, that notwithstanding the abrupt removal of the public deposits, notwithstanding the unexpected and unfair assaults upon some of the branches, particularly that of Savannah, to force them to suspend specie payments, it is beyond comparison the most solvent and safe of all the financial institutions in the Union. At this critical moment it has as much specie (ten millions) as all the other five hundred banks taken together, and I know from good authority that many Jackson men (this is the name adopted by themselves) have been very glad to be sprinkled with a few drops of the *venom* of this dangerous *reptile*.

If what is now taking place in this country were to occur in any European monarchy, those persons who insist upon all nations having a government cast in the republican mold, whatever may be the condition of their territory and population, their wealth and knowledge, their character and manners, would not fail to make it the text of their harangues against monarchical government. Holding up to view the picture of an unparalleled commercial prosperity, checked of a sudden by the caprice of the sovereign, they would prove that such is one of the unavoidable consequences of an opposition between the interest of the ruler and the welfare of the nation. They would demonstrate by geometrical syllogisms that it is the essence of monarchy to place authority in the hands of the weak and the foolish who to gratify their personal malice would not hesitate to hazard the happiness of millions. They would raise the cry of secret influence, of intrigue, which, according to them, is one of the attributes of monarchies. Unluckily for this theory, it is belied by facts under my own eyes in the most thorough and flourishing republic that has ever existed.

The selfishness of royalty, or more correctly speaking of courts, has hitherto begot much mischief and will continue to do so in the future; but it has met with its match in the bosom of republics, and above all under a system of *absolute* equality which distributes political power in *absolutely* equal quantities to the intelligent and the ignorant, to the most eminent merchant and author and to the brutal and drunken peasant of Ireland who is but just enrolled in the list of citizens. An *absolute* people, as well as an *absolute* king, may reject for a time the lessons of experience and the counsels of wisdom. A people, as well as a king, may have its courtiers. A people on the throne, whose authority is limited by no checks, may blindly and recklessly espouse the quarrels of its favorites of a day. Let those who doubt it come here and see it. Ignorance of the true interests of the country is not the exclusive prerogative of monarchies. The official papers of the Federal Executive in the affair of the Bank, so far as concerns a knowledge of the principles of government and the springs of the public welfare, are on a level with the measures of the government of Spain or Rome. And yet this Executive is the creature of the popular choice in the largest sense. It is not merely in monarchies that a dancer is to be seen in the post that belongs to a mathematician. The *camarilla!* Never have I heard it so much talked about as since I have been in this country. It is here called the *Kitchen Cabinet* and, admitting a fourth of what is said by the opposition to be true, it is difficult not to believe that its influence upon public affairs is greater than that of the ministerial cabinet.

But to return to the Bank. Congress met on the third of December and most of the State legislatures are now in session. Everywhere, and above all in Congress, the great, not to say the only, question agitated is that of the Bank. The subject of the discussions is the removal of the public deposits which the President has withdrawn from the Bank after a military fashion, having previously in the same spirit, removed from office the Secretary of the Treasury, Mr. Duane, who, although opposed to the Bank, considered the President's course illegal and rash. Thus far the manifestations of public opinion and the deliberative assemblies are extremely various and discordant. In New Jersey, a small and unimportant State, the Assembly has adopted, by a large majority, resolutions approving the acts of the Administration and instructing its delegates in Congress to support the President; notwithstanding which, Mr. Southard, one of the Senators from that State, has made an excellent speech on the other side of the question. The Assembly of New York, the first State in wealth and population, has adopted similar resolutions by a vote of 118 to 9. Some persons, to be sure, assert that this is because New York would like to have the mother bank. (New York is the chief seat of commerce in the United States. On this account it has some right to claim the parent bank. Philadelphia has the advantage of a location somewhat more central. The removal to New York would also require the transference of the mint and some other public offices to that city, at great expense. Philadelphia is, moreover, the city of American capitalists.) The youthful State of Ohio, whose growth borders on the miraculous (it now contains 1,100,000 inhabitants, although but fifty years ago it had not 6,000), Ohio, the Benjamin of the democracy, has strongly expressed the same wishes. The little State of Maine has done the same. The Administration party lately had a brilliant opportunity of displaying its sympathies and its hatred. The eighth of January, the anniversary of the battle of New Orleans, was celebrated by innumerable public dinners at each of which numerous toasts were drunk. President Jackson was the hero and the Bank was the scapegoat of the day. It would be impossible to imagine the flood of accusations, insults, and threats which was poured upon it, mingled with jests in the taste of the country upon Mr. Nicholas Biddle; thus, at one of these dinners the Bank was toasted as being *governed by Young Nick according to the principles of Old Nick.*

But the population of New England, particularly that of Massachusetts, is opposed to the Administration. In Virginia the same opinions seem to prevail, and it is the same with several of the old Southern States. The merchants and manufacturers of New York, Philadelphia, Baltimore, Boston, and a hundred other places have held meetings and adopted resolutions strongly censuring the conduct of the government toward the Bank, and accusing it of having caused the present crisis. Most of the Philadelphia banks have petitioned in favor of the Bank. Several banks at Boston and in Virginia have refused to take the public money in deposit; those of Charleston have been unanimous in this measure. The majority of persons of intelligence, experience, and moderation, and most of the merchants and manufacturers, are in favor of the Bank. The people, particularly in the Middle and Western States, and the operatives in the towns go for General Jackson.

In Congress the majority of the Senate is friendly to the Bank and the majority of the House is on the side of the Administration. The superiority in debate belongs to the defenders of the Bank. In the Senate, the three greatest statesmen in the country, Messrs. Clay, Webster, and Calhoun, are on this side of the question, and the speeches of Messrs. Clay and Calhoun have made a strong impression. In the House Mr. Binney, of Philadelphia, and Mr. McDuffie have pleaded the same cause with ability. On the other side there has been more high-flown declamation than reasoning. I have been struck with the resemblance between most of the speeches and newspaper essays directed against the Bank and our republican tirades of 1791 and 1792. There is the same declamatory tone, the same swollen style, the same appeal to the popular passions, with this difference, that the allegations made here are vague, empty, and indefinite, while with us fifty years ago the grievances were real. Most generally the pictures presented in these declamations are fantastical delineations of the moneyed aristocracy overrunning the country with seduction, corruption, and slavery in its train; or of Mr. Biddle wanting to be king. Amid this swarm of speeches and essays, one hardly ever meets with any indications of serious study or a tolerable knowledge of the subject; but I have been struck with the speech of Mr. Cambreleng, who has put forth some prudent suggestions as to the reforms required in the present system of banking.

For it must be confessed that this animosity of the President and the body of the people against the Bank of the United States, blind and unreasonable as it is, is founded on a real necessity, namely that of a complete reorganization of the banking system. When Congress renewed the charter of the Bank of the United States without modification in 1832 it committed an error. It should have seized this opportunity to place the currency of the country on a more solid basis; and if General Jackson had stayed within the terms of his veto message in which he declared that he was not opposed in principle to the establishment of a National Bank, but that the present Bank could not be retained without some modification, he might have become the benefactor of his country. He would not, indeed, have received Cobbett's congratulations, but he would have obtained the approbation of all statesmen and men of sense in the Old and the New World. However, whatever his friends may say, as the President did not foresee the distress which has befallen American commerce and, as nobody can doubt his patriotism, we need not absolutely despair of seeing him adopt this wise course.

The actual crisis abundantly proves the wretched condition of the currency, for the original cause of it was quite slight. It was merely the transfer from the vaults of one bank to those of another of ten millions, an inconsiderable sum relative to the amount of the business of the country. If the local banks, in spite of the control exercised by the Bank of the United States, had not previously passed all bounds, they would have been able, when the Bank of the United States was obliged by the withdrawing of the public money to contract its discounts, to have enlarged their own in the same proportion, since those same funds were transferred to their vaults. But the framework of these banks is so badly put together that it shakes at the slightest breath. The slight motion in the political and commercial atmosphere caused by the President's blow at the Bank in removing the public deposits was enough to make them totter. They are like a colossus with feet of clay which should have feet of gold, or, in other words, specie in their vaults.

The proportion of gold and silver metals, of which we have an excess in France, is here extremely small. In many

States, among others New York, there is an enormous quantity of bills of one, two, and three dollars. In South Carolina there are 25-cent, and even 12½-cent bills. In Pennsylvania, Virginia, and some other States, there are none of less than five dollars. The Bank of the United States emits none of less than that sum; but this minimum is too low. Most political economists, and particularly the English, lay it down as an axiom that the most perfect money is paper. This is true, if we suppose a nation in which any disturbance of industry—in consequence or apprehension of war, from foolish speculations, from glut or panic—is impossible. In such a land of Cockayne, such a terrestrial paradise, an unshaken confidence would prevail in all transactions and consolidate all interests. The metals would only serve to strike medals and to preserve inscriptions intended to commemorate this ineffable bliss. Paper would there be on a par with gold and even higher, as some English writers have maintained it should be. I do not know if there will ever be a nation in such a state of heavenly happiness; but I doubt it, because in the world of finance, as well as in the world of passion, I consider the Tender River a fable and pastorals a sport of fancy; but it is very evident that no such people exists now or will for some time to come. Now in the United States, the present banking system, like that of England from 1797 to 1821, or even 1825, is founded on this theory of the most perfect money. It is provided, indeed, that the banks shall pay gold for their paper on demand; but by the side of this clause, which tends to keep a certain quantity of the metals in the country, is inserted another which neutralizes it; it is the power of emitting bills in any number and of the sum of one, two, three, or five dollars. In prosperous times, the emission of paper is abundant, indefinite; as the necessity of a metallic standard ceases to be felt in proportion to the confidence which prevails, the metals disappear before the excess of paper; there is scarcely any left in the country. Since I have been in the United States I have not seen a piece of gold except in the mint. No sooner is it struck off than the gold is exported to Europe and melted down. When a crisis comes on, the demand for the precious metals increases rapidly, because everyone attaches more value to a positive standard than to paper, and the later the application of the remedy for the scarcity of metals, the longer does the crisis last and the more serious does it become.

In a new country, where capital cannot, of course, be abundant for capital of all kinds, whether of articles of food or precious metals, is the accumulated produce of labor—it is natural that the proportion of paper money should equal and surpass that of metallic money. The existence of paper money is even a great benefit to any country. In France we have the enormous sum of 600 million dollars in specie; in the United States 40 millions are sufficient for all the transactions of a commerce nearly as extensive as our own. In England the amount of specie at present does not exceed 220 millions, mostly in gold. Banknotes in circulation, which constitute the rest of the currency, amount at this time in the United States to 100 million, that is, two and a half times the amount of specie; in England to about the same as the specie which gives for the whole circulation of

The United States, 140 millions—
Of England, 440 millions.

If we had in France the industrial habits of the English and Anglo-Americans, 200 millions of circulating medium, half in paper and half in specie, would probably be sufficient for our operations; but considering our commercial inferiority, suppose that we should require 300 millions, of which two thirds should be metallic and one third paper, it would follow that we might advantageously employ 400 millions which are now unproductive in the form of specie, and which add nothing to our pleasures, our comfort, or our industrial capacity.

But if we might expect great benefit from banks of circulation and the paper which they would issue, it is evident that the Americans, in the present stage of their wealth and considering their actual capital, would find their advantage in putting some check upon themselves in this matter. It might then be proper to raise the minimum of bills of the Bank of the United States to ten, fifteen, or twenty dollars, as in England, where there is no paper less than the five pound note. The National Bank, if it were powerful enough, would keep the local banks in check and for this reason it is expedient to increase the capital. There would then be specie enough in the country for all purposes less than the paper minimum and in case of any disturbance the currency would be less readily deranged.

Nor is this the only point in which the charter of the Bank of the United States requires modification; its relations with the Federal government, as well as with the State governments, need to be modified; and some projects worthy of consideration, in this view, have been broached. It would also, probably, be expedient, as Mr. Cambreleng has remarked, to change the rules and regulations relating to private and public deposits and to provide that in future they should bear interest as they do in the Scotch banks. If this system were adopted by all the American banks, they would gain in solidity and they would embrace the interest of all classes and become provident institutions for the general good; while at present their direct profits, the dividends, fall exclusively to the shareholders, who belong to the wealthier classes, a fact which contributes not a little to their unpopularity.

Finally, it would be proper to consider to what degree the immediate advantages of credit might be extended to mechanics and farmers. In this respect the banks here are still absolutely aristocratic. The Americans have preserved in banking almost all the usages of their ancestors, the English. The American banks are now chiefly devoted to the use of speculators and merchants.

In the midst of so many contradictions, it is difficult to

foresee what will be the issue of the struggle. The friends of the Administration maintain that President Jackson and Vice President Van Buren are not only opposed to the Bank as it is, but to any National Bank, and that they will never yield. The *Globe,* the avowed organ of the President, has told Mr. Clay that unless he *can find a Brutus* (to assassinate General Jackson) the Bank will neither have the deposits nor a new charter. We may doubt, however, whether the President's mind is so decisively made up. After all, a majority of both houses can set at nought the *veto.* [Chevalier is, of course, wrong here; it would have taken a two-thirds majority to override a veto—J.W.W.] As for the Vice President, whom his opponents call the *cunning Van Buren,* as he aspires to succeed the President, many persons declare that his object is to gain the vote of the powerful State of New York by transferring thither the seat of the mother bank, but that he is too enlightened seriously to wish the destruction of an institution fraught with so much good to the country.

However this may be, it would be surprising if the present crisis were not followed sooner or later by a reaction in favor of the Bank of the United States with suitable modifications, or of another National Bank which, as Mr. Webster observed, would amount to the same thing if the shareholders of the present Bank are not sacrificed. The jealous democracy of this country has this advantage over other democracies, that in the main it has much good sense. The recollection of old sufferings caused by the abuses of the banking system and a jealousy of all pretensions to superiority have led it to give ear to much noisy declamation about the aristocracy of money, particularly when this has been mixed up with flattery of itself. It may have been led astray for a moment when its own prerogatives were the subject of discussion, as those sovereigns who assert the divine right of kings take fire in respect to theirs. Proud of its gigantic labors, it may have been tempted to believe that to it everything was possible and easy, that it had only to frown to cause the Bank to crumble into the dust at its feet without being itself shaken by the shock. But facts, positive, inexorable facts, now bear witness that it was mistaken, that it has trusted too much to its powers and its star, that the agency of the Bank of the United States is indispensable. The influence of facts has spread step by step even to the country people, who no longer find buyers of their produce. The argument is palpable and effectual; passion cannot long blind men of sense to such facts, for men of sense are those who do not give themselves up implicitly to abstractions and who admit that every theory which is point blank against fact is false or incomplete. This is the reason why good sense is worth at least as much in politics as spirit.

It is worth while to observe here that all the political difficulties in which the United States have become involved, and which have threatened the existence of the Union itself, have been settled by means of what are here called compromises, and in France *justes-milieux*. Thus was ended the serious dispute on the Missouri question which had well nigh set the Union in a flame. It was made a question whether Missouri should be received into the confederacy with a constitution sanctioning the institution of slavery. After a long and ineffectual debate, Mr. Clay moved that Missouri should be admitted unconditionally but that, at the same time, it should be declared that in future no new State lying north of 36° 30′ of latitude should be admitted into the Union with this institution; this proposition was received with general favor, and the admission of Missouri was carried. In the next session, however, a new quarrel arose between the North and the South, more violent and bitter than the former, in relation to an article in the constitution of Missouri prohibiting any free man of color from entering the State. Another compromise, proposed by Mr. Clay, finally settled the whole question in 1821 after it had kept the country in a flame for three years. In 1833 another compromise was made in respect to the tariff, the honor of which also belongs to Mr. Clay.

This question will sooner or later be settled in the same manner; the Union cannot do without a National Bank and it will have one.

There are some lucky persons who succeed in everything and there are some lucky nations with whom everything turns out well, even those events which seemed about to bury them in ruins. The United States is one of these privileged communities. When Villeroi came back to Versailles after his defeat, Louis XIV said to him, "Marshal, nobody is lucky at our time of life." Charles V also, as he grew old, said that fortune was like a woman and preferred young men to old ones. Louis and Charles were right so far as this, that when a man, young or old, has finished his mission, foresight, ability, and perseverance profit him little; he fails in whatever he undertakes; while he who has a mission yet to fulfill takes new strength from the most violent blows. This is true of nations as well as of individuals. The American people is a young people which has a mission to perform, nothing less than to redeem a world from savage forests, panthers, and bears. It moves with mighty strides toward its object, for it has not, like the nations of Europe, the burden of a heavy past on its shoulders. It may be checked in its career for a time by the present crisis, but it will come out of it safe and sound and more healthy than when it entered it. It will come out with increased resources, with a reformed banking system, and according to all appearances, even with an improved National Bank. May the nations of Europe not have to wait long for institutions which have so powerfully assisted England and America in their progress!

VI

Progress of the Struggle— New Powers

Length of the Debates in Congress — The Bank Must Withdraw — Old Dignities and Old Politics — New Dignities and New Politics — New Power of Industry

Baltimore, March 1, 1834.
Failures begin to be frequent in the United States, particularly in New York and Pennsylvania; the great commercial and manufacturing houses are shaking. Meanwhile the Senators and Representatives in Congress are making speeches on the crisis, its causes, and consequences. Three months have already been taken up in discussing the question whether the Secretary of the Treasury had or had not the right to withdraw the public deposits from the vaults of the Bank, without that institution having given any just cause of complaint and merely because it was strongly suspected of aristocratic tendencies. The resolutions which have given rise to these debates have been referred by the Senate to the Committee on Finance, and by the House to the Committee of Ways and Means. Debates will rise on the reports of these committees, on petitions and memorials and incidental matters, and, I am told, will last two or three months longer. It is at first glance hard to understand this slowness among a people which, above all things, strives to save time, and which is so much given to haste and despatch that its most suitable emblem would be a locomotive engine or a steamboat, just as the Centaurs were anciently confounded with their horses.

From all the large towns of the North, committees appointed by great public meetings bring to Washington memorials signed by thousands calling for prompt and efficient measures to put an end to the crisis. On the other hand, the partisans of the Administration find fault with the prolixity of the legislators. The calmness, or rather phlegm, which the Americans have inherited from their English ancestors, remains undisturbed in both houses of Congress and the solemn debate goes on. One speaker, for example, Mr. Benton, occupied four sessions, four whole days, with his speech, which led Mr. Calhoun to observe that the Senator from Missouri took up more time in expressing his opinion on a single fact than the French people had done in achieving a revolution. But these interminable delays ought not to be too lightly condemned, and for myself I only shrug my shoulders when I hear some impatient individuals asserting that Congress would be more expeditious were it not for the eight dollars a day which they receive during the session. This delay may seem irreconcilable with one of the distinctive traits of the American character, but in reality is imperiously demanded by the form and spirit of the government, by the institutions and political habits of the country.

The general discussion in Congress has no other object than to open a full and free public inquiry which enables each and all to have an opinion. It gives rise to a discussion of the question by the innumerable journals in the United States (where there are twelve hundred political newspapers), by the twenty-four legislatures, each composed of two houses, and by the public meetings in the cities and towns. It is an animated exchange of arguments of every caliber and every degree, of contradictory resolutions mixed up with applauses and hisses, of exaggerated eulogies and brutal invectives. A stranger who finds himself suddenly thrown into the midst of this hubbub is confounded and stupefied; he thinks himself present at the primeval or the final chaos, or at least at the general breaking up of the Union. But after a certain time some gleams of light break forth from these thick clouds, from the bosom of this confusion—gleams which the good sense of the people hails with joy and which light up the Congress. We see here the realization of the *Forum* on an immense scale, the *Forum* with its tumult, its cries, its pasquinades, but also with its sure instincts, and its flashes of native and untaught genius. It is a spectacle, in its details occasionally prosaic and repulsive, but, as a whole, in the mass, imposing as the heaving ocean.

In a country like this, it is impossible to avoid these delays; first, because it takes a long time to interchange words between the frontiers of Canada and the Gulf of Mexico and, secondly, because nothing is so dangerous as precipitation in a *Forum*, whether it only covers the narrow space between the *Rostra* and the Tarpeian Rock, or extends from Lake Champlain to the mouth of the Mississippi and from Illinois to the tip of Florida. Unfortunately the session in the *Forum* lasts longer than usual this time. The demagogues have set the popular passions in violent agitation. The sovereign people has allowed itself to be hypnotized by its flatterers, and it will require some time to be able to shake off the trance. The healing beam which will fix the gaze of the multitude and dissipate the charm that envelops them has not yet broken forth from the East or from the West; meanwhile the merchants and manufacturers, who are stretched upon the coals, writhe in vain; there is no answer to their cries.

The Bank, meantime, disappears from sight and keeps silence. It continues to attend to its own business and prudently confines itself to that alone. Its best policy is to avoid as much as possible making itself the subject of common talk. The demagogues have raised such a cry of monopoly and aristocracy that the people have come to believe the Bank a colossus of aristocracy, a prop of monopoly. These words *monopoly* and *aristocracy* are here what the word *Jesuits* was in France a few years ago. If the enemies of any institution can write on its back this kind of *abracadabra*, it is pointed at, hooted at, and hissed at by the multitude. Such is the magic power of these words that speculators employ them on all occasions as charms to draw customers. For example, at the head of the advertisements of steamboats you read in staring characters: NO MONOPOLY! ! ! It is pitiful to say that the Bank of the United States has a monopoly when there are no less than five hundred other banks in the country; by this course of reasoning one might convict the sun of enjoying a monopoly of light. And yet the multitude has believed it and believes it still. Now the best policy for those against whom such a storm of unpopularity is raised is to run for port, as sailors do in a gale of wind. The Bank has twice attempted to strike a blow by taking advantage of the mistakes of its enemies and both times the stroke has recoiled on itself.

The first time, the subject of dispute was a draft on the French government which was sold to the Bank last year by the Federal government and which France refused to pay; the draft was, therefore, protested and then paid by the correspondent of the Bank in Paris in honor of the endorser. In this affair the Executive of the United States committed two faults: [1.] It was an act of indiscretion to draw on the French government before the Chambers had made the necessary appropriation for paying the stipulated indemnity. [2.] Instead of drawing on the French government by a bill of exchange and selling the bill to the Bank without knowing whether it would be accepted, the Executive would have conducted itself with more propriety toward France, toward the Bank, and toward itself, if it had authorized the Bank to receive the moneys paid by the French government, in the capacity of its agent or attorney. By the commercial practice of all countries, and of this in particular, the Bank had a right to damages and it put in its claim. Its object in taking this step was much more to expose the errors of the Executive than to pocket the sum of $50,000 or $80,000. But its adversaries immediately raised the cry that the Bank was not contented with exacting enormous sums from the sweat of the people to the profit of the stockholders (observe that the dividends of the Bank are moderate, compared with those of other banking companies in the country, and that the Federal government is itself the largest shareholder); but that it was now attempting, by petty chicanery, to extort a portion of the public revenue and to bury the *people's money in Biddle's pockets*. To this reasoning, and it passes for demonstration, the multitude answered by imprecations against monopoly and the moneyed aristocracy and by renewed shouts of HURRAH FOR JACKSON!

A few days since, we witnessed another episode of this kind. The Bank is charged, by act of Congress, with the duty of paying the pensions of the old soldiers of the Revolution. It performs the service gratuitously, and it is notoriously a troublesome one. It has received several sums of money for this object and at this moment has about $500,000 in its vaults, intended for the next payments. The Administration, desirous of transferring this agency from the Bank, has demanded the funds, books, and papers connected with it. The Bank replied that it has been made the depository of this trust by act of Congress, and that it cannot, ought not, and will not surrender it, unless in obedience to an act of Congress. The Bank was right; the refusal was founded in justice. But mark the consequences: its adversaries express the greatest sympathy for these illustrious relics of the Revolution whom the arrogance of the Bank, they say, is about to plunge at the close of their career into the most dreadful misery. They pour forth the most pathetic lamentations over these glorious defenders of the country whom a *money corporation* is about to strip of the provision made for their declining years by the nation's gratitude. You may imagine all the noisy arguments and patriotic harangues that can be delivered on this text. On the fourth of February, the President sent a message to Congress in the same strain. All this is mere declamation, of the most commonplace and the most hypocritical kind; for who will prevent the deliverers of America from duly receiving their pensions, except those who shall refuse them drafts on the Bank which the Bank would pay at once? But a people hypnotized is not stopped by logic. It is at this moment believed by the multitude that the Bank has determined to kill the noble veterans of Independence by hunger. Once more, then, anathemas against monopoly, hatred to the moneyed aristocracy! HURRAH FOR JACKSON! JACKSON FOREVER!

Whenever, therefore, the Bank has allowed itself to be drawn into conflict, which is the enemy's country, it is pronounced to be in the wrong, though it were ten times right. On the contrary, when it has kept to its discounts and credits, it has always been able without opening its mouth to belie the charges of its enemies, who not only impute to it the atrocious crime of being suspected of aristocracy and monopoly, but attribute to it now the public distress which they denied the existence of a few months ago and which they are themselves the authors of. Very lately the Bank came to the relief of several local banks which were in danger of failing and a few days since it opened its coffers liberally to Allen & Company, one of the principal houses in the country, who, although having a capital much beyond the amount of its debts, was obliged by the pressure of the times to suspend payments; the failure of that house, which has no less than twenty-four branches, would have involved hundreds of others. This is the only way in which the Bank should assume the offensive. Such acts, without a word of comment, would secure it the favor and the support of all impartial and enlightened men and the gratitude of the commercial interest much more completely than the most eloquent protests against the measures of this or that secretary, or the most ingenious and able defense of itself.

I am more and more convinced that the United States will reap advantage from this crisis; sooner or later the reform of the banking system must result from it. Very probably, the National Bank, if it is maintained, and the local banks will hereafter be less absolutely separated from the

Federal and State governments; that is to say that the Federal and local governments will assume the control of the banks and consequently the banks will become a part of the governments. In this way many of the abuses of the banking system will be reformed and the legitimate and just influence of the banks will be strengthened. It would be easy to cite numerous facts which go to prove the tendency toward this result; thus in some of the States, the legislatures have established, or are establishing, banks in which the State is a shareholder to the amount of one half or two fifths of the capital, appoints a certain number of the directors, and reserves to itself an important control over the operations. There are some States, as for example Illinois, in which every other kind of bank is expressly forbidden by the constitution.

Republican publicists acknowledge only three classes of powers, the executive, legislative, and judicial. But it will soon be seen in the United States that there is also a financial power, or at least the banks will form a branch of government quite as efficient as any of the others. The Bank of the United States is more essential to the prosperity of the country than the Executive power as it is now organized. The latter conducts a little diplomatic intercourse, well or ill, with the European powers, nominates and removes some unimportant functionaries, maneuvers an army of six thousand men in the western wilderness, adds now and then some sticks of timber to the dozen ships of war that are on the stocks at Portsmouth, Boston, New York, Philadelphia, Washington, Norfolk, and Pensacola. All this might actually cease to be done without endangering the safety of the country and without seriously wounding its prosperity, that is, its industry. But take from the country its institutions for the maintenance of credit, or only that which controls and regulates all the others, the Bank of the United States, and you plunge it into a commercial anarchy which would finally result in political anarchy.

The word *politics* cannot have the same meaning in the

United States as in Europe. The United States are not engaged, like the nations of Europe, in territorial alliances and the preservation of the balance of a continent, nor are they entangled in treaties of Westphalia or Vienna. They are free from all those difficulties which in Europe arise from a difference of origin or religion, or from the conflict between rival pretensions, between old interests and new interests. They have no neighbor which excites their suspicions. Politics in the United States consists in the extension of commerce and the occupation by agriculture of the vast domain which nature has given them. In these points is involved the great mass of their general and individual interests; these are the objects which inflame their political and individual passions. As the banks are the soul of their commerce, their rising manufactures, and even their agriculture, it is evident that the success of their *politics* is intimately and directly connected with the right organization of their banking system. The real government of the country, that is to say, the control of its essential interests, is as much in the banks as in any body or power established by the Constitution. The time is come when this fact should be recognized and sanctioned. As among a military people the office of marshal or lord-high-constable is the first in the kingdom, so among a people which has nothing to do with war and has only to employ itself with its industry, that of president of the central bank, for example, ought to be a public charge, *political,* in the sense adapted to the condition and wants of that people—and one of the first rank in the country.

From this point of view, it may be said that what is now passing in the United States is a struggle in which the combatants are, on the one side, the military interest and the law, which have hitherto divided between them the control of public affairs, and on the other, the financial interest, which now claims its share in them; the two first have coalesced against the last and have succeeded for a time in raising the multitude against it, but they will fail in the long run since the multitude has more to gain from it than from them. It is said that when the committee of the New York merchants went to Washington to present a petition with ten thousand names in favor of the Bank, the President observed to them that they declared the grievances of the brokers, capitalists, and merchants of Wall Street and Pearl Street, but that Wall Street and Pearl Street were not the people. I do not know whether the story is true or not, but I know that such an answer would express the opinion of the dominant party. There is a school here which attempts to eliminate the wealthy classes from the people and which is just the reverse of the old school of European Tories which counts the people as only the higher classes and excludes from that rank the greater number of the nation. And nothing can be more unjust, for in order to measure the real importance of the men of Pearl Street and Wall Street, it is only necessary to consider what New York would be without them.

In fifty years the population of New York has increased tenfold, its wealth probably a hundredfold; its animating influences have been felt for hundreds of miles around. This unparalleled growth is not the work of lawyers and military men; the merit belongs chiefly to the industry, the capital, the intelligence, and the enterprise of that, numerically speaking, insignificant minority of Wall Street and Pearl Street. It is very easy to cant about the aristocracy of dollars and those filthy metals which men call gold and silver. And yet have not those vile metals ceased to be vile when they are the fruit of the industry and enterprise of those who possess them? If there is a country in the world where it is preposterous to prate about the aristocracy of dollars and about filthy metals, it is this. For here, more than anywhere else, everybody has some employment; whoever has capital is engaged in turning it to profit and can neither increase it nor even keep it without great activity and vigilance. A man's wealth is, therefore, very generally in the ratio of his importance, and even of his agricultural, manufacturing, or commercial capacity. The merchants are not without their faults; they are disposed to weigh everything in their money-scales, and a people governed entirely by merchants would certainly be one to be pitied. But a people governed by lawyers or by soldiers would be no happier and no freer. The policy of the Hamburg Senate in basely giving up unhappy political fugitives to the English executioner deserves the contempt of every man of honor; but would the rule of Russian or even of Napoleon's bayonets, or the babbling anarchy of the Directory, be less loathsome to those whose hearts beat with the love of liberty or with feelings of individual and national honor?

The revolutions of the ages which change religion, manners, and customs, modify also the nature of the powers that regulate society. Providence humbles the mighty when they obstinately shut their eyes to the new spirit of the age and raises up the lowly whom this new spirit fires. Four thousand years ago, it was one of the most important dignities in Egypt to have the charge of embalming the sacred birds or of spreading the litter of the bull Apis. In the Eastern empire the post of *protovestiary* was one of the first in the state and, not to go so far back, it was the ambition of many in France, hardly four years ago, to become *gentilhomme de la chambre*. Even today, among the great dignitaries who surround the King of England there is the *Groom of the Stole*, which literally means the servant in charge of the wardrobe.

Nobody nowadays embalms sacred birds, nobody spreads the litter of Apis. No one intrigues for the post of protovestiary or gentleman of the chamber and, from present appearances, I do not think that even the dignity of Groom of the Stole will long be an object of ambition in England. There are no longer lord-high-constables, or great vassals, or knights-errant, or peers of France in the old sense of the word. The French aristocracy, so brilliant fifty years ago, has fallen like corn before the reaper. The mansions of the old heroes have become factories; the convents have been changed into spinning works; I have seen Gothic naves in the best style of art transformed into workshops or granaries, and our brave troops have become peaceable laborers on the military roads.

Boards of petty clerks, whom the Castellans had employed to record their sovereign decrees, became in France *parlements* which braved the kings and assumed the guardianship of the laws of the realm. At present the forge masters of Burgundy and the Nivernais, the distillers of Montpellier, the clothiers of Sedan and Albeuf, have taken the place of the *parlements*. German princes who can boast of their fifty quarters dance attendance in the imperial, royal, or ministerial antechambers, while Their Majesties or Their Excellencies are conversing familiarly with some banker who has no patent of nobility and who even disdains to oblige his royal friends by receiving one. The East India Company, a company of merchants if ever there was one, has more subjects than the emperors of Russia and Austria together. If in the Old World, where the old interests had marked every corner of the land with their stamp, the old interests, the military and the law, are thus obliged to come to terms with the new interest of industry, with the power of money, how can it be possible that in the New World, where the past has never taken deep root, where all thoughts are turned toward business and wealth, this same power will not force its way into the political scene, in spite of the opposition of its adversaries and its envious rivals?

VII

Railroads in America

The Rage for Railroads in America — Universal Use of Railroads — Glance at Railroads in the United States

Richmond (Virginia), March 15, 1834. Three thousand years ago the kings of the earth were happy, happy as kings; but the old proverb is now become a falsehood. Then no Constantinople was coveted; the citadels of Antwerp and Ancona were not built. No one troubled himself about the frontier of the Rhine; simple Herodotus told marvelous tales, like those of the *Arabian Nights,* about the country which it watered. The banks of the Danube were trackless morasses; Vienna was not yet, nor of course the Treaty of Vienna. Peace reigned between the sovereigns, or at least their contests were altogether academical, philosophical, and literary. The good king Nectanebus, an enlightened prince, a patron of the arts, played charades with his neighbors, the mighty monarchs of Asia; he guessed all their riddles without their being able to solve his in turn; his glory was unmatched, his people rolled in prosperity. The condition of men of letters and science was, to be sure, somewhat of the meanest; grammarians and philosophers were sometimes dragged to market with halters on their necks, to be sold like cattle, a treatment to which none but Negroes are now subject. But if they were men of genius, their good star threw them into the hands of the best of masters, such as Xanthus, the kindest and most patient man the world has ever known, or good-natured princes, like Nectanebus, who knew how to appreciate true merit. Aesop, having become the property of this good king, soon got to be his counselor, friend, and confidant, revised his charades and riddles, and suggested new ones to the king in such a modest way that Nectanebus really believed himself the author of them. One day Nectanebus, by his advice, proposed to his rival monarchs this difficult problem: How would you build a city in the air? After they had puzzled their brains without success, Nectanebus prepared to give a solution of the question in the presence of the ambassadors of the Asiatic sovereigns solemnly convened; Aesop put some little boys in baskets which were carried up into the air by eagles trained for the purpose and the boys began to cry out to the astonished ambassadors; "Give us stone and mortar and we will build you a city."

This old story has often occurred to my mind since I have been in the United States and I have often said to myself, if Aesop's boys had been Americans, instead of having been subjects of King Nectanebus, they would have demanded materials, not for building a city, but for constructing a railroad. In fact there is a perfect mania in this country on the subject of railroads.

While at Liverpool, I went aboard the ship *Pacific* to engage a berth, and Captain Waite, a very worthy man who believes in God with all his heart and is not any the less on that account a very skillful commander and a most intrepid sailor, offered me the latest American newspapers. The first I opened happened to be the *Railroad Journal*. Soon after sailing I fell seasick and had scarcely a moment's relief till my arrival at New York; of all my recollections of the voyage, the most distinct is that of having heard the word *railroad* occurring once every ten minutes in the conversation of the passengers. At New York, I went to visit the docks for building and repairing vessels; after having examined the dry dock and two or three other docks, my guide, himself an enthusiast on the subject of railroads, carried me to the railroad dock where the ships are moved along a railway. In Virginia, I found railroads at the bottom of the coal mines, which are not, indeed, new to a European. At Philadelphia I visited the excellent penitentiary where everything was neat, quiet, and comfortable (if that word may be applied to a prison) in comparison with the abominable prisons in France, which are noisy, filthy, unhealthy, cold in winter and damp in summer. The warden, Mr. Wood, who manages the institution with great vigilance and philanthropy—after having shown me the prisoners' cells, the yards in which they take the air, the kitchen where the cooking is done by steam, and allowed me to visit one of the convicts, a poor fellow from Alsace —said to me, just as I was taking my leave: "But you have not seen everything yet, I must show you my railroad"; and in fact there was a railroad in the prison on the second floor, along which glided the cart in which food was brought to the prisoners.

Some days ago I happened to be in the little city of Petersburg, which stands at the falls of the Appomattox and near which there is an excellent railroad. A merchant of the city took me to a manufactory of tobacco in which some peculiar processes were employed. In these works was manufactured that sort of tobacco which most Americans chew and will chew for some time to come in spite of the severe, but in this matter just, censures of English travelers, unless the fashion of vetoes should spread in the United States and the women should set theirs on the use of tobacco with as unyielding a resolution as the President has shown toward the Bank. After having wandered about the workshops amid the poor little slaves by whom they are filled, I was stopping to look at some of these blacks, who appeared to me almost white and who had not more than one eighth of African blood in their veins, when my companion said to me, "As you are interested in railroads, you must see the one belonging to the works." Accordingly we went to the room where the tobacco is packed in kegs and subjected to a powerful pressure. The apparatus for pressing is a very peculiar contrivance—I will not now stop to describe it—the most important part of which is a movable railroad, suspended from the ceiling. Thus the Americans have railroads in the water, in the bowels of the earth, and in the air. The benefits of the invention are so palpable to their practical good sense that they endeavor to make an application of it everywhere and to everything, rightly or wrongly. When they cannot construct a real, profitable railroad across the country from river to river, from city to city, or from State to State, they get one up, at least as a plaything or until they can accomplish something better, under the form of a machine.

The distance from Boston to New Orleans is sixteen hundred miles, or twice the distance from Havre to Marseilles. It is highly probable that within a few years this immense line will be covered by a series of railroads stretching from bay to bay, from river to river, and offering to the ever-impatient Americans the service of their rapid cars at the points where the steamboats leave their passengers. This is not a castle in the air, like so many of those grand schemes which are projected amid the fogs of the Seine, the Loire, and the Garonne. It is a fact already half realized. The railroad from Boston to Providence is in active progress; the work goes on *à l'américaine*, that is to say, rapidly. From New York to Philadelphia, there will soon be not only one open to travel, but two in competition with each other, the one on the right, the other on the left bank of the Delaware; the passage between the two cities will be made in seven hours, five hours on the railroad, and two in the steamboat on the beautiful Hudson and the magnificent Bay of New York, which the Americans who are not afflicted with modesty compare with the Bay of Naples. From Philadelphia, travelers go to Baltimore by the Delaware and Chesapeake, and by the Newcastle and Frenchtown railroad, in eight hours; from Baltimore to Washington, a railroad has been resolved upon, a company chartered, the shares taken, and the work begun, all within the space of a few months. Between Washington and Blakely, in North Carolina, 60 miles of railroad are completed, from Blakely northward. A company has just been chartered to complete the remaining distance, that is, from Richmond to the Potomac, 70 miles, and the Potomac bears you to the Federal city, passing on the way Mount Vernon, a delightful spot, the patrimony of George Washington where he passed his honored old age and where his body now reposes in a modest tomb. Between Washington and Blakely, those who prefer the steamboats may take another route; by descending the Chesapeake to Norfolk, they will find another railroad, 70 miles in length, of which two thirds are now finished, and which carries them to Blakely, and even beyond. Blakely is a new town which you will not find on any map, born of yesterday; it is the eldest, and as yet the only daughter of the Petersburg railroad. From Blakely to Charleston, South Carolina, the distance is great, but the Americans are enterprising and there is no region in the world in which railroads can be constructed so easily and so cheaply; the surface has been graded by nature and the vast forests which cover it will furnish the wood of which the railroad will be made; for here most of these works have a wooden superstructure. From Charleston, a railroad 137 miles in length, as yet the longest in the world, extends to Augusta, whence to Montgomery, Alabama, there is a long interval to be supplied. From Montgomery, steamboats descend the River Alabama to Mobile, and those who do not wish to pay their respects to the Gulf of Mexico on their way to New Orleans will soon find a railroad which will spare them the necessity of offering this act of homage to the memory of the great Cortez.

Within ten years this whole line will be completed and traversed by locomotive engines, provided the present crisis terminates promptly and happily, as I hope it will. Ten years is a long time in these days and a plan whose execution requires ten years seems like a romance or a dream. But in respect to railroads, the Americans already have something to show. Pennsylvania, which by the last census, in 1830, contained only 1,348,000 inhabitants, has 325 miles of railroads actually completed, or which will be so within the year, without reckoning 76 miles which the capitalists of Philadelphia have constructed in the little States of New Jersey and Delaware. The total length of all the railroads in France is 95 miles, that is, a little more than what the citizens of Philadelphia, in their liberality, have given to their poor neighbors. In the State of New York, whose population is the most adventurous and the most successful in their speculations, there are at present only four or five short railroads, but if the sixth part of those which are projected and authorized by the legislature are executed, New York will not be behind Pennsylvania in this respect. The merchants of Baltimore, which at the time of the Declaration of Independence contained 6,000 inhabitants, and which now numbers 100,000, have taken it into their heads to make a railroad between their city and the Ohio, a distance of above 300 miles. They have begun it with great spirit and have now finished about one third of the whole road. In almost every section east of the Ohio and the Mississippi there are railroads projected, in progress, or completed, and on most of them locomotive steam engines are employed. There are some in the Alleghenies, whose inclined planes are really terrific because of their angle of climb; these were originally designed only for the transportation of goods, but passenger cars have been set up on them at the risk of breaking the necks of travelers. There are here works well constructed and ill constructed; there are some that have cost dear (from $40,000 to $50,000 a mile), and others that have cost little (from $10,000 to $15,000 a mile). New Orleans has one, a very modest one to be sure, only five miles long, but it will soon have others and, after all, it is ahead of old Orléans, for the latter has yet to wait till its capitalists, seized with some violent fit of patriotism, shall be ready to make the sacrifice of devoting some ten or twelve per cent of their capital to the construction of a railroad thence to Paris. Virginia, whose population is nearly the same as that of the Department of the North in France, and which is inferior in wealth, already has 75 miles of railroad fully completed and 110 in progress, exclusive of those begun this year. The Department of the North, where it would be quite as easy to construct them and where they would be more productive, has not a foot completed or in progress and hardly a foot projected. Observe, moreover, that I here speak of railroads alone, the rage for which is quite new in America, while that for canals is of very old date (for in this country fifteen years is an age) and has achieved wonders. There are States which contain 500, 800, or 1,000 miles of canals. We in France are of all people the boldest in theory and speculation and we have made the world tremble by our political experiments; but during the last twenty years we have shown ourselves the most timid of nations in respect to physical improvements.

VIII

The Banks—The Preservation of the Union

Truce Between the Parties — Possibility of a Compromise — The Democracy Must Prevail — The Bond of Union Grows Weaker — Probability of the Preservation of the Union — Changes Which It May Undergo — The Three Sections, North, South, and West

Washington, April 10, 1834.

The drama which has been taking place in the United States since the opening of the session has now reached the end of the first act. The two Houses have had under consideration the subject of the removal of the public deposits from the Bank of the United States to the local banks by the Executive and both of them have come to a decision. The Senate has declared by a majority of 28 to 18 that the reasons alleged by the Secretary of the Treasury in justification of the measure were neither satisfactory nor sufficient and, by a majority of 26 to 20, that the conduct of the President in this matter was neither conformable to the Constitution nor to the laws. This is the first instance, since the adoption of the Federal Constitution, of a censure of the Chief Executive of the nation by the Senate. The House has resolved, on its part, that the charter of the Bank ought not to be renewed, that the public deposits ought not to be restored to it, and that they should remain in the safekeeping of the local banks. The first resolve passed by a vote of 132 to 82; the majority for the two others was much less, 118 to 103, and 117 to 105. It has been resolved by a large majority, 171 to 42, that the conduct of the Bank should be made a subject of investigation, but this majority includes many friends of the Bank.

After these contradictory decisions which leave the majorities of the two Houses facing each other in opposition, there has been a truce. People want to know the result of two important elections. New York City is at this moment electing its mayor; Virginia, this coming April, will elect its legislature; New York is the most populous city of the Union and the most important commercial center; it is the city that the Administration party has catered to most and which it seeks to make the center of its strength in the next Presidential election. The Democratic party has had up to now a popular majority, but merchants, businessmen, and men of affairs have been nearly unanimously on the Opposition's side. Virginia, on the other hand, once one of the strongest supporters of General Jackson, has recently turned against him. The last Virginia legislature has opposed the old General; two months ago it forced Mr. Rives, who preceded Mr. Livingston as Minister to Paris, from his Senate seat because he had supported the President. Of all the States, Virginia has had the most illustrious body of representatives and her opinion has always carried great weight. Therefore, people wait anxiously to see if New York will continue to support General Jackson and if Virginia will persist in opposing him. Meanwhile each side is preparing a new campaign.

On what grounds will the new political struggle be fought? In the interests of the bank, I only hope that it will not be fought around that institution. The more vigorously it is defended, the more hateful it becomes to the democracy. Those Americans who feel an interest in their country and its institutions ought to make an effort to turn the debate toward some other point, for gradually both sides have become heated and exasperated in the struggle and already violence has been threatened. The most brilliant services have been forgotten, the purest characters trampled underfoot. The *Globe,* the avowed organ of the Administration, pours forth the vilest slanders on men such as Messrs. Clay, Calhoun, and Webster, of whom any country in the world would be proud. It has repeated and unhappily repeats still that the votes of the Senate have been bought by the Bank's gold. On the other hand, General Jackson, to whom it is impossible to deny the possession of eminent qualities, has been himself exposed to the vilest indignities. The gray hairs of that brave old man have borne the most scandalous insults. Attempts have even been made to throw ridicule on his victory at New Orleans, the most brilliant feat of arms in American annals, as if his glory were not the common property of the country. Some hotheads have even talked of recurring to violence. Commerce and enterprise have been struck numb. For want of means, the great public works of Pennsylvania have been in danger of being brought to a halt. But at present there appears to be a general wish to restore calm. The failure of a certain number of individuals, and especially of some banks, has proved a signal of alarm which has recalled everyone to a sense of the common danger, the general ruin that has threatened the country. There has been a failure of a bank in Florida, one in New Jersey, and two in Maryland, one of which, that of the Bank of Maryland in Baltimore, has caused a great sensation. The leading men of all parties have in good faith set themselves to search out some means of bringing the commercial crisis to an end. There is room to hope, therefore, that the debate will lose its bitterness, and at the same time will take a wider range. Instead of quarreling about the particular question of the Bank, it were to be wished that the higher questions of political economy should be discussed, such as that of a mixed currency in which there should be the proper mixture of paper and the metals necessary to give it stability, without keeping, as is the case in Europe, a large unproductive capital in the shape of specie; and that of a system of institutions of credit, banks of loan and discount, of deposit and exchange, powerful enough to serve as a spring and a support to the industry of the country, and yet so balanced in respect to each other and the powers of the government as not to be dangerous to the public liberties. A very able speech of Mr. Calhoun's has already drawn the general attention to the subject of financial reform, and one of the Senators friendly to the Administration, Mr. Benton, has embodied some of Mr. Calhoun's ideas in the shape of a bill to be presented to the Senate.

Everyone in the United States now agrees that to obtain a solid and stable currency it is necessary to keep a certain quantity of gold and silver in the country. It is perfectly understood that while there are paper dollars, silver dollars will disappear, that ten-dollar notes necessarily expel eagles, and that half-eagles will not stay where there are five-dollar bills. It is, therefore, proposed to abolish the issue of notes of less than ten or even twenty dollars, but all that Congress can do without the aid of a National Bank is to prohibit the reception by the collectors-of-the-customs of the bills of any bank which has in circulation notes of less than ten or twenty dollars; for Congress has no direct power over the local banks. This measure, however, would be insufficient; for the amount of money paid for customs bears a very small proportion to the whole circulation of the country and consequently would not affect the circulation in districts remote from the seacoast. The Administration does not deny the necessity of a police for controlling and regulating the banks; it seems disposed to effect it by means of some of the local banks which would act under the direction of the Secretary of the Treasury and which would gain certain privileges, such as that of being the depositories of the public money without paying interest. But this plan has some disadvantages; it would invest the Secretary, really the President, with a great discretionary power which is wholly at war with the political maxims of American government. It is a received truth in the United States that the sword and the purse ought not to be in the same hands. Besides, it is doubtful whether this control would be sufficiently powerful and sufficiently enlightened; and, finally, it would be difficult by means of this chain of local banks to answer one of the most pressing wants of the country, facility of exchange, because they are, and must be, as slightly connected with each other as the sovereign States from which they hold their charters. To exterminate small banknotes the surest agent would be a National Bank, and Congress has the power to establish one. This power, which is disputed because all its powers are disputed, would not be contested if it were stipulated that the Bank should obtain the consent of each State before establishing a branch within the State's limits. It would then be sufficient that the Bank should not receive the bills of any other bank which issued notes of less than ten or twenty dollars, or which received the bills of other banks that issued notes of less than the same minimum. In fine, a National Bank is an admirable instrument of exchange, and the most influential friends of the Administration are convinced of the necessity of an institution of the sort. I cannot believe that the President, and especially the Vice President, are really as much opposed to one as they have the air of being. As it is possible to conceive of a combination of circumstances which may reconcile its existence with the interests and views of Mr. Van Buren (such would be, for instance, the creation of a Bank of which the seat should be in New York instead of Philadelphia), it may be hoped that sooner or later, under one form or another, Mr. Van Buren may yield to the necessity of the case. It is true that out of hatred to the present Bank the prejudices of the multitude have been excited against the establishment of any bank at all and it is much more easy to rouse the popular passions than to control them when once let loose; this kind of game has resulted in the self-destruction of many a man's popularity. But in this matter the voice of the public interest and of individual interest will speak so loudly that it would be astonishing if it did not make itself heard by a people so much more sensible and reflecting than most European people. There is, then, in short, still some chance for a Bank of the United States.

Following are the principal features in which the economists of both parties seem to me to be at present tacitly agreed. The capital of a National Bank to be about 50 millions. The shares of the present Bank, representing a capital of 35 millions, to be exchanged at par for shares in the new Bank; the rest of the capital to be subscribed by the individual States, thus giving the new Bank a more truly national character. The rate of discount to be reduced from six to five per cent; Mr. Forsyth, a Senator friendly to the Administration, has demanded this modification. The laws relative to public and private deposits to be changed in conformity with the propositions of Mr. Cambreleng. The seat of the mother bank to be transferred perhaps to New York. The operations of the new Bank to be subjected to more strict regulations than those of the old Bank; the Bank to be required to keep on hand a larger amount of reserved profits, or some other provision borrowed from the bank of England to be adopted, in order to give more security to the institution.

THE BANKS—PRESERVATION OF THE UNION

It would not, probably, be impossible to unite a majority of the two Houses in favor of a plan which should embrace these features. But there is another subject about which little is said and upon which no one has yet publicly declared himself, although there are many who have thought much about it and it will not be easy to reconcile opinions upon it. How shall the Bank be governed? What relation shall there be between the administration of the Bank and the Federal and State governments? How and by whom shall the president of the Bank be chosen? This subject, about which there is a total silence, appears to me to be of such vital importance that I am convinced that what has occurred in the United States during the last six months would never have taken place if the nomination of the president of the Bank had been directly or indirectly in the hands of the President of the United States.

In Europe and particularly in France, the government of the banks is more or less in the hands and under the control of the king and the ministers. In America, in accordance with the principles of self-government, the Bank, like all the other industrial and financial institutions, has up to this time governed itself. The Federal government, owning one fifth of the shares, names one fifth of the directors; its powers stop there. The American axiom, which forbids the union of the sword and the purse in the same hand, is opposed to the exercise of a controlling influence over the choice of the president of the Bank by the President of the United States; and yet I am persuaded that the Democratic party will not be willing to hear of a Bank in the management of which it could not interfere.

The upper classes (*bourgeoisie*) are not here what they are in Europe; while in Europe they rule, here they are ruled. Democracy takes its revenge in America for the unjust contempt with which it has been so long treated in Europe. Now it is to these upper classes that the private shareholders of the Bank belong; it is the merchants, manufacturers, and capitalists who will always derive the most direct benefit from a National Bank, although all classes must indirectly derive great advantages from it. From the time when the upper classes sanctioned a completely universal suffrage without making any exception in favor of natural superiority, whether industrial or scientific, from the day when they consented that number should be everything and knowledge and capital nothing, they signed their own abdication. It is too late to agitate the questions whether this is absolutely a good or an evil, or whether it is good in the agricultural States with a scattered population, such as Ohio, Indiana, and Illinois, and evil in large and populous cities, the seats of a vast commerce, such as Philadelphia and New York. This is a matter already settled past recall; when the sword is surrendered, the vanquished must submit to take the law from the victor. In case, then, of the creation of a new National Bank, the shareholders must consent to receive their head, either from the President and Senate, as other public functionaries are appointed, or from the House of Representatives alone, or from some other similar source. If in a new or a somewhat modified Bank, the Federal and local governments should be stockholders to a large amount, this participation of the President or the House of Representatives, or of special delegates chosen by the States, in the management of the Bank, would appear altogether natural, even in the eyes of the most exclusive partisans of self-government. It remains to be seen whether, in this case, the Bank would not be more likely to become the instrument of party, a *den of intrigue and corruption*, a *golden calf*, a *monster*, as it is so often unjustly called, than in the present state of things.

If this quarrel should be terminated by a compromise, we may expect that it will be effected on the basis which I have presented. The upper classes will, perhaps, consider the conditions hard, but they should beware of rejecting them. It would be a great gain to them to obtain, under any form, a decisive sanction of a National Bank connected with the government and therefore incorporated with the interests of the country. Not only are numbers at present against the Bank, and numbers give the law here, but the Opposition is not so well organized as the Democratic party. The Opposition has, indeed, three leaders who do not always agree; the views of Mr. Calhoun of South Carolina do not coincide with those of Messrs. Clay and Webster on the subjects of the tariff and States' rights; and Mr. Clay, the son of the West, and Mr. Webster, who comes from Boston, the center of Federalism, differ on several constitutional questions. The Democratic party, on the contrary, is better disciplined; the two heads, General Jackson and Mr. Van Buren, present a formidable union of qualities and faculties. The old General is firm, prompt, bold, energetic; Mr. Van Buren, who sets up for the American Talleyrand, is mild, conciliating, prudent, and sagacious; his adversaries call him the little magician, the great manager, the designer of intrigues. While the pretensions of Messrs. Clay, Calhoun, and Webster are scarcely to be reconciled with each other and no one of them is willing to be second, Mr. Van Buren is ready with all his heart to serve under General Jackson now for the purpose of becoming his successor in the elections of 1836. A kingdom divided against itself cannot stand. But, if no compromise can be made, if the democracy is too untractable and the upper classes persist in claiming more than their position authorizes them to do, if the feelings, kept in a state of excitement, become exasperated on both sides and the contest be too much prolonged, the most frightful consequences may ensue. The Union itself may be endangered.

At the close of the War of Independence, the American confederacy occupied only a narrow strip along the Atlantic. Since that time the wave of an active, enterprising, and rapidly increasing population has rolled over the Alleghenies, the Ohio, the Mississippi, more recently over the Missouri, the Red River, the Arkansas, and I know not how far. Toward the south it is already sweeping over the Sabine and covering Texas, while toward the west, it has topped the Rocky Mountains and is approaching the Pacific shore. Instead of thirteen States, there are twenty-four, and the number will soon be increased to twenty-six. By the side of the old Atlantic strip, two other vast tracts with a more fertile soil have yielded up their riches to civilized man; one, at the west, comprises the great triangle lying between the Ohio, the Mississippi, and the Lakes, and the other at the south includes the fertile regions of Florida and Louisiana which under French and Spanish rule were a solitary wilderness. The geographic center of the Union fifty years ago was on the banks of the Potomac, on the spot where the city of Washington—that paper capital—now stands; it is now at Cincinnati and will soon be near St. Louis.

In proportion as the territory of the confederacy has been extended, the Federal bond has been weakened. It was nearly snapped asunder during the Nullification crisis, occasioned by the resistance of South Carolina to the tariff adopted under the influence of New England in order to protect her growing manufactures. If Congress had not satisfied the demands of South Carolina, Virginia would have made common cause with the latter and her example would have carried the whole South. The patriotic eloquence of Mr. Webster; the moderation of Mr. Clay and his prodigies of parliamentary strategy; the efforts of Mr. Livingston, then Secretary of State; the firm and, at the same time, conciliatory conduct of the President, who for the first time heard a bold defiance with patience; and the calm attitude of the Northern States—all prevented for the moment a general dissolution of the Union. But the germ of mischief remains. The charm of an indissoluble Union is broken. Ears have become familiar with the ominous word SEPARATION. A habit has grown up of thinking, and even of declaring, whenever the interests of the North and the South jar, that the cure-all will be a dissolution of the Union.

South Carolina keeps her militia organized and exacts from the State officers a special oath of allegiance. Georgia and Alabama contest the validity of treaties concluded between the Federal government and the Cherokee and Creek nations. Most of the States seek to extend the limits of their individual sovereignty. The doctrine of States' rights has even insinuated itself into the bosom of orthodox Philadelphia, for I see by the journals that a States' rights dinner is announced there. These symptoms may become full of danger in a moment of universal excitement. When the passions are at the helm, there is no pause in the course. What, for instance, would be the event if Nullification should find an echo in the same States of the North where it has lately been so firmly rejected? It is they that have the most direct interest in the establishment of a National Bank; it is they that suffer most from the financial combinations of General Jackson and from the objections of Southern statesmen against the constitutionality of a bank. Although no allusion is made to this danger, it is evident that the solicitude of many persons has been aroused by it and it is fortunate that it is so, for a more general disposition to conciliatory measures is the consequence.

The principle of separation is engaged in a deadly conflict with the spirit of centralization or consolidation. Hardly was the Constitution signed, when twelve additional articles or amendments were immediately adopted, almost all of which contained restrictions on the powers and attributes of the Federal government. At the same time the authority of Congress to charter a bank and give it powers within the territories of the States, was contested. On this point, however, the principle of union was victorious and the Bank was established. Next, the right of the Federal government to engage in internal improvements was denied, and Congress, after a long struggle, has been compelled to resign its claims; General Jackson willed it and it was done. The National Road which extends from Washington to the western wilderness and for which appropriations have been annually voted, each professing to be the last, shows what the Federal government could do and wished to do. Even the uniform system of weights and measures seems to be on the point of being broken up, in spite of the express provisions of the constitution. Pennsylvania has undertaken, nobody knows why, to establish regulations on this point contrary to the general usage (an act has been passed by the Pennsylvania legislature providing that two thousand pounds shall make a ton).

The public debt is now paid; that is one Federal tie the less. The Bank, assailed afresh, is on the point of falling; that is an immense loss to the Federal principle. The Supreme Court of the United States, one of the bulwarks of the Union, is assaulted. The vast domain of the West, the national property, seems in danger of being given up to individual States, for this disposition is one of the favorite topics of the Democratic party.

But if centralization comes off the worse in Federal politics, it has the better within the States. The principal States are engaged in constructing vast systems of internal communication; they are establishing for themselves financial systems, and many of them are about to set up great banks which shall exercise within their respective limits the salutary influence possessed by the Bank of the United States throughout the whole Union. Thus each State, as it detaches itself from the Federal Union, organizes more fully its own powers and binds more firmly together its imperfectly combined elements. But, on the other hand, industry and the spirit of enterprise restore to the Union the strength which political jealousy and party quarrels tend to take away from it. There is not a family in the North that has not a son or a brother in the South; the community of interests daily grows stronger. Commerce is a centripetal force; along the whole Atlantic coast there is only one mart, New York; there is only one of importance on the Gulf of Mexico, New Orleans; and the relations of New York and New Orleans make these two cities, instead of rivals, mutual supports. The railroads and the steamboats spread over the country the meshes of a net not easily broken. Great distances vanish; before long it will be easy to go from

Boston to New Orleans in eight days, less time than is generally required to go from Brest to Marseilles.

When we reflect on the extent of territory the Roman Empire preserved for centuries, we cannot doubt the possibility of maintaining a certain degree of unity on the American territory, immeasurably vast as it appears to an eye accustomed to the divisions of the map of Europe. The Romans had not attained that degree of perfection in the means of communication which we now possess. Not only had they no knowledge of steamboats and railroads and the telegraph, but they had few highways and were unacquainted with the use of carriages hung on springs. The progress of commercial and financial arts makes it more easy to manage the financial concerns of the universe now than it was to administer those of a province in the time of Caesar. I cannot, therefore, make my mind believe that the Union will be broken up into fragments, driven in different directions and dashing one against another.

And yet it is very possible that the Union will not continue long on its present footing. Are the relations established between the States by the Constitution of 1789 the most perfect that can be devised now? Ought not the unforeseen formation of the two great groups of the West and the Southwest be followed by some modification of those relations? Would not the subdivision of the general confederacy into three subordinate confederacies, conformable to the three great territorial divisions, the North, the South, and the West, with a more intimate union between the members of each group, have the effect of satisfying the advocates of States' rights, without endangering the principle of union? Would not this arrangement be the means of giving more elasticity to the Union? Could not the existence of three partial confederacies be reconciled with that of a central authority, invested with the undisputed powers of the present Federal government—one army, one navy, one diplomatic representation abroad, one common right of citizenship, one Supreme Court, and, as far as possible, one system of customs, and one Bank? These are questions which it will, perhaps, be worth while to examine some day, and even at no distant day. But it would be desirable that they be approached and discussed with calmness. If they should be raised unexpectedly in a period of irritation and bad feelings, they would be the signal of an explosion, of a deplorable catastrophe. Union gives strength. North America, one parceled out into hostile fragments, would be of no more weight in the balance of the world than the feeble republics of South America.

IX

The First People in the World

Pretensions of Every Nation to Superiority — Pretensions of the Americans — Superiority Passes from People to People — New Peoples — Russia and the United States — English Opinions of the United States — The Social System of the United States Superior in Respect to the Condition of the Laboring Classes

Philadelphia, April 24, 1834.
Which is the first people in the world? There is no nation which does not make pretensions to this superiority. Who in France has not sung in the words of Béranger, "Queen of the world, oh my country! oh France!" in the full conviction that the French nation was predestined to be forever at the head of the human race, to eclipse all others in peace and in war? For myself, before I had crossed the frontier, I believed profoundly, with a religious faith, that we were not only the most generous and chivalric of people, the most intellectual and ingenious, the first in the fine arts, the most amiable and brilliant, but also that we were

the most enlightened, the first in political and industrial arts, the most inventive and the most practical, in short, the model nation, perfect and unrivaled. Notwithstanding the rains and fogs of Paris, I supposed our climate the mildest and the most serene in the world. In spite of Landes and Champagne, I considered it undeniable that our soil was the most fertile, our scenery the most picturesque in the world. Trusting to the reports of our industrial exhibitions, I was ready to swear that we had left our English neighbors a hundred leagues behind, that their manufacturers, to avoid being reduced to beggary by our competition, would soon be obliged to come over to learn how to smelt and refine iron, how to spin cotton, how to manufacture steel, how to manage the most gigantic establishments in the most economical manner, how to despatch mountains of merchandise beyond the sea most expeditiously.

After having crossed the frontier one gradually lowers these magnificent pretensions; patriotism becomes purer and stronger. In visiting foreign parts one sees what is wanting to the prosperity and glory of his country and how it might be possible to add some jewels to her crown. Thus it does not require long observation to see that if England might borrow much from us, we have not less to learn from her. The English are not only more skillful manufacturers and better merchants than we are, but they possess in a higher degree than we do those qualities which enable men, once having conceived grand projects, to carry them into execution. The English have that practical sagacity and that unending perseverance by which our Titan-like battles of the Revolution and the Empire, our impetuous and devoted enthusiasm, our unparalleled victories, our unmatched triumphs, were reduced to treaties of Vienna, that is to say, were made to result in our own humiliation and in the enthronement of Great Britain on the apex of the European pyramid. The English have less of the gift of speech, but more capacity for action than we have. And it is owing to this that they have found means to extend their colonial possessions while all other nations were losing theirs. What they lost in the West, they have recovered in the East tenfold. They possess that political sense to which they owe the peaceful settlement during the last three years of questions that seemed destined to shake the granite foundations of their island and bury it in the sea. They have achieved their Reform; they have abolished the monopoly of the East India Company; they have reconstructed the Bank; they have abolished slavery. During this period, we have been revolving about questions of secondary importance without being able to make a decision. We do not know how to deal with monopolies which, in comparison with the colossal privileges of the East India Company, are grains of sand; we, who have given to the world the most conclusive arguments in favor of liberty of commerce!

If in Paris we consider ourselves, in all, and for all, and forever, the model for all people, at London the opinion is not less exclusively and decidedly in favor of the English. In London the Duke of Wellington is called the conqueror of Napoleon, which, indeed, is true to the letter, but is nevertheless perfectly ridiculous, although Lord Wellington is certainly an extraordinary man. I have seen Englishmen pettishly shake their head when they were told that the sky of England was foggy; with a little malice, one can make them maintain that they need not envy the climate of Italy and that even the atmosphere of Manchester, where the sight of the sun is a rarity, has charms—in spite of the slanders of its detractors—even for those who have breathed the air of Naples. At Madrid, that heroic people which seems to be awaking at last from its long lethargy has not lost the habit of believing in the supremacy of Spain; and there they dream that they are yet in the glorious days of Charles V when the sun never set on the Spanish dominions. We can pardon this in noble Castilians, but I believe that even Don Pedro and Don Miguel, those interminable Pretenders, have each an official journal which tells them daily that a breathless universe has its eyes fixed on their ragged armies and that the destinies of the world are settled at Santarém and Setubal. At Constantinople, in the capital of an empire which exists only because the European powers cannot agree on the division of the spoils, they call us Europeans *Christian dogs*. In Rome the people still call themselves Romans, and this ridiculous misnomer really makes the populace across the Tiber in old Rome believe that military glory is yet the lot of the country and that the *Romans* will soon resume the character of lords of the world, magnanimously raising the humble and crushing the pride of the powerful (*parcere subjectis, etc.*)! In Vienna, on the contrary, everybody thinks that Rome is no longer in Rome, but that it is, of right and in fact, in the archducal capital; that the emperor is heir by lineal descent to Augustus and Trajan. The device of an early prince of the house of Austria, A.E.I.O.U. (*Austria est imperare orbi universo;* the empire of the world belongs to Austria), attests that this pretension is almost as old as the house of Hapsburg. In Prussia, meanwhile, the young nobles, proud of having studied at the great universities of Jena and Berlin and of having worn the sword in an army once that of Frederick the Great, affect an utter disdain for the Austrians. Elated by the rapid extension of their country, which has not, however, yet reached its full growth, the Prussians look upon their sandy land as the cradle of a new civilization. It seems that the waters of the Spree have miraculous qualities and that whoever has not tasted them has but four senses instead of five. At St. Petersburg and Moscow, no one doubts that the sword of the emperor, thrown into the scales of the world's destinies, would at once overbear the opposite balance. Perhaps we of western Europe have done all that we could in filling the Russians with these high notions of the influence of the Czar. In Russia, the flatteries of the eighteenth century are taken seriously and the inner circle of the aristocracy imagine, on the faith of the greatest enemy of despotism, that today enlightenment comes from the North. What an enlightenment! May Europe be solidly united to form a dike strong enough that it comes to nothing more.

Thus in Europe each nation arrogates to itself the first rank. I do not see why the Americans should be more modest than people on the other side of the Atlantic. The miracles which they have accomplished in fifty years give them a right to be proud. They, also, in their turn, are persuaded that they are the first people in the world, and they boast loudly of their pre-eminence.

The fact is there is no chosen people on whom superiority is entailed for ages. The Jewish people, among whom this notion of predestination seems to have been most deeply rooted, has for centuries afforded the most melancholy refutation of the doctrine. Since the age of Richelieu and the Revolution of 1688—that is, since Spain has fallen asleep—France and England have been at the head of civilization and have divided supremacy between themselves; the one ruling by theory, the other by practice; the one giving the tone in taste, arts and manners, the other in politics. But what were France and England three centuries ago in the time of Charles V, when the generals of that emperor and king slew Bayard at Rebecque, made Francis I prisoner at Pavia and the Pope prisoner in Rome, while four thousand miles farther west, Cortez was conquering for Charles the proud empire of Montezuma? Prussia, who now shares the dominion of Germany and who is worthy of that dignity, who is the youthful, the aspiring, the ambitious Germany, full of the future, as Austria is the patriarchal, sober, prudent, conservative Germany, clinging to the past and the old—what was Prussia three generations ago? What shall we all be, French, English, Prussians, and Austrians three centuries hence, or perhaps one hundred years hence? Who can say that some northern blast, finding us divided, enfeebled by our divisions, will not have laid low those who are now so high and haughty? Who knows if the vigorous race which is now bursting forth from this virgin soil will not then have passed us in their turn, as we have outstripped our predecessors? Who can say whether the two gigantic figures that are now rising above the horizon—that in the East with one foot on Moscow and one just ready to fall on Constantinople, the other in the West, as yet half hidden by the vast forests of the New World, whose huge limbs stretch from the mouths of the St. Lawrence to those of the Mississippi—who can foresee whether these youthful Titans who are watching each other across the Atlantic and already touch hands on the Pacific will not soon divide the empire of the world?

Civilization is a treasure to which each generation adds something in transmitting it to its heirs and which passes from hand to hand, from people to people, from country to country. Setting out from Asia it was four thousand years in reaching the borders of the Atlantic Ocean. Woe to the nations that, having become depositories of the treasure, instead of keeping it with watchful care and laboring to increase it, lay it down by the roadside and waste their time and strength in foolish quarrels! They will soon be robbed of their trust! The Americans are the most enterprising of men and the most ambitious of nations; if we continue to be swallowed up in our barren disputes, they are the people to snatch from us while we are unaware the precious charge of the destinies of our race and to place themselves at the head of its march.

Each people has its qualities, developed by education, which at certain moments shine with peculiar brilliancy, like a beacon light to which the eyes of mankind look and by which its march is guided and which always command the esteem or love or respect of others. The people of the United States most undeniably have theirs. No people is so peculiarly fitted by its intrinsic character, as well as by the circumstances of its territory and the condition of its population, for democratic institutions. The Americans possess, therefore, in the highest degree, the better features of democracy, and they have also its inseparable defects; but if there is something in them to blame, there is still more to praise. There is much here for a European to learn, for one who comes to seek, not subjects for fault-finding, satire, and sarcasm (which have become vulgar commonplaces since the small coin of Voltaire and Byron has passed through so many hands), but positive facts which might be imitated in our old countries with the necessary modifications required by the difference between our circumstances and the condition of America. Almost all English travelers in this country have seen a great deal that was bad and scarcely anything good. The portrait they have drawn of America and the Americans is a caricature which, like all good caricatures, has some resemblance to the original. The Americans have a right to deny the jurisdiction of the tribunal, for they have a right to be tried by their peers and it does not belong to the most complete aristocracy in Europe, the English aristocracy, to sit in judgment on a democracy. Yet all the English travelers in America have belonged to the aristocracy by their connections or their opinions, or have aspired to it, or aped its habits and judgments that they might seem to belong to it.

A Yorkshire farmer or a Birmingham mechanic would certainly pass a very different judgment. He would probably be as exclusively disposed to praise as the most disdainful tourists have been to blame. And the farmers and mechanics count for something in the numbers of the English population and in the elements of the British prosperity. Suppose an Ohio or Illinois farmer, after having sold his flour and salt pork to advantage, should enact the nabob for six months in England and on his return should describe, with the rude eloquence of the West, the distress of the British operatives, the corn laws, the poor rates, the frightful condition of the Irish peasantry, the impressment of sailors, the sale of military offices and, to complete his picture of manners, should add a boxing match, a scene of the guests at a dinner rolling dead drunk under the table, the sale of a wife by her husband in open market; if he should give such a picture to his countrymen as a political and moral portrait of England, the English would shrug their shoulders, and with reason. Yet his story would be founded on facts and could not be said to be actually false in any particular. Now such a story would be an exact counterpart of most of the representations of America by English travelers. Do not unto others what you would not have others do unto you.

There is one thing in the United States that strikes a stranger on stepping ashore and is of a sort to silence his sentiments of national pride, particularly if he is an Englishman: it is the appearance of general ease in the condition of the people of this country. While European communities are more or less cankered with the sore of pauperism for which their ablest statesmen have as yet been able to find no healing balm, there are no poor here, at least not in the Northern and Western States which have protected themselves from the leprosy of slavery. If a few such individuals are seen, they are only an imperceptible minority of dissolute or improvident persons, commonly people of color, or some newly landed emigrants who have not been able to adopt industrious habits. Here nothing is more easy than to live and to live well by labor. Objects of the first necessity, bread, meat, sugar, tea, coffee, fuel, are in general cheaper here than in France and wages are double or triple. I happened, a few days ago, to be on the line of a railroad in process of construction where they were throwing up some embankments. This sort of labor, which requires only muscle, not skill, is commonly done in the United States by Irish newcomers who have no resource but their arm, no quality but muscular strength. These Irish laborers are fed and lodged, and here is their bill of fare: three meals a day and at each meal plenty of meat and wheat bread, coffee and sugar at two meals, and butter once a day; in the course of the day, from six to eight glasses of whiskey are given them according to the state of the weather. Besides which they receive for pay forty cents a day under the most unfavorable circumstances, often from sixty to seventy-five cents. In France the same labor is worth about twenty-four cents a day and the laborers feed themselves.

This positive and undeniable fact of general ease is connected with another which gives it a singular importance in the eyes of a European who is the friend of progressive reforms and the enemy of violence: the prevalence of radicalism in politics. The term *democrat*, which elsewhere would fill even republicans with terror, is here greeted with acclamations, and the adjective *democratic* is zealously claimed by every party as its exclusive property. But this is the only kind of property which is called in question. It is true that material property rapidly disappears in this country unless it is preserved by the most constant vigilance and renewed with untiring industry. But as long as it exists, it is the object of profound respect—which, I must confess, has rather surprised me. I should have expected that social theory here would have borrowed some notions from the predominant political theory; but there are those in Europe, not there considered the boldest speculators on this subject, who here could be looked upon as the most audacious innovators. From this simple statement, it seems natural to infer that valuable lessons are to be learned here by those who seek to solve the great question that now agitates Europe, the amelioration of the greatest number. It would be interesting to inquire into the causes of this state of things, and to examine whether, with certain modifications, it could not be transferred to Europe, and particularly to France. I shall return to this subject.

X

The Yankee and the Virginian

How Emigration Moves West — Two Great Streams of Emigrants — Character of Each — Part Played by Europe — Virginian Type — Yankee Type — Yankee Predominance in the Last Half Century — The Virginian May in Turn Get the Upper Hand — Advantages of the Contrast of Character — Two Types in History — Nations of Three Types — Excess of Unity in France

Charleston, May 28, 1834.
The great flood of civilization which has poured over the vast regions of the West, the South, and the North, from the Great Lakes to the Cape of Florida, has flowed on with a wonderful power and an admirable regularity. Emigration has taken place from east to west along the whole line of march. The inhabitants of New England, after having first spread themselves over their original territory and founded the new States of Maine and Vermont, have thrown themselves into the State of New York; thence, keeping as much as possible along the northern frontier of the United States, they have extended all along the coasts of Lake Ontario and Lake Erie and overrun the vast delta between the Ohio and the Upper Mississippi which now contains the States of Ohio, Indiana, and Illinois, and the Territory of Michigan. The emigrants from New York and Pennsylvania have spread themselves comparatively little beyond the limits of their own territory, which is very extensive and was thinly peopled in 1783. They have, however, furnished a small contingent to the great army of emigration from New England and have helped to occupy the country, some in Michigan, others in Ohio and Indiana.

Virginia, after having settled her western part with her own sons, has given birth to Kentucky and then, acting the same part in the South as New England in the North, has sent forth to the Gulf of Mexico those numerous swarms that have invaded the Southwest. North Carolina has taken part in this task and has besides a child of her own in Tennessee. Georgia and South Carolina have contributed to create Alabama and Mississippi, and Tennessee and Kentucky have in turn furnished offshoots for Missouri and Arkansas.

Thus the States where there are no slaves have brought forth a family of truly democratic republics—that is to say, with an essentially farming population, holding no slaves, and, excepting the vine, cultivating all the products of temperate Europe. These young States are founded on equality and the subdivision of property, for most of the farms do not exceed 80 to 160 acres. The Southern States, on the other hand, have created aristocratic republics, based on slavery and the accumulation of property in a few hands, still more exclusively agricultural than the Northwestern States and chiefly occupied in cultivating cotton, a precious commodity, which now furnishes for exportation, inclusive of what is consumed in the North, an annual value of forty or fifty million dollars.

Thus, among all the columns of emigration, two particularly attract attention and form of themselves the main body of the army; the others are only auxiliaries. These two great masses are the New England and the Virginia columns.

That part of Virginia which was most peopled during the war of Independence has a low and nearly level surface and a sandy and, in general, very poor soil. Along the rivers there are tracts formerly productive, but even these have been exhausted by the cultivation of tobacco. The large landowners of this state must have been early led to think of quitting their plantations for the fertile lands of Kentucky, occupied then by warlike savages who made them their favorite hunting grounds. Some bold and hardy pioneers, at the head of whom was old Boone, first ventured across the mountains with their rifles and bravely sustained a bloody contest with the Indians. After many desperate fights in which more than one unknown hero fell under the bullet or the tomahawk of some red-skinned Hector, after numerous assaults in which more than one matron enacted the part of our Jeanne Hachette, after many alarms and much suffering, the genius of civilization won out. At the call of the pioneers, roused by the fame of their exploits, the planters of the coast set out on their pilgrimage. They arrived with their slaves, cleared and cultivated large tracts in the midst of which they led a patriarchal life, surrounded by their servants and flocks, following with ardor the chase of wild beasts and sometimes of Indians, and too often spending the proceeds of their crop in betting on the speed of their horses, of which they are very proud and whose pedigree is better known to them than their own. More recently, when the demand for cotton had increased in England in consequence of improvements in the steam engine and machinery in general, and when the steamboat had opened the way into the heart of the Mississippi Valley, they have moved southward, always taking their slaves with them; a prospect of future wealth and prosperity was thus opened for the South.

The industrious sons of New England likewise bade farewell to the rocky and ungrateful soil of their birthplace. Loading a wagon with a plough, a bed, a barrel of salt meat, the indispensable supply of tea and molasses, a Bible, and a wife, and with his axe on his shoulder, the Yankee sets out for the West, without a servant, without an assistant, often without a companion, to build himself a log cabin deep in the woods, six hundred miles from his father's roof, and to clear away a spot for a farm. The first of these wanderers went from Connecticut, *the land of steady habits,* Puritans among Puritans.

The Virginian and the Yankee have planted themselves in the wilderness, each according to his nature. The part they have taken in founding the new States of the West explains the fact so often mentioned of fifty or sixty members of Congress being natives of Virginia or Connecticut. In this conquest over nature, Europe has not remained an idle spectator; she has sent forth vigorous laborers who have co-operated with the sons of New England, for slavery fills them with horror and drives them from the men of the South. Many Irish and Scotch, a number of Germans, Swiss, and some French are now settled in Michigan, Ohio, Indiana, and Illinois. The traveler who descends the Ohio, passes on the way Gallipolis, a French settlement, Vevay, a Swiss village, and Marietta, so called in honor of the unfortunate Marie Antoinette. The terminations in *burg* are scattered among Indian names, Jacksonvilles, Washingtons, and Columbias. But the co-operation of Europeans does not deprive the Yankees of the principal share in the honor of the work; they began it, they have borne and still bear the burden and heat of the day. In comparison with them, the European has been only the eleventh-hour-man, the apprentice, the hireling. The fusion of the European with the Yankee takes place but slowly, even on the new soil of the West; for the Yankee is not a man of promiscuous society; he believes that Adam's oldest son was a Yankee. Enough, however, of foreign blood has been mingled with Yankee blood to modify the primitive character of the New England race and to form a third American type, that of the West, whose features are not yet sharply defined but are daily assuming more distinctness; this type is characterized by its athletic forms and ambitious pretensions and seems destined ultimately to become superior to the others.

The Yankee and the Virginian are very unlike each other; they have no great love for each other and are often at variance. They are the same men who cut each other's throats in England under the name of Roundheads and Cavaliers. In England, they patched up a peace by the interposition of a new rule which was neither Stuart nor Cromwell. In America, where there was no power to mediate between them, they would have devoured each other as they did in England, had not Providence thrown them wide apart, one party at the South, the other at the North, leaving between them the territory now occupied by the mediating (*justes-milieux*) States of New York and Pennsylvania with their satellites, New Jersey and Delaware.

The Virginian of pure race is frank, hearty, open, cordial in his manners, noble in his sentiments, elevated in his ideas; he is a worthy descendant of the English gentleman. Surrounded from infancy by his slaves who relieve him from all personal exertion, he is rather indisposed to activity, even indolent. He is generous and profuse; around him, but more in the new States than in impoverished Virginia, abundance reigns. When the cotton crop has been good and the price is high, he invites everybody, excepting only the slaves that cultivate his fields, to partake in his wealth without much thought of next year's produce. To him the practice of hospitality is at once a duty, a pleasure, and a happiness. Like the patriarchs of the East or the heroes of Homer, he spits an ox to regale the guest whom Providence sends him and an old friend recommends to his attention, and to moisten this solid repast he offers Madeira—of which he is as proud as of his horses—which has been twice to the East Indies and has been ripening full twenty years. He loves the institutions of his country, yet he shows with pride his family plate, the arms on which, half effaced by time, attest his descent from the first colonists and prove that his ancestors were of a good family in England. When his mind has been cultivated by study and a tour in Europe has polished his manners and refined his imagination, there is no place in the world in which he would not appear to advantage, no destiny too high for him to reach; he is one of those whom a man is glad to have as a companion and desires as a friend. Ardent and warm-hearted, he is of the stuff from which great orators are made. He is better able to command men than to conquer nature and subdue the soil. When he has a certain degree of the spirit of method, and I will not say of will (for he has enough of that), but of that active perseverance so common among his brethren of the North, he has all the qualities needful to form a great statesman.

The Yankee, on the contrary, is reserved, cautious, distrustful; he is thoughtful and pensive, but equable; his manners are without grace, modest but dignified, cold, and often unprepossessing; he is narrow in his ideas but practical; and, possessing the idea of the proper, he never rises to the grand. He has nothing chivalric about him, and yet he is adventurous and he loves a roving life. His imagination is active and original, producing, however, not poetry, but drollery, what is called here "Yankee notions." The Yankee is the laborious ant; he is industrious and sober, frugal, and, on the sterile soil of New England, niggardly; transplanted to the promised land in the West, he continues moderate in his habits, but is less inclined to count the cents.

In New England he has a large share of prudence, but once thrown into the midst of the treasures of the West he becomes a speculator, a gambler even, although he has a great horror of cards, dice, and all games of hazard and even of skill, except the innocent game at bowls. He is crafty, sly, always calculating, boasting even of the tricks which he plays upon the careless or trusting buyer because he looks upon them as marks of his superior sagacity; he is, moreover, well provided with rationalizations to lull his conscience. With all his nice subtleties, he is, nevertheless, expeditious in business because he knows the value of time. His house is a sanctuary which he does not open to the profane; he is little given to hospitality, or rather he displays it only on rare occasions and then he does so on a great scale. He is a ready speaker and a close reasoner, but not a brilliant orator. For a statesman, he wants that greatness of mind and soul which enables a man to enter into and love another's nature and leads him naturally to consult his neighbor's good in consulting his own. He is individualism incarnate; in him the spirit of locality and division is carried to the utmost. But if he is not a great statesman, he is an able administrator, an unrivaled man of business. If he is not suited to command men, he has no equal in acting upon things, in combining, arranging, and giving them a value.

There are nowhere merchants of more consummate ability than those of Boston, but it is particularly as the colonist of the wilderness that the Yankee is admirable. Fatigue has no hold on him. He has not, like the Spaniard, the capacity to bear hunger and thirst, but he has the much superior faculty of finding at all times and in all places something to eat and to drink, and of being always able to contrive a shelter from the cold, first for his wife and children and afterward for himself. He grapples with nature in close fight and, more unyielding than she, subdues her at last, obliging her to surrender at discretion, to yield whatever he wills, and to take the shape he chooses. Like Hercules, he conquers the hydra of the pestilential morass and chains the rivers; more daring than Hercules, he extends his dominion not only over the land, but over the sea; he is the best sailor in the world. The ocean is his tributary and enriches him with the oil of her whales and with all her lesser fry. Wiser than the hero of the twelve labors, he knows no Omphale who can seduce him, no Deianira whose poisoned gifts can balk his searching glance. In this respect he is rather a Ulysses who has his Penelope, counts upon her faith, and remains steadfastly true to her. He does not even need to stop his ears when he passes near the Sirens, for in him the tenderest passions are deadened by religious austerity and devotion to his business. Like Ulysses in another point, he has a bag full of tricks. Overtaken at night by a storm in the woods, in a half hour, with no other resource than his knife, he will have made a shelter for himself and his horse. In winter, caught in one of those snowstorms which are unknown among us, he will construct a sled in the twinkling of an eye and keep on his way, like an Indian, by watching the bark of the trees. Thus to the genius of business, by means of which he turns to profit whatever the earth yields him, he joins the genius of industry which makes her prolific, and that of mechanical skill which fashions her produce to his wants. He is incomparable as a pioneer, unequaled as a settler of the wilderness.

The Yankee has set his mark on the United States during the last half century. He has been eclipsed by Virginia in the councils of the nation, but he has in turn had the upper hand throughout the country and eclipsed her on her own soil; for in order to arouse the Virginian from his Southern indolence, it has been necessary that the Yankee should come to set him an example of activity and enterprise at his own door. But for the Yankee, the vast cotton plantations of the South would still be an uncultivated waste. It was a Yankee, Eli Whitney, who toward the end of the last century invented the cotton gin which has made the fortune of the South. To give an enterprise success in the South, some Yankee must come a thousand miles to suggest the idea to the natives and carry off the profit before their eyes. New England has given only two Presidents to the Union, both popular on the eve of their election, both unpopular on the morrow, both rejected at the end of their first term, while all the others have been natives of Virginia or South Carolina and have been re-chosen for a second term. But then what a revenge has she taken in business matters, at the North and the South, in the East as well as the West! Here the Yankee is a true Marquis of Carabas. At Baltimore as well as at Boston, in New Orleans as well as at Salem, in New York as well as at Portland, if a merchant is mentioned who has made and kept a large fortune by sagacity and forecast, you will find that he is a Yankee. If you pass a plantation in the South in better order than the others, with finer avenues, with the Negroes' cabins better arranged and more comfortable, you will be told, "Oh! that is a Yankee's; he is a *smart man!*" In a village in Missouri, by the side of a house with broken windows, dirty in its outward appearance, around the door of which a parcel of ragged children are quarreling and fighting, you may see another, freshly painted, surrounded by a simple, but neat and nicely whitewashed fence, with a dozen of carefully trimmed trees about it, and through the windows in a small room shining with cleanliness you may espy some nicely combed little boys and some young girls dressed in almost the last Paris fashion. Both houses belong to farmers, but one of them is from North Carolina and the other from New England. On the western rivers, you will hear a boat mentioned which never meets with an accident and in which all travelers and merchants are eager to take their passage; the master is a Yankee. At New Orleans, alongside the levee, you may be struck with the fine appearance of a ship which all the passers-by stop to admire; the master is also a Yankee.

The pre-eminence of the Yankee in the colonization of the country has made him the arbiter of manners and customs. It is from him that the country has taken a general tone of austere severity that is religious and even bigoted; because of him all sorts of amusements, which among us are considered innocent relaxations, are here proscribed as immoral pleasures. It is he that has introduced Prison Reform, multiplied schools, founded Temperance Societies. It is through his agency, with his money, that the missionaries endeavor silently to found colonies in the South Seas for the benefit of the Union. If one wished to form a single type, representing the American character of the present moment as a single whole, it would be necessary to take at least three fourths of the Yankee and to mix with it hardly one fourth of the Virginian.

Actually, the material work of settlement is well advanced. The physical basis of society is laid. On this base it is necessary now to raise a social structure of a form yet unknown but which, I am fully convinced, will be on a new plan, for all the materials are new; besides, neither humanity nor Providence ever repeats itself. Which of the two, Yankee or Virginian, is best suited to execute this new task?

I cannot tell; but it seems to me that the Virginian is now about to take his turn and that, in the phase which the United States are now on the point of entering, the social qualities of the Virginian will win the advantage which naturally belonged to the laborious Yankee in the period of settling the forest. In a word, I believe that, if the Union lasts and the West continues to form a united mass from the falls of Niagara to New Orleans, this third type of the West, which is growing and aspires to rule over the others, will take a great deal from the Virginian and very little from the Yankee.

It is no small advantage to a people to combine within itself two types with different characteristics when they unite harmoniously in composing a common national character. A people of which all the individual members are referable to a single type is among nations what a celibate is among individuals; it is a sort of hermit, its life is monotonous. The strongest and sweetest feelings of human nature are dormant in it; it remains stationary; nothing spurs it forward. Such was ancient Egypt.

A people consisting of two types, on the contrary, when neither has an oppressive superiority over the other, enjoys a complete existence; its life is a perpetual interchange of ideas and sensations, like that of a married pair. It is fecund; it has the power of reproducing and regenerating itself. Each of the two natures alternately acts and is acted upon, without ever being inactive. By turns each gains the superiority and yields to the other; thus, according to circumstances, different qualities come into play. Two natures mutually support and relieve each other, they stimulate each other, and through this wholesome rivalry the nation that combines them in itself reaches high destinies.

History shows that the progress of humanity has been constantly promoted by the reciprocal action and reaction of two natures or two races, sometimes friends, oftener enemies or rivals. The most general fact in the history of our civilization is the struggle between the East and the West, from the expedition of the Argonauts and the war of Troy to the battle of Lepanto and the siege of Vienna by the Turks. In this great drama, it was not merely to shed rivers of blood that Providence has dashed against each other Europeans and Asiatics, Greeks and Persians, Romans, Carthaginians, and Parthians, Saracens and Franks, Venetians, Turks, and Poles; blows have not been the only thing exchanged between Europe and the Orient. If you wish to know, you Westerners, what you have gained from contact with the East, even when you have met sword in hand, look around you; most of the fruit trees that enrich your fields, the vine which gladdens the heart, the silk and cotton that adorn your houses and your persons, these are the spoils of your Eastern wars; sugar and coffee, the cultivation of which has changed the political balance of the world, were brought into Europe from the East, one by yourselves, the other by the Arabs when they made themselves masters of Spain. The mariner's compass, which has given a new continent to civilization and established the dominion of man over the before unconquered deep, was the gift of the East. Your arts and your sciences are of Oriental origin; the secrets of Algebra were stolen from the Moors of Spain by a monk; your numerical system, the basis of all your financial improvements, bears the name of the Arabs; your chivalry was brought from Asia by the Crusaders. Your Christianity, the father of modern Europe, would not have existed in the West had not the Roman legions conquered Judea, which contained its seed, had not the Roman Empire contained the school of Alexandria in which that seed could blossom, and had not the Rome of the Caesars been raised as a pedestal for the successors of St. Peter from which they might rule over the East and the West.

Behold the Roman people; its noble career was a continual succession of wars followed by as many assimilations of the conquered, alliances, real marriages, which always gave it a new vigor. It begins with the double figure of

Romulus and Remus; then follow the Romans and Sabines, at least the Sabine women, then Rome and Alba, next Rome and the Latins, finally Rome and Carthage. It might be called a young sultan who carries off a captive at the point of the sword and makes her his favorite until he grows tired of her, or until he finds another more worthy of his love. It goes on in this way, changing, and daily rising in the sequence of its choices, until it meets with Greece, which becomes not an object of a passing caprice but a legitimate bride. This marriage of Greek and Roman natures gave splendor and joy to imperial Rome and rest to the world. Its destiny once entwined with that of Greece, the Roman people paused to enjoy, and for this purpose substituted the rule of the Caesars for the republican constitution, and Greek rhetoricians and players and emperors, voluptuous like the disciples of Epicurus, or philosophers like Pericles, for the stern and severe aristocracy of earlier days.

What is the history of Greece but a continual oscillation between the austere Lacedaemon and the brilliant Athens, between the country of Lycurgus and Leonidas, and that of Solon, Aspasia, and Alcibiades? United, they acquired an indomitable energy and supported the shock of all Asia. Unfortunately they had too little feeling of a common nationality and too much of local jealousy. Almost perpetually divided, they never completely extended their sway over Greece itself. When the Greek race was about to reach its apogee, neither was destined to lead it there. For that Providence raised up a man in the North before whom *the earth was silent*.

One could say the same of the history of Europe, that after the German conquests it resumed this double thread in the English and French people, and that the major part of the progress of our civilization has been occasioned by the rivalry of these illustrious competitors or by their friction during their brief truces. Finally, the great achievements of the life of the whole human race offer us the spectacle of two natures, each ruling the other in its turn, one in ascendance, the other in eclipse, turn by turn, until now most often at war, sometimes in harmony, each always animated by contact with the other.

So long as a nation comprises an indefinite number of types mixed together without order and without rank, it resembles a body not yet in a state of consistency. It has no definable character, no fixed destination. It is incapable of achieving anything great in the world. Thus from the time of the war of the old German electors against the Holy Empire and of the treaty of Westphalia, which sanctioned their independence and broke in pieces the former unity of the nation, Germany continued under an eclipse until the rise of the house of Brandenburg from the midst of the anarchy of the little German States, when a rival was given to the house of Austria and a strong dualism established.

Dualism is not, however, the only mode in which a society can be constituted, at once solid and elastic. When a third type exists whose superiority is admitted by the others or which partakes sufficiently of the nature of each to serve as a bond and a mediator between them, the social organization is then in a high degree vigorous; for then the harmony between the two primitive types has ceased to be an abstraction, it takes on flesh and bone. In some cases this third personage of the drama becomes so indispensable to the action that it must be supplied at any price and its great prerogatives devolve on a transient actor. Thus in Greece the Boeotian federation led by Thebes played this part during a short period. With a great many peoples, the role has been filled by an aristocracy which has served as a check to both parties in turn. An aristocracy worthy of the name is eminently qualified for this task, because it combines the two natures in itself, feels the reaction of their passions influencing itself, and has the energy necessary either to curb or spur them on, as the case requires.

There is no country in which dualism is more admirably developed than in the United States. Each of the two natures has an open field, each a distinct career of industry.

Each possesses in the highest degree the qualities necessary for its peculiar position. Considered in respect to a triple type, the United States are not less favorably situated; the young giant that is growing up in the West seems destined to fulfill the prophecy *the last shall be first*, and to hold together the North and the South in his vigorous grasp.

In France, for the last fifty years, the desire for unity which has always been a natural impulse with us has taken on the character of a fever; unity and perfection have become synonyms for us. We have poured everything into a melting pot and have patterned everything after a single mold. We have established a political system which centers France in Paris and in which the move of a single wheel at the center moves eighty-six wheels in the provincial departments, five hundred wheels in the subdivisions of those departments, and forty thousand wheels in the communes. By greatly exaggerating the grand principle of unity, we have organized France as if it were not a powerful kingdom but the province of an empire. We have admirably arranged ourselves to be conquered in a single battle by some enemy chief who would rule us by some agent in Paris.

We, also, have two distinct types, that of the North and that of the South. Instead of employing the principle of centralization as a means of developing both and giving them a free and harmonious action, we have endeavored to confound them in a narrow and sterile unity. We have especially thwarted the most reasonable and legitimate wishes of the South, which has been overborne and crushed by the North. It takes its revenge, indeed, in furnishing us with most of our statesmen, much as Ireland has the privilege of giving premiers to England; but like Irish ministers in England, our Southern statesmen, ungrateful sons of a neglected mother, govern wholly in the interest of the North, as if France contained only towns and had no rural population, as if we were chiefly a manufacturing and only after the fact an agricultural people, and, what is worse, as if we were a society of philosophers and not a nation longing for religious faith and political enthusiasm.

It was fortunate for our national independence during the crisis of our great revolution that the Constituent Assembly created at the convention a central control for all territorial matters by abolishing all the great corporate bodies and all the great private perquisites which existed in the old regime. If there had been one insurrection more, we would have been defeated and perhaps broken up into small parts. But now that the danger is passed, would it be impossible to find a combination which, without completely destroying central order, would give the provinces a little of that strength which they seek in vain since they have been shattered by the institution of eighty-six regional departments? Is it not possible, from now on, to govern France in a way that will satisfy the interests, the ideas, and the sentiments of the South without doing violence to the North?

XI

Captain John Smith

His Youth — His Adventures on the Continent and in the Levant — His Captivity — His Return to England — Takes Part in a Colonial Venture — Arrival in Virginia — He Is Made Prisoner by the Savages and Saved from Death by Pocahontas, Daughter of King Powhatan — His Exploits — The Founder of Virginia — Present State of France Compared with the Condition of England Then — Scientific Expeditions

Richmond (Virginia), May 25, 1834. Captain John Smith was born in 1579 at Willoughby in Lincoln County, England. From his earliest youth he astonished his playmates and even his schoolmaster by the daring of his escapades. He was thirteen years old when he was seized by the desire to go to sea. To this end, he sold his books and his toys, whatever would provide him with some small means. He was ready to leave when his father died and because of this he fell under the guardianship of matter-of-fact men to whom the romantic genius of a young man seemed but sentimental folly; they kept careful watch on him, but his independent spirit could not bear these narrow confines. When he was about fifteen, so that he might learn some sense, he was placed in the office of a merchant who spared him neither hard work nor lessons.

The merchant to whom Smith had been apprenticed was one of the leading men of business in Lynn. He did a large maritime business and young Smith had hopes that his master might send him on trips, trips at sea. But without waiting to talk about going to sea, he ran away; with ten shillings in his pocket he left the merchant and his business without so much as taking leave. His lucky star led him to a young lord who was setting out with a large entourage to make the grand tour of Europe. Smith entered his service, but not for long. After a few months, he became disgusted with his new master and joined the Dutch Army. There he spent three or four years; then, at the urgings of a Scottish gentleman who promised him excellent letters of recommendation to the court of King John, he crossed the sea again and went to Scotland. Disappointed in his expectations there, he left the court and returned to his native town. Soon, horrified at the narrowness of the lives of his neighbors, he went to live alone deep in the forests, taking books on military tactics and military history, a horse, and a sword. There he passed his time between the study of war and exercise at arms without seeing a soul other than an Italian groom employed by the Count of Lincoln.

At this moment he came into part of his father's estate and, with the means to travel, he felt again the desire to see the world. So Smith started anew. Arriving in Flanders, he was robbed by four French thieves. He pursued them, found one, fought with him, wounded him, made him confess his crime, and then set out on a trip with some money which an old friend of the family had given him. He followed the coastline of France from Dunkirk to Marseilles, visiting arsenals and forts, and then set sail for Italy.

Unfortunately for him he found himself alone, an Englishman and a heretic, in the midst of a company of pilgrims who were making a pilgrimage to Rome. A storm struck the boat, and the pilgrims, seeking some sinner who was responsible, threw Smith, like some modern Jonah, into the sea. He had the good luck to reach by swimming the island of Sainte-Marie, near Nice. At Nice he stayed just long enough to join another ship ready to set sail for Alexandria and which, in mid-passage, falling into a fight with a richly laden Venetian ship, attacked it, boarded it, and despoiled it. Smith was set ashore at Antibes with his part of the booty, crossed Italy, passed the Gulf of Venice, arrived in Styria, a province of Austria, and ended by joining as a volunteer in the service of the emperor, then at war with the Turks.

Smith was not only brave and intrepid, he was enormously resourceful. He found a way to force the Turks to give up the siege of Olympia and even gained the rank of captain in a regiment of Count Meldritch, a Transylvanian. After this show of prowess, Smith was at the siege of Regal in Transylvania; the siege had dragged on a long while when one day a herald presented himself at the camp of the Christians to announce that Turbashaw, a Turk renowned for his valor, defied the bravest of them to single combat, just, he said contemptuously, to divert the ladies and to pass away the time. Among the Christian soldiers it was decided by lot that Smith would be the one to meet the challenge of the Turk. The meeting was formally arranged; the Turkish ladies lined the ramparts of Regal; the army of the besiegers was drawn up in formal ranks; trumpets blared forth. Smith slew the Turk. Another Turkish knight chose to revenge Turbashaw; Smith slew him too. A third Turk stepped forth from the ranks, a giant, the terrible Mulgro. At the first encounter, Smith was nearly dropped by the blow of a battle-axe; the Turks sent up a cry of joy, the Turkish ladies on the battlement clapped their hands; they were still cheering and applauding when Mulgro, run through by a sword-thrust, fell helpless to the ground and Smith lopped off his head. Soon after the city was taken.

But armies have their day. A little later the Christians were routed; Smith was left for dead on the field of battle; the richness of his armor led the Turks to believe he was a man of some distinction and he was treated as one who was worth a considerable ransom. As soon as he was well, he was forced to march like a slave to a Turkish city. There he was bought by a pasha who sent him as a present to a lady whose favor he sought in Constantinople, saying, the cheap braggart, that Smith was a Bohemian knight whom he had conquered in battle. This fraud brought only evil to the pasha; the lady knew Italian and Smith spoke it too. Smith recounted his adventures, his victories and his defeats; the lady, outraged by the deceit of the pasha, became sympathetic with Smith in his misfortunes, stirred by the accounts of his noble deeds and dangers, moved, as one of Smith's biographers puts it, like Desdemona. Smith was hoping for a bit of quiet and happiness when the lady, whether to divert the suspicions of her mother or to teach the Turk a lesson, sent Smith to her brother, a nobleman whose estate was by the Sea of Azov.

The lady pressed her regard for Smith on her brother; she wished him to understand her feelings for the captive; but her noble brother was outraged that a Christian dog had touched the heart of his sister. Smith, expecting a cordial reception, was not an hour at the brother's estate before he was beaten, stripped, and had his hair shaved off. An iron collar was put round his neck and, dressed in a hair shirt, he was sent to work the fields with the other Christian slaves of his master. Each day his barbarous ruler came to inspect the work of his prisoner and to heap abuse and blows on him. Once Smith found himself alone with him; when his master reprimanded him for the way in which he had threshed the grain, Smith knocked him senseless into a pile of manure with a blow of the flail and, seizing the fallen bridle, leaped onto his master's Arabian horse and fled. When he had reached the desert he found his way as best he could and after sixteen days' traveling arrived at Hexapolis on the River Don, where he found a Russian post. The Russians received him generously. The Princess or Baroness Palamata, whether out of charity or affection, showered Smith with evidences of her interest. Refreshed, Smith set out for Transylvania, where his friends wept with joy on seeing him and lined his purse with money. From there he returned to England, passing on the way Germany, France, Spain, and the Kingdom of Morocco.

He arrived in his country just as an expedition was setting forth to establish a colony in America. Urged to take part, he joined. Smith was then twenty-eight years old. The expedition slipped down the Thames on December 19, 1606, and entered Chesapeake Bay on April 26, 1607. On May 13 the company debarked on a peninsula where it founded the colony of Jamestown. Today, the traveler who sails up the James River in a steamboat can see on this peninsula a tower in ruins and the debris of a cemetery wall which are quickly passed. That is all that remains of the first settlement.

Smith had a group of mediocre men for his companions, men who could not tolerate his superiority. Hardly had they left the Thames when he was accused of plotting to make himself king of the colony. On this absurd pretext he was thrown in the brig during the crossing. After debarking, when the sealed instructions sent with the expedition were opened, it was discovered that the government of the colony was confided in a Council of seven persons and that Smith was one of the seven. His colleagues, nevertheless, excluded him from the Council on the grounds of his presumed plot. Without the power of obtaining his demand, he asked to be tried. He was patient, then, and explored the region around Jamestown, mounting the rivers, making acquaintance with the native tribes, and paying visits to King Powhatan, the most powerful of the savage chieftains. During this time, the colony was badly administered. No planning, no provision was made for the winter which was coming; little or no planting; no military precautions against the Indians, with whom some quarrels over small matters had already raised bad feelings. One day Powhatan's braves made a surprise attack on the colony; one man was killed; seventeen were wounded; discontent broke out against the Council, and especially against Wingfield, who was then the president. Smith took advantage of the occasion to demand a proper trial, which no one dared longer to refuse him. He was acquitted on all points and Wingfield was ordered to pay him two hundred pounds sterling in damages, which Smith generously handed over to be spent on the general good of the colony. After this gesture he was the darling of the group; all the colonists received Communion together the same day as a sign that they were willing to let bygones be bygones; then Captain Newport, who had led them from England, set sail with his fleet, leaving the colony of 105 people.

But scarcity set in and with it sickness; then, what is worse than disease, internal strife. Fifty colonists died a miserable death. In the midst of this general despair, Wingfield, the president of the Council, in concert with some of his friends, resolved to seize secretly the last ship which the colony had and flee to England. The plot was discovered; Wingfield was deposed and another president elected to his place. This one had the good sense to let himself be guided by Smith, whose moment had come. Smith drew up a plan of work, assigned each one his task, and was obeyed. Houses were raised; the town was well fortified and guarded; he himself set an example to the workers, laboring harder than any. It was not enough to have shelter for the winter; there had to be provisions too. Smith set out to discover food supplies, especially corn which the Indians grew. On one of these excursions he fell in with a large tribe who made an idol of him and gave him as a ransom to their god I don't know how many bushels of corn along with venison, and he hastened back to Jamestown. He appeared there at the appropriate moment; Wingfield had taken up his schemes again with success and this time he had to fight to bring the conspirators to their senses. From that time on, power was securely in the hands of Smith.

Hardly had he restored order than he gave free rein to the inspirations of his adventurous imagination, perhaps more than was suitable for a man on whose head rested the safety of the colony. One day he left to explore the Chickahominy River; after having sailed up it as far as possible, he left his ship and the majority of the party hidden in a creek, sheltered from all danger, and continued in a canoe

—just himself with two whites and two Indians. Unfortunately those he had left behind him forgot their instructions to stay out of sight. They left the ship, contrary to orders, and were attacked by a party of Indians under the command of Opechancanough, brother of Powhatan, who was on the lookout for Smith. One of the men was captured and made to tell what direction the captain had taken; the others were able to make the ship and save themselves.

Smith, meanwhile, had arrived at the head of the river. Opechancanough took him by surprise during the night and killed the two Englishmen. Smith was surrounded by two hundred warriors and had received a flesh wound in the thigh. He defended himself with the shrewdness of the serpent and the strength of a lion; he killed three of his attackers and, tying the hands of one of his two Indians with his garters, he used him as a shield. He fought his way through his astonished enemies, got into the open, and headed for his canoe, but on the way he floundered into an impassable swamp and there sank up to his waist with his Indian. Such was the fear with which he filled the savages that, even in this situation, none of them dared approach him until he had thrown away his arms. He was half dead from cold. The Indians took him back to his camp, put him near the fire, and massaged him until he had recovered the use of his limbs.

Smith thought he was dead. The corpses of his companions were beside him, scalped. He thought to take a compass from his pocket and show it to Opechancanough. The savage could not conceal the astonishment he felt at this needle that always moved. Since he had no notion of transparent glass, he was even more surprised that it was impossible to seize the needle with his fingers, although he could see it perfectly. In order further to excite the Indian chieftain and his warriors, Smith began to tell them all that he knew about astronomy, about the movement of the celestial bodies, about the size and shape of the earth and the sea, about the sun and the moon. His audience was dumfounded. But savage instinct took the upper hand again; when Smith was finished talking, he was tied to a tree. The Indians gathered in a circle about him and fixed their arrows to shoot him. Smith was going to die!

Instead of giving the signal which would be the sign to loose their arrows at Smith's breast, Opechancanough ordered them to spare the prisoner for now. He wanted to parade his prize before the court of the Indian princes, his cousins, and especially before Powhatan, who was king over all; for all the Indian leaders had formed a confederation in the area of the James River, just as twenty years ago the German princes formed a confederation along the Rhine, and, like Napoleon, Powhatan was their sovereign protector.

Smith's courage, his physical prowess, and the wealth of his spirit made the Indians think him an extraordinary man, as if he were a superman. His capture was celebrated by ceremonies without end, ceremonies filled with all the ritual that the savage imagination could fancy. Great care was taken that he was given the best of food, so that he began to believe that they were fattening him up in order finally to eat him. Medicine men came to cast the devil out of him; they prayed to the Great Spirit in order to divine his final decision about Smith. To receive him, Powhatan spread out all the luxury that the wilds can offer. When Smith appeared before this great chief, one queen rinsed his hands with water; another queen, playing the role of a servant, presented him with a feathered headdress. Smith was led from village to village and it all ended with the proposal that he join the Indians and lead the attack on Jamestown. On this condition they offered him as many women and as much land as he desired. When he refused, the kings and wise men held a council; they decided that Smith should die and that the sentence of execution should be carried out at once.

All was made ready. Two stones were put at the feet of Powhatan and Smith was stretched out on them. The chiefs ranged themselves all about. A profound silence fell on the people behind them. Powhatan himself wished to execute the sacrifice. He approached with his great club; he raised it to deliver the fatal blow. The end of hope!

Suddenly a girl—women were always Smith's guardian angels—leaped forth from the crowd. She placed her head between the head of Smith and Powhatan's weapon; it was the eldest daughter of the king, his loveliest daughter, the beautiful Pocahontas. Raising her arms toward her father, she begged him with her tears to spare the captive. At first the king was indignant, but he so loved Pocahontas that he could not cause her pain. He looked at his warriors and sought in their eyes the resolution which he lacked; he saw there only compassion. "Let him live," he said. The next day Smith was on the way to Jamestown with two guides. He was to send Powhatan, as a gesture of peace, two muskets and a grindstone.

Now delivered from captivity, Smith spent himself on the affairs of the colony and when all was in order began his explorations once again. He traveled up the Potomac and explored amid a thousand perils most of the rivers which flow into the Chesapeake. His constant courage, the religious terror which he inspired in the savages, and especially the noble assistance of Pocahontas always saved him —him and the colony—like some miracle. Pocahontas needed only to find her Chateaubriand to become as famous as Atala. As young and as beautiful as Atala, she was more heroic, and it was not only a man that she had saved. Young as she was (she was then only twelve or thirteen years old), it often happened that she would make during the night long marches, alone, through the woods and the swamps, through the wild storms which in Virginia are terrible, finally to arrive to warn Smith and the colonists of plots against them by the Indians. Other times, when the colonists were dying of hunger, Pocahontas would appear like some beneficent spirit, with bearers loaded with foodstuffs, and would disappear after seeing them fed. Up to that time no other colony was able to establish itself on the American continent north of the Gulf of Mexico; Providence supplied the helping hands of this mysterious maiden in order finally to plant a colony there. Greece would have erected an altar to such a one and made her a goddess equal to Diana, the goddess of the forests, and Minerva, the goddess of wisdom.

The colonists went about it differently. When Smith was not there, they abducted Pocahontas in order to have a hostage against her father, Powhatan. Then, after having held her for some time, they planned, with her and with Powhatan's consent, to find a husband for her. Eventually he was found in one of them, John Rolfe, who took her to England. Pocahontas, the lovely, the modest, the heroic Pocahontas, became therefore Mrs. Rolfe, a bourgeois wife in London and Brentford. At the age of twenty-one she died quite prosaically of consumption at Gravesend, just as she was preparing to return to America. Perhaps if she had ended more tragically, she would have been the heroine of twenty epic poems.

The high adventures of Captain John Smith are as numerous and as astonishing as those of Hercules; and after his naive account (like Caesar, he wrote his Memoirs) of a feast given him by the ladies of the court of Powhatan one can believe that he lacked none of the adventures of the son of Jupiter, even those which cannot be told. One time he surpassed Hercules' victory over Antaeus by strangling singlehanded a great giant of an Indian chief and carrying him on his shoulders to Jamestown. Another time, Opechancanough had him surrounded with seven hundred men; Smith suddenly seized the chief by his hair, dragged him, trembling and humiliated, into the midst of the Indians, who were frozen with surprise, and made them all lay down their arms. The difficulties he overcame are innumerable; he won out against famine and sickness, the snares and the arrows of the savages, the rebelliousness of one group of the colonists and the complaints and disaffection of others who sighed after the fleshpots of Egypt, against the sloth and the stupidity of the adventurers who flowed into the colony only in search of gold, against the treason of some, Germans and Swiss, who went over to Powhatan, where they thought they could get a better price. Everything was against him, everything, to the point of revolt and assassination by steel or by poison. There was no extremity he did not have to face. One day, seeing him in an agony of despair, his companions were desolate at having failed his faith. His perseverance and his courage finally triumphed over all. By the grace of his unceasing efforts, the colony was securely established; several towns were founded; and after two years' stay in Virginia, grievously wounded by an explosion of a barrel of gunpowder, he left Jamestown, never to return. After he had left, the colony still had much to undergo, but it had taken root and soon was to prosper.

Such was the beginning of Virginia. When the War for Independence was declared, Virginia was the most powerful of the States. Without the institution of slavery, which holds it back like an iron ball shackled to its feet, it would still be the foremost State. It was Virginia which gave the American Revolution Washington, Jefferson, Madison, Monroe, and many other illustrious political leaders. The generous and chivalric traits which distinguish the Virginian character derive in part from the memories which the example and the lessons of Captain John Smith left in the hearts of his adventurous companions.

If I go into the life of John Smith in such detail, it is not only because of the interest which attaches to the life of an extraordinary man, but also because of the analogy which our moment in history bears to his.

His was a time of political and religious crisis, of civil war and revolution. It was the time of the reconstruction of Europe by the treaty of Westphalia. The head of Charles I fell then; then another dynasty was ready to rise in England. It was a time when the Protestant party spoke of making a republic of France. Imaginations were aroused, excited; men's minds were in a state of ferment. Wise men then believed that the world was coming to an end. It was not just a world that was ending, it was a New World being born, and the pains which afflicted the Old World were the pangs of birth.

Suppose that men like Smith had been forced to stay in England. With his lively imagination, his ebullient energy, his great will power, he would have been inevitably led into politics, then the most pressing matter. And how could a man of his quality have failed to put himself at the head of a party to overthrow the country?

To speak more plainly: England was then in fact in the throes of a revolution which perhaps would not have occurred if two men, endowed like Smith with devouring imaginations and wills of iron, had not been kept in England. These two men were John Hampden and Oliver Cromwell. They wished to go to America but the king prevented them. A few years later, one of the two had destroyed the royal power, such at least as the Stuarts meant it to be; a little later the other would kill his king.

Now, there is in the world, in Europe, between the Pyrenees and the Rhine, between the ocean and the Alps, a country where the qualities of John Smith, and the accompanying defects of those qualities, are present in abundance. In this country a youthful passion abounds, full of audacity and ambition, ready to worship every phantom that is put before it, avid for action and danger, tormented by the desire for strong emotions and seeking them wherever it can find them, even in conspiracies and civil war. In this country, a dozen changes in the government in the course of forty years have destroyed respect for power, have depreciated experience, have sown disquiet and unrest in the souls of men. The system of education which has prevailed there has been essentially speculative, literary, and poetic; instead of calming the emotions, instead of fixing them on positive ideas and positive facts, it tends on the contrary to increase, to double, their adventurous disposition.

Might one conclude from this that one of the conditions of order and happiness for this country, for our noble France, would consist in spending this youthful ardor on the world, in the name of science and art, or else to found new empires?

XII

Lowell

Losses of the Jacksonians — View of Lowell — Rise of American Manufactures — Founding of Lowell — Lowell Railroad — Influence of Manufactures on the Happiness and the Morality of the People

Lowell (Massachusetts), June 12, 1834. The municipal elections which took place in New York two months ago and the legislative elections in Virginia which occupied the whole month of April have revealed to the Opposition its whole strength. Its success was unexpected, particularly in New York; I say success, although the newly elected mayor belongs to the Administration party, because the Opposition has the majority in both houses of the Common Council, the Board of Aldermen and the Board of Assistants, who govern in reality. The Opposition has since continued to gain ground. There are some able statesmen in the Senate who are also skillful parliamentary tacticians; they knew that by irritating the President they might force him to commit some act of imprudence, and this motive was not without its weight in the adoption by the Senate of resolutions censuring his conduct in regard to the Bank. The old General has felt this censure very keenly and replied to it by a protest, which his best friends consider a mistake, and which the Senate refused to have entered on its journal. It is a matter of surprise that Mr. Van Buren, whose sagacity all admit, did not interpose his influence to prevent the sending of this message. One of the fundamental maxims of American politics is, as I have already said, that the sword and purse should not be united in the same hands; that is, that the President, to whom the Constitution has entrusted the military force of the Republic, should not also be the keeper of the public money. This, I repeat, is an axiom which underlies all discussion. The President's protest clashes with this sacred doctrine. It became necessary, therefore, to follow up the protest by an explanatory message, which the Opposition calls a recantation, and which in truth is one. This retractation or explanation has not, however, destroyed the effect of the first message, and the consequence has been a hesitation in the Democratic ranks. The Virginia elections, which were then going on, show that they were influenced by it, and some other elections of less importance have for the most part turned out unfavorably to the Administration.

In Albany, the headquarters of Mr. Van Buren's friends, the Opposition has carried the municipal elections. The partisans of the Administration have, as if in sport, added fault to fault. These past few days a committee of the House of Representatives appointed to examine into the doings of the Bank, of which the majority were Jackson men as the Administration has the upper hand in that body, committed a series of blunders. There was a paper war between the committee and the directors of the Bank in which the former were completely unhorsed and had no better resource than the brutal idea of ordering the president and directors of the Bank to be taken into custody by the sergeant-at-arms. Such an action has revolted everyone. The majority, lately so compact, already shows signs of falling apart. Several recent votes show that the Opposition is gaining ground. One might say that the prudent, those, to use the words of the great master of diplomacy, *whose watches go faster than those of their neighbors,* are getting ready to desert. Outside the halls of Congress, the Opposition is organizing energetically for the general congressional elections, which are to take place next autumn; it is making preparations in the spirit of one who feels sure of victory and is determined that it shall be a decisive one. In New York, for example, the Common Council has removed all Jackson men from municipal office; all have been replaced by anti-Jackson men. Hospital commissioners, inspectors of weights and measures, commissioners for public transportation and road building, all, even down to the street cleaners, have been swept out of office. The mayor, who is a Jackson man, will have an anti-Jackson secretary because that officer is chosen by the Common Council. These removals are rude measures, but the friends of the Administration have no right to complain, for they set the example on a larger scale by removing hundreds of custom-house officers and postmasters. Without pretending to justify these violent acts, it should be said that something more is involved than merely removing an adversary to make way for a friend. The Opposition wants the inspectors of streets to be anti-Jackson men because the sweepers they employ have a vote; just as the Administration insists that all postmasters be Jackson men because in the country they have a certain influence.

It is less than a year since General Jackson visited the great towns of the North. He was received with acclamations such as neither North or South America had ever before seen. Washington never excited half the enthusiasm; not Bolívar, Pizarro, nor the great Cortez was ever saluted with such pompous epithets. It was an apotheosis. Not a year has gone by, and already abuse has succeeded to the most extravagant praise. A few days ago, I was grieved to read some unbecoming pleasantries upon the old General's scars. What will be held sacred if honorable wounds, all received in front, fighting for one's country, are to become a subject of low jests? The war of the President on the Bank was certainly unjust and disastrous to the country. The measures taken in his name against that institution were impolitic and unauthorized by law. The violent passion and imperious temper displayed by him in the affair cut a curious figure in the seat that had been occupied by sages like Washington and his successors. All this is true; but when we look back on fifty years of public services, we are filled with grief and indignation to think that, at the end of so long a career, insult and ingratitude will be, perhaps, his only reward. Can he have been raised so high, only that his fall should be so great? Is he destined to furnish another proof of the instability of popular favor in every age and all countries? But instead of dwelling on these unpleasant reflections, I will rather describe the scene now exhibited literally under my windows.

Lowell is a city eleven years old and it now contains fifteen thousand inhabitants, inclusive of the suburb of Belvedere. Twelve years ago it was a barren waste in which the silence was interrupted only by the murmur of the little river of Concord and the noisy dashings of the clear waters of the Merrimack against the granite blocks that suddenly obstruct their course. Today there are huge factories, five, six, or seven stories high, each capped with a little white belfry which strongly contrasts with the red masonry of the building and which stands out sharply against the dark hills on the horizon. There are small wooden houses, painted white, with green blinds, very neat, very snug, very nicely carpeted, and with a few small trees around them, or brick houses in the English style, that is to say simple but tasteful without and comfortable within; on one side, fancy-goods shops and milliners' rooms without number, for the women are the majority in Lowell, and vast hotels in the American style, very much like barracks (the only barracks in Lowell); on the other side, canals, waterwheels, waterfalls, bridges, banks, schools, and libraries, for in Lowell reading is the only recreation and there are no less than seven journals printed here. The rigid spirit of Puritanism has been carried to its utmost in Lowell, owing to the great number of young girls collected together in the factories. In 1836 a man was fined by the municipal authorities for being a common fiddler; he was treated as if he had outraged the public morals, the magistrates fearing that the pleasures of the dance might tend to corruption of manners. All around are churches and meetinghouses of every sect, Episcopalian, Baptist, Congregationalist, Methodist, Universalist, Unitarian, etc., and there is even a Roman Catholic chapel. Here are all the edifices of a flourishing town in the Old World, except the prisons, hospitals, and theaters. Everywhere one hears the noise of hammers, of spindles, of bells calling the hands to their work or dismissing them from their tasks, of coaches and six arriving or starting off, of the blasting of rocks to make a millrace or to level a road; it is the peaceful hum of an industrious population whose movements are regulated like clockwork; a population not native to the town, and one half of which at least will die elsewhere, after having aided in founding three or four other towns; for the full-blooded American has this in common with the Tartar, that he is *encamped*, not established, on the soil he treads upon.

Massachusetts and the adjoining small States of New England contain several manufacturing towns similar to Lowell, but none of them on so large a scale. An American well acquainted with the character of his countrymen gave me the following account of the origin of these towns, and of Lowell in particular. "In 1812," he said, "the United States declared war against Great Britain to defend the honor of their insulted flag. Boston and the rest of New England opposed the war and thus drew upon themselves the reproaches of their brethren of the Middle and Southern States. The fact is that they were quite as sensitive as the rest of their countrymen to any insult offered their flag by the mistress of the ocean; the patriotism of the New Englanders is above suspicion; they began the war of Independence, and they supported the principal burden of that war. They were, likewise, resolved to have satisfaction for the outrages committed by England, for it was they who had the greater number of seamen impressed by the English; New England comprises only one sixth of the whole population of the Union, but owns half of the shipping of the country, or 700,000 tons out of a little more than 1,400,000. But they did not wish to have recourse to the cannon's mouth. A commercial people, they had much to lose and nothing to gain by a maritime war; a clear-sighted race, they saw that God was on the side that could muster the largest armies and the most numerous navy. In a word, war appeared to them to be a barbarous, old-fashioned means, unworthy of their inventive wit. The Yankees never do anything like other people. They always have some contrivance in store that nobody else would ever have thought of. After a careful examination, the Yankee said to himself, 'The best mode of warfare against the English will be to attack the sources of their wealth; now what is the principal source of the wealth of Great Britain? Its manufactures. Among its manufactures which are the most productive? Why the cotton. Well then, we will set up spinning works and manufactories of cottons; this will be our war on Great Britain.'

"Ten or twelve years were spent making experiments, in preliminary preparations and attempts to form a class of operatives and to make machinery. In 1823 the Merrimack corporation began operations at Lowell, where the Merrimack River has a fall of thirty-two feet, creating a vast source of power, and has been followed by the Hamilton, Appleton, Lowell, Suffolk, Tremont, Lawrence, and other companies in succession."

Such is Lowell. Its name is derived from that of a Boston merchant who was one of the first promoters of cotton manufacture in the United States. It is not like one of our European towns that was built by some demigod, a son of Jupiter, or by some hero of the Trojan war, or by the genius of an Alexander or a Caesar, or by some saint attracting crowds by his miracles, or by the whim of some great sovereign like Louis XIV or Frederick, or by an edict of Peter the Great. It is neither a pious foundation, nor an asylum for fugitives, nor a military post; it is one of the speculations of the merchants of Boston. The same spirit of enterprise which a year ago suggested the idea of sending a cargo of ice from Boston to Calcutta round Cape Horn to cool the drink of Lord William Bentinck and the nabobs of the India Company has led them to build up a town here, wholly at their own expense, with all the buildings required by the wants of a civilized community, in order to be able to manufacture white cottons and calicoes; and they have succeeded, as they ordinarily succeed in their speculations. The annual dividends of the manufacturing companies in Lowell are generally from ten to twelve per cent.

The manufacture of cotton in America, which dates only from the last war with England, is growing rapidly, although the modifications of the tariff required by the attitude of South Carolina last year have somewhat tended to check the manufacturing spirit. Boston seems destined like Liverpool to have its Lancashire behind it. As watercourses abound in New England, according to the general nature of the region, steam engines may be dispensed with for a long time to come. This part of the country is not at all fertile, and it took all the perseverance and obstinacy of even the Puritans to introduce the comforts of life into it. It is rugged, rocky, mountainous, and bleak, consisting of the first ridges of the Alleghenies, which extend all the way to the Gulf of Mexico, continually receding from the Atlantic as they stretch southward. The inhabitants have an extraordinary mechanical genius; they are patient, attentive, and inventive; they must succeed in manufactures. Rather they have already succeeded and Lowell is a miniature Manchester. More than thirty thousand bales of cotton, or one sixth of the whole domestic consumption, are consumed in Lowell, without mentioning several manufactories of broadcloths, woolens, and carpets. To strengthen the resemblance between their city and Liverpool, the Boston merchants determined to construct a railroad twenty-six miles long from Boston to Lowell; there was already a canal, as there is one between Liverpool and Manchester, but this has been found insufficient, as it was at Liverpool and Manchester. They would not permit this road to be constructed in the usual hasty and provisional manner of American works, but determined to have something Roman, and their engineers have given it to them and have certainly made the most solid railroad in the world. They have only left out the beautiful masonry, the arches of hewn stone, the columns, and all the monumental architecture which makes the Liverpool and Manchester railroad one of the wonders of modern times; these magnificent ornaments yield no dividends. Yet the Boston and Lowell railroad in its Roman or Cyclopean simplicity will cost $56,000 a mile.

In traveling through the neighborhood of Manchester, one is struck with wonder at the sight of the great spinning works. To see those huge white buildings by moonlight, projecting themselves on the dark background above the plain, those hundreds of windows from which stream the brilliant rays of gaslights, those lofty chimneys, higher than the highest obelisks, one is tempted to think them palaces, abodes of pleasure and joy. Alas! the delusive splendor! alas! the whited sepulchers! All this fairy illusion vanishes when one crosses their doorsill, sees the haggard looks and ragged clothes of the crowd that fills these vast structures, beholds those poor children whom Parliament vainly strives to protect against their prolific fathers, who are incessantly begetting new competitors, and against the lash of their overseers. On arriving at Lowell, the first impression of pleasure caused by the sight of the town, new and fresh like an opera scene, fades away before the melancholy reflection, will this become like Lancashire? Does this brilliant glare hide the misery and suffering of the worker, hide those degrading vices engendered by poverty in manufacturing towns, drunkenness and prostitution; does popular sedition hang over the heads of the rich by a frail thread which an ordinary accident and slight imprudence, or a breath of the bad passions, would snap asunder? This question I hasten to answer.

XIII

The Factory Girls of Lowell

Results of Mechanical Inventions — The Locomotive Engine — Wages in Lowell — Factory Girls — American Manners — Measures of the Companies to Maintain Public Morality in Lowell — French Manners — Will Good Morals Last at Lowell? — Moral and Political Influence of Western Lands — Algeria

Boston, June 22, 1834.
War, the last argument of kings and peoples, war, in which they put forth their strength with pride, is surely not the greatest exhibition of human power. A field of battle may excite terror or a feverish enthusiasm, pity or horror; but the creative power of man is more imposing than human strength employed in slaughter and destruction. The Pyramids or the colossal temples of Thebes, the Coliseum or Saint Peter's of Rome, reveal a higher grandeur than a field of battle covered with desolation and death, were it strewn with three hundred thousand bodies, as in those two great struggles in which our fathers, under Meroveus and Charles Martel, presented a barrier to the career of the barbarians and saved the Western world from the encroachments of the East. The power of man, like that of God, is not less

visible in small things than in great. There is nothing in the physical order of things of which our race has a better right to boast than mechanical invention, by means of which man subdues the wild power of nature or develops its latent energy. By the aid of mechanical contrivances, this poor weak creature, reaching out his hands over the immensity of nature, takes possession of unchained rivers, of the torrential winds of heaven, of the tides of the sea. By them he drags forth from the secret bowels of the earth hidden stores of fuel and of metals, and masters the subterranean waters which dispute his dominion. By machinery he turns each drop of water into a reservoir of steam, that is, into a magazine of power, and thus he changes the globe, in comparison with which he seems but an atom, into a laborious, untiring, submissive slave, performing the heaviest tasks under the eye of its master. Is there anything which gives a nobler idea of the power of man than the steam engine in the form in which it is applied to produce motion on railroads? It is more than a machine, it is almost a living being. It moves, it runs like a racehorse at the top of his speed. More than this, it breathes; the steam which issues periodically from the cylinders, condensed into a white cloud, resembles the quick breathing of the racehorse. A steam engine has a complete respiratory apparatus which acts like our own by expansion and compression; it wants only a system of circulation in order to have life.

One evening in Virginia, some hours after sundown, I was looking at a distant locomotive engine approaching along the Petersburg and Roanoke railroad, one of the many fine works which Mr. Robinson, the engineer, still quite a young man, has executed in Virginia and Pennsylvania. The engine came on at its usual rate of speed through a narrow clearing cut for the road in one of the primitive forests, formerly the domain of the great king Powhatan and his copper-colored warriors. The chimney yawned out at the top like the gaping mouth of some great beast; it threw out thousands of sparks. Although still at a distance, the noise of the quick breathing of the cylinders could be heard distinctly. In the darkness, in so wild a place, in the bosom of a vast wilderness and the midst of a profound silence, it was necessary either to be acquainted with mechanics, or to be filled with the superstition of the ages, not to believe this flying, panting, flaming machine was a winged dragon vomiting forth fire and flame. A short time ago some Brahmins, the fathers of ancient science, seeing a steamboat stem the current of the sacred Ganges, really believed that it was some strange animal recently discovered by the English in some distant land.

In our modern societies the improvements of machinery have given us manufactures which promise to be a source of inexhaustible prosperity and well-being to mankind. English manufactures alone yield about eight hundred million yards of cotton stuffs annually, or about one yard for each inhabitant of the globe. If this amount of cloth had to be produced without machinery, by hand, it is probable that each of us would hardly be able to card, spin, and weave his yard a year, so that the whole time of the whole human race would be occupied by a task which, by the aid of machinery, is accomplished by five hundred thousand arms in Great Britain. From this fact we may conclude that when the manufacturing system shall be completely organized, a moderate amount of labor by a small part of the human race will be sufficient to produce all the material comforts for the whole. There can be no doubt that it will be so some day; but this beautiful order of things is still in the future. The manufacturing system is a new thing; it is expanding, and as it matures it will improve. The staunchest pessimists cannot deny this, yet we should expose ourselves to the most cruel disappointments if we imagined that the progress of improvement can be otherwise than slow, step by step. There are seven-leagued boots in fairy tales, but none in history.

Temporarily the manufacturing system involves the most terrible consequences, which it would be useless to enumerate here. Who has not sounded its depths with terror? Who has not wept over it? It is the cancer of England, a cancer so cruel that one is sometimes tempted to think that all the ability displayed of late by British statesmen in attempts at domestic reform will prove a dead loss.

The introduction of the manufacturing system into a new country, under the empire of circumstances very different from ours, is an event worthy of the closest attention. No sooner was I recovered from a sort of giddiness with which I was seized at the sight of this extemporaneous town of Lowell, hardly had I taken time to touch it, to make sure that it was not a pasteboard town, like those which Potëmkin erected for Catherine along the road to Byzantium, when I set out to find out how far the creation of manufactures in this country had given rise to the same dangers in regard to the welfare and morals of the working class and in regard to the security of the rich and public order, as in Europe. Through the polite attention of the agents of the two principal companies (the Merrimack and the Lawrence), I was able to satisfy my curiosity. The cotton factories alone employ six thousand persons in Lowell. Of this number nearly five thousand are young women from seventeen to twenty-four years of age, the daughters of farmers from the different New England States, particularly Massachusetts, New Hampshire, and Vermont; they are here far from their families and on their own. Seeing them pass through the streets, morning and evening and at mealtimes, neatly dressed; finding their scarfs, and shawls, and the green silk hoods which they wear as a shelter from the sun and dust (for Lowell is not yet paved) hanging in the factories between vases of flowers and shrubs which they cultivate, I said to myself, this, then, is not Manchester. When I was informed of the rate of their wages, I understood that it was not at all like Manchester. The following are the average weekly (that is, six days of work) wages paid by the Merrimack corporation last May.

For picking and carding .... $\begin{cases} 3.00 \text{ Dolls.} \\ 3.10 \\ 2.78 \end{cases}$

For Spinning 3.00

For weaving .... $\begin{cases} 3.10 \\ 3.12 \end{cases}$

For warping and sizing .... $\begin{cases} 3.45 \\ 4.00 \end{cases}$

In the cloth-room (measuring and folding).... 3.12

These numbers are, I repeat, averages. The wages of skilled hands amount to $5.00 and sometimes nearly $6.00. Note that last March, in consequence of the crisis occasioned by the President's quarrel with the Bank, there was a general reduction of from $.30 to $.40 a week. You know how much smaller are the wages of women than of men; there are few women in Europe, outside of some of the great cities, who can earn more than $.20 a day or $1.00 a week. It must be remembered also that in the United States the necessaries of life are not only much cheaper than in England, but even than in France, so that a great many of these girls can save $1.00 or $1.50 a week. After spending four years in the factories, they may have a little fortune of $250 or $300. When they have a dowry, they quit the factory and get married. Out of one thousand females in the Lawrence mills, only eleven are married women, and nineteen widows.

In France, it would be difficult to conceive of a state of things in which young girls, generally pretty, should be separated from their families, fifty or a hundred miles from home, in a town in which their parents could have no one to advise and watch over them. It is a fact, however, with the exception of a small number of cases which only prove the rule, that this state of things has yet had no bad effects in Lowell. The manners of the English race are totally different from those of us French; all their habits and all their notions wholly unlike ours. The Protestant education, much more than our Catholic discipline, draws round each individual a line over which it is difficult to step. The consequence is more coldness in domestic relations, the more or less complete absence of a full and free expression of the stronger feelings of the soul, but, in turn, everyone is obliged and accustomed to show more respect for the feelings of others. What among us would pass for a youthful imprudence, a pretty trick, is severely frowned upon by the English and Americans, and particularly by the Americans of New England, who are, as has been said, double-distilled English. Nobody in this country, then, is surprised to see the daughters of rural proprietors, after having received a tolerable education, quit their native village and their parents, take up their residence fifty or a hundred miles off, in a town where they know no one, and pass three or four years in this state of isolation and independence. They are under the safeguard of the public faith. All this presupposes an extreme reserve of manners, a vigilant, inexorable, and rigid public opinion. It must be acknowledged that under this rigorous system there is a somber hue, an air of listlessness, thrown over society; but, when one reflects on the dangers to which the opposite system exposes the daughter of the poor who has no one to look out for her, when one counts the victims, however slight may be his sympathies for humanity, it is difficult to deny that Anglo-American prudery, all things considered, is fully worth our ease and freedom of manners, whatever may be their attractions.

The manufacturing companies exercise the most careful supervision over these girls. I have already said that twelve years ago Lowell did not exist. When, therefore, the factories were set up, it also became necessary to provide lodgings for the workers. Each company has built for this purpose a number of houses within its own limits, to be used exclusively as boarding houses for them. These are under the care of a matron who is paid by the company at the rate of one dollar and a quarter a week for each boarder, that sum being taken out of the weekly wages of the girls. These housekeepers, who are generally widows, are each responsible for the conduct of her boarders, and they are themselves subject to the control and supervision of the company in the management of their little communities. Each company has its rules and regulations, which are not merely paper-laws but are carried into execution with all that spirit of vigilant perseverance that characterizes the Yankee. I will give you a short summary of one of these codes, for they seem to me to throw great light on some of the most striking peculiarities of this country. I will take those of the Lawrence company which is the most recently formed; they are a revised and corrected edition of the rules and regulations of the other companies. They bear the date May 21, 1833.

The first Article of the general rules is as follows:

> All persons employed by the Company must devote themselves assiduously to their duty during working-hours. They must be capable of doing the work which they undertake, or use all their efforts to this effect. They must on all occasions, both in their words and in their actions, show that they are penetrated by a laudable love of temperance and virtue, and animated by a sense of their moral and social obligations. The Agent of the Company shall endeavor to set to all a good example in this respect. Every individual who shall be notoriously dissolute, idle, dishonest, or intemperate, who shall be in the practice of absenting himself from divine service, or shall violate the Sabbath, or shall be addicted to gaming, shall be dismissed from the service of the Company.
>
> Article 2: All ardent spirits are banished from the Company's grounds, except when prescribed by a physician. All games of hazard and cards are prohibited within their limits and in the boarding-houses.

THE FACTORY GIRLS OF LOWELL

The following articles from 3 to 13 determine the duties of the agent, assistant agent, foremen, watch, and firemen. Article 13 directs that every female employed by the company shall live in one of the company's boarding houses, attend divine service regularly at one of the churches in the city, and rigidly observe the rules of the Sabbath. Article 14, the last, contains an appeal to the operatives on the necessity of subordination and on the compatibility of obedience with civil and religious liberty.

There is, besides, a special rule relative to boarding houses. It recounts that the company has built those houses and lets them at a low price, wholly for the good of the hands, and that the company, therefore, imposes certain duties on the persons who hire them. It makes them responsible for the neatness and comfortable condition of the houses, the punctuality and good quality of the meals, good order and harmony among the boarders. It requires that the matrons shall receive no persons as boarders who are not employed in the company's works and obliges them to keep an account of the behavior of the girls. It also prescribes that the doors shall be shut at ten and repeats the injunction of attendance at divine worship.

These regulations, which among us would excite a thousand objections and would be in fact impracticable, are here regarded as the most simple and natural thing in the world. They are enforced without opposition or difficulty. Thus in regard to Sunday, for instance, which with us is a holiday, a day of amusement and gaiety, it is here a day of retirement, meditation, silence, and prayer. In the United States, the theaters are generally closed on Sunday, out of respect for the rules of the Sabbath; the only exception to this custom is among the French population of Louisiana. In New England, religious scruples on this point are carried further than elsewhere; thus in Boston a city ordinance prescribes the shutting up of the theaters on Saturday evening because, according to some precisionists, the Sabbath begins at sunset on that day. This is one of the features in which the French type most strongly contrasts with the Anglo-American. In a moral and religious point of view, there prevail among us a laxity and a toleration which offer a counterpart to the American *let-alone* principle in political matters; while the principle of political authority which has always been established in great vigor among us under all forms of government, monarchy, empire, or republic, corresponds to the austere reserve of American manners, to their rigid habits of life, and to the religious severity which exists here by the side of the great multiplicity of sects. So true is it, that both order and liberty are essential to human nature and that it is impossible to establish a society on one of these principles alone! If you abandon a portion of the social institutions exclusively to the spirit of liberty, be assured that the principle of order will take no less exclusive possession of some other portion. Yield up to liberty the whole field of politics and you are compelled to give religion and manners wholly up to order. Leave manners and religion to liberty, and you find yourself obliged to strengthen the principle of order in politics, under pain of suffering society itself to fall into ruins. Such are the general laws of equilibrium which govern nations and the universe of worlds.

Up to this time, then, the rules of the companies have been observed. Lowell, with its steeple-crowned factories, resembles a Spanish town with its convents; but with this difference, that in Lowell, you meet no rags nor Madonnas, and that the nuns of Lowell, instead of working *sacred hearts,* spin and weave cotton. Lowell is not amusing, but it is neat and decent, peaceable and sage. Will it always be so? Will it be so long? It would be rash to affirm it. Up to now the life of manufacturing has elsewhere proved little favorable to the preservation of severe morals. So it has been in France, as well as in England; in Germany and Switzerland, as well as in France. A few days ago I received from one of my friends who was passing through Arau (in the district of Argovie) the following lines:

I have seen the new industry which is invading the mountains and snatching its workers from the fertile fields. I can see also how much industry emancipates and at the same time how much it demoralizes. In passing a stranger, the peasant or the worker no longer salutes him; the young girl no longer murmurs her "God bless you," but looks at him boldly and smiles invitingly.

However, since there is a close connection between morality and well-being, it may be very probable that while the wages shall continue to be high at Lowell, the influences of a good education, a sense of duty, and the fear of public opinion will be sufficient to maintain good morals. Will wages, then, continue to be what they are? There are some causes which must tend to reduce them; the tariff which protects American industry is progressively decreasing; by July 1, 1842, it will be reduced to a maximum of twenty per cent. But, on the other hand, as the work processes become more perfect, the laborers grow more skillful; the capitalists are realizing their capital investments and consequently will no longer expect to realize ten or twelve per cent. A certain lowering of wages is very possible, even after that of last March, because labor is paid in the Lowell factories better than it is in the surrounding country; but there must be limits to cutting wages. In Europe, work is often wanting for the hands; here, on the contrary, hands are wanting for the work. While the Americans have a vast domain in the West, a common fund from which by work each may draw for himself and by himself an ample heritage, an extreme fall of wages is not to be thought of.

In America as in Europe, competition among the leading workmen tends to reduce their wages; but the tendency is not increased in America, as in Europe, by the competition among the laborers, that is by a surplus of hands wanting work, for the West stands open as a refuge to all who are unemployed. In Europe, a coalition of workmen can mean only one of two things: raise our wages or we shall die of hunger with our wives and children—which is an absurdity; or raise our wages, otherwise we shall take up arms—which is civil war. In Europe, there is no other possible construction to be put upon it. But in America, on the contrary, such a coalition means, raise our wages or we go to the West. Every coalition which does not amount to this in the minds of the associates is merely the whim of the moment, an affair of little importance. This is the reason why coalitions which in Europe are often able to shake the most strongly organized power present no real danger to the public peace in this country, where authority is disarmed. This is the reason why European countries, burdened with an excess of population, need for their safety and welfare a West into which each may overflow in its own manner. This also is the reason why France is right in keeping Algeria.

XIV

The Bank and Slavery

Preparations for the Elections — The Bank Question — How Slavery Offers a Way to Save the Bank — The States' Rights Party — Concessions by the North in Regard to Slavery

Elmington (Virginia), August 24, 1834. The elections of members of the House of Representatives will take place in New York, Pennsylvania, and Ohio, the principal States in the Union, next October and November. Although the members then elected will not take their seats until the session which begins in December, 1835, yet great importance is attached to the results of these elections, even in respect to the approaching session of Congress. Both sides are making ready with the greatest activity; both parties have chosen their text. As the harangues against the aristocracy of money have aroused the prejudices of the laboring classes, who form the majority of voters, against the Bank, the watchword of the Opposition is no longer ostensibly the Bank. But it says to the voters, referring to the recent acts of the President against the Bank, and the doctrines which on this occasion he put forth in his messages: "The Executive power is guilty of gross usurpation; hasten to the rescue of the Constitution from its monstrous encroachments. It is no longer a question of the Bank; it is a question of our liberties, bought by the blood of our fathers, which an audacious soldier, surrounded by a train of servile place-men, has with impunity made a mockery of." This is certainly the best ground for the Opposition to take; for General Jackson, in the affair of the Bank, as in most other circumstances of his life, has cared little for forms. He has gone straight to his object, without stopping to consider where he put his foot.

The Administration party, which well knows how unpopular the Bank is with the multitude since this unpopularity is chiefly its own work, talks Bank and nothing but Bank. "The Opposition," they say, "is mocking you when it calls upon you to save the Constitution and the laws. What do they care for the Constitution and the laws? It is the Bank that they wish to save. Down with the Bank! General Jackson, *the Hero of two Wars,* who pushed back English bayonets from the Union at the peril of his life, wishes to free the soil of the country from this prop of tyranny and corruption. The Bank is nothing but English influence which seeks to enslave you. It is now to be seen whether you will be freemen or worshipers of the Golden Calf. In spite of the hypocritical protestations of the parasites of the Bank, remember at the polls that the question, the only question, the whole question, is Bank or no Bank." At bottom, what the Administration party says is true; the Opposition has not given up the cause of the Bank. The question which is at issue and which is to be settled by the elections is, in fact, the question of the Bank. But whose fault is it, if the Opposition today has good reason to call the citizens to the defense of the Constitution?

The leaders of the Democratic party felt, moreover, that their policy, which consisted in setting up the local banks in opposition to the National Bank, would necessarily fail and that the financial and commercial interests of the country, comprising the local banks themselves, must in the long run rally round the Bank of the United States. The abuse which they had heaped upon the latter would, therefore, fall directly upon the local banks. It was impossible that the democratic multitude would not see that it had much more just grounds of complaint against the local banks than against the Bank of the United States, by which nobody ever lost a dollar. Accordingly, after having hesitated a long time, the heads of the party seem ready to take the bold stand of openly denouncing all banks. Bank-bills, they say, are nothing but wretched rag-money; eulogies of gold and silver are now the order of the day. Gold is called *Jackson money*. The United States mint has been actively employed in striking gold coins, half-eagles and quarter-eagles. The principal journals of the Jackson party pay the daily wages of their journeymen printers in gold; the warm friends of the Administration affect to carry gold pieces in their pockets; and as only paper is generally used here in business transactions, even of the most trifling amount, you may be certain that a man who is seen with gold in his hands is a Jackson man. The President lately made a visit to his country house, the Hermitage, in Tennessee, and paid his expenses all along the road in gold, and the *Globe*, his official organ, took care to inform the public of it. At a dinner given in his honor by the citizens of Nashville, he proposed this toast: "Gold and silver, the only currency recognized by the Constitution!"

This apotheosis of gold and silver, abstractly considered, is all very well. Up to now the metals have made too small a proportion of the currency of the United States. Gold, particularly, was never seen. At its last session Congress removed one of the obstacles to keeping gold in the country and substituting it for small banknotes by raising its legal value. How far this act will achieve its goal of keeping a certain quantity of gold in the country, I know not; but I am persuaded that the only prompt and effectual means of sweeping away the small bills will be a National Bank.

The prudent and experienced men of the party will certainly resist a formal declaration of war against all banks; but it is hardly to be avoided that in the Democratic party the most rash and the most violent should give the law to the men of moderation and experience. In this event, Mr. Van Buren will need all his skill to preserve discipline in the ranks. He is too well acquainted with the commercial situation of the United States to allow himself to dwell one moment on such a project as the destruction of the banks. His creed is the overthrow of the Bank of the United States, not because it is a bank, but because, in his view, its existence is contrary to the Constitution.

The tactics of the Opposition have already given them success in some partial and unimportant elections, but even if they should have the majority in the next Congress it would be but half a victory, for the Bank would not be preserved. Many persons who have joined the Opposition because its watchword was the Constitution and the laws would have kept aloof had they seen the name of the Bank joined with them, so rooted is the jealousy of this useful institution. Admitting, then, that the Opposition triumphs in the coming elections, it will be necessary to set some new springs in motion in order to save the Bank. It is easy at present to point to one on which the friends of the Bank will not fail to rely.

The Union, homogeneous as it is in regard to language and general character, is subdivided, as I have already said, into three groups, daily becoming more and more strongly marked. North of the Potomac the States are poor in soil, but rich in commerce and manufactures; in 1833, out of $108,000,000 the ports of the North imported $96,000,000. Deducting the imports of New Orleans, those of all the Southern States were only of the value of $2,700,000. The exports of the South are much greater than its imports. In the North are the great commercial towns, Boston, New York, Philadelphia, and Baltimore, and the secondary ports of Salem, Portland, New Bedford, Nantucket, and Providence. There, also, are almost all the manufactures of the Union. These States do not admit slavery, with the exception of Maryland, where slaves are on the decrease, and the Lilliputian State of Delaware, where slavery has, in fact, almost disappeared. South of the Potomac, between the Atlantic and the Mississippi, are the slaveholding States, wholly agricultural, and the only part of the country in which cultivation is conducted on a great scale, producing cotton, rice, sugar, and tobacco, without mechanical industry and having little commerce except the coasting trade, the foreign trade being in the hands of the North. In the West, reaching from the Great Lakes southward and lying on the Ohio and the Mississippi, is a tract of the highest fertility in which, since Independence, have grown up the new States of Ohio, Indiana, and Illinois, besides Michigan, which is now on the point of becoming a State. These are also agricultural States, producing corn and cattle of all kinds, yielding whiskey and salted provisions, cultivated by free hands, and in which property is so subdivided that each family has its own farm.

Of these three groups, the North is most interested in the existence of a central Bank. It is there, also, that the financial machinery of the Union is most thoroughly understood, and there it is most fully recognized that such a Bank is one of its most indispensable wheels. But the North alone, even with the support of some commercial towns in the South and West such as New Orleans and Cincinnati, does not make up a majority. Even in the North, in the rural districts back of New York and Philadelphia, a jealousy of the commerce of the cities prevails which is worse than injustice, for it is ingratitude, which displays itself by a blind hostility to the Bank. In a word, although the question of a National Bank is considered almost a question of existence by the great commercial capitals of the North, without whose enterprise that region would still be little better than a wilderness, yet the North is far from being unanimous in favor of such an institution, and even if it were the North would not alone be able to save it.

The North, then, must seek allies in the South or the West. There are some symptoms of the increase of the Opposition in the West, but this is only because the question of the Bank has been temporarily left out of view. The West favors neither the Bank nor banks. The hatred of these eminently democratic States to the banking system is formally written into the constitutions of Indiana and Illinois, by which banks are expressly prohibited, unless the State think proper to establish one itself with its own funds; a measure which each has already made preparations to adopt. It is to the South, then, that the North must look for help.

The inhabitants of the South and the North differ from each other in many ways (see Chapter X). To a certain degree there are the same analogies and the same contrasts between the North and the South as between England and France. I asked a fellow countryman, established at Richmond, whose patriotism had not been cooled by a long absence from France, why he preferred Richmond to the Northern cities which, in some respects, are more favorable to business. "Because," he replied, "the Virginians are the French of America." The South, like France, is most distinguished for brilliant qualities, the North, like England, for the solid; great ideas have their origin more in the South; good execution belongs more to the North. The North is gifted with English perseverance, at once the pledge and the condition of success; the South, like us, is easily moved, but easily discouraged—all ardor at the outset, but disconcerted by a check from any unforeseen obstacle. It was a matter of general surprise through the Union last year that the South Carolinians had completed, and completed in a good style, a railroad from Charleston to Augusta; the distance is equal to that from Havre to Paris. From the intermixture of Northern with Southern men in Congress, we find in that body a spirit of calculation and practical good sense combined with a lively imagination and large views; the well-balanced combination of these opposite qualities explains the union of boldness and wisdom which generally characterizes the acts of that body. Until recently, when the West has suddenly loomed up and taken its stand by the side of these two rivals, the domestic politics of the United States have consisted in maintaining the balance between the North and the South.

There are grave political differences between the North and the South. The North has more respect for the Federal bond and is disposed to tighten rather than to relax it. The South has the opposite tendency. The South is opposed to the tariff, to the system of internal improvements by the Federal government, to whatever tends to enlarge the influence of the Federal authority. "The lighter is the Federal yoke," says the South, "the more easily it will be borne, the less cause there will be to fear that any of the members of the confederation will be tempted to shake it off." "By relaxing too much the Federal bond," says the North, "you destroy it. If you go on thus, even for a short time, the Union will be dissolved indeed and will exist only in name; the slightest accident will then be enough to abolish even the name." In all these quarrels, however, even in that of Nullification, when a part of the South threatened to break the Federal compact, they have hitherto come to an understanding. Concessions have been made by both sides, but more often by the North than by the South. As they have so long continued to preserve a Union, there is room to hope that they will still be able to live together for a long time to come.

THE BANK AND SLAVERY

The general leaning of the South to an interpretation of the Constitution most favorable to the sovereignty of the States has led many of the Southern politicians to maintain the doctrine of the unconstitutionality of the Bank, although in opposition to a formal decision of the Supreme Court of the United States, the Chief Justice of which, Judge Marshall, is more revered throughout the Union than any other Southern man, and even more so in the South than elsewhere. The Constitution, say the States' rights purists, does not give Congress power to establish a Bank of the United States. On the other hand, if they are ticklish as to what they call the encroachments of one branch of the national government, the Congress, they are not less so about those of which the Opposition accuses another branch, that is, the President. Thus at the same moment that they combat the Bank, they combat the President also, on account of his measures against the Bank. This third party is numerous in Virginia.

Now allowing the conclusions of the States' rights party relative to the Bank to be founded on a strict interpretation of the law, they are none the less inadmissible in practice. And as it is impossible in the United States to give currency to the maxim, *let the colonies perish rather than principle,* the North entertains the hope that the States' rights party, following the example of some of its leaders such as Mr. Calhoun and Mr. McDuffie, will relax a little the rigor of its theories. The Administration, on the other hand, is doing its utmost to preserve the theoretical notions of Virginia on the Bank question in all their original purity on their native soil, and Mr. Van Buren, who is farsighted, lately sent the following toast to a Fourth of July dinner in that State: "Unqualified war on the Bank of the United States."

The North, fortunately for itself, has a means of acting upon the South, through slavery. This requires some explanation. At the time of the Declaration of Independence (1776), slavery existed in all the States. During the war of the Revolution, Pennsylvania, in 1780, adopted a plan which soon exterminated it within her limits; Massachusetts, in 1781, proclaimed slavery to be incompatible with the laws already existing; the other States of New England, and finally New York and the other States north of the Potomac, with the exception of Delaware and Maryland, adopted measures similar to those of Pennsylvania. This was an easy matter for these States; their slaves did not form more than one twentieth or one fifteenth of the whole population. But it was a very different affair in the South, where the proportion of slaves was six or seven times greater and where all the rural labor and menial services were performed by slaves. The institution of slavery was, therefore, permitted to stand in the South. The acquisition of Louisiana and Florida enlarged the number of slave States; and, by an oversight which will one day be bitterly rued, slavery has been permitted in some of the new States, such as Missouri, where it would be easy to do without the blacks. In 1790, there were 660,000 slaves (not counting those in the Northern States) distributed in six States, one Territory, and the Federal District; in 1830 there were 2,000,000 in twelve States, two Territories, and the Federal District. The white population of the slave section in 1790 was 1,250,000, or as 190 to 100; in 1830 it was 3,760,000, or as 186 to 100. The proportional increase of the slave population would appear still greater if we added the free blacks and struck out the States of Delaware and Maryland. In 1830 the number of slaves in Louisiana and South Carolina was greater than that of the whites.

In our days, slavery is a scourge in every country where it exists; of this the people of the United States, in the South as well as in the North, are convinced. But how to put an end to it? The bloody experiment of Santo Domingo and its fatal consequences to the majority of the blacks themselves offer no encouragement to immediate emancipation. The great experiment which the English government is making in its colonies is not yet advanced enough to afford any light. Besides, the English colonies contain only about one third of the number of slaves now in the United States. The indemnity allowed to the owners amounts to about $125 a head, which for 2,500,000, the present number in the United States, would amount to about $312,000,000. And supposing the slaves once emancipated, what shall be done with them? This question is the most embarrassing of all to one who is acquainted with the wretched condition of the free blacks in the United States. On the other hand, the difficulties increase with the progress of time, and the Southern States are, or think they are, obliged to adopt measures in regard to the black population which may be defended by the plea of necessity, but which are nevertheless excessively harsh. Some are surprised that the slave and the free black are more severely dealt with by the laws of the Southern States than by those of a colony belonging to an absolute monarchy, Cuba for instance; and that, for example, it should be prohibited under pain of fine and imprisonment to teach them to read or write. The contrary would be much more surprising. In a country where there is perfect liberty for the free class, it would be impossible to sustain slavery unless by the severest legislation. If the slave should read in your constitutions and bills of rights, "that all men are born free and equal," how can it be that he would not be in a standing conspiracy against you? It is fair to observe that in the United States the slaves, though intellectually and morally degraded, are humanely treated in a physical point of view. They are less severely tasked, better fed, and better taken care of than most of the peasants of Europe. Their rapid increase attests their easy condition.

In spite of all the precautions against an insurrection of the blacks, the solicitude of the Southern States continually increases. From the first of this month the blacks in the English West Indies, which are within three days' sail of the United States, are partially free. Between those islands and Southern and Northern ports there is an active commerce, and communication is frequent. Finally, the religious proselytism which carried the measure of emancipation in England has its organs in the United States. There are not wanting philanthropists in Boston, Philadelphia, and Ohio who are always ready to facilitate the escape of runaway slaves. Last winter, while I was at Richmond, forty or fifty slaves disappeared, and there is no doubt that what are here called the *fanatics* of Philadelphia or New England furnished them the means of flight.

The question of slavery, then, is of all others the most deeply interesting and alarming to the Southern States. Whenever it has been raised, even indirectly and secondarily, they have reacted vehemently; the moment it is touched, their voice is heard; this is their weak side; here the North has a hold on them.

In regard to slavery, the Northern States have never departed from a policy of compromise. The North's conduct may even appear like shameful connivance to Europeans not aware that the most precious treasure of North America, that is to say the Union, is at stake. The Northern States have written into law all that the South has demanded; they have granted the Southern master the right to claim his runaway slave before their own courts, so that the republican soil of the North does not enjoy the privilege which belongs to some of the monarchical countries of Europe, that of giving liberty to whoever sets his foot upon it. The North has permitted slavery to be maintained in the Federal District, in Washington, at the foot of the Capitol steps. The North, seeing the South in a flame on the Missouri question, stifled its just repugnance to her admission. The North, which has an interest in the recognition of Haiti, has yielded that point because the South declares that it would be an encouragement to the slaves to revolt. Thus, to maintain harmony in the Union, the North has pushed its concessions even to silencing its religious feelings, its principles of liberty, its commercial interests. As the Union promotes the good of all, all ought to be ready to make sacrifices to preserve it, and it would be just for the South to renounce its theories about the constitutionality of a National Bank, theories which are belied by long practice and which have been formally condemned by judges of whom the South itself is proud.

Some months ago the public clamor imposed silence on the Abolition Societies in the North, whose object is the abolition of slavery in the South. The newspapers contain details of the devastation and pillage committed about a week ago by a handful of vagrants—taking as their pretext some imprudence by the Abolitionists—on the poor, inoffensive colored people for three consecutive July nights in New York and Philadelphia. Far be it from me to accuse the Opposition, which has the majority in these two cities, of having been an accomplice of these wretches! Yet I believe I state a fact when I say that those terrible riots, in which houses, schools, and churches were plundered and pulled down by the dozen every evening, and in which peaceable persons of color were robbed and personally abused, would have been more energetically repressed, had not the North, above all things else, been eager to punish the Abolitionists and to show to the South that it had nothing in common with them. The North, in a word, has given and continues to give to the South every conceivable guarantee on the subject of slavery. The South, which may one day need not merely the passive forbearance but the active aid of the North against insurrection, should consider if the North exacts too much in return by asking toleration for the Bank, an institution indispensable to the North and from which the South itself has received nothing but favors.

XV

The Elections

The Jacksonian Party Recoups Its Losses — Decisive Results in New York — New Acts of Hostility by the President Against the Bank — Hatred of Moneyed Men on Both Sides of the Atlantic

New York, November 11, 1834. The fall elections have taken place in most of the States. They have resulted favorably for the Democratic party and the President. Last April the mayor of New York, who is a Jackson man, was chosen by the tiny majority of 181 votes out of 35,147 and the Opposition won a majority in the Common Council. The majority in favor of General Jackson is now, 2,400. Several causes have contributed to produce this result.

The name of the Bank, whose cause is closely connected with that of the Opposition, sounds more and more odious to the ears of the multitude. This is unjust, but it is a fact. Some of the late measures of the Bank have redoubled the animosity of the Democratic party toward it. It refused to show its books to the committee of inquiry appointed by the House of Representatives, unless in the presence of the officers of the Bank, and its enemies have persuaded the multitude that the *Monster* dared not reveal the secrets of its den to the representatives of the people. The Bank persists, according to the custom of the commercial world, in demanding damages on account of the protest by the French government of the bill of exchange sold to the Bank by the Administration and has withheld the dividends due the United States on their stock. The purpose is merely, say the officers of the Bank, to bring the question of damages before the proper tribunal. But the Democratic party takes this act as the text for its tirades against the Bank. "Behold it," they say, "setting itself above the laws, taking the execution of justice into its own hands and under false pretenses laying hold of the public money." In both these cases it is quite possible that the right is wholly on the side of the Bank, but appearances are against it, and nothing can be more injurious to it in a country governed by universal suffrage. Many of its friends, admitting that the course of the Bank has been strictly legal, would have preferred that a more prudent policy had been adopted, both for the interest of the Bank itself and of the Opposition.

The silence of the principal speakers in Congress, who are almost all in the ranks of the Opposition, has contributed not a little to its losses since the close of the session. The friends of the Administration in Congress, and especially in the Senate, were beaten in debate; they felt it themselves; their whole appearance was a formal confession of defeat; the whole party was disconcerted by the hesitation and embarrassment of its leaders. Since the thirtieth of June, the rank and file of the party have had time to rally; they have restored their ranks beyond the reach of the fire of Messrs. Clay, Calhoun, and Webster, and they have gained a victory which four months ago they could not have hoped for.

Finally, the revival of business in the country has also turned to the disadvantage of the Opposition. During the April elections in New York, the community was just recovering from a crisis; all classes had suffered and were still suffering. It was difficult to deny that this temporary distress had been caused by the President's attack on the Bank, by what he himself called an experiment. Commerce is now active again, autumn business has been good, and everything encourages the expectation of a not less favorable state of the spring trade. General Jackson's experiment seems, then, to have succeeded, and a great number of persons who belong to the Democratic party as their natural element, and who had quitted it in the spring, have naturally fallen back into its ranks.

But it is necessary to seek elsewhere to understand the full meaning of the Administration's victory. The Opposition has not actually been driven from its former positions, but the Jackson party has maintained the greater number of those it before occupied and has stood particularly firm in Pennsylvania and New York. In a word, to judge by the elections that have already taken place, the House of Representatives in the session that begins at the close of 1835 will be, like the present House, composed of a majority of Jackson men. The Opposition, however, has gained rather than lost. It carried the State of Maryland by a considerable majority and has even won the Democratic State of Ohio, upon which it hardly calculated; ten representatives out of nineteen from that State belong to the Opposition, and although the governor is a Jackson man, the majority of the State legislature is anti-Jackson, an important circumstance because the legislatures elect the Senators in Congress.

The elections in Pennsylvania, where the Opposition lost two representatives, have surprised no one, but those in New York have run contrary to all calculations. I know some well-informed Jackson men who had shrewdly judged the results of previous elections and who did not expect a majority of more than three or four hundred in the city; as I have observed, they had one of twenty-four hundred. The Opposition thought it could contest the State and relied upon carrying the city. It is certainly extraordinary that the commercial interest should be beaten in the first commercial city in the New World; such a result does no honor to the system which has caused it. The unexpected triumph of the Opposition in Ohio had redoubled their confidence in New York. They had celebrated with a great show the junction of the young giant of the West with the anti-Jackson forces. One of the magnificent steamboats belonging to the New York and Albany line, called the *Ohio,* had been sent up the river with cannon, and the roar of its guns had been mingled with the shouts of the towns and villages on the Hudson. A little model of the frigate *Constitution,* the palladium of the Opposition in New York, was publicly paraded before the eyes of the multitude. A packet boat had been sent up the Erie canal from Albany and made the new and flourishing towns—which at once give and take life, activity, and wealth from that great artery of the State —resound with salvos of artillery in honor of Ohio. But now the cannon of the Opposition is silent; only that of Tammany Hall is heard. The little frigate which during the elections was hung up before Masonic Hall, the headquarters of the Opposition, no longer displays the colored lights with which her rigging was illuminated every night. The streets of New York, which do not indeed require it, receive no additional light except from the Jackson processions which parade nightly by torchlight.

The New York elections are not only important in their results, but also on account of the disorder which prevailed while they were going on. During the last six months, the spirit of anarchy has raised its head in the United States in such a manner as to inspire serious alarm, even among those not prone to be timid. You know what happened in New York during the April elections; later, in July, the city became for several nights the scene of a series of outrages against the poor blacks. In August the same excesses were committed in Philadelphia under the same pretext and with no less audacity and perseverance; then came the brutal assault on the Ursuline convent in Charlestown, when the retreat of peaceful nuns devoted to the education of young girls was attacked, plundered, and burnt down, without the Selectmen of the town having the power or the courage to make head against the rioters and without the leading citizens, taken by surprise by this act of savage intolerance, venturing to interfere. Hardly a month since, there was also an incendiary conflagration at Philadelphia on the evening of the election; six houses were burnt and the firemen were driven off by the rioters, as at Charlestown, by main force. The same evening, an event of an even more grave character occurred; several muskets were discharged by some of the Opposition whom the mob had assailed with stones, several persons were wounded, and one or two killed. A week before, during the primary elections, an obscure and peaceable individual was killed by a stab with a dagger.

A repetition of these scenes of disorder was feared in New York, but nothing of the sort occurred. Nearly 36,000 voters exercised their right of suffrage without any disturbance, although both parties were highly excited. The merit of this wise conduct is due wholly to the people; the Common Council had, indeed, taken extraordinary measures for the preservation of the peace, but what is here considered extraordinary hardly comes up to the ordinary in Europe. If the multitude in the United States abstain from acts of violence, it is because they choose to do so; if they preserve order, it is because they love order. Three hundred constables more or less, in a city of 260,000 like New York, could do nothing. Some persons, however, attribute this moderation of the democracy wholly to its confidence in success and insist that if there had been any symptoms of the elections going the other way the streets would have been thronged, as in April, by bodies of men armed with clubs.

The fate of the Bank has been decided by these elections. In fifteen months its charter expires and the Bank will die, to be revived before long under a new form when a new series of commercial disasters shall have convinced the most incredulous that they cannot get along without it. It is worthy of note that it falls by the hands of the two States that owe it the most, New York and Pennsylvania. The blindness of Pennsylvania in particular is inexplicable. Who would expect this stupid fury in drying up the sources of its own prosperity? For without Philadelphia capital, the interior districts of the State would yet be a wilderness; its one thousand miles of canals and railroads, its innumerable bridges, the finest wooden structures in the world, its numerous roads, the manufactures and mines which now enrich it, would not exist. Some persons assert that Pennsylvania, which begins with Philadelphia, perhaps the most enlightened and refined city in the United States, ends with a rural population of German origin, the most ignorant in North America. The conduct of the Pennsylvanians in regard to the Bank is not calculated to change the opinion of these severe judges. The able Correa, for some time Portuguese Minister to the United States, once said, on returning from a trip to the western part of Pennsylvania, that this State reminded him of the Sphinx, which had the head of an angel and the body of a beast. This saying is often quoted in the United States. As for the New York electors, it may be supposed that if the seat of the mother bank were in their capital, the votes of the town and the State would have turned out very differently.

The only chance left for the Bank is that the portion of the South which is under the influence of Virginia should condescend to lend it a helping hand. Such an act of generous compassion on the part of the South is not probable, but it is not absolutely impossible. I have often been present at discussions between men of the South and the North in which the Northerners have said to their opponents: "Without us you would be at the mercy of your slaves; it is our union with you which will prevent them from rising and cutting your throats." The Southerners answered: "We will take it upon ourselves to keep down our slaves; we shall have no need of your help against any attempts at insurrection for a long time to come. All we ask of you is, not to stir them up to revolt. But as for you, why you are yourselves overwhelmed by a flood of ultra-democracy. Your workmen give you the law. Before long you will be glad to get the aid of the South to restore the balance which your universal suffrage has destroyed." The South now has a fine opportunity to exercise in the North this moderating power which it boasts that it possesses.

THE ELECTIONS

Frederick the Great, having gained a victory over the Imperialists just after the battle of Fontenoy, wrote to Louis XV: "I have just paid the draft which Your Majesty drew on me at Fontenoy." General Jackson has honored the bill drawn on him by the New York electors more promptly. A circular has been directed by the Secretary of the Treasury to the receivers of the public money prohibiting the reception of certain drafts on the branch banks. These drafts were issued merely because it was physically impossible for the president and cashier of the mother bank to sign five- and ten-dollar notes fast enough to supply the place of those that were worn out or torn in the course of circulation. They have the same form as banknotes and pass like them, although the charter of the Bank makes no mention of them. This act of the Administration will, however, do no injury to the Bank; for if it is obliged to withdraw all these drafts, amounting to seven millions, from circulation, there is nothing to prevent its issuing bills to the same amount.

The Bank is prepared for every event. The amount of its bills in circulation, including the drafts on the branches, does not exceed 17 millions, and its means in specie or other ready capital exceed 20 millions. It will merely be necessary for the president, Mr. Biddle, and the cashier, Mr. Jaudon, who were already crowded with business, to devote three or four hours a day to signing bills; for the branch drafts were only designed to relieve them from this duty. The order of the Secretary of the Treasury amounts, therefore, merely to a task inflicted on those gentlemen.

On both sides of the Atlantic there is at present a reaction against the aristocracy of money. While here the eternal chorus of NO BANK! DOWN WITH THE BANK! NO RAG-MONEY! is forever displayed on the liberty poles and the flags of the democracy, among us the bankers are denounced as jackals from the national tribune by our most able speakers. Do those who hope that industry will soon raise itself to political influence and dignity deceive themselves then? Or are the industrial classes themselves, and particularly those who are at their head, the financial class, yet unconscious of their future destiny, and too slow to shake off the bad habits which they contracted when the sword was law and work was the lot of slaves and serfs? Do not these Princes of Industry pay too little regard to those lofty and noble sentiments which are well worth the privileges of the nobility, and without which no supremacy could ever be sustained? To engage in public affairs with dignity, one's hands must be clean, the public good must be prized above money bags; and yet, such is the state of commercial dealings in our day that, without inheriting a double share of generosity and patriotism, it is difficult to escape from them without becoming contaminated and callous. How many honorable men are there in the industrial ranks who groan over the customs to which they are obliged to conform, over the examples which they are obliged to imitate? The Bank of the United States must pay the penalty of the vices which even in our day degrade commerce, but which henceforth will belong only to history. It is punished for the sins of others. This great institution has not itself deserved the reproach of cupidity; the services it has rendered to the country are immense; those which it has rendered itself, that is to say, its profits, have been moderate.

I must, however, do America the justice to observe that, although the desire to make money is universal, yet in the principal and older commercial centers there is more honesty and less selfishness than among us. American selfishness is less contracted than ours; it does not stoop to petty meannesses; it operates on a more liberal scale. There are certainly wild speculators, blind and desperate gamblers here also; but the objects of their schemes are almost always enterprises of public utility. The spirit of speculation in the United States has strewn this vast country with useful works, canals, railroads, turnpikes, with factories, farms, villages, and towns; among us it has been more rash, wild, and foolish, and much less productive in useful results. It is with us mere stock-jobbing, without any good influence on the prosperity of the country; it is a game in which the dice are loaded, in which the credulous lose the earnings of years in a fever-fit of a moment. Its only results are ruin and despair, and if it contributes anything to the people it is the cells of the madhouse. These are sad truths, but truths which it may be useful to utter.

XVI

Pittsburg

French Settlements at Pittsburg — View of Pittsburg — Its Industry — How Cities Are Founded in the United States — The Trinity of Church, School and Press, and the Bank

Pittsburg, November 24, 1834.

Seventy-six years ago to the day, a handful of Frenchmen sorrowfully evacuated a fort which stood on the point of land where the Allegheny and Monongahela mingle their waters to form the Ohio. The French, with their faithful allies the Indians, had made a vigorous resistance; they had defeated the expedition sent against them in 1754 and forced Washington, then a lieutenant colonel in the Virginia militia, to surrender Fort Necessity. They had routed the troops of the boastful Braddock and spread terror, the memory of which is not yet forgotten, through the English colonies. But the destiny of France was then in the hands of him who of all her kings will be most severely judged by the tribunal of history. Under that most dissolute and selfish prince, France—sacrificed to the paltry intrigues of the bed-chamber, humbled at home—could not triumph abroad. The French were, therefore, obliged to abandon

Fort Duquesne; on that day, November 24, 1758, one of the most magnificent schemes ever projected was annihilated.

France had then possession of Canada and Louisiana; we were then masters of the two finest rivers, the two largest and richest basins of North America, that of the St. Lawrence and that of the Mississippi. Between these two basins nature has raised no barrier, so that in the rainy seasons canoes can pass from Lake Michigan into the Illinois River and continue without any obstruction to the Gulf of Mexico. The plan of our heroic pioneers, priests, sailors, and soldiers had been to found the empire of New France in this great valley. Beyond a doubt, this idea had attracted the attention of Louis XIV, and its execution was begun by the erection of a chain of posts, the sites of which were admirably chosen. There is no country in the world which comprises such an amount of so highly fertile land; none which offers natural routes of communication comparable to the network of navigable rivers and streams spread over this great region. There is none more healthy, for—with the exception of a few areas subject to autumnal fevers, but which rapidly lost this character when brought under cultivation—there are only two infected spots, New Orleans and Natchez, in which during a few months in the year yellow fever occasionally makes its appearance. The sums swallowed up by one of the foolish wars of Louis XV would probably have been amply sufficient to accomplish this noble project. But the enterprise, although pushed forward with admirable zeal and sagacity by agents on the spot, encountered only indifference from the ministers at home, the great point of whose policy was to know who was to be the favorite mistress of His Most Christian Majesty on the morrow. The capture of Fort Duquesne was soon followed by the conquest of all Canada by the English; and in 1763, by the treaty of Paris (these treaties of Paris never bode us any good), France, exhibiting an example of that complete submission and flat despair which our history exhibits so often and the English so rarely, ceded the basin of the St. Lawrence and the left bank of the Mississippi to England with one hand, and the right bank of that great river to Spain with the other.

Thus it came to pass that the empire of New France, like so many other magnificent schemes conceived in our country, existed only on paper, or in the visions of youthful officers, full of sagacity and boldness, and intrepid missionaries, heroes alike without a name, whose memory is honored only in the wigwam of some poor exiled Indian chief. Fort Duquesne is now become Pittsburg; in vain did I piously search for some relics of the French fortress; there is no longer a stone or a brick on the Ohio to attest that France once bore sway here.

Pittsburg is at present essentially pacific; if cannon and balls are seen here, it is because a trading people make it a rule to supply the market with whatever is in demand. The cannon are new, fresh from the mold, and equally available to the Sultan Mahmoud, or the Emperor of Morocco, or the government of the States—whoever will pay for them. Pittsburg is a manufacturing town which will one day become the Birmingham of America; one of its suburbs has already received that name. It is surrounded, like Birmingham and Manchester, with a dense, black smoke which, bursting forth in volumes from the foundries, forges, glass-houses, and the chimneys of all the factories and houses, falls in flakes of soot upon the dwellings and persons of the inhabitants. It is, therefore, the dirtiest town in the United States. Pittsburg is far from being as populous as Birmingham, but it exhibits proportionally a greater activity. Nowhere in the world is everybody so regularly and continually busy as in Pittsburg; I do not believe there is on the face of the earth, including the United States, where in general very little time is given to pleasure, a single town in which the idea of amusement so seldom enters the heads of the inhabitants. Pittsburg is, therefore, one of the least diverting cities in the world. There is no interruption of business for six days in the week, except during the three meals, the longest of which occupies hardly ten minutes; and Sunday in the United States, instead of being as with us a day of recreation and gaiety, is according to the English custom doubly strong with the Anglo-Americans, consecrated to prayer, meditation, and silence. By means of this energetic assiduity in work common to all ages and classes and by the aid of numerous steam engines which labor like humble slaves, the inhabitants of Pittsburg create an amount of products altogether disproportionate to their number. The nature, bulk, and weight of the products manufactured at Pittsburg make this disproportion more striking; for—whether it be that American industry, still new, cannot give the finish required for articles of luxury and ornament, or that the Americans have the good sense to discern at a glance that the manufacture of objects of the first necessity or of essential use is more profitable than that of the trinkets with which civilization loves to adorn herself wherever there is wealth, and even where there is none—only the ruder and coarser kinds of work are done in Pittsburg.

Although Pittsburg is at this moment the first manufacturing town in the Union, it is still far from what it is destined one day to become. It is situated in the middle of extensive coal fields, the beds of which are easily worked. The district east of Pittsburg furnishes much pig iron which is brought hither to be converted into malleable iron, or into all kinds of machines, tools, and utensils. Pittsburg has, then, coal and iron within reach; that is to say, power and the lever by which the power is to be applied. The market for its products is still more vast than its means, for the whole basin of the Mississippi, with all its lateral valleys which on our continent would be basins of the first class, lies open to it. The population, which improves in its condition as rapidly as it increases in numbers, creates an indefinite demand for the engines and machines, hollow ware, nails, horseshoes, glass, tools and implements, pottery, and stuffs of Pittsburg. It needs axes to fell the primitive forests, saws to convert the trees into boards, ploughshares and spades to turn up the soil once cleared. It requires steam engines for the fleet of steamers which throng the western waters. It must have nails, hinges, latches and other kinds of hardware for houses; it must have white lead to paint them, glass to light them; and all these new households must have furniture and bed linen, for here everyone desires physical comfort.

Thus Pittsburg is beginning to be what Birmingham and St. Etienne are, and what several places in the departments of Aveyron and Gard will become when we become more enterprising and use the proper exertions to develop all the resources now buried in the bowels of our *belle France*, for so it is called everywhere abroad. Furthermore, Pittsburg is and must be a commercial center, a great market. Standing at the head of steam navigation on the Ohio, it is directly or indirectly, that is through the more central cities of Cincinnati and Louisville, the natural *entrepôt* between the upper and lower country, the North and the South. Pennsylvania has spared no pains to secure and extend the advantages resulting from this situation. It has made Pittsburg one of the pivots of its great system of internal improvements, which was undertaken with such boldness and has been pursued with such perseverance. Pittsburg is connected with Philadelphia by a line of railroads and canals nearly four hundred miles long, and the numerous branches of the Pennsylvania Canal give it access to all the most important points in the State. A direct communication with Lake Erie is, indeed, wanting, but there will soon be a double and triple one. A railroad three hundred miles long is projected between Baltimore and the Ohio; one third of the distance is already completed; the legislature of Pennsylvania has made it a condition that the western terminus of this work shall be at Pittsburg. A canal, for which the plans and drawings were furnished by General Bernard, is to connect Chesapeake Bay by the way of Washington with the Ohio; the same condition in favor of Pittsburg has been prescribed in this case.

Pittsburg is one of the few American towns which owe their birth to war. It was at first one of the chain of French forts and was afterward occupied by the English as a frontier post against the savages. In 1781, Pittsburg consisted of a few houses under the protection of the cannon of Fort Pitt. The origin of Cincinnati was similar. Both commenced with a fortress, but—more fortunate than some of our great commercial towns, such as Havre, which is stifled in the embrace of its fortifications—Pittsburg and Cincinnati have obliterated all traces of their origin. Of Fort Pitt, which the English constructed just above the site of Fort Duquesne, nothing remains but a small magazine which has been converted into a dwelling house; another trace of the martial epoch (which here forms the mythological age) is the name of Redoubt Alley, which is taken from a battery once erected there to sweep the Monongahela. At Cincinnati, Fort Washington has been razed and on its site now stands a bazaar built by Mrs. Trollope. Not one of the least singular changes that have taken place in America within a half century is the difference between the old mode of founding a town and the way at present they are made to rise out of the ground.

Some weeks ago I visited the anthracite coal district in Pennsylvania. Anthracite, a mineral carbon deposit, is the most convenient kind of fuel and is at present in general use all along the Atlantic coast from Washington to Boston, and its introduction has produced a domestic revolution. Six or seven years ago, when the demand for it was suddenly very much increased, the district which contains the coal beds became the subject of speculation, at first prudently conducted, but finally growing wild and extravagant. The speculators vied with each other in tracing out the plan of whole cities. I have seen detailed plans, with straight streets and fine public squares scrupulously provided for, of cities which do not actually consist of a single street, of towns which hardly contain three houses. This frenzy gave birth, however, to one town of three thousand inhabitants, Pottsville, to ten or twelve railroads, great and small, to several canals, basins, and mining explorations that have proved fairly successful. As for the projected cities, several of them have really become flourishing villages, although the dreams of their founders have not proved true.

In this anthracite region, in the manufacturing districts of the Northeast, along the New York canals, and in all parts of the West, a traveler often has an opportunity of seeing the process of building towns. First rises a huge hotel with a wooden colonnade, a real barracks in which all activity, rising, breakfasting, dining, and supping, are regulated by the sound of a bell with military precision, uniformity, and rapidity, the hotelkeeper being, as a matter of course, a general or at least a colonel of the militia. The barroom is at once the exchange where hundreds of bargains are made under the influence of a glass of whiskey or gin, the clubroom which resounds with political debate, and the theater of preparations for civil and military elections. At about the same time a post office is established. In the early stages the hotelkeeper commonly acts as postmaster. As soon as there are any dwelling houses built, a church or meetinghouse is erected at the charge of the growing community; then follow a schoolhouse and a printing press with a newspaper, and soon after appears a bank, to complete the threefold representation of religion, learning, and industry.

A continental European in whose mind the existence of a bank is intimately associated with that of a great capital city, is very much surprised, even for the hundredth time, at finding one of these institutions in a spot yet in the intermediate state between a village and the primitive forest inhabited by bears and rattlesnakes. On the banks of the Schuylkill, which has lately been canalled and which, flowing from the coal region, empties itself into the Delaware near Philadelphia, may be seen, at the point where navigation begins, the beginnings of a town built during the time of the mining speculations. Port Carbon, for that is its name, consists of about thirty houses standing on the declivity of a valley and disposed according to the plan of the embryo city. Such was the haste in which the houses were built that there was no time to remove the stumps of the trees that covered the spot; the standing trees were partially burnt and then felled with an axe, and their long, charred trunks still cumber the ground. Some of them have been converted into piles for supporting the railroads that bring down the coal to the boats; the blackened stumps, four or five feet high, are still standing, and you make your way from one house to another by leaping over the prostrate trunks and winding round the standing stumps. In the midst of this strange scene appears a large building with the words, *Office of Deposit and Discount,* SCHUYLKILL BANK. The existence of a bank amid the stumps of Port Carbon surprised me as much as the universal neatness and elegance of peaceful Philadelphia, or the vast fleet which is constantly receiving and discharging the products of all parts of the world at the quays of New York.

I return to the triple emblem of the church, the school with the printing press, and the bank. A society which is formed around such a nucleus must differ more and more from contemporary European society, which was formed chiefly under the auspices of war and by a succession of conquests following one upon another. American society, taking labor for its point of departure, based upon a condition of general material well-being on one side, and upon a system of common elementary education on the other, and moving forward with the religious principle for its lodestar, seems destined to reach a degree of prosperity, power, and happiness much superior to what we have attained with our semi-feudal organization and our fixed antipathy against all moral rule and all authority. It presents, doubtless, especially in the newer States, many imperfections and it will have to submit to various modifications; this is the lot of all unfinished works, even when God Himself is the maker. But a few errors and follies are of little import in the eyes of those whose thoughts are occupied with the great interests of the future rather than with the paltry troubles of the present hour. Of little moment are the disgust and disappointment that a European of delicate nerves may have to encounter, if, for the purpose of killing time, he ventures upon a Western steamboat, or into a Western tavern; so much the worse for him, if he has fallen into a country where there is no place for an idle tourist seeking only amusement! Let the foreigner smile at the simplicity and extravagance of national vanity. That patriotic pride, rendered excusable by brilliant success, will be moderated; the errors and the follies are daily correcting themselves; the unavoidable rudeness of the backwoodsman will be softened as soon as there are no more forests to fell, no more swamps to drain, no more wild beasts to destroy. The evil will pass away and is passing away; the good remains and grows and spreads, like a grain of mustard.

XVII

General Jackson

The Revolution Worked by General Jackson — His Military Successes — His Character — His Bold Tactics — His Embarrassments

Louisville (Kentucky), December 15, 1834. You must have been astonished in France at the President's message on the French debts. Here the sharp and reckless tone of some of the press had prepared the public mind for some energetic demonstration; but the message has exceeded the hopes of those who wished to assume an attitude of defiance in regard to France and the fears of those who dreaded some imprudent step. Had such a paper come from any former President—from Washington to John Quincy Adams—it would have been looked upon as an expression of the sentiments of a majority of the American people. Neither of them would have been willing so to commit the United States without being sure that the national will really required it. Their rule of action would have been to let themselves be pushed on by the nation, rather than to draw it after them or to go beyond it; and this, in fact, is more conformable to notions of self-government. They would have had the question profoundly discussed by the cabinet, not only orally, but in writing, as Washington did at the time of the establishment of the first bank in 1791. They would have personally consulted some of the leading statesmen of the country of all parties and all interests. They would have listened patiently to the representations of those upon whom the heavy burden of war would have fallen most directly, the merchants of Boston, New York, Philadelphia, Baltimore, Charleston, New Orleans, and other large ports; and finally, after having weighed all objections, measured all difficulties, if they had been convinced that the interest and honor of their country absolutely required the appeal to the last argument, they would have reluctantly addressed the challenge to their oldest ally and friend, to the firmest stay of liberty and improvement in the Old World.

General Jackson has changed all this; the rules of conduct and the policy of his Administration are no longer those established by the wisdom of his predecessors. Some may maintain that this change is for the better; on this point, the future, and no distant future, will decide. But the fact of a change is undeniable. General Jackson possesses in the highest degree the qualities necessary for conducting partisan warfare. Bold, indefatigable, always alert, quick-sighted, with an iron will and a frame of adamant, devoted to his friends, harsh and terrible to his enemies, making light of obstacles, passionately fond of danger, his campaigns against the Creeks and Seminoles were marked by the most brilliant success and his resistance to the English army under Pakenham at New Orleans was heroic. By these exploits and the enthusiasm which military services excite in all countries, General Jackson found himself the most popular man in the Union when the founders of national independence disappeared and he naturally became the candidate for the presidential seat. Objections were made to his unbending temper, the impatience of contradiction which he had shown throughout his whole career, his obstinacy in following his own impulses despite the law, and his disposition to use the sword of Alexander rather than to conform himself to the delays of constitutional forms. His natural propensities, strengthened by the habits of military command and by the peculiarities of that kind of warfare in which he had been engaged, must, it was urged, have become ungovernable; and it would be impossible for him to acquire that moderation which is necessary in the exercise of civil authority. It was predicted that in politics, as in war, he would be zealous for his friends, implacable toward his adversaries, violent against whoever should attempt to check his course; that, instead of being above party quarrels, he would come down into the arena in person. His arrest of a judge in New Orleans, the execution of the militiamen, and of the two Englishmen, Arbuthnot and Ambrister, his invasion and conquest of Florida in time of peace, his anger and threats when Congress was deliberating upon charges founded on these summary acts, were all dwelt upon.

But his chivalric character, his lofty integrity, and his ardent patriotism seemed sufficient guarantees for his conduct. For reasons of domestic policy which it would take too much time to explain, many enlightened men who had at first treated the idea of supporting him for the presidency with ridicule gave in to the plan, trusting that they should be able to exercise a salutary influence over him. His fiery temper seemed in fact to be calmed by his elevation; the recollection of his oath of office which, at the moment it was made, was made in good faith, was yet fresh. He had conscientiously resolved to observe the principles consecrated by Washington, Jefferson, and the other patriarchs of America to keep himself scrupulously within the narrow limits of prerogative, as he had traced them or allowed them to be traced out for him; to follow the current of public opinion, without seeking to bar its course or divert it from its regular channels; to be moderate, patient, and calm. During his first term, he continued pretty faithful to his resolution, to his professed principles, and to the advice of those who raised him to his seat. But this state of constraint was insupportable to him; it is too late to reform at the age of sixty years.

Besides, not all temperaments, or, I should say, the distinctive qualities of all men, can adapt themselves to that high sphere of serenity in which he who governs others should move. Such a conformity was even more difficult for General Jackson than for any other man; the turbulence and impetuosity of youth had not been tempered in him either by age or by the fatigues of war. And in a country where universal suffrage prevails, political disputes are of a character to exhaust the patience of an angel. Step by step, then, the stormy propensities of the Tennessee planter were seen returning. The character of the bold, daring, restless, obstinate, fiery, indomitable partisan chief, of the conqueror of the Creeks and Seminoles, gradually broke through the veil of reserve, caution, gravity, and universal good will which had covered it and tore in pieces the constitutional mantle in which his friends had taken so much pains to wrap him.

At length, in 1832, South Carolina furnished a natural occasion for giving the rein to his warlike propensities, which had been curbed for four years. That State had, on its own authority, declared the Tariff Act of Congress null and void and had armed its militia to sustain its Nullification Ordinance. The President immediately began preparations for war, retaining however the language of moderation, and obtained an act of Congress (the Force Bill) authorizing him to employ all means to maintain the laws of the United States. When this storm was laid, General Jackson was proclaimed the savior of the Constitution; and perhaps sufficient care was not taken to prevent a very natural mistake by an old soldier and to make him sensible that the congratulations of a grateful people were addressed less to his warlike attitude than to the pacific measures taken under his auspices. In the heat of debate and the shout of acclamation that followed the restoration of order, the old military leaven began to ferment in the President's heart and without a pause he rushed into a vigorous campaign against the Bank. This was a war almost without provocation, certainly without a just cause, and for some time it appeared that the General would be worsted. But he held his own and neither bent nor broke. In this affair he was the same Old Hickory that the Indians had found always and everywhere on their trail, whom they could neither tire nor surprise and upon whom they could get no hold, either by force or fraud. The last congressional election assures him victory, and the Bank is condemned to the fate of the Creeks and Seminoles, of Mr. Clay and Mr. Calhoun, of the Spanish government of Florida, and of the English General Pakenham.

The intoxication of success seems to have restored all the fire of his youth and, at an age when other men look only toward repose, he requires new perils and new trials. Last winter, Mr. Clay declared in the Senate that if phrenology were a true science President Jackson must certainly have the bump of combativeness, for his life had been nothing but the perpetual exercise of that passion; at fourteen years of age against the English; then against his neighbors, the first settlers of Tennessee, not a very tractable race, who handled the knife, the sword, the pistol, and the rifle with as much promptness as himself; next against the Indians, the English, the Indians again, and the inoffensive Spaniards; then against Mr. Clay, Mr. Calhoun, and South Carolina; and finally, for want of other adversaries, he was engaged in a bout with the Bank. The General seems, in fact, to be possessed with the demon of war; for no sooner had he put his foot on the throat of the Bank than he required a new enemy, and finding in America none but vanquished adversaries, or objects unworthy of his anger, he flings down the glove to France. Thus far the defiance thrown out to France is merely the expression of General Jackson's humor. But, unluckily, this act of an individual emanates from a man who is President of the United States until the fourth of March, 1837, and who is even more pertinacious in his enmities than in his friendships. Unluckily too, the defiance has been inserted in a solemn document which is looked upon in Europe as a true indication of the sentiments of the American people. And finally, the man who has put the United States in this posture has just made an experiment which shows the degree to which he can lead the people to espouse his personal quarrels.

His tactics in politics, as well as in war, is to throw himself forward with the cry of, *Comrades, follow me!* This method succeeded admirably in the case of the Bank. If he had recommended to Congress to withdraw the public deposits from that institution, he would certainly have failed; Congress would have declared against it. He therefore boldly took the first step himself and ordered the removal, in opposition to the advice of the majority of his cabinet, two months before the meeting of Congress, without the slightest possible pretense of the urgency of the measure. "I will take the responsibility," he said. The Secretary of the Treasury refused to execute the order because he considered it a fatal abuse of power, and he was dismissed. The majority of the House of Representatives and, in the last elections, of the people, have sanctioned these dictatorial acts. General Jackson has, indeed, lost most of his friends in the enlightened classes and among the business community, but he cares little for individuals, however distinguished; by virtue of universal suffrage, it is numbers that rule here.

Will the bold policy by which he carried the multitude against the Bank be as successful now that he attempts to excite against France? It may be compared to one of those feats of strength in which one may succeed the first and even the second time, but will break his back the third. General Jackson may possess that sort of popularity which is irresistible for a short time, but the duration and solidity of which are in the inverse ratio to its intensity and brilliance. This, however, is mere conjecture. One thing is certain, that the General has the majority in the House of Representatives, and from what is known of the composition of the next Congress there is every appearance that he will keep it during the term of his Presidency; while the Opposition, which now has the majority in the Senate, may lose it after the present session. Besides, it is not plain to me that the Opposition will be unanimous in censuring the measures of General Jackson in regard to France. The opponents of General Jackson, as well as his friends, are obliged to court their common sovereign, the people. Now in all countries the multitude are very far from being cosmopolites; their patriotism is more lively and warm, but it is also more brutal, more unjust, and more arrogant than that of the higher classes. In France, they cry with enthusiasm, *Our country before all things!* Here the word is, *Our country, right or wrong!* which is the perfection of national selfishness.

As General Jackson is not, however, a madman or a fool, it is difficult to imagine that he wishes the United States to pass at once from a close friendship to a state of war with France. If he thinks that France has exceeded all reasonable bounds of delay, that she has exhausted all the patience she had a right to expect from an old ally, from a nation whose independence was bought with our blood and our treasure, why is he not content with proposing measures of commercial restriction? A duty upon our goods would also be a means of paying the twenty-five millions. He knows that if France has more to lose than the United States in a war of tariffs, the United States, whose commerce and navigation are much more extensive than ours, have more to lose in a real war whose theater would naturally be the sea. But which class in the United States will suffer most by a war? The commercial, certainly. Who own the vessels and the goods? Oh! the merchants and shipowners who vote against the General and his friends, the adversaries whom he detests and despises; the traders of Boston who beheaded his statue on the bows of the frigate *Constitution;* those of New York who have had caricature medals struck at Birmingham holding up his government to hatred and contempt; the capitalists of Philadelphia, friends of Mr. Biddle and admirers of Mr. Clay. General Jackson troubles himself very little about the interest of such fellows as these.

On the contrary, an increase of the tariff, whatever should be the motive of it, would particularly hurt the Southern States and would be very unwelcome there. As it is the South that produces cotton, the principal article of export from the United States to France, the reprisals which the French government would not fail to make would fall chiefly upon the South. Now the Democratic party at present needs the support of the South and is courting Virginia in particular, the most influential of the Southern States. The success of the plans of the Democratic party, that is to say, the election of Mr. Van Buren to the presidency, depends much upon the attitude taken by Virginia, not in 1836, the year of the election, but the present year, not tomorrow but today. Public opinion is yet undecided in Virginia; it is desirable, at any price, to prevent it from leaning in any degree to the side of the Opposition, and it is well understood that Virginia will not consent to laying any special burdens on the South. The Virginia legislature is now in session and one of its first acts will be the choice of a Senator in Congress. If Mr. Leigh, the present Senator, is chosen, then it will be committed in favor of the Opposition and perhaps lost to the Democratic party. The loss of the legislature may involve that of the State; the loss of Virginia may involve that of the South. Considerations of this kind have much more weight here than would be imagined in Europe. In the midst of the changing institutions of this country, politicians live only from hand to mouth.

It sometimes happens that European governments are clogged in their foreign policy by domestic difficulties. General Jackson would have been more cautious if he had only realized that such is the position of the French government at this moment. But be assured that he also has his domestic embarrassments which affect his measures. This is more peculiarly the case with him than with any other President, because he is more a man of party, more entangled in party meshes, than any of his predecessors. Congressional intrigues and sectional interests create the same difficulties here, particularly for an Administration like his, which among us result from an ill-balanced population and the burden of the past. The French government may be confident of this and ought to act conformably.

XVIII

Public Opinion

Public Opinion in America Differs from That of Europe — Democratic Government — The Senate

Louisville, December 22, 1834.
The first impression produced in the United States by General Jackson's message was astonishment. It was a truly theatrical gesture that no one anticipated. In Europe, I suppose that it will have excited more than surprise and it

will be a matter of wonder how a measure so rash and reckless could have come from a government which from its origin has been characterized by tact and prudence. I have already attempted to explain this mystery and have said that this quasi declaration of war was altogether an individual affair of General Jackson, that in this, as in everything else, he has acted on his own impulse. The intelligent men who surrounded him at the beginning and who moderated his fiery temper no longer have any influence. One after another has been separated from him and several, such as Mr. Calhoun, who during his first term was Vice President, are now his irreconcilable enemies. His position as the head of the Democratic party, obliges him, therefore, to supply some fuel for the furious passions which recent struggles have kindled.

It would be a mistake to judge the reception of a document of this character in this country by what would happen under similar circumstances in Europe. Public opinion has not the same arbiters here as in European society; what is called public opinion in Europe is the generally current opinion among the middling and higher classes—that of the merchants, manufacturers, men of letters, and statesmen, those who having inherited an assured income devote their time to study, the fine arts, and, unfortunately too often, to idleness. These are the persons who govern public opinion in Europe, who have seats in the chambers, fill public offices, and manage or direct the most powerful organs of the press. They are the polite and cultivated, accustomed to self-control, more inclined to skepticism than fanaticism, and on their guard against the impulses of enthusiasm; to whose feelings all violence is repugnant, all rudeness and all brutality offensive; who cherish moderation often even to excess and prefer compromises and half measures. Among persons like these General Jackson's message would have met with universal condemnation, or rather, if General Jackson had taken his ideas from such as they, he would never have dictated such a message.

The minority which in Europe decides public opinion, and so is sovereign, is here deposed and, driven from post to post, has come to influence opinion only in a few salons in the large cities and has no greater power than is allowed to minors, women, and idiots. Until the accession of General Jackson, it had, however, exercised some influence over all the Presidents, who were generally scholars and all of whom, aside from their party connections, were attached to the minority by family and social relations and by their habits of life. Up to the present time, the educated class had also preserved some influence over the two Houses; but now it has completely broken with the President, or rather the President has broken with it; it has no longer any credit, except with one of the Houses, since the Senate still consists of men who belong to it by their superior intelligence, education, and property. The democracy does not fail, therefore, to stigmatize the Senate as an aristocratic body and to call it the House of Lords. The mass which in Europe bears the pack and receives the law has here put the pack on the back of the enlightened and cultivated class which, among us on the other hand, has the upper hand. The farmer and the mechanic are the lords of the New World; public opinion is *their* opinion; the public will is *their* will; the President is *their* choice, *their* agent, *their* servant. If it is true that those who hold power in Europe have been too much disposed to use it in promoting their own interests, without consulting the wishes and the welfare of the mass beneath them, it is no less true that the classes which wield the scepter in America are equally tainted with selfishness and take less pains to disguise it. In a word, North America is Europe stood on its head. European society, in London and Paris as well as at St. Petersburg, in the Swiss republic as well as in the Austrian empire, is aristocratic in this sense: that even after all the great changes of the last fifty years it is still founded more or less absolutely on the principle of inequality or a hierarchy of ranks. American society is essentially and radically a democracy, not in name merely but in deed. In the United States the democratic spirit is infused into all the national habits and all the customs of society; it besets and startles at every step the foreigner who, before landing in the country, had no suspicion to what a degree his every nerve and fiber had been steeped in aristocracy by a European education. It has effaced all distinctions except that of color; for here a shade in the hue of the skin separates men more widely than in any other country in the world. It pervades all places, one only excepted, and that the very one which in Catholic Europe is consecrated to equality, the church; here all whites are equal, everywhere, except in the presence of Him in whose eyes the distinctions of this world are vanity and nothingness. In Roman Catholic countries, the churches, vast structures, are open to all without distinction; each takes his seat where he pleases; all ranks are mixed together. In the United States the churches are very numerous and very small, being built by joint-stock companies. They are appropriated to the exclusive use of the proprietors, with the exception of one free-seat for the poor, each one's share of property being designated by an enclosed space or a pew. The whole floor of the church is thus occupied by pews and the gallery is generally divided in the same manner, though a part of the latter is generally open and free to all. Each pew is sold and transferred like any other property; the price varies according to the town, the sect, or the situation. The proprietors pay an annual tax for the support of public worship, lighting and warming the church, and the minister's salary, the amount of the tax being proportioned to the value of the pew. Sometimes the church itself owns the pews and the rent covers the expenses of the public worship. According to this system, the place occupied by the worshipers depends on their wealth, or, at least, on the price they are able or willing to pay for their pews. In this regard, Catholics in the United States have followed the example set by the Protestants.

Strange inconsistency! Or rather solemn protest, attesting that the principle of rank is firmly seated in the human heart by the side of the principle of equality, that it must have its place in all countries and under all circumstances!

Democracy everywhere has no soft words, no suppleness of forms; it has little address, little of management; it confuses moderation with weakness, violence with heroism. Little used to self-control, it gives itself unreservedly to its friends and sets them up as idols to whom it burns incense; it utters its indignation and its suspicions against those it suspects, rudely, and in a tone of anger and menace. It is intolerant toward foreign nations; the American democracy in particular, bred in the belief that the nations of Europe groan ignobly under the yoke of absolute despots, looks upon them with a mixture of pity and contempt. When it looks across the Atlantic, it affects the superior air of a freeman looking upon a herd of slaves. Its pride kindles at the idea of humbling the monarchical principle in the person of the *tyrants who tread Europe underfoot.*

It may, then, be expected that public opinion here will approve the message, both as to its manner and matter, that it will consider it full of moderation and propriety. It is probable that most of the men and the journals of the Opposition will fear to censure it openly and boldly. Not even the Jackson men themselves are unanimously in favor of it; the speakers and writers of the Opposition consider themselves and are bound to pay homage to the sovereign people; they are all obliged to court the multitude, which is not very manageable in regard to points of national dignity and vanity. A certain number of journals and political men have expressed their views as to the occasion and the consequences of a declaration of war with some independence and have been able to reconcile their patriotism with a lofty courtesy toward the oldest and the most faithful ally of America. But these are exceptions to the general rule. Some of the best informed and most influential of the Opposition journals have, to the general astonishment, suddenly turned right-about-face and welcomed the part of the message relative to France with acclamations. Thus they appear more democratic than the democracy, furious upon a point of honor, ready to sacrifice everything in order to obtain redress for an outrage to which, after twenty years, they have just become sensible. He who yesterday was a peaceful and reasonable writer is today a thunderbolt of war, can talk of nothing but the violated national dignity, thinks only of fanning the flame. The secret of this sudden change is this: if the United States were at war, they would spend a great deal of money, and a bank would then be indispensable to the Federal government. Now *a* bank and *the* Bank is at bottom all one. This is what is called policy, cleverness, but it remains to be seen if the Democratic party will be the dupe of such arts and if those who are most interested in the existence of the Bank, that is, the merchants of New York, Boston, and New Orleans, and even those of Philadelphia, wish to have a bank at any price.

Happily for the peace of the world, the majority of the Senate of the United States consists of men eminent for their experience, their ability, and their patriotism, who judge the interests of their country on grounds of high policy, and who, among other questions, will not fail to consider this: whether it would not be the worst of all means of securing the liberty of the seas, an object which they have at heart, for the French and American navies to destroy each other. They do not hesitate, when circumstances require it, to take a stand above the demands of an ephemeral popularity and to meet the difficulties face to face. A handful of firm and eloquent men in this illustrious assembly was sufficient last winter to sustain the shock of the popular masses and to check and bear them back. The Senate has only to continue equal to itself to deserve well of its country and of mankind.

XIX

Cincinnati

The Location and a View of Cincinnati — Factories — Slaughtering of Hogs — The Water System — General Harrison — Dependent Condition of Public Officers

Memphis (Tennessee), January 1, 1835. Cincinnati has been made famous by Mrs. Trollope, whose aristocratic feelings were offended by the pork trade which is carried on here on a great scale. From her accounts many persons have thought that everybody in Cincinnati was a pork merchant and the city a mere slaughterhouse. The fact is that Cincinnati is a large and beautiful town, charmingly situated in one of those bends which the Ohio makes, as if unwilling to leave the spot. The hills which border the *Belle Rivière* (as the French call the Ohio) here recede from the river and form a lofty plain which they wall about on all sides except the one where the Ohio serves as a moat; on this plain, man could build a spacious city beyond the reach of terrible floods. Geologists, who have no faith in the favors of the fabled Oreades, the nymphs of mountains, will attribute this tableland merely to the erosion of the mountains in the diluvian period by the river Licking, now a modest little stream which descending from the highlands of Kentucky empties itself into the Ohio opposite Cincinnati. However this may be, there is not in the whole course of the river a single spot which offers such attractions to the founders of a town.

The architectural appearance of Cincinnati is very nearly the same as the new sections of an English town. The houses are generally brick, most often three stories high, with the windows shining with cleanliness, each designed for a single family and regularly placed along well-paved and spacious streets, sixty feet in width. Here and there the prevailing uniformity is interrupted by some more imposing edifice, and there are some houses of hewn stone in very good taste, real miniature palaces, with neat porticoes, inhabited by the aristocratic portion of Mrs. Trollope's hog merchants, and several very pretty mansions surrounded with gardens and terraces. Then there are the public common schools where girls and boys together learn reading, writing, arithmetic and geography, under the joint direction of a master and a mistress. According to the official report of the trustees and visitors of the common schools, dated July 30, 1833, there were then in Cincinnati 6,000 children between the ages of six and sixteen, exclusive of 230 children of color, for whom there is a separate school. About 2,300 children attended the common schools and 1,700 private schools. The number of common schools is 18, under the care of 12 masters and 5 assistants, 6 mistresses and 7 assistant mistresses. The masters receive $400 a year, and the assistants $250; the schoolmistresses $216, and their assistants $168. These salaries are thought to be too low.

In another direction you see a small, plain church, without sculpture or paintings, without colored glass or Gothic arches, but snug, well carpeted, and well warmed by stoves. In Cincinnati, as everywhere else in the United States, there is a great number of churches; each sect has its own, from Anglican Episcopalianism, which enlists under its banner the wealth of the country, to the Baptist and Methodist sects, the religion of the laborers and Negroes. On another side stands a huge hotel which from its exterior you would take for a royal residence but in which, as I can testify, you will not experience a princely hospitality. Or a museum, which is merely a private speculation, as all American museums are, and which consists of some few crystals; some mammoth bones, which are very abundant in the United States; an Egyptian mummy; some Indian weapons and dresses and a half-dozen wax figures, representing, for instance, Washington, General Jackson, and the Indian Chiefs, Black Hawk and Tecumseh; a figure of Napoleon afoot or on horseback; a French cuirass from Waterloo; a collection of portraits of distinguished Americans, including Lafayette and some of the leading men of the town; another of stuffed birds, snakes preserved in alcohol, and particularly a large living snake, a boa constrictor or an anaconda. One of these museums in Cincinnati is remarkable for its collection of Indian antiquities, taken from the huge caves of Kentucky or from the numerous mounds on the banks of the Ohio, several of which were on the site of Cincinnati. This museum has one show which I never saw anywhere else; it is a representation of the Infernal Regions, to which the young girls of Cincinnati resort in quest of that excitement which a comfortable and peaceful, but cold and monotonous, manner of life denies them. This strange spectacle seems to afford a delicious agitation to their nerves and is the principal source of revenue to the museum.

As for the banks, they are modestly housed at Cincinnati, but a plan of a handsome edifice, worthy of their high fortune and sufficient to accommodate them all, is at present under consideration. The foundries for casting steam engines, the yards for building steamboats, the noisy, unwholesome, or unpleasant workshops are in the adjoining village of Fulton, in Covington or Newport on the Kentucky bank of the river, or in the country. As for the enormous slaughter of hogs, about 150,000 annually, and the preparation of the lard which follows, the town is not in the least incommoded by it; the whole process takes place on the banks of a little stream called Deer Creek which has received the nickname of *the Bloody Run* from the color of its waters during the slaughtering season, or near the basins of the great canal which runs from Cincinnati to Dayton in the center of the State and which they plan to extend much farther, all the way to Lake Erie. Cincinnati has, however, no squares planted with trees in the English manner, no parks nor walks, no fountains, although it would be very easy to have them. It is necessary to wait for the ornamental until the taste for it prevails among the inhabitants; at present the useful occupies all thoughts. Besides, all improvements require an increase of taxes, and in the United States it is not easy to persuade the people to submit to this. Cincinnati also stands in need of some public provision for lighting the streets, which the repugnance to taxes has so far prevented.

For about twenty years Cincinnati has had a system of waterworks for supplying the inhabitants with water. For an annual rate of about eight or twelve dollars a family, each has a quantity amply sufficient for all its needs. A steam engine on the banks of the river raises the water to a reservoir on one of the hills near the city, three hundred feet high; from there it is conducted in iron pipes in every direction. The height of the reservoir is such that the water rises to the top of every house and fireplugs are placed at intervals along the streets to supply the engines in case of fire. Several of the new towns in the United States have waterworks, and Philadelphia, among the older cities, has an admirable system of works which, owing to a series of unsuccessful experiments, has cost a large sum. At the moment there is under discussion a plan for supplying Boston with water, which will cost several millions because the water must be brought from a distance. New York is also engaged in a similar work, the expense of which will be about five millions. The Cincinnati waterworks have not cost much above $150,000, although they have several times been completely reconstructed. It is generally thought in the United States that the waterworks ought to be owned by the towns, but those in Cincinnati belong to a company and the water rate is, therefore, higher than in Philadelphia and Pittsburg. The city has three times been in negotiation for the purchase of the works and has always declined buying on advantageous terms; the first time the establishment was offered for $35,000, the second time for $80,000, the third time, $125,000 was asked, and $300,000 or $400,000 will finally be paid for it. In this case, as in regard to lighting the streets, the principal cause of the refusal of the city to buy was the unwillingness to lay new taxes.

Cincinnati, approached from the water, has an imposing appearance, still more so when it is viewed from one of the neighboring hills. The eye takes in the windings of the Ohio and the Licking, which comes into it at right angles, the steamboats that fill the port, the basin of the Miami Canal with the warehouses that line it and the locks that connect it with the river, the whitewashed spinning works of Newport and Covington with their tall chimneys, the Federal arsenal above which floats the starry banner, and the numerous wooden spires that crown the churches. On all sides the view is terminated by ranges of hills, forming an amphitheater still covered with the vigorous growth of the primitive forest. This rich verdure is here and there interrupted by country houses surrounded by colonnades provided by the forest. One is happy to say that those who people this panorama live in the midst of plenty; they are industrious, sober, frugal, thirsting after knowledge, and if, with a very few exceptions, they are entirely strangers to the delicate pleasures and elegant manners of the refined society of our European capitals, they are equally ignorant of its vices, dissipation, and follies.

At first glance one does not perceive any difference between the right and left bank of the river; from a distance, the prosperity of Cincinnati seems to extend to the opposite shore. This is an illusion; on the right bank, that is, in Ohio, there are none but freemen; on the other side, there is slavery. You may descend the river hundreds of miles with slavery on the left and liberty on the right, although it is the same soil and equally capable of being cultivated by the white man. When you enter the Mississippi you have slavery on both sides of you. A blind carelessness or, rather, a fatal weakness in the rulers and a deplorable selfishness in the people have allowed this plague to fasten itself on a country where there was no need of tolerating its existence. Who can tell when and how and through what sufferings it will be possible to eradicate it?

I met with one incident in Cincinnati which I shall long remember. I had observed at the hotel table a man of medium height, stout and muscular, about sixty years of age, yet with the active step and lively air of youth. I had been struck with his open and cheerful expression, the amenity of his manners, and a certain air of command which appeared through his plain dress. "That," said my friend, "is General Harrison, clerk of the Cincinnati Court of Common Pleas"—"What! General Harrison of Tippecanoe and the Thames?" "The same; the ex-general, the conqueror of Tecumseh and Proctor; the avenger of our disasters on the Raisin and at Detroit; the ex-governor of the Territory of Indiana, the ex-Senator in Congress, the ex-Minister of the United States to one of the South American republics. He has grown old in the service of his country, he has passed twenty years of his life in those fierce wars with the Indians in which there was less glory to be won, but more danger to be encountered, than at Rivoli and Austerlitz. He is now poor, with a numerous family, neglected by the Federal government, although still vigorous because he has the independence to think for himself. As the Opposition is in the majority here, his friends have thought of coming to his relief by removing the clerk of the Court of Common Pleas, who was a Jackson man, and giving him the place, which is a lucrative one, as a sort of pension. His friends in the East talk of making him President of the United States. Meanwhile we have made him clerk of an inferior court." After a pause my informant added, "At this poor table you may see another candidate for the presidency who seems to have a better chance than General Harrison; it is Mr. McLean, now one of the judges of the Supreme Court of the United States."

Examples of this abandonment of men whose career has been in the highest degree honorable are not rare in the

United States. I had already seen in New York the illustrious Gallatin, who, after having grown old in the service of the Republic, after having been for forty years a legislator, a member of the cabinet, a minister abroad, after having taken an active part in every wise and good measure of the Federal government, was dismissed one fine day without so much as a thank-you and would have terminated his laborious career in poverty, had not his friends offered him the place of president of one of the banks in New York. The distress of President Jefferson in his old age is well known—and how he was reduced to the necessity of asking permission of the Virginia legislature to dispose of his estate by lottery; while President Monroe, still more destitute, after having spent his patrimony in the service of the state, was forced to seek the charity of Congress; and these are the men to whom their country owes the invaluable acquisitions of Louisiana and Florida! A system of pensions is unknown in the United States. No provision is made for the old age of eminent men who accept the highest offices in the state, although it is impossible for them to lay up anything out of their comparatively moderate salaries, and several of them have seen their fortunes disappear along with their health in public service. Public functionaries are treated like menial servants. The system of domestic life is such in the United States that every American, in private life, treats the humblest of his white domestics with more respect than most of them show, in public life, to officers of the highest rank. On every occasion and in a thousand ways, the latter are reminded that they are nothing but dust, and that a frown of the people can reduce them to nothing.

The way in which Americans treat their public officers is the logical consequence of the principle of popular sovereignty; but I think it consistent neither with reason nor justice. If it is true that nations have an inalienable right to determine in their own interests the rules which will set limits to power, it is equally true that men of superior abilities and worth have a natural and sacred right to be invested with high powers and functions. If it is criminal to sport with the welfare of the mass, it is no less so to trample underfoot the wise and good. And if those whom talents and zeal for the public good call to important posts are repulsed by the prospect of ingratitude and contempt, to what hands shall the care of the commonwealth be confided? What will then be the fate of the sovereign people? There is no less despotism in a people who, impatient of all superiority, repay the services of illustrious citizens only with neglect and capriciously throws them aside like so much garbage, than in an Asiatic prince who reduces all to the same level of servitude, treats all with the same insolence and brutality, and considers virtue and genius overpaid by the honor of being permitted to kneel on the steps of his throne.

In conformity with the prevailing ideas on the subject of offices and officers, no sort of provision has been made for the protection of the latter. They are removable without any kind of pretense or formality, without being informed of the ground of their removal and without any reason being given to the public. In this way a terrible rod of tyranny hangs over them, although under the mild and moderate administration of former Presidents little use was made of it; but, since the accession of General Jackson, a regular system of removal from office has become the practice, and office has become the reward of party service. It has been publicly declared that *to the victor belong the spoils*. President Jackson has filled all the custom-houses and post offices with his creatures, and this policy has been followed in individual States, counties, and towns. At every change of opinion, the state changes its executive officers; the legislators change their secretaries, printers, and even their messengers; the courts, their clerks; the towns, their treasurers, their inspectors of markets, weights and measures, and even their rubbish-men and watchmen. Men in office now understand that the preservation of their places and the bread of their families are hazarded at every municipal, State, or Federal election, according as they hold the town, State, or general government. Formerly they took no part in election maneuvers, the Presidents having expressly forbidden the officers of the Federal government to meddle with them; at present they are the most active agents in them. The President has now at his command an army of sixty thousand voters dependent on his will, whose interests are bound up in his and who are mere tools in his hands. So true is it that extremes meet, that by pushing to excess a single principle, however true, we shall come to conclusions which, practically speaking, amount to the opposite of the principle itself. Thus by drawing out too fine the principle of the popular sovereignty, we may come nearer and nearer to tyranny and the oppression of the people. Is not this a proof that logic is not always reason, and that truth is often, if not always, found in the harmonious combination of seemingly contradictory principles?

XX

Cincinnati

Industry of the People — Industrial Feudalism — Concerning Patronage — Absence of a Leisure Class — Sharp Surveillance in That Regard Everywhere in the United States — Why Americans Do Not Please Certain European Travelers — Recognition Which Posterity Will Give Americans

Natchez (Mississippi), January 4, 1835. Cincinnati contains about forty thousand inhabitants, inclusive of the adjoining villages. Although founded forty years ago, its rapid growth dates only about thirty years back. It seems to be the rendezvous of all nations; Germans and Irish are very numerous and there are some

CINCINNATI

Alsacians; I have often heard the harsh accents of Rhenish French in the streets. But the bulk of the population which gives tone to all the rest is of New England origin. What makes the progress of Cincinnati more surprising is that the city is its own creation. Other towns which have sprung up in the United States in the same rapid manner have been built on shares, so to speak. Lowell, for example, is an enterprise of Boston merchants who, after having raised the necessary funds, collected the workmen and told them, "Build us a town." Cincinnati has been gradually extended and embellished almost wholly without outside aid, by its own inhabitants, who have for the most part arrived on the spot poor. The founders of Cincinnati brought with them nothing but sharp-sighted, wakeful, untiring industry, the only patrimony which they inherited from their New England fathers, and the other inhabitants have scrupulously followed their example and adopted their habits. They have chosen Franklin as the patron saint of their city and adopted Poor Richard's maxims as a fifth gospel.

Cincinnati is, as I have said, admirably situated. This is true of its geographical position, but, if you follow rivers on the map and consider the natural resources of the soil, you will find that there are several points on the long line of the rivers of the West as advantageously placed, both for trade and manufactures, and that there are some even more favored. Pittsburg, which has within reach both coal and iron, that is to say, the daily bread of industry; which stands at the head of the Ohio, at the starting point of steam navigation, at the confluence of the Monongahela and the Allegheny, one coming from the south and the other from the north; Pittsburg, which is near a great network of lakes, appears as the pivot of a vast system of roads, railroads, and canals, several of which are already completed. Pittsburg was marked out by nature at once for a great manufacturing center and a great mart of trade. Louisville, built at the falls of the Ohio, at the head of navigation for the largest class of boats, is a natural medium between the commerce of the upper Ohio and that of the Mississippi and its tributaries. In respect to manufacturing resources, Louisville is as well provided as Cincinnati, and the latter, setting aside its enchanting situation, seemed destined merely to become the market of the fertile strip between the Great and Little Miami rivers.

But the power of men, when they decide to will something and will it perseveringly, is sufficient to balance and conquer the power of nature. In spite of the superior advantages of Louisville as an *entrepôt*, in spite of the manufacturing resources of Pittsburg, Cincinnati is able to maintain a population twice that of Louisville and half as large again as that of Pittsburg in a state of well-being which equals, if it does not surpass, the average condition of each of the other two. The inhabitants of Cincinnati have established this prosperity among themselves, by the instinctive reaction with which the sons of New England are filled by their eminently practical and calculating genius. A word to the wise is sufficient, they say. But cleverer than the wisest, the Yankees understand each other without a word and by a tacit consent direct their common efforts toward the same point. In the United States *to work Boston fashion* means to do anything with perfect precision and without words. The object which the Cincinnatians have had in view, almost from the origin of their city, has been nothing less than to make it the capital or great interior mart of the West. The indirect means which they have employed have been to secure the manufacture of certain articles which, though of little value separately considered, form an important aggregate when taken together; getting the start of their neighbors with that spirit of diligence that characterizes the Yankees, they have accordingly distributed the manufacture of these articles among themselves. This plan has succeeded.

Thus, with the exception of the pork trade, one is surprised not to see any of the large-scale industry which has made the fortune of the manufacturing towns of England

and France. The Cincinnatians make a variety of household furniture and utensils, agricultural and mechanical implements and machines, wooden clocks, and a thousand objects of daily use and consumption, soap, candles, paper, leather, etc., for which there is an indefinite demand throughout the flourishing and rapidly growing States of the West and also in the new States of the Southwest, which are wholly devoted to agriculture and in which, on account of the existence of slavery, manufactures cannot be carried on. Most of these articles are of ordinary quality; the furniture, for instance, is rarely such as would be approved by Parisian taste, but it is cheap and neat, just what is wanted in a new country where, with the exception of a part of the South, there is general ease but little wealth and where plenty and comfort are more generally known than the little luxuries of a more refined society. The prosperity of Cincinnati, therefore, rests upon the sure basis of the prosperity of the West, upon supplying articles to fill the basic needs of the bulk of the community; a much more solid foundation than the caprice of fashion upon which the branches of industry most in favor with us depend. The intellectual also receives a share of attention. In the first place, there is a large typefoundry in Cincinnati, which supplies the demand of the whole West and that army of newspapers printed in it. According to the usual English or American mode of proceeding, the place of human labor is supplied as much as possible by machinery, and I have seen several little contrivances here that are probably not to be found in the establishments of the Royal Press or of the Didots. Then there are several publishing houses; they issue nothing but publications in general demand, such as school and religious books and newspapers. By means of this variety of manufactures which taken separately appear of little consequence, Cincinnati has taken a lead from which it will be difficult to remove her, for in this matter priority is no trifling advantage. The country trader who sells a little of everything is sure to find almost anything he wants in Cincinnati. Therefore he goes there before any other place in order to lay in his stock of goods. Cincinnati is thus in fact the great central mart of the West; a great quantity and variety of produce and manufactured articles flow through here, notwithstanding the natural superiority of several other sites, either in regard to the extent of water communication or mineral resources.

M. Charles Fourier has characterized the spirit of the nineteenth century by the term *industrial feudalism*. The human race, according to some, has thrown off one yoke only to bear another, less burdensome perhaps, but also less noble. The warlike lords of the Middle Ages have passed away but the industrial lords have come to take their place, the princes of manufactures, banks, and commerce. These new masters will spread less distress and privation through life, but also less glory. They will increase the body's pittance, but diminish the soul's. At the sight of the great factories of England, of some of those on the European continent, and of those which are multiplying so rapidly in New England in that wonderful creation the city of Lowell, one is tempted to think that industrial feudalism is already established in the Old World and is creeping beneath democratic institutions, like the snake under the grass, in the New. Those who do not believe that the human race can go backward, and who prefer to rock themselves in the cradle of hope, rather than yield to flat despair, while they admit this tendency as a fact, console themselves by the contemplation of its other characteristic features, at the head of which they place the general spirit of emancipation which carries all before it. If in England, for instance, there are in the factories a thousand germs of despotism, there are in the working classes a thousand germs of resistance, in the population a thousand germs of liberalism; there are Trades' Unions, there are radicals. Neither of these opposite forces will alone decide the destinies of the future. From their opposing impulses will result a single force, different from both, yet partaking of both. The force of emancipation will make what to some seems about to become feudalism simply patronage.

Patronage has not finished its career upon the earth. It will endure while Providence continues to cast men in different molds; it will continue for the good of the weak and the poor, for that of the class of men, so numerous in southern Europe, for example, who require the support of somebody more powerful than themselves. But it will be modified in character, growing successively less and less violent and more and more mild. The inferior has been a slave, a serf, a paid freeman; he may, after a time that is impossible to predict, become an equal partner without ceasing to be inferior. However this may be, there is no germ of industrial feudalism in Cincinnati, there are no great factories or workshops. Industry is divided there, pretty much as the soil is among us. Each head of a family, with his sons and some newly arrived emigrants as assistants and servants, has his domain. Cincinnati is, therefore, as republican in its industrial organization as in its political. This subdivision of manufactures has hitherto been attended with no inconvenience because in the vast West, whose growth is visible to the eye, production cannot at present keep pace with consumption. But how will it be in a century, or perhaps in fifty years? Will not the condition of industry in Cincinnati undergo some great change, or rather will not the whole country undergo a complete change of character and condition which will involve a reorganization of the industrial system?

The moral aspect of Cincinnati is delightful in the eyes of him who prefers work to everything else, with whom work can take the place of everything else. But whoever has a taste for pleasure and display, whoever needs occasional relaxation from business in gaiety and amusement, would find this beautiful city with its picturesque surroundings an impossible place to stay. It would be still more so for a man of leisure, desirous of devoting a large part of his time to the cultivation of the fine arts and the rest to pleasure. For such a man, indeed, it would not be possible to live here. He would find himself denounced on political grounds, because men of leisure are looked upon in the United States as so many steppingstones to aristocracy, and anathematized by religion, for the various sects, however much they may differ on other points, all agree in condemning pleasure, luxury, gallantry, the fine arts themselves. Now the United States are not like some countries in Europe, particularly France, where religion and the pulpit can be braved with impunity. Hemmed in by the laborious habits of the country, by the axioms of politics and religion, a man must either resign himself to the same mode of life with the mass or seek a soil less unfriendly to his tastes in the great cities of New York, Philadelphia, or New Orleans, or even in Europe. There is, therefore, no such thing in Cincinnati as a leisure class, living without any regular profession on their inheritance or on the wealth acquired by their own enterprise in early life, although there are many persons of wealth having one hundred thousand dollars and more. I met a young man there, the future heir of a great fortune who, after having been educated at West Point and received a commission, had retired from the service in order to live at home. Wearied out with his solitary leisure, burdened with the weight of his own person, he could find no other relief than to open a fancy-goods shop.

Everywhere in the United States where there are no slaves, and outside the large towns of the seacoast, a strict watch is kept up in regard to persons of leisure, obliging those who might be seduced by a taste for this kind of life to fall into the ranks and work, at least until age makes repose necessary. Public opinion is on the lookout to banish any habits of dissipation, however innocent, that might get a footing in society and make a life of leisure tolerable. Religious and philanthropical societies, instituted under various names, take upon themselves the task of enforcing the decrees of public opinion; like vigilant sentinels, they compel a rigid observance of the austerities, or—if you choose—the *ennuis*, of Sunday; they labor to suppress intemperance and gaming, the spirit of which, if once diffused among a people so wholly devoted to money-making, might lead to the most fatal consequences. These societies and committees pursue their task with a more than British perseverance, and sometimes with a puritanical fanaticism. When Mr. John Quincy Adams became President, he had a billiard table placed in the President's house, and such is the real or affected abhorrence here of anything called a game that this billiard table was actually one of the arguments against the re-election of Mr. Adams. "It is a scandal, an abomination of abominations," was the general cry. Mr. Adams, whose private character is above suspicion, was, if we must believe the Opposition journals of the day, a teacher of immorality because he had a billiard table in his house, and General Jackson has doubtless caused that scandalous piece of furniture to be broken up and burnt since he has become master of the White House.

Anywhere else this rigor would be called intolerance, inquisition. Here it is submitted to without a murmur, and few persons are really annoyed by it, or show that they are. The American can support a constant and unrelaxing devotion to labor. He does not feel the need of amusement and recreation. The silence and retirement of his Sunday seem to be a more effectual relaxation for him than the noisy gaiety of our festivals. To put it better, one might even say that he lacked the capacity for pleasure. All his faculties and energies are admirably and vigorously combined for production; he is devoid of those without which pleasure is not enjoyment and amusement is but a painful effort. Work for work, he prefers that which pays to that which costs.

Such a social organization is incomparable for a pioneer people. Without this devotion to business, without this constant direction of the energies of the mind to useful enterprise, without this indifference to pleasure, without those political and religious notions which imperiously repress all passions but those whose objects are business, production, and gain, can anyone suppose that the Americans would ever have achieved their great industrial prowess? With any other system less exclusively oriented toward production, they would yet, perhaps, be meditating the passage over the Alleghenies. Instead of having that great domain of the West, immense in its extent and resources, already cleared and cultivated, furrowed with roads and dotted over with farms, they would probably be still confined to the sandy strip that borders the Atlantic. It must be allowed that this ardent and entire devotion to business gives the nation a strange aspect in the eyes of a European. And this explains the fact that Americans have found so little favor with foreign tourists who have visited their country. But, in return, they are sure of the gratitude of that innumerable posterity for whom they are preparing with such energy and sagacity an abode of plenty, a land of promise. This posterity, it is said, will change the habits of their fathers, will adopt new tastes, and even new institutions. So be it! It is of little consequence whether Americans of the twentieth or the twenty-first century shall retain the national character, customs, and laws of Americans of the nineteenth. The more interesting question is whether the Americans of our day do not fulfill, as perfectly as human nature is capable of doing, the mission which Providence has entrusted to them, that of acting as a nation of pioneers and subduers of the forest, and if they do not deserve to be excused, like all nations and individuals, for having the defects inherent in their good qualities. The question thus stated will be easily answered by everyone who sets any value on the interests and welfare of the future.

XXI

Western Steamboats

Influence of the Means of Communication on Civilization and Liberty — The West's Situation Before the Steamboat — Invention of the Steamboat — Description — Passengers — Life Aboard — Accidents and the Little Attention Given Them — Real Rulers in the West — Importance of the West

New Orleans, January 8, 1835. One of the points in which modern society differs most from the ancient is, certainly, the facility of traveling. Formerly it was possible only for a patrician to travel. To travel then, just as to be a philosopher, one had to be rich. Merchants moved in caravans, paying tribute to the Bedouins of the desert, to the Tartars of the steppes, to petty princes perched like eagles in castles built at the mountain passes. Instead of the English stagecoach or the post chaise rattling at high speed over the paved road, they had the old Asiatic litter or palanquin, still preserved in Spanish America, or the camel, ship of the desert, or four bullocks yoked to the slow wagon, or for the common citizens or the iron warriors, the horse; instead of those sumptuous steam packets, genuine floating palaces, the small and frail bark, pursued by robbers on the rivers and by pirates on the sea, the sight of which extorted from the Epicurean Horace the exclamation of terror,

Illi robur et aes triplex—Circa pectus erat.

The roads were then rough and narrow paths, made dangerous by brigands, by monsters of the forest, or by precipices. A long train of luggage, provisions, servants, and guards was necessary, and from time to time the traveler rested with some hereditary friend of his family, for then there were no comfortable hotels in which today, by the means of money, he can get all he needs and can command the help of attentive servants. If there were any public shelter then, it was some filthy den, like the caravansaries of the East, wretched, bare, and comfortless, where he found nothing but water and a roof, or like the inns of Spain and South America, which are a happy mean between a caravansary and a stable. The great bulk of mankind, slaves in fact and in name, were then attached to the land, chained to the soil by the difficulty of locomotion.

To improve the means of communication, then, is to promote a real, positive, and practical liberty; it is to extend to all the members of the human family the power of moving about and using the world which has been given to all as a common patrimony; it is to increase the rights and privileges of the greatest number as truly and as amply as could be done by electoral laws. I would go further—it is to establish equality and democracy. The effect of the most perfect system of transportation is to reduce the distance not only between different places, but between different classes. Where the rich and the great travel only with a pompous retinue, while the poor man who goes to the next village travels painfully alone over mud and sand and rocks and through thickets, the word equality is a mockery and a falsehood, and aristocracy stares you in the face. In India and China, in Mohammedan countries, in half-Arabian Spain and her former American colonies, it matters little whether the government is called a republic, an empire, or a limited monarchy; the peasant and the laborer cannot there persuade himself that he is the equal of the soldier, the Brahmin, the mandarin, the pasha, or the noble, whose retinue runs over him or covers him with mud. In spite of himself, he is filled with awe at its approach and servilely bends before it as it passes him. In Great Britain, on the contrary, in spite of the wealth and the great privileges of the nobility, the mechanic and the laborer who can go to the office and get a ticket for the railroad cars, provided they have a few shillings in their pockets, and who have the right, if they will pay for it, of sitting in the same vehicle, on the same seat, with the baronet or the peer and duke, feel their dignity as men and touch, as it were, the fact that there is not an impassable gulf between them and the nobility.

Because of these considerations, I would find it difficult to believe that a government could be tyrannical which would devote itself zealously to the task of opening roads through the country and diminishing the time and expense of transportation. Is it not true that ideas as well as goods circulate along the great highways, the canals, and the rivers, and that every traveling clerk is more or less a missionary? Those who are possessed with the retrograde spirit know full well that the answer is yes. They favor no projects of internal improvement; they fear an engineer almost as much as they do a publisher of Voltaire. Since it is undeniable that one of the first railroads in Europe was constructed in the Austrian empire, since the imperial government has opened many fine roads from one end of its possessions to the other, and since it is encouraging the introduction of steamboats on the Danube, I may venture to conclude that Metternich deserves a better reputation than he enjoys on this side of the Rhine. You know, on the other hand, that during the short ministry of M. de Labourdonnaye, in 1829, the surveys and plans of various roads in Vendée disappeared from the archives and have never since been found. Only a few months ago in Puebla—one of the free and sovereign States of the Mexican confederacy, whose government, however, enjoys a high reputation for ignorance and bigotry—the representatives of the people, animated with a holy wrath against those ruthless unbelievers (mostly foreigners) who have pushed the sacrilegious spirit of innovation so far as to set up a line of stagecoaches between Veracruz and Mexico and to repair the great road between the two cities, imposed an annual tax of $135,000 upon them and prohibited their taking any tolls within the limits of the State.

There is a region where, by simply perfecting the means of water transportation, a revolution has been produced, the consequences of which on the balance of power in the New World are incalculable. It is the great valley of the Mississippi, which had, indeed, been conquered from wild beasts and Redskins previous to the invention of Fulton but which, without the labors of his genius, would never have been covered with rich and populous States. After the conquest of Canada had put an end to the brilliant but sterile exploits of the French on the Ohio and the Mississippi, the Anglo-Americans, then subjects of the king of Great Britain, began to expand. The first settlers seated themselves in Kentucky and occupied the soil for agricultural purposes. In a short time they had effaced from its surface the slight traces which the French, almost exclusively engaged in hunting, had left of their passage. Instead of the little and restless but indolent race produced by a cross of French with Indian blood, the newcomers, avoiding all mixture with the natives, produced a laborious and energetic population that on this fertile soil and like its natural productions acquired those gigantic proportions which characterize the Western Virginian, the Kentuckian, and the Tennesseean, no less than the trees of their forests. Without ever laying aside their rifles, which forty years ago were carried to divine service in Cincinnati itself, they cleared and brought under the plough the fertile tracts which were converted into fine farms for themselves and their rapidly multiplying families. They had to pass days of terror and distress and, in many an encounter with the Indians from whom they conquered the wilderness, more than one husband and more than one father fell under the rifle fire of the Red men, were dragged into the most wretched captivity, or underwent the horrid torments of the stake. The name of Blue Licks still sounds in the ears of Kentucky like that of Waterloo in ours. Before the decisive victory of Fallen

Timbers gained by General Wayne, two American armies, under the command of Generals Harmar and St. Clair, were successively defeated with great slaughter. The story of this long struggle between the whites and the Red men is still repeated in the barrooms of the West.

In 1811, although the formidable Tecumseh and his brother the Prophet had not yet been conquered by General Harrison, the American had extended his undisputed empire over the most fertile districts of the West. Here and there villages had been built; and the forest everywhere showed clearings in the midst of which stood the log house of some squatter or some more legal proprietor. On the left bank of the Ohio, Kentucky and Tennessee had been erected into States and western Virginia had been settled. A current of emigration had transported the industrious sons of New England to the right bank of the river and by their energy the State of Ohio had been founded and already had nearly 250,000 inhabitants. Indiana and Illinois, then mere Territories, gave fair promise for the future. The treaty of 1803 had added to the Union our Louisiana, in which one State and several Territories with a total population of 160,000 souls had already been organized. The whole West, at that time, had a population of nearly 1,500,-000: Pittsburg and Cincinnati were considerable towns. The West had, then, made rapid progress, but separated as it was from the Gulf of Mexico by the circuitous windings and the gloomy swamps of the Mississippi, from the eastern cities by the seven or eight ridges that form the Alleghany Mountains, destitute of outlets and markets, its further progress seemed to be arrested. The embryo could grow but slowly and painfully for want of the proper channels through which the sources of life might circulate.

At present, routes of communication have been or are being made on all sides, connecting the rivers of the West with the eastern seaboard, where stand the great marts, Boston, New York, Philadelphia, Baltimore, Richmond, and Charleston. Previously, there was not one which was practicable through the whole year and there was not capital enough to undertake one. All the commerce of the West was carried on by the Ohio and the Mississippi, which is, indeed, still and probably always will be the most economical route for bulky objects. Western boatmen descended the rivers with their corn and salt meat in flatboats, like the Seine coal boats; the goods of Europe and the produce of the Antilles were slowly transported up the rivers by the aid of the oar and the sail, the voyage consuming at the least one hundred days, sometimes two hundred. One hundred days is nearly the length of a voyage from New York by the Cape of Good Hope to Canton; in the same space of time France was twice conquered, once by the allies and once by Napoleon. The commerce of the West was, therefore, necessarily limited and the inhabitants, separated from the rest of the world, had all the rudeness of the forest. It was in such a time that the vernacular expression was coined which describes the Kentuckian as half horse, half alligator. The number of boats which made a round-trip voyage once a year did not exceed ten, measuring on an average about one hundred tons. Other small boats, averaging about thirty tons, carried on the local trade between different points on the rivers, besides which there were numerous flatboats which never made the return voyage. Freight from New Orleans to Louisville or Cincinnati was six, seven, and even nine cents a pound. At present the passage from Louisville to New Orleans is made in about eight or nine days and the return voyage in ten or twelve; freight is often less than half a cent a pound from New Orleans to Louisville or Cincinnati.

In 1811, the first steamboat in the West, built by Fulton, started from Pittsburg for New Orleans; it bore the name of the latter city. But such are the difficulties in the navigation of the Ohio and Mississippi, and such was the imperfection of the first boats, that it was nearly six years before a steamboat ascended from New Orleans, and then not to Pittsburg, but to Louisville, six hundred miles below it. The first voyage was made in twenty-five days and it caused a great stir in the West; a public dinner was given to Captain Shreve, who had solved the problem. Then, and not before, was the revolution completed in the West and the hundred-day boats were supplanted. In 1818, the number of steamboats was 20, making an aggregate of 3,642 tons; in 1819 the whole number that had been built was 40, of which 33 were still running; in 1821, there were 72 in actual service. In that year the *Car of Commerce*, under Captain Pierce, made the passage from New Orleans to Shawneetown, a little below Louisville, in ten days. In 1825, after fourteen years of trials and experiments, the proper proportion between the machinery and the boats was finally settled. In 1827, the *Tecumseh* ascended from New Orleans to Louisville in eight days and two hours. In 1829, the number of boats was 200, with a total tonnage of 35,000 tons; in 1832, there were 220 boats making an aggregate of 40,000 tons, and at present there are 240, measuring 64,000 tons. According to statements made to me by experienced and well-informed persons, the whole amount of merchandise annually transported by steamboat between New Orleans and the upper country is at least 140,000 tons. The trade between the basins of the Ohio, the Tennessee, and the Upper Mississippi, not included in this amount, forms another considerable mass. To have an idea of the whole extent of the commerce on the western waters, we must also add from 160,000 to 180,000 tons of provisions and various objects which go down in flatboats. This amount is, indeed, enormous, and yet it is probably but a trifle compared with what will be transported on the rivers of the West twenty years from now; for on the Erie Canal, which compared with the Mississippi is a line of but secondary importance, and at a single point, Utica, 420,000 tons passed in a period of seven months and a half.

Such is the influence of routes of communication on which cheapness is combined with dispatch. In Mexico, where nature has done so much and where, in return, man has done so little, in those countries where natural resources are, perhaps, tenfold greater than those of the United States, but where man is a hundredfold less active and industrious, transportation is effected wholly on the backs of mules or men, even on the plains. The annual amount of the transportation from Veracruz, the principal port, to Mexico City, the capital of the country, does not, therefore, amount to 6,000 tons, and the descending freight is much less.

Western steamboats look very much like the Vigier baths on the Seine; they are huge houses of two stories. (The *Homer*, a noted boat built by Mr. Beckwith of Louisville, one of the most skillful builders in the West, has a third story.) Two large chimney columns vomit forth torrents of smoke and thousands of sparks; from a third a whitish cloud breaks forth with a loud noise; this is the steam-pipe. In the interior they have that coquettish air that characterizes American vessels in general; the cabins are showily furnished and make a very pretty appearance. The little green blinds and the snugly fitted windows, pleasingly contrasting with the white walls, would have made Jean-Jacques sigh with envy.

Their capacity is sometimes 500 to 600 tons, but ordinarily 200 to 300. Their length varies from 100 to 150 feet. Notwithstanding their dimensions and the elegance with which they are fitted out, they cost but little, the largest boats being built for about $40,000, including their engines and furniture. A boat of the same dimensions would cost nearly $100,000 in France; this is owing to the low price of the timber, the coarseness of the steam engines, which, on account of the cheapness of fuel, there would be no advantage in making with more nicety, and the skill of the mechanics—the Americans excel in working in wood. A very nice boat 100 feet long, of the legal measurement of 100 tons but carrying 150, only costs from $7,000 to $8,000. It is estimated that the large boats cost about $100 a ton, legal measurement, and the small ones, $80. But if these elegant craft cost little, they do not last long. Whatever care is taken in the choice of materials and for the preservation of the boat, it is rare that they wear more than four or five years. An old captain, lately giving me an account of a boat about the construction of which he had taken great pains, told me with a deep sigh that "she died at three years." The magnificent vegetation of the West, those tall, straight trees by the side of which our European oaks would look like dwarfs, growing rapidly on the thick layer of soil deposited in the diluvian period by the rivers of the great valley, last just in proportion to the time occupied by their growth. And in this case, as in regard to human glory and the splendor of empires, the rule holds good that time respects only what it has founded.

The number of passengers these boats carry is considerable; they are almost always crowded, although there are some such as the *Henry Clay*, the *Homer*, and the *Mediterranean* which have two hundred beds. I have found myself, with seventy-two others, on one of these boats which could accommodate only thirty cabin passengers. A river voyage was formerly equivalent to an Argonaut expedition; at present it is one of the easiest things in the world. The rate of fare is low; you go from Pittsburg to New Orleans for fifty dollars, all found, and from Louisville to New Orleans for twenty-five dollars. It is still lower for the boatmen who run down the river in flatboats and return by steamer; there are sometimes five or six hundred of them in a separate part of the boat, usually on a lower deck, where they have shelter, a berth, and a place to cook, and pay from four to six dollars for the passage from New Orleans to Louisville; they are, however, obliged to help take in wood. The rapidity with which these men move about has contributed not a little to the extension of commerce in the West. They can now make three or four trips a year instead of one, an important consideration in a country where there is a shortage of labor. On the downward voyage, their place is occupied by horses and cattle, which are sent to the South for sale, and by slaves, human cattle destined to enrich the soil of the South with their sweat, to supply the loss of hands on the sugar plantations of Louisiana, or to make the fortune of some cotton planters. Virginia is the principal seat of this traffic, "the native land of Washington, Jefferson and Madison, having become," as one of her sons sorrowfully observed to me, "the Guinea of the United States."

Excellent as these boats are, great as is the service they render America, when the first feeling of curiosity is once satisfied, a long confinement in one of them has little to attract a person of a cultivated mind and refined manners. There are few Europeans of social polish, and even few Americans of the upper class in the eastern cities, who, on escaping from one of these floating barracks, would not feel disposed under the first impulse of ill humor to certify the correctness of Mrs. Trollope's views of western society. There is in the West a real equality, not merely an equality to talk about, an equality on paper; everybody that has on a decent coat is a gentleman; every gentleman is as good as any other and does not conceive that he should put himself out to oblige his equal. He is occupied entirely with himself, and cares nothing for others; he expects no attention from his neighbor and does not suspect that his neighbor can expect any from him. In this rudeness, however, there is not a grain of malice; there is on the contrary an appearance of good humor that disarms you. The man of the West is rude, but not sullen or quarrelsome. He is sensitive, proud of himself, proud of his country, and to excess, but without silliness or affectation. Remove his cover of vanity and egoism and you will find him ready to oblige you and even generous. He is a great calculator, and yet he is not cold; he is capable of enthusiasm. He loves money with a passion, yet he is not avaricious and is often prodigal. He is rough because he has not had time to soften his voice and cultivate the grace of manners. If he appears ill-bred, it is not from choice, for he aspires to be considered a man of breeding, but he has been obliged to occupy himself much more with the cultivation of the earth than of himself. It is perfectly natural that the first generation in the West should bear the impress of the severe labors it has so energetically and perseveringly pursued. If these reflections, however, are consoling for the future, they cannot give to a life aboard the Ohio and Mississippi steamboats any charms for him who sets value on amiable and engaging manners.

Besides, the voyage on the Mississippi is more dangerous than a passage across the ocean; I do not mean merely from the United States to Europe, but from Europe to China. You are exposed to the risk of explosions and fire and, in ascending, to running against snags and planters. Then there is the danger of your boat falling afoul another running in an opposite direction in a fog, to say nothing of the inconvenience of getting aground on sand bars. Add to these things the monotonous aspect of the country along the river, the solitude of its flat and muddy banks, the filthy appearance of its yellow and turbid waters, the strange habits of most of the travelers crowded into the same cage with yourself, and you may conceive that, in course of time, such a situation becomes extremely unpleasant. The Louisiana planters, therefore, who go North in the hot season in search of a fresher and purer air than that of New Orleans, make their annual migrations by sea, aboard the fine packet ships which run regularly between that city and New York.

Explosions of the boilers are frequent, either on account of the ignorance and lack of skill of the engineers, or on account of the defective nature of the boilers themselves, and they are always attended with serious injury because the boats are so crowded with passengers. A few days ago, sixty persons were killed and wounded aboard a single boat, but these accidents do not occur in well-managed boats, on which no reasonable economy has been spared in the purchase of the machinery and the wages of the engineers. Some law containing provisions similar to those in force in France is required here, but to be practical it must apply to the whole valley, which would only be the case with an act of Congress. Public opinion, however, would not permit Congress to meddle with the matter and the cry of Federal encroachment on States' rights would be raised at once. One State only, Louisiana, has passed a law on the subject, but it is very defective and I doubt that it is enforced. Preventive measures are what is wanted, inspection of the machinery and licensing of competent engineers, while the law of Louisiana only provides for the punishment of the captain on board whose boat an accident happens, with a special penalty in case he should be engaged in some game of chance at the time of the accident.

There is a good number of cases of fire aboard the steamboats and many have perished this way, although the river is not very wide. The *Brandywine* burned near Memphis in 1832, and every soul on board, to the number of 110, was lost. Americans show a singular indifference in regard to fires, not only in the steamboats, but also in their houses; they smoke without the least concern in the midst of half-open cotton bales loaded on a boat; they ship gunpowder with no more precaution than if it were so much maize or salt pork and leave objects packed in straw right in the way of the torrent of sparks that issue from the stacks. The accidents caused by the trunks of trees in the bed of the river, called logs, snags, sawyers, or planters, according to their position, have been very numerous; attempts have been made to prevent these kinds of disasters by strengthening the bows and by bulkheads which double the hull in that part. The Federal government has two *snag-boats,* constructed with great ingenuity, which are employed in removing these obstructions from the rivers, but the bordering States, whose taxes are very light, have contributed nothing toward these objects. The machinery of the boats of the Federal government, the *Heliopolis* and the *Archimedes,* contrived by Captain Shreve, has done much toward clearing the channel, but there is still much to be done.

The chances of accident might be diminished in various

ways by well-directed measures and at a moderate expense. The character of the river is now well understood and there are many engineers in the United States who can manage the Great Father of Waters. Unluckily the Federal government, which does not know what to do with its money (for it has now on hand a surplus of eleven millions), is checked by a doctrine with which, one cannot tell why, the Democratic party has become possessed, which forbids the general government from engaging in public works within the limits of the individual States. Thus, although the whole Union is interested in the improvement of the navigation of the western rivers, the Federal government does not venture to undertake it with energy and on a liberal scale. General Jackson's predecessor, Mr. Adams, was a warm friend to the action of the government in internal improvements. He thought, like Mr. Clay and other men of superior abilities, that the progress of the young States of the West would be very much accelerated, to the advantage of the whole Union, if the central government would undertake to execute, in whole or in part, a system of public works of general interest. But one of the watchwords of the opponents of Mr. Adams was, *No Internal Improvements!* and the very States which would have been most immediately benefited rallied to this cry. So utterly can party spirit blind the most clear-sighted of men to their own interests.

If accidents of so serious a nature succeeded each other with such frequency in Europe, there would be a general outcry. The police and the legislative power would vie with each other in their efforts to put a stop to them. Steamboats would become the terror of travelers, the public would abandon them, and they would be left deserted on the rivers. The consequences would be the same, to a degree, around the large eastern cities, because society there is beginning to be regularly organized and a man's life counts for something. In the West, the flood of emigrants, descending from the Alleghenies, rolls swelling and eddying over the plains, sweeping before it the Indian, the buffalo, and the bear. At its approach the gigantic forests bow before it, as the dry grass of the prairies disappears before flames. It is for civilization what the hosts of Genghis Khan and Attila were for barbarism; it is an invading army and its law is the law of armies. The mass is everything, the individual nothing. Woe to him who trips and falls! he is trampled down and crushed underfoot. Woe to him who finds himself on the edge of a precipice! The impatient crowd, eager to push forward, crowds him, forces him over, and he is at once forgotten, without even a half-suppressed sigh for his funeral oration. *Everyone for himself!* The life of the true American is the soldier's life; like the soldier he is encamped, and at that, in a flying camp, here today, fifteen hundred miles off in a month. It is a life of vigilance and strong excitement; as in a camp, quarrels in the West are settled summarily and on the spot by a duel fought with rifles, or knives, or with pistols at arm's length. It is a life of sudden vicissitudes, of successes and reverses; destitute today, rich tomorrow, and poor the day after, the individual is blown about with every wind of speculation, but the country goes on increasing in wealth and resources. Like the soldier, the American of the West takes for his motto, *Victory or death!* But to him, victory is to make money, to get dollars, to make a fortune out of nothing, to buy city lots at Chicago, Cleveland, or St. Louis and sell them a year afterward at an advance of a thousand per cent; to carry cotton to New Orleans when it is worth twenty cents a pound. So much the worse for the conquered; so much the worse for those who perish in the steamboats! The essential point is not to save some one individual or even some hundreds; what is essential in respect to steamers is that they should be numerous; staunch or not, well commanded or not, it matters little if they move at a rapid rate and are navigated at little expense. The circulation of steamboats is as necessary to the West as blood is to the human system. The West will beware of checking and fettering it by regulations and restrictions of any sort. The time is not yet come, but it will come later.

There are certain feelings in the human heart that must show themselves in some form or another. Repressed at one point, they will break out at another. Respect for the authority of government, which until the time of our revolution had so firmly cemented European society together, has constantly been on the wane on this side of the Atlantic, and in the West it is perfectly nil. There the authorities, for so they are called, have as little power as pay; there are governors who govern nothing, judges who are very liable to be brought to judgment themselves. The chief magistrate is pompously styled in the constitutions of these new States as commander-in-chief of the army and navy of the State. Pure mockery! for it is at the same time provided, except in time of war and especially in time of peace, that he has hardly the power of appointing a corporal. Yet the feeling of discipline and obedience does not die; it is instinctively transferred to those men who are in fact the generals of the great migration. If little concern is felt in regard to the governor of the State, everybody is docile and obedient to the innkeeper, the driver of the coach, and the captain of the steamboat; with them no one ventures to maintain the principles of self-government. All rise, breakfast, dine, sup, when the landlord or his lieutenant general, the barkeeper, thinks fit to ring the bell or beat the gong; it is just as it is in a camp. They eat what is placed before them without ever allowing themselves to make any remark about it. They stop at the pleasure of the driver and the captain without showing the least symptom of impatience; they allow themselves to be overturned and their ribs to be broken by the one, they suffer themselves to be drowned or burnt up by the other, without uttering a complaint or a reproach; the discipline is even more complete than in the camp. It has been said that the life of founders of empires, from the times of Romulus to that of the buccaneers, consists of a mixture of absolute independence and passive obedience.

The society which is now founding itself in the West has not escaped this common law.

This part of the United States, which was a mere wilderness at the time of the Declaration of Independence, and on which no one spent a thought when the capital was fixed at Washington, will be, by the next census, the most powerful of the three great sections of the Union. Before long, it will singly be superior to the other two taken together; it will have the majority in Congress, it will govern the New World. Already the old division into North and South is becoming secondary and the great division of the Union will soon be into the East and the West. The present President is a man of the West. The Democratic party has just held a convention at Baltimore to agree upon the selection of candidates for the next presidential election. Mr. Van Buren, who is from the East, has been chosen, but although he had the unanimous vote of the convention he seems about to find a formidable competitor in the bosom of his own party in the person of Mr. White of Tennessee. On the subject of the vice-presidency there was an animated debate in the convention; some proposed Mr. Rives from the South, others Mr. Johnson from the West. Mr. Rives passes for a man in every respect superior to his opponent; his diplomatic services have been highly esteemed by his countrymen. Mr. Johnson is honest and loyal, without question, but there is great doubt, or rather there is no doubt at all, about his abilities. The only claim set up by his friends is a *strong suspicion* that he killed the celebrated Indian chief Tecumseh at the battle of the Thames. But then Mr. Johnson is from the West and he has been preferred to his rival, even at the risk of offending Virginia, whose influence in the South is well known. Mr. Van Buren has agreed to this combination on the ticket—perhaps he engineered it—because he would rather risk the loss of the South than the West.

This, then, is what the West has become. When we reflect that the only visible instrument of this progress is the steamboat, we can understand that for men there the whole of politics is comprised in material advance and the interests which grow out of it.

XXII

The Means of Communication

Geographic, Political, and Economic Divisions of the Union — The Resulting System of Internal Improvements — Lines Running East to West — Erie and Pennsylvania Canals, etc. — Communications Between the St. Lawrence and Mississippi Valleys — Ohio Canal and Others — Improvements in the Two Rivers — Communications Along the Atlantic Coast — Coasting Trade — Railroad and Steamship Lines — Communications Connecting the Major Cities — Internal Improvements in the Coal Mining Areas — Miscellaneous Internal Improvements — The National Road — Character of Internal Improvements in the U.S. — American Engineers — Internal Improvements Strengthen the Union — Necessity for European Governments to Carry Out Great Enterprises in Communication

Buffalo (New York), July 9, 1835. The territory of the United States consists: [1.] of the two great inland basins of the Mississippi and the St. Lawrence, which run, the former from north to south towards the Gulf of Mexico, the latter from south to north toward the gulf to which it gives its name; [2.] on the eastern side, of a group of smaller basins which empty into the Atlantic Ocean, the principal being those of the Connecticut, Hudson, Delaware, Susquehanna, Potomac, James, Roanoke, Santee, Savannah, and Alatamaha rivers. The Allegheny Mountains, which are called the backbone of the United

States because they lie along the length of the continent, form a natural watershed, dividing the great inland basins from the eastern group of small basins. On the west, the valleys of the St. Lawrence and Mississippi are bounded by the Mexican Cordilleras, which here are called the Rocky Mountains. At the foot of this chain spreads out a wide desert, bare of vegetation, which it is said can never be peopled by man except in some oases.

Almost the whole Anglo-American population is as yet on the left of the Mississippi. On the right bank there is only one State, Missouri, one of the least important of the confederacy, and one Territory, Arkansas, which will soon become a member of the Union. [Chevalier forgot that Louisiana also lies on the right bank of the Mississippi River —J.W.W.] The Allegheny chain does not reach a great height; it is hardly as lofty as the Vosges, while the Rocky Mountains exceed in elevation the Pyrenees and even the Alps.

The Allegheny system, although of no great height, rises from a wide base, nearly 150 miles as the bird flies. Viewed as a whole, it consists of a number of small valleys separated by as many ridges, stretching with uniformity nearly from one end of the chain to the other, from the shores of New England, where the mountains are washed by the sea, to the Gulf of Mexico, in the neighborhood of which they gradually decline. These alternations of ridges and valleys form a series of parallel furrows which one can follow on the terrain, with few breaks, for a distance of twelve or fifteen hundred miles. The geological formations are arranged nearly exactly along with these furrows through great distances; there are, however, exceptions to the rule, for sometimes the same layer is seen to pass from one furrow to another, always cutting the former at a very acute angle.

Notwithstanding this general character of regularity, these cavities are not hydrographical basins or river valleys, whichever one wishes to call them. But the rivers, instead of hollowing out beds between two successive ridges and thus passing off to the sea, frequently pass from one valley to another, breaking through the weak points of the ridges. These openings or gaps, as they are called here, are highly useful as routes for roads, canals, and railroads, enabling the engineer by following the course of the rivers to flank heights which it would have been almost impossible to top. Of all these openings the most interesting is that made by the Potomac through the Blue Ridge at Harpers Ferry, which Jefferson, in his Virginian enthusiasm, said was worth a voyage across the Atlantic.

The United States may then be divided hydrographically into two distinct regions, one to the east, the other to the west of the Alleghenies; or into three: [1.] the Mississippi valley [2.] the valley of the St. Lawrence with the Great Lakes [3.] the Atlantic coast. This vast country may also be divided into the North and the South. It has two commercial capitals, New York and New Orleans, which are as it were the two lungs of this great body, the two galvanic poles of the system. Between these two divisions, the North and the South, there are radical differences both in a political and an industrial point of view. Society in the South is built on slavery; in the North, on universal suffrage. The South is a great cotton plantation, yielding also some subsidiary articles such as tobacco, sugar, and rice. The North acts as a factor or agent for the South, selling the productions of the latter and furnishing her in return with those of Europe; as a sailor, carrying her cotton beyond the sea; as an artisan, making all her household utensils and farming tools, her cotton gins, her sugar mills, her furniture, wearing apparel, and all other articles of daily use, and providing her also with corn and salted provisions.

From this it follows that the great public works in the United States must have the following object: [1.] to connect the Atlantic coast region with the region beyond the Alleghenies; that is, to unite the rivers—such as the Hudson, the Susquehanna, the Potomac, the James, or its bays, such as the Delaware and the Chesapeake—either with the Mississippi or its tributary the Ohio, or with the St. Lawrence or Lake Erie, or with Lake Ontario, whose waters are carried by the St. Lawrence to the ocean; [2.] to form communications between the Mississippi and St. Lawrence valleys, that is, between one of the great tributaries of the Mississippi, such as the Ohio, the Illinois, or the Wabash, and Lake Erie or Lake Michigan, which of all the great lakes of the St. Lawrence basin reach farthest south; [3.] to connect together the northern and southern poles of the Union, New York and New Orleans.

Independent of these three new systems of public works, which are in fact in progress and even partly completed, there are numerous secondary lines intended to make access to the centers of consumption more easy or to open outlets from certain centers of production; from these arise two new classes of works: one includes the various canals and railroads which, starting from the great cities as centers, radiate from them in all directions, the other comprises similar works executed for the transportation of coal from the coal regions.

I. EAST-TO-WEST LINES ACROSS THE ALLEGHENIES

The works which have almost wholly occupied, and still chiefly occupy, the attention of statesmen, economists, and businessmen in the major cities of the United States are those designed to form communications between the East and the West. There are on the Atlantic coast four principal cities which have long striven with each other for supremacy: Boston, New York, Philadelphia, and Baltimore. All four aim to secure the command of the commerce of the new States which are springing up in the fertile regions of the West. They have struggled with different degrees of success, but always with a rare intelligence. They have not, however, been equally favored in their natural advantages.

Boston is too far north; she has no river which permits her to stretch her arms far toward the West, and she is surrounded on all sides by a hilly country, across which rapid communication is difficult and construction expensive. Philadelphia and Baltimore are blocked by ice almost every winter and this obstruction is, for Baltimore, a drawback from the other advantages of her position—her greater nearness to the Ohio, her more central latitude, and the beauty of her bay, which is over 250 miles long and receives numberless streams, the Susquehanna, Potomac, Patuxent, Rappahannock, etc. Philadelphia is badly placed; Penn was seduced by the beauty of the Schuylkill and the Delaware. He thought that the broad plain which spread out nearly three miles between their waters would afford an admirable site for a city with carefully laid out streets whose warehouses, easy of access, would permit thousands of vessels to load and unload at once. He forgot to secure for his city a great hydrographical basin capable of consuming the merchandise which it should import and of sending in return the products of its own labor. He neglected to make an examination of the Delaware, which he took for a great river but which, unluckily, is not so. If he had founded the City of Brotherly Love on the banks of the Susquehanna, it might have maintained a long struggle against New York.

New York is, then, the queen of the Atlantic coast. This city stands on a long, narrow island between two rivers (the North River and the East River); ships of any burden and in any numbers may lie at the wharves; the harbor is rarely closed by ice; it can be entered by small vessels with all winds and by the largest ships at all times except when the wind is from the northwest. New York has, besides, the invaluable advantage of being situated on a river for which some great cataclysm has dug out a bed through the primitive mountains, uniformly deep, without rocks, without rapids, almost without a slope, and cutting through the most solid mass of the Alleghenies at right angles. The tide, slight as it is on this coast, flows up the Hudson to Troy,

160 miles from its mouth; and such is the nature of its bed that whale-ships are fitted out at Poughkeepsie and Hudson, of which the former is 75 and the latter 116 miles above New York, and that except in the lowest stage of the water vessels of nine-feet draft can go up to Albany and Troy in any tide.

New York possesses in addition great advantages in respect to the character of its population. Originally a Dutch colony, conquered by the English, and lying in the neighborhood of New England, she presents a mixture of the solid qualities of the Saxon race, of the Dutch phlegm, and of the enterprising shrewdness of the Puritans. This mixed breed understands admirably how to turn to account all the advantages which nature has bestowed on the city.

Hardly was the War of Independence at an end when the great men whose patriotism and courage had brought it to a happy close, filled with ideas of the wealth yet buried in the bosom of the then uninhabited West, began to form plans for rendering it accessible by canals. If it is true that Prussia in the time of Voltaire resembled two garters stretched out over Germany, the United States in the time of Washington and Franklin, and it is only fifty years since, might be likened to a narrow riband thrown upon the sandy shore of the Atlantic. Washington at that time projected the canal which has since been begun according to the plans of General Bernard and which seeks the West by following the Potomac; but from want of capital and experienced engineers, what in our day has become a long and fine canal was then merely a series of side-cuts around the Little Falls and Great Falls of the Potomac. At the same time, the Pennsylvanians made some unsuccessful efforts and spent considerable sums in ineffectual attempts to render the Schuylkill navigable and to connect it with the Susquehanna. In the State of New York, some short cuts, some locks and sluices, were then the only prelude to greater schemes. The works undertaken at that time and during the fifteen first years of the present century could not be completed, or failed in the expected results. One work only was successfully executed, the Middlesex Canal, which extends from Boston to the river Merrimack at Chelmsford, a distance of twenty-seven miles.

The War of 1812 found the United States without canals and almost without good roads; their only means of communication were the sea, their bays, and the rivers that flow into them. Once blockaded by the English fleets, they could not only not communicate with Europe and India, but even among themselves, between State and State, between city and city, between New York and Philadelphia for instance. All contact was cut off. Their commerce was annihilated and the sources of their capital dried up. Bankruptcy smote them like a destroying angel, sparing not a family.

First Line: Erie Canal

The lesson was hard, but it was not lost. The Americans, to do them justice, know how to profit by the teachings of Providence, especially if they pay dear for them. The project of a canal between New York and Lake Erie, which had already been discussed before the war, was eagerly taken up again after the peace. De Witt Clinton, a statesman whose memory will be forever hallowed in the United States, succeeded in inspiring his countrymen with his own noble confidence in his country's great destiny and the first stroke of the spade was made on the fourth of July, 1817. In spite of the evil forebodings of men distinguished for their sagacity and public service; in spite of the opinion of the venerated patriarch of democracy, Jefferson himself, who declared it necessary to wait a century longer before undertaking such a work; in spite of the remonstrances of the illustrious Madison, who wrote that it would be an act of folly on the part of the State of New York to attempt, with its own resources only, the execution of a work for which all the wealth of the Union would be insufficient;

notwithstanding all opposition, this State which did not then contain a population of 1,300,000 inhabitants began a canal 428 miles in length and eight years later, in 1825, completed it at a cost of $8,400,000. Since then it has continued to add numerous branches, covering almost every part of the State with a network of canals. In 1836, the State had completed 656 miles of canal, including slackwater navigation, at the expense of $11,962,712, or $18,235 per mile. [Rather than convert Chevalier's figures in francs and leagues back into dollars and miles, T. G. Bradford used the official statement of the Canal Board, February 23, 1837, and I have followed his lead. The text as it now stands does not include the Black River Canal and the Genesee Valley Canal begun in 1837, adding 168 miles and $3,000,000—J.W.W.]

The results of this work have surpassed all expectations. It opened an outlet for the fertile districts of the western part of the State which had before been cut off from communication with the sea and the rest of the world. The shores of Lake Erie and Lake Ontario were at once covered with fine farms and flourishing towns. As far as Lake Michigan, the stillness of the primitive forest was broken by the axe of New York and New England settlers. The State of Ohio, which is washed by Lake Erie and which before had had no connection with the sea except by the long southern route down the Mississippi, had now a short and easy communication with the Atlantic by way of New York. The territory of Michigan was settled; it now contains 100,000 inhabitants, and will soon take its rank among the States. Transportation on the Erie Canal alone exceeded 400,000 tons in 1834 and it must nearly reach 500,000 tons in 1835. The annual amount of tolls from the canals, and at moderate rates, is about $1,500,000. The population of the city of New York increased in the ten years from 1820 to 1830 by 80,000 souls. New York has become the third, if not the second, port in the world and the most populous city in the New World. The illustrious Clinton lived long enough to see the success of his plans, but not to receive the brilliant reward which the gratitude of his countrymen intended for him. He died on February 11, 1828, at the age of 59, and but for this premature death he would probably have been chosen President of the United States.

The Erie Canal is no longer sufficient for the commerce which throngs it. In vain do the lockmasters attend night and day to the signal horn of the boatmen and perform the process of locking with a quickness that puts our slowness to shame. There is no longer enough room in the canal, whose dimensions are rather limited. (It is 40 feet wide on the surface and 4 feet deep; the locks are 95 feet long and 15 feet wide. The Languedoc Canal is 90 feet wide, and 6½ feet deep, with locks 115 feet long, 36 feet wide in the center, and 18 feet at each end. The English canals are generally of about the dimensions of the Erie Canal.) The impatience of commerce, with whom time is money, is not satisfied with a rate of speed about fourfold that which is common on our canals. Merchandise of all sorts, as well as travelers, flows in at every point in such quantities that railroads have been constructed along the borders of the canal to rival the packet boats in the transportation of passengers only. There is one from Albany to Schenectady, 15 miles long, which, though not well built, cost about $550,-000. A second which will be finished in 1836 runs from Schenectady to Utica and is 78 miles long. A third railroad is being built from Rochester to Buffalo by way of Batavia and Attica, about 80 miles, and it is probable that before long the line will be completed from one end of the canal to the other.

A still greater undertaking is already underway: a company chartered about three years ago will begin next spring the construction of a railroad from New York City to Lake Erie through the southern counties of the State. On account of the circuitous route made necessary by the uneven nature of the ground, the length of this road will be about 340 miles. Meanwhile the canal commissioners have not slept. In July, the Canal Board, in compliance with an act of the legislature, directed the construction of a double set of lift locks on the whole line so that there might be as little delay as possible in the passage of boats, and the enlargement of the canal so that the width shall be 70 feet and the depth 6 feet, with a corresponding increase in the dimension of the locks; larger boats may then be used, the speed may be increased, and perhaps it will be practicable to use steam tow-boats. The cost of this work is estimated at about $12,500,000.

Finally, to make herself more entirely mistress of the commerce of the West and to penetrate her own territory more completely, the State of New York is about to commence a new branch of the Erie Canal (if we may call a work whose entire length will be 120 miles a branch) which will form an immediate connection with the Ohio River. This canal is to run from Rochester, the city of millers, following the course of the Genesee, with a rise of 979 feet and then a fall of 78 feet to Olean on the Allegheny River, 270 miles from its junction with the Monongahela at Pittsburg. The main canal from Rochester to Olean is only 107 miles in length, but there is a branch to Danville. The Allegheny in its natural state is navigable only during a few months in the year; the total distance from New York to Pittsburg by this route is 800 miles.

When there could no longer be a doubt of the speedy completion of the Erie Canal, Philadelphia and Baltimore felt that New York was going to become the capital of the Union. The spirit of competition aroused in them a spirit of enterprise. They wished also to have their routes to the West, but both had great natural obstacles to overcome. By means of the Hudson, which had forced a passage through the heart of the mountains, New York was freed from the greatest difficulty in the way of establishing communication between the East and the West, that of topping the crest of the Alleghenies. Between Albany, where the Erie Canal begins, and Buffalo, where it meets the lake, there are no high mountains. For a similar service Baltimore could not look to the Patapsco, nor Philadelphia to the Delaware; neither of these cities can approach the West by the basin of the Great Lakes, unless by a very circuitous route; they are too far off. It became necessary for them, therefore, to climb the loftiest heights and then to descend to the level of the Ohio with their works.

Second Line: Pennsylvania Canal

What is called the Pennsylvania Canal is a long line of 400 miles, starting from Philadelphia and ending at Pittsburg on the Ohio. It was begun simultaneously with several other works at the expense of the state of Pennsylvania in 1826. It is not entirely a canal. From Philadelphia, the Columbia railroad, 81 miles long, runs to the Susquehanna at Columbia. A canal, 172 miles long, comes after the railroad and ascends the Susquehanna and the Juniata to the foot of the mountains at Holidaysburg. To get from Holidaysburg to the other side of the mountains, there is a portage railroad, 37 miles long, with great inclined planes, sometimes exceeding a ten per cent grade which does not, however, deter travelers from going over them. (The maximum of inclination allowed by our *Administration des Ponts-et-Chaussées* [Board of Public Works] is 1:200; in the great lines executed at the expense of government, the inclination has generally been kept below 1:333, which is the maximum adopted in the fine railroad from London to Birmingham.) From Johnstown, the western terminal of this railroad, a second canal goes to Pittsburg, 104 miles. This route is subject to the inconvenience of three transshipments, one at Columbia at the end of the railroad from Philadelphia, the second and third at the ends of the portage railroad. One of these may be avoided by means of two canals constructed by incorporated companies, namely, the Schuylkill Canal which extends up the river of that name and the Union Canal which forms a junction between the upper Schuylkill and the Susquehanna. The distance from Philadelphia to Pittsburg by this route is 435 miles, or 35 miles more than by the other route.

The Pennsylvania Canal, begun in 1826, was finished in 1834. The State has connected it with a general system of canals which embraces all the principal rivers of the State, especially the Susquehanna with its two great branches, the North Branch and the West Branch, and is also underway with works for a canal connecting Pittsburg with Lake Erie, at Erie, a town founded by our Canadian countrymen and by them called Presqu'île. Pennsylvania has executed, then, in all about 820 miles of canals and railroads, of which 118 are railroads, at a cost of about $25,000,000 exclusive of sums paid for interest. Average cost per mile, $35,000; average cost per mile of canals, $32,500; average cost per mile of railroads, $48,000.

This is much more than the cost of the New York works, although the dimensions of the works are the same and the natural difficulties were not much greater in one case than in the other. It is owing to bad management in Pennsylvania. The Pennsylvanians had no Clinton to guide them. An unwise economy, forced upon the canal commissioners by the legislature, prevented them from securing the services of able engineers, and to save some thousands of dollars in salaries they have had to spend millions repairing what was badly done, or in doing badly what more able hands would have executed well at less cost.

Third Line: Baltimore and Ohio Railroad

Still less than Philadelphia could Baltimore think of a continuous canal to the Ohio. Wishing to avoid the transshipments which are necessary on the Pennsylvania line, the Baltimoreans decided on the construction of a railroad from their city to Pittsburg or Wheeling, the whole length of which would be about 360 miles. It is now finished as far as Harpers Ferry on the Potomac, a distance of 80 miles, and the company seem to have given up the design of carrying it farther. Here it will connect with the Chesapeake and Ohio Canal, of which I shall speak below, as the Columbia railroad connects with the Pennsylvania Canal. It is probable that, on approaching the crest of the Alleghenies, the canal will in turn give way to a railroad across the mountains and thus the Maryland works will be similar to the Pennsylvania line.

Fourth Line: Chesapeake and Ohio Canal

The plan which had been cherished by Washington, of making a canal along the Potomac which would one day cross the mountains to the Ohio, was resumed when New York taught the country that it was ripe for the boldest enterprises of public works. John Quincy Adams, then President of the United States, favored the project with all his might. At that time it was not a settled principle that the Federal government had no right to engage in internal improvements. The old idea which Washington had cherished of making the political capital of the Union a great city was not less to the taste of Mr. Adams and his friends. It was, therefore, resolved to undertake the Chesapeake and Ohio Canal, and a company was incorporated for this purpose. Congress voted a subscription of $1,000,000; the city of Washington, without commerce, without manufactures, with its population of 16,000, subscribed the same sum. The other little cities of the Federal District, Georgetown and Alexandria, having both together a population of about 10,000 furnished $500,000; Virginia contributed $250,000, Maryland $500,000; and $600,000 were raised by individual subscriptions. The work was begun July 4, 1828. The next year, by aid of a loan of $3,000,000 from Maryland, this great work will be carried to the coal beds of Cumberland at the foot of the mountains; the length of this division is 185 miles, the estimated cost $8,500,000, or $46,000 per mile. The execution is on a bold scale and superior to that of the works before mentioned; its dimensions exceed those generally adopted in the proportion of 3 to 2, which gives a larger section in the ratio of 9 to 4.

Fifth Line: The James River Canal to the Kanawha

Virginia, formerly the first State in the confederacy, but now fallen to the fourth in rank and already outstripped by Ohio, which did not exist during the War of Independence, is at length roused to action and has determined to profit by the lessons which have come to her from the North. A company whose means consist of little more than the subscriptions of the State and of the capital, Richmond, is about to open a canal from the East to the West. The James River, which flows into Chesapeake Bay, is navigable for vessels of 200 tons to the foot of the plateau on which Richmond stands in so charming a situation. To the east of the mountains the canal, starting from Richmond, will follow the course of the James River and to the west will descend the Kanawha, one of the tributaries of the Ohio, to Charleston at the head of steamboat navigation. The Allegheny crest will be passed by a railroad 150 miles long; the canal itself will be about 250 miles long.

South Carolina, stirred up by the example of Virginia, is engaged in a great railroad from Charleston to Cincinnati on the Ohio, but it is still in the planning stage. The people of Cincinnati are enthusiastically interested in this scheme. Georgia is also dreaming of a great railroad from the Savannah River to the Mississippi at Memphis; but this project has not assumed a substantial shape. North Carolina does nothing and projects nothing. If she ever becomes rich, it will not be because she has seized fortune by the forelock, but because fortune has come to her bedside.

Sixth Line: Richelieu Canal

The Canadians are constructing on their territory a canal which will form another communication between the East and the West, that is, between the Hudson and the St. Lawrence, between New York and Quebec. The great fissure which forms so fine a bed for the Hudson between New York and Troy does not end there, but stretches on toward the north to the St. Lawrence, constituting the basin of Lake Champlain, which is a long and narrow cavity in the midst of the mountains and the bed of the Richelieu River. Between Lake Champlain and the Hudson there is only a ridge 54 feet above the level of the former and 134 above that of the latter. The Richelieu River, which issues from the northern end of the lake and flows into the St. Lawrence, is broken by rapids, and a lateral canal, 12 miles long and of sufficient dimensions to receive lake craft, will be opened here in the course of a year; the cost will be $350,000; the distance from New York to Quebec by canals, rivers, and lakes is 540 miles. The railroad from St. John, where the rapids of the Richelieu begin, to Laprairie on the St. Lawrence, opposite to Montreal, a distance of 16 miles, effects for Montreal what the canal does for Quebec; it cost about $160,000, or $10,500 per mile. The distance from Montreal to New York is 360 miles.

II. LINES OF COMMUNICATION BETWEEN THE MISSISSIPPI VALLEY AND THAT OF THE ST. LAWRENCE

There is no mountain chain between these two valleys. The basin of the Great Lakes, whose waters together form the St. Lawrence, is separated from the valley of the Mississippi only by a spur of the Allegheny system, not more than 450 feet high, and sinking rapidly down toward the west, so as to be but a few feet above the surface of Lake Michigan. During the rainy season, when the streams are swollen and the marshes of the watershed are flooded, our Canadian countrymen pass in boats from Lake Michigan into the Illinois River. The breadth of this dividing spur is more considerable than its height. It is not a ridge or crest, but rather a tableland which imperceptibly merges by gentle slopes into the plains that surround it. Its level summit is filled with marshes and therefore offers great facilities for feeding the canals which cross it; farther west, where it is scarcely higher than the rest of the country, it is often as dry as the surrounding prairies.

First Line: Ohio Canal

Only one work connecting the two valleys is as yet completed. This is the Ohio Canal, which crosses that State from North to South, extending from Portsmouth on the Ohio to Cleveland, a little city, completely new, which has sprung up on the shores of Lake Erie since the canal was built. It is 334 miles long and cost nearly $4,500,000, or about $13,500 per mile. This is low, yet the locks are all of hewn stone; the ground, however, was very favorable. The work was done at the expense of the State and at the same time that Pennsylvania and Baltimore, following New York, started to undertake internal improvements. This young State with its population of farmers, which has not a single engineer within its limits and none of whose citizens had ever seen any other canal than those of New York, has thus, with the aid of some second-rate engineers borrowed from New York, constructed a canal longer than any in France, with more skill and intelligence than was displayed by Pennsylvania despite the scientific lights of Philadelphia. This farming population of Ohio, almost wholly of New England origin, has a business instinct, a practical shrewdness, and a readiness to exercise all trades without having learned them that would be sought in vain in the Anglo-German population of Pennsylvania. The legislators under whose direction the public works were executed in both States were, as is usual in the United States, a perfect copy of the mass of their constituents with all its good and bad qualities. The Ohio canal commissioners added to a noble disinterestedness an admirable good sense, and to them is due the greater part of the glory of having planned and executed it. They were farmers and lawyers who set themselves about making canals naturally, easily, and without even a suspicion that in Europe no one dares to undertake such a work without long preparation and scientific study. Now it is no longer an art in that State to plan and construct canals, but a mere trade; the science of canalling is there become quite an affair of the common people. The first-comer in a barroom will explain to you, over his glass of whiskey, how to feed the summit level and how to construct a lock. All our mysteries in civil engineering are here fallen into the hands of the public, very much as the methods of descriptive geometry are to be found in the workshops, where they had been handed down by tradition ages before Monge gave them the sanction of theory.

I have said before that Ohio, Indiana, and Illinois form a great triangle wholly comprised within the Mississippi valley with the exception of a narrow strip along the lakes belonging, of course, to the St. Lawrence basin. The general slope of the surface is from north to south; the streams run mostly in that direction; this is especially true of the great tributaries of the Ohio. This arrangement of the secondary valleys is no less favorable to the construction of canals between the lakes, on the one side, and the Ohio and Mississippi on the other, than the configuration and humidity of the dividing tableland.

Second Line: Miami Canal

Ohio has constructed another canal which, starting from Cincinnati on the Ohio, runs north to Dayton and is called the Miami Canal. It is 65 miles long and cost nearly $1,000,000, or $15,400 a mile. By the aid of a grant of land from Congress and the State's own resources, it is now being extended to the Mad River and as far as Defiance on the Maumee River, the site of a fortress of that name built by

General Wayne after his celebrated victory over the Indians. The Maumee, which was called by the French *the Miami of the Lakes,* is one of the principal tributaries of Lake Erie and is to be canalled by the State. The distance from Dayton to Defiance is 125 miles; estimated cost, $2,750,000, or $22,000 per mile.

Third Line: Wabash Canal

Ohio and Indiana with the aid of a grant of land from Congress have undertaken in concert a canal which will connect the Wabash, one of the tributaries of the Ohio, with the Maumee. The greater part of the canal will be parallel to the two rivers, or in their beds; the length of the whole work will be 382 miles, of which 195 are in Indiana and 87 in Ohio. The greater portion of the Indiana section along the Wabash has been completed, but Ohio has not yet been able to commence her portion because, owing to an absurd system of establishing boundaries, the mouth of the Maumee, whose whole course is in Ohio, will fall on the land of the future state of Michigan. (No one can look at a map of the United States without being struck by the appearance of the straight lines constituting the frontiers of most of the States; this method of bounding a territory by meridians and parallels of latitude is absurd since it requires an infinite number of geodesic operations, which have not been executed, and cannot be so for a long time. Meridians and parallels do very well for the divisions of the heavens; but for the earth there are no suitable boundaries but the beds of rivers, or watersheds in the mountain chains.) Ohio protests against this arrangement; Michigan stands firm to her claims. Both sides have voted the sums needful for war and both have taken arms; hostilities have even been begun, but the interference of the Federal government has led the parties to consent to an armistice. In this quarrel Ohio has reason on her side, but Michigan appeals to the letter of the law as favorable to her. It is probable that in creating

Michigan a State, Congress will attach this strip to Ohio, to which it is so important. In this unsettled state of things, Ohio has suspended the execution of her part of a work which will give new importance to the mouth of the Maumee.

Fourth Line: Michigan Canal

The project of a canal from Chicago at the southern end of Lake Michigan to the head of steam navigation, that is, to the foot of the falls in the Illinois River, has long been discussed. By means of a cut of 26 feet the canal should be, it is said, quite easy to construct; by means of a cut 26 feet deep at a maximum the watershed of the canal can be brought down to the level of Lake Michigan, which then could serve as a reservoir for the canal. It will be 96 miles long and will traverse a level or slightly undulating country, bare of trees and still known by the name given it by the French Canadians, Prairie. It is proposed to construct this canal of larger dimensions than are common in the United States so as to make it navigable by lake craft and steamboats. It is one of the most useful works ever undertaken in the world.

Fifth Line: Western Pennsylvania Canal

The canal which Pennsylvania has begun between the Ohio and the town of Erie, to be 112 miles long, for feeding which extensive works have already been constructed around Lake Conneaut, will make another very short line of water communication between the basins of the Mississippi and the St. Lawrence.

Other Lines

Lastly, two canals are about to be undertaken which will connect the Pennsylvania works with those of Ohio and, consequently, form new connections between the Mississippi and the St. Lawrence. One of these is the Sandy and Beaver Canal which, beginning at the confluence of the Big Beaver with the Ohio, follows the Ohio to the mouth of the Little Beaver, ascends the valley of this stream, and passes down that of the Sandy River to the Ohio Canal at Bolivar. It will be 90 miles long. From Bolivar to New York by the Ohio Canal, Lake Erie, Erie Canal, and the Hudson, the distance is 785 miles; by the new canal the distance from Bolivar to Philadelphia, that is to the ocean, is only 512 miles. The Mahoning Canal leaves the Ohio Canal at Akron, following the valleys of the Little Cuyahoga, the Mahoning, a tributary of the Big Beaver, and the Big Beaver to the Ohio River; it is about 90 miles in length; the distance from Akron to the Ohio River is 115 miles.

The generally level character of the terrain of Ohio, Indiana, and Illinois is not less favorable to the construction of railroads than to that of canals. But as capital is scarce in this new and barely cultivated country, few enterprises of much importance have up to now been undertaken. The financial companies and institutions which have always preceded the introduction of canals and railroads have, however, been already established and are prosperous; their success is the omen of the approach of the latter. In the absence of companies the States are ready to adopt the most extensive schemes of public works; for the American of the West is not a whit behind the American of the East in enterprise. At present, I know only one railroad actually in process of construction beyond the Ohio River and that does not seem to be pushed forward with much activity; it is the railroad which is to run from Dayton on the Miami Canal to Sandusky on the bay of that name in Lake Erie; the length will be 153 miles. Many others have been projected in this region, and Indiana has had surveys made for a railroad extending across the State from north to south, or from New Albany on the Ohio River to some point on Lake Michigan. In 1836, the legislature of Indiana adopted a general system of public works, for the execution of which it authorized a loan of $10,000,000. The system embraces the canalization of the Wabash and White rivers, the connection of the Wabash with the Maumee, and of Lake Michigan with the same river by canals, and a canal across the center of the State from Evansville by Indianapolis to the Wabash and the Erie Canal. Appropriations were made by the same law for railroads from Madison and Jeffersonville on the Ohio to the Wabash Canal and in aid of the Lawrenceburg and Indianapolis railroad which has been undertaken by a company.

WORKS FOR IMPROVING THE NAVIGATION OF THE OHIO, MISSISSIPPI, AND ST. LAWRENCE

To this head belong the works executed in the beds of the rivers themselves. The Mississippi is the *beau idéal* of rivers in regard to navigable facilities. From St. Louis to New Orleans, a distance of nearly 1,200 miles, there is water enough for steamers of 300 tons throughout the year. Its yellow and muddy waters flow in a deep, although very circuitous, channel and its general breadth is from 800 to 1,000 yards in places where it is not expanded to a much greater width by low, flat islands, thickly covered with trees. There are no sandbanks in this part of the channel, yet there are formidable dangers in the way of the inexperienced navigator; these are the trunks of trees that have been carried away from the banks, as I have already mentioned, and in the removal of which the Federal government employs steam snag-boats, the *Heliopolis* and *Archimedes;* these boats are provided with a peculiar machinery by means of which they drag the trees up from the bed and saw them into pieces of no consequence.

Captain Shreves, who has the command of these boats and who invented the machinery, is also employed in constructing in the Ohio submerged dams of loose stones which have the effect of increasing the depth of water in the dry season. He is at present engaged with a flotilla of steamboats in opening the bed of Red River, one of the great tributaries of the Mississippi, which the drift timber has choked up and covered over through a distance of 165 miles. At Louisville, the Ohio River, whose bed has generally a very slight inclination, descends 22 feet in two miles, so as to be impassable for steamboats except during the season of high water. The Louisville and Portland Canal has been constructed by a company to avoid this obstruction; it is about a mile and three quarters long and cost $750,000. It receives the largest boats at a rate of toll which for the *Henry Clay* amounts to $175 and for the *Uncle Sam* $190. It has been proposed that Congress should buy this canal and make the passage toll-free; the importance of the navigation of the Ohio would justify the measure.

The St. Lawrence differs essentially from the Mississippi; instead of an expanse of muddy waters, it presents a clear blue surface to the eye. The Mississippi traverses a low, uninhabited and uninhabitable region where the soil consists entirely of sand, or rather of mud deposited by the river floods; not a stone as large as a fist is to be found and only a few bluff points are to be met with, which are above the reach of high water and on which the pale inhabitants struggle unsuccessfully with the pestilential emanations of the surrounding swamps. The St. Lawrence flows through a broken, hilly, and sometimes rugged country with a fertile soil, everywhere healthful, sprinkled with flourishing villages which attract the eye of the traveler from a distance by their newly whitewashed houses and their churches built in the French style with their spires covered with tin. The Mississippi, like the Nile, has its annual overflow, or rather it has two each year, but the spring floods are much more considerable. The St. Lawrence, owing to the vast extent of the lakes which serve as a reservoir and feeder to it, always preserves the same level, the extreme range of its rise and fall being only about twenty inches. From the beauty of its waters, from their prodigious volume, from the country which it waters, and from the groups of isles scattered over it, the St. Lawrence would be one of the first rivers in the world in the eyes of the artist, but in those of the merchant it is of quite a secondary importance. Its transparent waters hardly hide the numerous rocks; the navigation is interrupted first by the Falls of Niagara and, after it leaves Lake Ontario, by numerous rapids, cataracts, or rocks between that lake and Montreal. None but an Indian or a French Canadian would dare to descend that portion of the river in a canoe. At several points the most powerful steamer would be unable to make head against the current.

The spirit of emulation which has prevailed among the States of the Union has extended to the British Provinces, to the English population which, leaving the lower part of the river to the French, has occupied Upper Canada. The inhabitants of this Province have embraced the opinion that if the chain of communication which is broken by the cataracts and rapids could be made whole, much of the produce which now finds its way to the Mississippi, or to the Pennsylvania and New York canals, would seek a more convenient vent by the St. Lawrence, and that British manufactures would take the same route up the river, through the ports of Quebec and Montreal, to the Western States. One canal has, therefore, already been executed around the falls of the Niagara which forms a communication between Lakes Erie and Ontario; the Welland Canal is 28 miles in length, exclusive of 20 miles of slack-water navigation. It is navigable by lake craft of 120 tons, and has cost $2,000,-000, nearly the whole of which was furnished by the Upper Province, Lower Canada and the mother country having contributed a very trifling sum.

Since that work has been completed, the river below Lake Ontario has been surveyed and it has been found that the aggregate length of the points not passable by steamboats of 10-feet draft is only 30 miles, pretty equally divided between the two provinces. Upper Canada, which contains hardly 250,000 inhabitants, with no large towns and with little capital, has begun her portion of the work along the rapids within her limits. This work will be large enough to admit the passage of steamboats drawing 9 feet and having a burden of 500 tons. I saw the laborers at work along the Long Saut Rapids at Cornwall, where there will be a cut of 13 miles long; the estimated cost of this section is $1,250,000. The French population of Lower Canada, swallowed up in political quarrels the result of which cannot be foreseen, neglects its essential interests in pursuit of the imaginary interests of national pride. It has done nothing toward continuing, within its limits, the great work which has been begun by the poorer province of Upper Canada.

III. LINES OF COMMUNICATION ALONG THE ATLANTIC

First Line: Inland Channels by the Sounds and Bays Along the Atlantic

Upon examining the coast of the United States from Boston to Florida, it will be seen that there is almost a continuous line of inland navigation, extending from northeast to southwest in a direction parallel to that of the coast, formed in the North by a series of bays and rivers and in the South by a number of long sounds or by the narrow passes between the mainland and the chain of low islands that lie before it. The necks of land that separate these bays, rivers, and lagoons are all flat and narrow. From Providence (42 miles south of Boston) to New York are Narragansett Bay and Long Island Sound, together 180 miles long. From there, to reach the Delaware, you go to New Brunswick at the head of Raritan Bay, where you encounter the New Jersey isthmus, a level tract not more than 40 feet above the level of the sea and 35 to 40 miles wide. This neck is now cut across by the Raritan and Delaware Canal, a fine work, navigable by small coasting craft, 43 miles long exclusive of a navigable feeder of 24 miles, all lately executed by a company in less than three years at a cost of about $2,500,000.

This canal terminates at Bordentown on the Delaware. From there, one descends to Delaware City, 70 miles below Bordentown and 40 below Philadelphia. There the isthmus which divides the Delaware from the Chesapeake is cut through by a canal whose highest point is only 12 feet above the surface of the sea; this is the Chesapeake and Delaware Canal, built, like most, of dimensions suitable to coasting vessels. The cost was very great, about $2,600,000; length 13½ miles. Having entered the Chesapeake, one may continue to Norfolk, which is about 200 miles. From there—to reach the sounds and inland channels along the coast of North Carolina, South Carolina, and Georgia —a number of improvements have been made, the principal one being the Dismal Swamp Canal, 20 miles long, whose summit level is only 10 feet above the level of the sea. This is also adapted for coasting vessels. The works which are intended to continue the navigation beyond the sounds connected with the Dismal Swamp Canal have not been completed. To the south of the Chesapeake the line is, therefore, imperfect; but steamboats run from Charleston to Savannah by the channels and lagoons between the mainland and the low islands which yield the famous long-staple cotton.

Second Line: Communication Between the North and South by the Maritime Capitals

Parallel to the preceding line, which is designed for the transportation of bulky articles, is another farther inland for the use of travelers and lighter and more valuable merchandise, one on which steam is becoming the only motive power both by land and by water: by land on railways, and by water in steamboats. You go from Boston to Providence by a railroad 42 miles long which cost $1,500,000, or $33,000 a mile. From Providence to New York, passengers are carried by steamboats in from 14 to 18 hours; some boats have made the passage in 12 hours. In passing from Narragansett Bay to the Sound, it is necessary to double Point Judith where there is commonly a rough sea, to avoid which a railway is now in progress from Providence to Stonington, a distance of 47 miles. A third railroad, the utility of which seems questionable (since the boats in the Sound move at the rate of 15 miles an hour), is projected from a point on Long Island opposite Stonington to Brooklyn, a distance of 88 miles.

Between New York and Philadelphia, you go by steamboat to South Amboy on Raritan Bay, 28 miles, whence a railroad extends across the peninsula to Bordentown and down along the Delaware to Camden, opposite Philadelphia. In summer a steamboat is taken at Bordentown, but in winter the Delaware is frozen over and the railway is then used through the whole distance to transport the crowd that is always going and coming between the commercial and financial capitals of the United States, between the great mart and the exchange of the Union, between the North and the South. An ice-boat lands the traveler in Philadelphia a few minutes after he has left the cars at Camden. This railroad is 61 miles long and cost $2,300,000, or $38,000 a mile. It has but one track most of the way. I met many persons at Philadelphia who remembered having been two and sometimes three long days on the road to New York; it is now an affair of seven hours which will soon be reduced to six. Two railroads, each belonging to a different group, one of which is completed and the other nearly so, will form, with the exception of an interval of several miles, a second line across the peninsula from New York to Philadelphia. One extends from Philadelphia to

Trenton, 26 miles; the other from Jersey City, opposite New York, to New Brunswick, 30 miles; if, therefore, rails were laid between New Brunswick and Trenton, a distance of 28 miles over a perfectly level plain, land communication between New York and Philadelphia would be complete; but up to now the State of New Jersey has refused to authorize this connection because it received a considerable sum from the Camden and Amboy company for the monopoly of the travel.

From Philadelphia to Baltimore, the route is continued by steamboat to Newcastle and by a railroad 16¼ miles long from there to Frenchtown across the peninsula, where another steamboat takes the traveler to Baltimore in 8 or 9 hours after starting from Philadelphia. The Newcastle and Frenchtown railroad cost $400,000, or $24,500 a mile. The navigation of the Chesapeake and Delaware is sometimes interrupted by ice and it has, therefore, been thought that it would be useful to have a continuous railroad from Philadelphia. There would also be a saving of time, for the present route is somewhat circuitous. Different companies have undertaken different portions of this work, which will pass by Wilmington on the Delaware and Havre de Grace, a city founded by the French on the Susquehanna near its mouth in Chesapeake Bay. The whole distance by this route is only 93 miles instead of 118, the distance by the present line, and the passage will occupy 5 or 6 hours instead of eight or nine. From Baltimore southward two routes offer themselves; you may take the steamboat to Norfolk, a distance of 200 miles which is accomplished in 18 or 20 hours, where another boat ascends the James River to Richmond still more rapidly, a distance of about 135 miles in 10 hours; or you may go from Norfolk to Weldon on the Roanoke by a railroad 77 miles long of which two thirds are completed.

From Baltimore you may also go to Washington by a branch of the Baltimore and Ohio railroad, and from there by steamboat down the Potomac to a little village, 15 miles from Fredericksburg, from which a railroad is now in progress to Richmond. It will be 58 miles long and will cost only $12,000 a mile, including the engines, cars, and depots. From Petersburg, 20 miles from Richmond, a railroad extends to Blakely on the Roanoke, 60 miles, and the interval between Petersburg and Richmond will soon be filled up. The Petersburg and Roanoke railroad, which is shorter than the post road follows with very little deviation an old Indian trail, a remarkable fact, which was told me by the able engineer Mr. Moncure Robinson. It extends almost entirely on the surface of the ground and without embankments through the sandy, uncultivated plains, intersected by the pools of stagnant water which uniformly border the sea from the Chesapeake to Cape Florida and are annually infested by the fever of the country. The whole region is most admirably adapted for railroads constructed almost wholly of wood. The surface is graded by nature and the sandy soil offers an excellent foundation for the wooden frame on which the rails are placed. The still-virgin forests of pine and oak afford an inexhaustible supply of timber for the construction of the railways, free to whoever wishes to use it. But if the land is perfectly suited, the population is far from being so. In this sterile tract, the inhabitants are thinly scattered; there are only a few villages here and there on the rivers. Large towns, in which alone the necessary capital would be found, do not exist and the aid of Northern capitalists has been necessarily resorted to. Philadelphia capital has been largely employed in the construction of the Petersburg and Richmond railroads and without it the great line between the South and the North will not be continued across North Carolina, one of the poorest States in the confederacy, and connected with the works completed or in progress in Georgia and South Carolina.

There is, therefore, a great void of 325 miles between the Roanoke and Charleston, the chief city of South Carolina, or rather of 275 miles between the Roanoke and Columbia, the capital of that State. From Charleston, a railroad 136 miles long extends through the uncultivated and feverish zone of sand and pine barrens to the cotton region; it terminates at Hamburg on the Savannah River opposite Augusta, which is the principal interior cotton market; the cost of this work was only about $9,500 a mile including some cars, etc. Its construction is peculiar in this respect, that where its level is above that of the surface recourse has been had to piles instead of embankments. The railway, thus perched upon stilts from 15 to 25 feet high, certainly leaves something to be desired in regard to the safety of travelers; but it was necessary to construct it and to do so with a very small capital, and in this respect it has been successful. The receipts have already been sufficiently large to permit the company gradually to substitute embankments of earth for the frail props on which it formerly rested. Another singular circumstance about it is that it was constructed almost entirely by slaves. This road was undertaken with the purpose of diverting to Charleston part of the cotton which descended the river Savannah to the town of the same name. It has fully answered the expectations of its projectors.

From Augusta, the Georgia railroad has lately been begun and will traverse some of the most fertile cotton districts in the State; it will extend to Athens, a distance of 115 miles. To continue the line from North to South, or from Boston to New Orleans, it would be necessary to prolong this railroad in the direction of Montgomery, Alabama, from where a steamer takes the traveler to Mobile on the Alabama River. Between Mobile and New Orleans there are regular lines of steamboats running through Mobile Bay, Pascagoula Sound, and Lakes Borgne and Pontchartrain. The last four miles between the latter lake and New Orleans are passed over in a quarter of an hour on a railroad which the Louisiana legislature calls in its bad French *chemind coulisses*.

Such is, with its gaps, the line between the North and South, the most advanced today. It will not be the only one, but as civilization establishes itself farther west and capital multiplies, several new routes will be formed, receding more and more from the coast.

The Baltimore and Ohio railroad is connected at Harpers Ferry with the Winchester railroad, 30 miles long, which runs up the bed of one of those long valleys that separate the successive ridges of the Allegheny Mountains from each other. That in which Winchester stands is one of the most regular and fertile of these great basins and is celebrated under the name of the Virginia Valley. Although, therefore, the Winchester railroad was constructed only for the purpose of giving the produce of Winchester and its vicinity an easy access to the market of Baltimore, yet it may one day become a link in the great chain of communication extending through the Valley from north to south. A company has already been chartered for continuing the work to Staunton, a distance of 96 miles. Another line from the South to the North which will, perhaps, be connected with that of the Great Virginia Valley has been projected at New Orleans and authorized by the legislatures of Louisiana and the other States through which it will pass; it is a railroad from New Orleans to Nashville, the capital of Tennessee, and I am assured that the work will soon begin. This line aspires to nothing less than competition with the magnificent river lines of the Ohio and the Mississippi in the transportation of passengers and cotton.

IV. LINES RADIATING AROUND THE MAJOR CITIES

First Center: Boston

Three railroads extend from Boston in different directions; the first, 26 miles long, to the manufacturing city of Lowell, which thus becomes a suburb of Boston, and the second, 44 miles, to Worcester, the center of an important agricultural district. The former cost $60,000 a mile, the latter $32,000. The third road is the Providence railroad, already mentioned above as one of the links in the great chain from North to South. The Lowell railroad enters into competition with the Middlesex Canal; the Worcester road is to be continued to the Hudson River, where it will terminate opposite Albany. It will also be connected with the city of Hudson, 30 miles below Albany, by a railroad extending from West Stockbridge. It will thus become to Boston a Western railroad, which name it has in fact received. A company has been authorized to execute the portion between Worcester and Springfield, a distance of 54 miles, the whole distance from Boston to Albany being 160 miles. The Eastern railroad, a fourth work, is about to be undertaken, passing through Lynn, famous for its boots and shoes; Salem, a little city which carries on an extensive trade with China; Ipswich, Beverly, and Newburyport, toward Portland, the principal town in the northern extremity of the Union.

Second Center: New York

Radiating from New York are: [1.] the railroad to Paterson, an important manufacturing town at the falls of the Passaic, 16 miles long; [2.] the New Brunswick railroad, already mentioned, which serves as a route of communication with several important points, especially Newark, and for the transportation of provisions for the New York market from part of New Jersey; [3.] the Harlem railroad, almost exclusively for passengers; [4.] the Brooklyn and Jamaica railroad on Long Island, 12 miles long, designed both for pleasure excursions and for transporting articles of consumption to the markets of New York.

Third Center: Philadelphia

Around Philadelphia, in addition to the great works extending to Columbia, Amboy, and Baltimore already mentioned, are: [1.] the Trenton railroad; [2.] the Norristown and Germantown road, designed for passengers and for the accommodation of some manufacturing villages, such as Manayunk, 16 miles long; [3.] that of West Chester, a branch of the Columbia railroad, 9 miles long, designed for the supply of the markets of the city. There are also several railroads running through the city whose rails are laid on the level of the street and on which only horse-cars are used.

Fourth Center: Baltimore

Besides the Baltimore and Ohio railroad with its Washington branch, Baltimore is also about to have a railroad through York to the Susquehanna opposite Columbia, the length of which will be 73 miles. The object of this road is to contest with Philadelphia the commerce of the valley of the Susquehanna. The Pennsylvania Canal with its many branches is a complete canal system, above Columbia, for this river and its tributaries. But below Columbia there are several rapids and shoals which interrupt the navigation of the river, except for downward-bound boats at high water. The Philadelphia merchants, fearing that all the works executed at a great expense by Pennsylvania would turn out less to their benefit than to that of the people of Baltimore, as the latter have openly boasted, for a long time opposed both the canalization of the Susquehanna from Columbia to its mouth and the permission to construct that section of a railroad from Baltimore to Columbia which would lie within the limits of Pennsylvania. Their opposition has, however, been at last overcome and charters have been granted authorizing the construction of both works. The railroad company, to which Maryland has just made a loan of $1,000,000, is pushing the railway ahead with great activity.

Fifth Center: Charleston

Some short canals have been cut to facilitate the access to Charleston from the interior, but they are in a bad state and are of little importance.

Sixth Center: New Orleans

Independent of the short railway of five miles from Lake Pontchartrain to New Orleans, there are several other works, such as the Carrolton railroad, which is a little longer, and two short canals extending from the city to the lake. Some cuts have also been made between the lagoons and marshes of the lower Mississippi. These canals, dug in a wet and muddy soil, have presented serious difficulties in their construction. They are of no interest in regard to their extent or importance.

Seventh Center: Saratoga

The springs of Saratoga, in the State of New York, are visited for two or three months in the summer by an immense number of visitors who swarm there like bees. There is not a master of a family in easy circumstances in Philadelphia, New York, and Baltimore who does not feel obliged to pass 24 or 48 hours with his wife and daughters among this crowd in their Sunday's best and to visit the field where the English army under General Burgoyne surrendered its arms. There are at present two railroads to Saratoga; one from Schenectady, 22 miles long, a branch of the Albany and Schenectady road, and another from Troy on the Hudson, 25 miles long. After the season is over they serve for the transportation of fuel and timber.

V. WORKS CONNECTED WITH COAL MINES

The bituminous coal mines of Chesterfield, near Richmond, are connected with the James River by a short railway adapted only for horses, which is 12 miles long and cost $15,000 a mile, including the cars, depots, etc. Once delivered at the river, the coal is easily transported along the whole coast, where it comes into competition with the English and Nova Scotia coals.

The anthracite beds of Pennsylvania are responsible for the construction of a much more extensive series of works. At present hardly any fuel is consumed on the coast for domestic and manufacturing purposes other than anthracite coal, which is found only in a small section of Pennsylvania between the Susquehanna and the Delaware. It gives a more intense and sustained heat than wood, which had also become very dear, and is much better suited to the rigorous winters which are experienced in the United States along the latitude of Naples. Anthracite is also much preferable to bituminous coal, the only sort in use with us; it makes no smoke and is much cleaner, not soiling the carpets and drapery. The fire is easily kept up and a grate needs to be filled only two or three times during the whole twenty-four hours to maintain a fire night and day. It spares the servants a great deal of trouble, so they prefer it; and on this point, as on several others, their opinion is more important than that of their masters. The only inconvenience attending it is that it sometimes gives off a sulphurous smell. It is also beginning to take the place of wood in the steamboats. The anthracite trade has, therefore, become considerable, and several canals and railroads have been made or are being made to transport the fuel from the mines to the points of consumption.

The principal of these lines are the following: [1.] The Schuylkill Canal, which extends from Philadelphia to the vicinity of the mines about the head of the Schuylkill. Its length from Philadelphia to Port Carbon is 108 miles; it cost, inclusive of the double locks, $3,000,000, or $28,000 a mile, and yields a net income of 20 to 25 per cent; 400,000 tons of coal are annually brought down upon it. [2.] The Lehigh Canal runs from the Delaware to the mines near the heads of the Lehigh; it is 46 miles long and cost $1,560,000, or $34,000 a mile. [3.] The lateral canal along the Delaware starts from Easton, at the mouth of the Lehigh, and ends at Bristol, the head of navigation for sea vessels. It transports to Philadelphia the coal that is brought down the Lehigh Canal; it is 60 miles long, and cost $1,238,000, or $20,600 a mile. This work was executed by the State of Pennsylvania and has been enumerated before among the State works. [4.] The Morris Canal starts from Easton and ends at Jersey City, opposite New York. It serves the New York market with coal. The change of level is here for the most part effected, not by locks, but by inclined planes, the operation of which is very simple; the length of this is 102 miles, the cost $2,650,000, or $25,000 a mile. [5.] The Delaware and Hudson Canal extends from the Roundout Creek on the Hudson near Kingston, 90 miles above New York, to the anthracite mines near the upper Delaware. The coal is brought down to the canal at Honesdale from the mountains on a railroad 16 miles long; the canal is 109 miles long and cost $2,250,000, or $20,000 a mile; the railroad cost $300,000, or $17,500 a mile. [6.] The Pottsville and Sunbury railroad is designed to bring down to the Schuylkill the products of the mines lying in the heart of the mountains between the Susquehanna and the heads of the Schuylkill. It is remarkable for the boldness of the inclined planes, some of which have an inclination of 25 and 33 per cent, and which are worked by very ingenious and economical contrivances. It is 45 miles long and cost $1,120,000, or $25,000 a mile. [7.] The Philadelphia and Reading railroad, now in progress, will enter into competition with the Schuylkill Canal; it is 56 miles long and cost, including the necessary apparatus, $26,300 a mile. It is proposed to continue it to Pottsville, 35 miles from Reading; there would then be a continuous railroad from Philadelphia to the center of the Susquehanna valley.

Beside these seven great lines, several mining companies have constructed various railways of less importance which branch from them in different directions. At the end of 1834, there were 165 miles of these smaller works, constructed at an expense of about $1,125,000, which added to the 542 miles and $13,280,000 of the seven works above enumerated, gives a total of 707 miles and $14,400,000 or, deducting the Delaware Canal, which has been counted before, of 647 miles and $13,162,000.

The aggregate length of all the works which I have already enumerated, including only those that are finished or far advanced, is 3,025 miles of canal and 1,825 miles of railroad, made at a cost of above 112 millions. If we add several detached works, such as the Ithaca and Oswego, the Lexington and Louisville, the Tuscumbia and Decatur (Alabama) railroads, and various canals in New England, Pennsylvania, Georgia, etc., we shall have a total of 3,250 miles of canal and 2,000 miles of railroad, constructed at an expense of upwards of 120 million dollars.

The impulse is, therefore, given; the movement goes on with increasing speed; the whole country is covered in every direction. If I were to attempt to enumerate all the railroads for which the routes are under survey, which have been or are on the point of being authorized by charters from the several legislatures, for which the subscription is about to be opened or has already been filled, I should be obliged to mention all the towns in the Union. A town of 10,000 inhabitants which has not its railroad looks upon itself with that feeling of shame which our first parents experienced in the terrestrial paradise when, after having eaten of the fruit of the tree of knowledge, they saw that they were naked.

I have spoken here only of the best means of communication—canals and railroads—not of common roads. If I had undertaken to speak of these, I should have mentioned above all the great work called the National or Cumberland Road, which, starting from Washington or, strictly speaking, from Cumberland on the Potomac, strikes the Ohio at Wheeling and extends westward across the center of Ohio, Indiana, and Illinois to the Mississippi. It has been constructed wholly at the expense of the Federal government and up to the present time $5,400,000 have been allotted to it. Begun in 1806, it is now nearly finished to

Vandalia in Illinois. A dispute between Illinois and Missouri about what city it should end at has delayed the completion of the last division. From Washington to Vandalia is 800 miles, from Cumberland to Vandalia, 675 miles. The doctrine of the unconstitutionality of Congress engaging in internal improvements having prevailed since the accession of General Jackson to the presidency, Congress has offered the National Road to the States within which it lies and they have accepted it on condition of its being first put in a state of perfect repair. Several of the States have also spent considerable sums in improving the condition of their own roads. South Carolina, for instance, has devoted about a million and a half to this object.

The public works of the United States are generally managed with economy; the costs which I have cited testify to that, because they are much less than that of similar works in Europe although the wages of labor here are two or three times higher than on the old continent. The canals constructed by the States are, nevertheless, pretty well finished; their dimensions are less than those of our canals, but greater than those of England; the locks are almost always of hewn stone. (On some of the canals the locks are partly of wood and partly of stone; these composite locks are economical and easily kept in repair, and deserve to be introduced in other countries. On many canals the locks are wholly of wood.) The bridges, viaducts, and aqueducts are generally wooden superstructures resting on abutments and piers of common masonry. The river dams are always of wood. The railroads constructed by the States, those of Pennsylvania in particular, have been built at a great expense; they have a double track with stone viaducts and some tunnels; the rails are wholly of iron, resting on stone blocks or sleepers. The Lowell railroad company also wished to have its road constructed in the most solid manner. It has used granite lavishly, which I believe superfluous if not useless. The Baltimore and Ohio railroad has two tracks, but except for a short distance is on wood.

In the Northern States and near the large towns, most of the railroads have an iron edge rail and a roadway prepared for two tracks, but with only one track laid. Such are the Worcester, Providence, and Amboy railways, and such will be the Philadelphia and Reading road; but the rails rest upon wooden crosspieces which, apart from their cheapness, have some advantage over stone sleepers in regard to wear of the cars, superior ease of motion, and greater facility of repairs. Those railroads in the North on which there is less travel and which are more remote from the large towns, and all those of the South, have but a single track, with no preparation for a second, and consist of an iron bar about two inches wide and half an inch thick resting on longitudinal sleepers.

On most of the American railroads, the inclinations are much greater than what in Europe are usually considered the *maxima*. A rise of 35 feet to the mile, for instance, seems moderate to American engineers and even 50 feet does not frighten them. Experience has shown that these inclinations, the latter of which is double the *maximum* established by our engineers, do not endanger the safety of travelers. They do, indeed, diminish the rate of speed, unless additional power is applied at certain points to increase the force of traction; but the Americans think that these inconveniences are more than overborne by the reduction of the first cost of construction. The curves are also greater; on the Baltimore and Ohio railroad, on which locomotives are used, there are several with a radius of 400 or 500 feet, but the consequence is that on this road the average rate of speed does not exceed 12 or 13 miles an hour, only half as great as that on the Liverpool railroad but twice as great as that of a coach on an ordinary road. In general, however, the American engineers endeavor to avoid curves of less than 1,000 feet radius. In France the Board of Public Works, in their surveys and plans, have fixed upon 2,700 feet as the *minimum*.

On some of the American railroads, however, even the

rules of European science have been exceeded; on the Lowell railroad the *minimum* radius is 3,000 feet; on the Boston and Providence railroad there is no curve of a radius less than 6,000 feet. The rate of velocity on the American railroads is as various as the manner of their construction and the amount of their inclinations and curvatures. On the Boston and Lowell road the rate is nearly 25 miles an hour; on the Boston and Providence and Worcester roads it is about 20 miles; on the Camden and Amboy railroad the mean velocity has been reduced to 15 miles; on the Charleston and Augusta road, it is only about 12; and it is still less on the Baltimore and Ohio railway.

One of the chief means of economy in the construction of these works in this country is the use of wood for bridges. The Americans are unequaled in the art of constructing wooden bridges; those of Switzerland, about which so much has been said, are clumsy and heavy compared with theirs. The American bridges have arches of 100 and 200 feet span; the bridge over the Schuylkill at Philadelphia consists of a single arch of 300 feet span; and they are not less remarkable for their cheapness than for their boldness. The bridge over the Susquehanna at Columbia is 6,000 feet long and cost $130,000; it is roofed over and has two carriageways and two side-ways for foot passengers. In general the wooden superstructure of a covered bridge with a double carriageway may be built at the rate of $8,000 to $14,000 per 600 feet, according to the locality and the character of the work; a similar structure with us would be built of hewn stone, and would cost at least $200,000 to $300,000. The masonry is generally of uncut stone, or of undressed hewn stone, and is not, therefore, expensive. Three different plans are followed in the construction of bridges: one is that of a carpenter called Burr; a second that of Colonel Long; and the third, which is the newest, most interesting, and most suitable for railroads on account of its firmness, is that of Mr. Town; they are all remarkable for requiring scarcely any iron. There are, however, some bridges of hewn stone on American railroads. Such is the Thomas Viaduct over the Patapsco on the Baltimore and Ohio railroad, wholly of fine granite; it is 700 feet long, and cost only $120,000, although it has two roadways and is 60 feet high.

The greatest difficulty which Americans have encountered in the execution of their public works was not to procure the necessary capital, but to find men capable of directing operations. In this respect also, New York has done the Union signal service. The engineers who were trained in the construction of the Erie Canal have spread the benefits of the experience acquired in that work over the whole country. Mr. Wright, the most eminent among them and still the most active of American engineers notwithstanding his advanced age, has been engaged in the superintendence of an inconceivable number of undertakings. His name is associated with the construction of canals from the Chesapeake to the Ohio, from the Delaware to the Chesapeake, from the Hudson to the Delaware, from the James to the Kanawha; on the St. Lawrence, and even on the Welland; as well as with those of the railroads just mentioned. Within the last ten years the number of able engineers in the United States has become considerable, and they have written the records of their skill and science on the soil of their country. General Bernard contributed not a little to this result by carrying with him into the New World the most improved processes of European art and setting an example of their application. Mr. Moncure Robinson, also a pupil of the French schools of science, who excels in the art of combining great economy with great solidity and neatness of execution, has constructed the inclined planes of the portage railroad over the Allegheny and has built the Chesterfield, Petersburg, and Roanoke, the Little Schuylkill, and the Winchester railroads; he is, at present, engaged on the Pottsville and Sunbury, the Philadelphia and Reading, and the Fredericksburg and Richmond roads. Major McNeil has just finished the Boston and Providence railway and is engaged on the Stonington and the Baltimore and Susquehanna roads. Mr. Douglass, after having completed the Morris Canal and the Brooklyn and Jamaica railroad, is preparing, for the coming season, the operations on the New York waterworks. Mr. Fessenden, who has executed the Worcester railroad, is now engaged on the Eastern and Western railroads on the right and left of Boston. Mr. Knight, the principal engineer of the Baltimore and Ohio railroad, is occupied in devising plans for topping the Alleghenies. The late Mr. Canvass White assisted in the construction of the Louisville and Portland Canal and had finished the fine canal from the Raritan to the Delaware not long before his death. Mr. Allen has built the Charleston and Augusta railroad. Mr. Jervis, who is now directing a part of the great works of canalization in New York, constructed the Carbondale and Honesdale road.

To supply the lack of men of science demanded by the spirit of enterprise the Federal government authorizes the officers of the engineer corps and of the topographical engineers to enter into the service of the companies. It also employs them itself in surveying routes and preparing plans or constructing works on its own account. General Gratiot, the chief engineer, therefore, performs the duties of president of a board of public works (*directeur-général des ponts et chaussées*). Colonels Albert and Kearney, of the topographical engineers, take an active part in the construction of the great canal from the Chesapeake to the Ohio, of which the Federal government is the principal shareholder. Captain Turnbull superintends the canal from Georgetown to Alexandria; Captain Delafield the works on the National Road and Captain Talcott the improvements of the navigation of the Hudson. Colonel Long passes from route to route and conducts at one time the surveys from Memphis to Savannah, at another those from Portland to Montreal and Quebec. On the other hand, architects become engineers, and Mr. Strickland of Philadelphia and Mr. Latrobe of Baltimore superintend the construction of the railroad between these two cities; and even simple merchants take upon themselves the responsibility of great works, as in the case of Mr. Jackson of Boston, who is in fact chief engineer of the Lowell railroad.

The spectacle of a young people, executing in the short space of fifteen years a series of works which the most powerful States of Europe with a population three or four times as great would have shrunk from undertaking, is in truth a noble sight. The advantages to the public prosperity which result from these enterprises are incalculable, and the political effects are not less important. These numerous routes, which are traversed with so much ease and speed, will contribute to the maintenance of the Union more than a regularly balanced national representation. When New York shall be only six or eight days from New Orleans, not merely for the rich and privileged, but for every citizen, every laborer, disunion will be impossible. Distance will be annihilated, and this colossus, ten times greater than France, will preserve its unity without an effort.

It is impossible not to turn my thoughts back to Europe and to make a comparison by no means favorable to the great kingdoms which occupy it. The partisans of the monarchical principle maintain that it is as powerful in promoting the greatness and welfare of peoples and the progress of the human race as the principle of independence and self-government which prevails on this side of the Atlantic. For myself, I believe them to be right, but it is necessary that some tangible proof of the correctness of their opinion should be given if we do not wish that the contrary doctrine should make converts. It is by the fruits that the tree must be judged. European governments dispose of the property and the persons of more than 250 millions of men, that is, a population twenty times greater than that of the United States at the time these great works were begun. The extent of territory which demands their care is not quite four times as great as that at present occupied by the States and the organized Territories. The millions which European nations raise so easily for war, that is to say, to destroy and slaughter each other, would not certainly be wanting to their princes for the execution of useful enterprises. The latter have only to will it and all the peoples of Europe will be so completely blended together in interests, feelings, and opinions that the whole continent would be like a single state and a European war would be looked upon as no less sacrilegious than a civil war. By putting off the day of these useful works, do not the sovereigns give countenance to the reasonings of those who assert that the cause of kings is irreconcilable with the cause of nations?

XXIII

Labor

French Attempts to Colonize America — The English Colonial System — American Society is Entirely Oriented Toward Work — Haste — Organization of Labor Peculiar to America — Organization Proper for France — Canada — Algiers

Lancaster (Pennsylvania), July 20, 1835. There can be no success or happiness without special devotion to some one end. Individual or nation—to be successful and prosperous, beware of attempting everything! Human nature is finite and, like it, you must set some bounds to your wishes and efforts. *Learn how to limit yourself and to be content* is the precept of wisdom. If it is a wise rule, then Americans are at least partially wise, for they practice it partially. In general, the American is little disposed to be contented; his idea of equality is to be inferior to none, but he endeavors to rise in only one direction. His only means, like his only thought, is to subdue the material world; or, in other words, his means is industry in its various branches, business, speculation, work, action. To this sole object everything is subordinate, education, politics, private and public life. Everything in American society, from religion and morals to domestic usages and daily habits of life, is bent in the direction of this aim common to each and every one. If there are some exceptions to this general rule, they are few and belong to two causes: first, American society, absorbed as it is in its work, is not destined to remain forever imprisoned in this narrow circle, and it already contains the germs of its future destiny, whatever it may be, in the centuries ahead; secondly, human nature, however finite, is not single and no force in the world can stifle its eternal protest against exclusiveness in taste, institutions, and manners. Speculation and business, work and action, these, then, under various forms, are the special task which Americans have chosen with a zeal that amounts to fanaticism. This was marked out for them by the finger of Providence in order that a continent should be brought under the dominion of civilization with the least possible delay.

I cannot reflect without sorrow that once France seemed called to take part in this great mission with the two nations between whom God has placed it, morally between in regard to character and institutions as well as physically between in respect to geographical position, namely the English and Spaniards. While Spain, then queen of the world, grasped South America and the vast empire of Mexico, civilized, sword in hand, the native tribes, and built those monumental cities which will bear witness to its genius and its power ages after the calumnies of its slanderers shall have been forgotten, while England was planting some insignificant colonies on the barren shore of North America, France was exploring the vast basin of the Father of Waters and taking possession of the St. Lawrence, compared with which our Rhine, *tranquille et fier,* is but a modest rivulet; we were crowning with fortifications the steep rock of Quebec, building Montreal, founding New Orleans and St. Louis, and here and there subduing the rich plains of Illinois. At that time, we occupied the most fertile, best watered, and finest portion of North America, the part best suited to become the seat of a magnificent empire, in harmony with our notions of unity. Our engineers, with a sagacity for which the Americans now express the greatest admiration, had marked out by fortresses the sites most suitable for large towns. Our flag floated over Pittsburg (then Fort Duquesne), Detroit, Chicago, Erie (then Presqu'île), Kingston (then Fort Frontenac), Michillimackinac, Ticonderoga, Vincennes, Fort Charters, Peoria, and St. John, as well as over the capitals of Canada, and over Louisiana. Then our language might have set up its claim to be the universal language; the French name bade fair to become the first, not only in the world of ideas by art and letters, like the Greek, but also in the material and political world by the number of individuals who would take pride in bearing it, by the immensity of the territory over which its dominion stretched, like the Roman. Louis XIV in the days of his deification, in the Olympus which he had built himself, meditated this noble destiny for his people and his race. With a lofty pride he seemed to read their future triumphs on the pages of fate. But there is left to us who are separated from him only by a single century, there is left, alas! nought but vain and impotent regrets. The English have driven us forever, not only from America, but also from the East Indies, where that great prince had given us a footing. The descendants of our fathers in Canada and Louisiana struggle in vain against the British flood that swallows them up; our language is drowned in the same deluge; even our names for the cities we founded and the regions we discovered are corrupted in the harsh throats of our fortunate rivals and are too Saxonized to be any longer recognized. We have ourselves forgotten there even was a time when we could have claimed to rule the New World; we no longer remember the generous men who devoted themselves to secure dominion for us. To preserve the name of the heroic La Salle from oblivion, it has become necessary for the American Congress to raise a monument to his memory in the rotunda of the Capitol, between those to William Penn and John Smith. We have had no stone for him among all our innumerable sculptures; our painters have covered miles of canvas with their colors but have not drawn a line in honor of him.

Meanwhile new powers, the upstarts of Europe, defy us, elbow us, and crowd us in. In vain did the genius of the second Charlemagne restore to us the capital of the first and the finest provinces of Clovis; capital and provinces have been snatched from us almost immediately. One step more downward and we should have been forced forever back among the secondary states, the worn-out and decrepit nations, with no successors to receive and sustain with honor the inheritance of our fathers' glories. What is it that has thus degraded a great people and robbed it of its well-earned future? In an absolute monarchy like ours, it was enough that we should be ridden by such a prince as Louis XV, who had inherited nothing from his great ancestor but his vices; it was enough that during fifty years France was the plaything of his infamous selfishness and the shameful imbecility of his creatures. Absolute governments may sometimes produce wonders in a short space of time, but they are exposed to cruel reverses. Had we been the conquerors in America, instead of having been conquered by the English, what would have been the consequences? To judge what the people of New France would have been by what the Canadians and the Creoles of Louisiana are, the boldness and rapidity of the progress of civilization would have been much less than it has been. When it is proposed to conquer nations on the field of battle, France may enter the lists with confidence; but when it is proposed to subdue nature, the Englishman is our superior. He has firmer sinews and more vigorous muscle; physically he is better made for labor; he carries it on with more perseverance and method; he becomes interested in it and obstinately bent upon it. If he meets any obstacle in his task, he attacks it with the devouring passion which a Frenchman can feel only in the presence of an adversary in a human form.

With what zeal and devotion has the Anglo-American fulfilled his mission as a pioneer in a new continent! Behold how he makes his way over the rocks and precipices; see how he struggles face to face with the rivers, with the swamps, with the primeval forests; see how he slaughters the wolf and the bear, how he exterminates the Indian, who in his eyes is only another wild beast! In this conflict with the external world, with land and water, with mountains and the pestilential air, he appears full of that impetuosity with which Greece flung itself into Asia at the voice of Alexander; of that fanatical daring with which Mahomet inspired his Arabs for the conquest of the Eastern empire; of that delirious courage which animated our fathers forty years ago when they threw themselves upon Europe. On the same rivers, therefore, where our colonists floated, carelessly singing in the bark canoe of the savage, they have launched fleets of superb steamers. Where we fraternized with the Redskins, sleeping with them in the forests, living like them on the chase, traveling in their manner over rugged trails on foot, the persevering American has felled the aged trees, guided the plough, enclosed the fields, substituted the best breeds of English cattle for the wild deer, created farms, flourishing villages, and opulent cities, dug canals, and made roads. Those waterfalls which we admired as lovers of the picturesque and the height of which our officers measured at the risk of their lives, those he has shut up for the use of his mills and factories, regardless of the scenery. If these countries had continued to belong to the French, the population would certainly have been more gay than the present American race; it would have enjoyed more highly whatever it might have possessed, but it would have had less comfort; and wealth and ages would have passed away before man had become master of those regions which have been reclaimed in less than fifty years by the Americans.

If we examine the acts passed by the local legislatures at each session, we shall find that at least three fourths relate to the banks, which provide credit for the worker; to the establishment of new religious societies and churches which are the citadels where the guardians of industry keep watch; to routes and means of communication, roads, canals, railways, bridges, and steamboats which facilitate the access of the producer to the markets; to primary instruction for the use of the mechanic and the laborer; to various commercial regulations; or to the incorporation of towns and villages, the work of these hardy pioneers. There is no mention of an army; the fine arts are not so much as named; literary institutions and the higher scientific studies are rarely honored with notice. The tendency of the laws is above all to promote industry, material labor, the task of the moment. In the States that are somewhat older, the laws are always marked by their respect for property because the legislature feels that the greatest encouragement to industry is to respect its fruits. They are especially conservative of landed property, either from a lingering remembrance of the feudal laws of the mother country, or because they are anxious to preserve some element of stability in the midst of the general change; yet the laws generally pay less regard to the rights of property than is the case in Europe. Woe to whatever is inactive and unproductive, if it can be accused on however slight a foundation of resting upon monopoly and privilege! The rights of industry here have precedence over all others, efface all others, and it is on this account that, except in the affair of public credit in which the towns and States pique themselves on the most scrupulous exactness in fulfilling their engagements, in every dispute between the capitalists and the producer, the latter almost always has the better.

Everything is here arranged to facilitate industry; the

towns are built on the English plan; men of business, instead of being scattered over the town, occupy a particular quarter devoted exclusively to them in which there is not a building used as a dwelling house and nothing but offices and warehouses to be seen. The brokers, bankers, and lawyers here have their cells, the merchants their counting-rooms; here the banks, insurance offices, and other companies have their chambers, and other buildings are filled from cellar to garret with articles of merchandise. At any hour, one merchant has but a few steps to go after any other, or after a broker or a lawyer. This, it will be seen, is not according to the Paris fashion, by which a great deal of precious time is lost by men of business in running after one another; in this respect, Paris is the worst arranged commercial city in the world. New York is, however, inferior in this particular to London or Liverpool; it has nothing like the great docks and the Commercial House.

The manners and customs are those of a working, busy society. At fifteen, a man is engaged in business; at twenty-one he is established, he has his farm, his workshop, his counting-room, or his office, in a word his employment, whatever it may be. Twenty-one is also the age at which he gets married, and at twenty-two he is the father of a family and consequently has a powerful stimulus to excite him to industry. A man who has no profession and—which is nearly the same thing—who is not married enjoys little consideration; he who is an active and useful member of society, who contributes his share to augment the national wealth and increase the numbers of the population, he only is looked upon with respect and favor. The American is brought up with the idea that he will have some particular occupation, that he is to be a farmer, artisan, manufacturer, merchant, speculator, lawyer, physician, or minister, perhaps all in succession, and that if he is active and intelligent he will make his fortune. He has no conception of living without a profession, even when his family is rich, for he sees nobody about him not engaged in business. The man of leisure is a variety of the human species which the Yankee does not suppose to exist and he knows that, though rich today, his father may be ruined tomorrow. Besides the father himself is, as is customary, engaged in business and does not think of passing on his fortune; if the son wishes to have one at present, let him make it himself!

The habits of life are those of an exclusively working people. From the moment he gets up, the American is at his work, and he is absorbed in it till the hour of sleep. He never permits pleasure to distract him; public affairs alone have the right to take him for a few moments. Even mealtime is not for him a period of relaxation when he might rest his weary brain in an intimate and restful environment. It is only a disagreeable interruption of business, an interruption which he accepts because it is inevitable, but which he cuts short as much as possible. In the evening, if no political meeting requires his attendance, if he does not go to discuss some question of public interest, or to a religious meeting, he sits at home, thoughtful and absorbed in his meditations, whether on the transactions of the day or the projects of tomorrow. He refrains from business on Sunday because his religion commands it, but it also requires him to abstain from all amusement and recreation—music, cards, dice, or billiards—under penalty of sacrilege. On Sunday an American would not dare to receive his friends. His servants would not consent to it, and on that day he can hardly secure their services for himself at an hour also convenient to them. A few days ago, the mayor of New York was *accused* by one of the newspapers of having entertained on Sunday some English noblemen who came from England in their own yacht to give the American democracy a strange idea of British tastes. The mayor hastened to declare publicly that he was too well acquainted with his duties as a Christian to entertain his friends on the *Sabbath*. Nothing is, therefore, more melancholy than the seventh day in this country; after such a Sunday, the labor of Monday is a delightful pastime.

LABOR

Approach an English merchant in his counting-room in the morning and you will find him stiff and dry, answering you only by monosyllables; accost him at mail-time and he will be at no pains to conceal his impatience; he will dismiss you without always taking care to do it politely. The same man in his drawing room in the evening, or at his country house in summer, will be full of courtesy and attention to you. The Englishman divides his time and does only one thing at a time. In the morning he is wholly absorbed in business; in the evening he plays the man of leisure, relaxing and enjoying life; he is a gentleman, having before his eyes the English aristocracy, a perfect model to form his manners, and to teach him how to spend his fortune with dignity and grace. The modern Frenchman is a confused mixture of the Englishman of the evening and the Englishman of the morning; in the morning a little of the former, in the evening a little of the latter. The old French model was the former, or rather, to do each one justice, was the original after which the English aristocracy has formed itself. The American of the North and the Northwest whose character now sets the tone in the United States is permanently a man of business; he is always the Englishman of the morning. You may often find the Englishman of the evening on the plantations of the South, and some are beginning to be met with in the great cities of the North.

Tall, slender, and light of figure, the American seems built expressly for labor. He has no equal for dispatch of business. No one else can conform so easily to new situations and circumstances; he is always ready to adopt new processes and implements or to change his occupation. He is a mechanic by nature. Among us there is not a schoolboy who has not composed a ballad, written a novel, or drawn up a republican or monarchical constitution. In Massachusetts and Connecticut, there is not a laborer who has not invented a machine or a tool. There is not a man of any importance who has not his scheme for a railroad, a project for a village or a town, or who has not some grand speculation in the drowned lands of the Red River, in the cotton lands of the Yazoo, or in the cornfields of Illinois. Eminently a pioneer, the American type, he who is not more or less Europeanized, the pure Yankee, in a word, is not only a worker, he is a migratory worker. He has no root in the soil; he is a stranger to the worship of one's birthplace and family home; he is always in the mood to move on, always ready to start in the first steamer that comes along from the place where he had just now landed. He is devoured with a passion for movement, he cannot stay in one place; he must go and come, he must stretch his limbs and keep his muscles in play. When his feet are not in motion, his fingers must be in action; he must be whittling a piece of wood, cutting the back of his chair, or notching the edge of the table, or his jaws must be at work grinding tobacco. Whether it be that continual competition has given him the habit, or that he has an exaggerated estimate of the value of time, or that the unsettled state of everything around him keeps his nervous system in a state of perpetual agitation, or that he has come so from the hands of nature —he always has something to do, he is always in a terrible hurry. He is fit for all sorts of work except those which require a careful slowness. Those fill him with horror; it is his idea of hell. "We are born in haste," says an American writer, "we take our education on the run; we marry on the wing; we make a fortune at a stroke and lose it in the same manner, to make and lose it again ten times over in the twinkling of an eye. Our body is a locomotive going at the rate of twenty-five miles an hour; our soul, a high-pressure engine; our life is like a shooting star, and death overtakes us at last like a flash of lightning."

In the hotels and on board the steamboats, the door of the dining hall is crowded at the approach of a mealtime. As soon as the bell sounds, there is a general rush into the room and in less than ten minutes every place is occupied. In a quarter of an hour, out of three hundred persons, two hundred have left the table, and in ten minutes more not an individual is to be seen. On my passage from Baltimore to Norfolk, in the winter of 1834, I found that despite the cold three fourths of the passengers had risen at four o'clock, and at six, being almost the only person left abed and feeling sure that we must be near our port, I got up and went upon deck; but it was not until eight o'clock that we came in sight of Norfolk. On mentioning the fact afterward to an American, a man of sense who was on board at the same time and who, wiser than I, had lain abed till after sunrise: "Ah, sir," said he, "if you knew my countrymen better, you wouldn't be at all surprised at their getting up at four o'clock to arrive at nine. An American is always on the lookout lest any of his neighbors should get the start of him. If one hundred Americans were going to be shot, they would contend for first place, so strong is their habit of competition."

"Work," says American society to the poor; "work, and at eighteen you shall get, you a simple worker, more than a captain in Europe. You shall live in plenty, be well-clothed, well-housed, and able to save. Be attentive to your work, be sober and religious, and you will find a devoted and submissive wife; you will have a more comfortable home than many of the higher classes in Europe. From a journeyman, you shall become a master; you shall have apprentices and dependents under you in turn; you will have credit without stint, become a manufacturer or agriculturist on a great scale; you will speculate and become rich, found a town and give it your own name, you will be a member of the legislature of your State or alderman of your city, and finally member of Congress; your son shall have as good a chance to be made President as the son of the President himself. Work, and if the fortune of business should be against you and you fall, you shall soon be able to rise again, for a failure is nothing but a wound in battle; it shall not deprive you of the esteem or confidence of any one, if you have always been prudent and temperate, a good Christian and a faithful husband."

"Work," America says to the rich, "work and do not stop to think of enjoying your wealth. You shall increase your income without increasing your expenses; you shall enlarge your fortune, but it shall be only to increase the sources of labor for the poor and to extend your power over the material world. Be simple and severe in your exterior, but at home you may have the richest carpets, plate in abundance, the finest linens of Ireland and Saxony; externally your house will be on the same model with all others of the town; you will have neither livery nor equipage, you will not patronize the theater, which tends to relax morals; you will avoid play; you will sign the articles and pledges of the Temperance Society; you will not even indulge in good cheer; you shall set an example of constant attendance at your church; you shall always show the most profound respect for morals and religion, for the farmer and mechanic around you have their eyes fixed upon you; they take you for their model; they still acknowledge you to be the arbiter of manners and customs, although they have taken from you the political scepter. If you give yourself up to pleasure, to parade, to amusement, to dissipation and luxury, they also will give rein to their gross appetites and their violent passions. Your country will be ruined, and you will be ruined with it."

It is possible to imagine various social systems differently organized but equally favorable in theory to the promotion of industry. We might imagine a society organized for work under the influence of the principle of authority; that is, a society composed of a gradation of ranks; we might conceive another constituted under the auspices of the principle of liberty or independence. To organize any given people *a priori* for purposes of industry, it is necessary, under penalty of giving birth to a Utopian scheme, to consult the circumstances of its origin and the condition of its territory, to know where it has been and where it is going.

With the people of the United States, an offshoot of the English stock and imbued with Protestantism to the marrow of their bones, the principle of independence, of individualism—of competition, in fine—could not but be successful. The iron hearts of the Puritans, the *Ultras* of Protestantism, could not fail to find this principle congenial to them. That is why the sons of the Eastern States which were peopled by the Puritans have played the chief part in the occupation of the great valley of the Mississippi.

The civilization of the West (particularly the Northwest, that portion of the West where slavery does not exist) has sprung from the secret and silent co-operation of two or three hundred thousand young farmers who started, each on his own account, from New England, often alone, sometimes with a small company of friends. This system would not have succeeded with Frenchmen. The Yankee alone with his wife in the wilderness is self-sufficient. The Frenchman is eminently social; he could not bear the isolation in which the Yankee moves at ease. Although alone, the Yankee is moved to passion by the work he has conceived and set himself to do; the Frenchman can only become interested in an industrial enterprise in connection with others whose concurrence with him is evident and palpable, or rather he is not moved by any material task, for he reserves his affections and sympathies for living objects. It is quite impossible for him to fall in love with a *clearing,* to feel the same transports at the success of a manufacturing process as for the safety of a friend or the happiness of a mistress; but he is capable of applying himself to the task with ardor if his characteristic passions, his thirst for glory and his pride, are aroused by human contact. If it were proposed, then, to settle colonies with Frenchmen, it would be necessary to put little reliance on individual efforts. In all things a Frenchman must feel his neighbor's elbow as in a line of battle. To colonize a new land, one could throw Americans there in isolation; they would form little centers around which constantly expanding circles of population and cultivation would grow up. But if the new settlers were Frenchmen, it would be necessary to carry with them a society ready made, social bonds already established, or at least a regular social framework to which to attach the social strands; that is, they must have, at starting, the great circle with its center strongly marked.

Canada is almost the only colony that has been founded exclusively by Frenchmen, and a complete social organization was carried thither. Once the country was explored, the royal fleet landed the *seigneurs* who had received fiefs from royal grants. They were followed by vassals transplanted from Normandy and Brittany, among whom the lands were distributed. At the same time the fleet deposited an appointed clergy, endowed with ample domains and the right of collecting tithes. Next came traders and companies who were given the monopoly of the fur trade and the commerce of the colony. In a word the three orders, the clergy, nobility, and third estate, were imported ready-made from Old France into New. The only thing which the colonists left behind them was the poverty of the greatest number. The system was a good one for that period; the principle of order and hierarchy which prevailed there under the only form possible was in keeping with the character of the people. The proof of this is to be found in the fact that Canada has flourished under this system which the English conquerors have never changed and the population has increased in the midst of general ease. I have never seen anything which better presents the image of *aurea mediocritas* than the pretty villages on the banks of the St. Lawrence. They do not exhibit the ambitious prosperity of the United States; they are much more modest; but if there is less show, there is also more contentment and happiness. Canada reminded me of Switzerland; there is the same aspect of calm contentment and quiet happiness. One would talk of Canada were it not by the side of the American colossus; its development would attract attention were it not for the miraculous expansion of the United States. Neither would it be right to assert that the progress of Canada has been in spite of the colonial system; the dispute about the *because* and the *although* is easily settled in this case. All that was burdensome about the original system remains untouched and there is no complaint against it. The seignorial dues, the tithe, and the various monopolistic privileges still exist in full vigor and, incredibly, do not appear in the interminable list of ninety-three grievances lately drawn up by the Canadians against the ruling regime.

In France—thank God!—there are no more *seigneurs,* no more vassals, no more tithes; the three orders are abolished; there is not even royalty any longer in the absolute sense; but we do have a government under three divisions which has at its disposal resources far more unfailing, means of action far more energetic. This central power, the only one which now exists, should step in and give directions here, there, or anywhere that royalty and the various orders gave theirs. We will not found a colony at Algiers, or anywhere else, unless the government takes charge and fills the role, save for those modifications required by time and circumstance, played in Canada by the nobility and the clergy. The intermediaries which before existed between the Crown and the mass of the people have disappeared. Part of their prerogatives can and ought to return to the people, just as has been done with regard to the internal administration of the country, because the nation, now more enlightened and more apt at self-direction, has not the need to the same degree as in the past of rule handed down from above. Yet, certainly, the major part of the prerogatives of the powers of old should go to swell that of the central power, and not be purely and simply annulled. With us, the French, such as we are today, it would be for the general good if the government had the major share of the inheritance of influences from the past, especially in the matter of colonization. Nothing is more difficult than to colonize; it is an entirely new creation. The proper role of a colony is to be a minor; in the United States, where self-government is pushed to its logical extreme, the continental colonies which they call territories are treated as minors until they have reached a population of sixty thousand; now for every minor a tutor is indispensable.

Without doubt a government which wishes to establish colonies should seek the co-operation of capitalists, but one is mistaken if one waits on them, in relation to Algiers, for large efforts or great results. In the matter of colonial companies we are no more advanced than in the time of Louis XIV; perhaps less; I look in vain in France for something which can be compared today to our India Companies of past days.

I do not wish to play the role of prophet, much less the prophet of disaster; moreover, at the distance I am from Algiers, I should speak only with extreme care. Yet I am persuaded that with the policy of laissez-faire or do-nothing adopted by the government we are not on the way of planting a French population there. Moreover, until the time has come when two hundred or three hundred thousand Frenchmen are there, our control will only be ephemeral, at the mercy of some uninformed vote of the Chamber, or a ministerial caprice, or a single threat of war; and, to say what has force in this positive century, Algiers will cost us dearly with no return at all.

If I am not completely wrong, those who emigrate to Algiers under a system of individual emigration can be, save with a few exceptions, only the refuse of our great cities. There will be none of the flower of our country and of our factories, young cultivators or robust workers like those who, musket in hand, make the glory of our army; those would have the force and the will power to take possession of the land as one takes possession of civilization, by tilling the soil and hard work. Our honest countrymen and our intelligent workers are deaf to the call of the colonial companies; they have good reason not to believe the promises of speculators. They will not expatriate themselves to establish a French regime on the soil of Africa unless an enlightened government calls them in a high and clear voice; but they would pour there if they saw organized there, under the patronage and the guarantee of the state, a nucleus of true colonists.

Every year about two thousand soldiers resign from the Regency (but it is still the Regency!) to return to their homes and to become workers or peasants again. What a blessing it would be for Algiers if they could return, where they want to return, after having been to France to get a wife. With the widespread ambition today to become a man of property, it would not be impossible to attract them by giving them land, tools, and small houses which the army itself could have built. Settled on large farms or in villages around which each of them could have his own field and which in time of need could provide an impregnable blockhouse, they would provide a nucleus around which the French people would soon grow and the existence of which would encourage the companies finally to take their enterprises seriously. If they were left their arms and their uniforms, they would constitute a peacetime militia who would not fear the Arabs and whom the Arabs would hold in awe. Who could disapprove if Algiers, conquered by our army, should become our patrimony? Our soldiers have paid for Algiers at the same price the first American settlers purchased the West, that is, with their blood.

XXIV

Money

Money Among the English and the Americans — System of Honor — Its Present Impossibility in France — Payment for Public Services — Free Services in France — Standard of Living for Public Servants in the United States — Influence of Industrial Progress on the Salaries of Public Officials — No Marriages for Money in the United States — No Misers

Sunbury (Pennsylvania), July 31, 1835. In a society devoted to production and trade, money must be regarded with other eyes than among a people of military spirit or one nourished in classical studies and learned speculations. Among the latter, it must be looked upon, theoretically at least, as vile metal. With them honor and glory are more powerful and more common motives of action than interest; they are the coin with which many persons are content, the only coin which many persons are ambitious to acquire. In an industrious society, on the other hand, money, the fruit and object of labor, is not to be despised; a man's wealth is the measure of his capacity and of his consideration among his fellow citizens. Whatever may be the cause, the fact is certain that money is not the same thing here that it is with us; it weighs here where with us it has no weight; it appears openly here, where with us it would be hidden. When I was in England, I was surprised at the number of notices on the docks threatening, for instance, a fine for certain offenses, with a promise of half to the informer. If a prefect of the police should offer such a premium to informers among us, our blood would boil with indignation. In this country the same practice prevails and seems to be still more frequent. When a crime is committed, the authorities offer a reward of $100 or $200 to whoever will make known or deliver up the criminal. In Philadelphia I saw the governor of the State and the mayor of the city endeavoring to outbid each other in promises. A murder had been committed during one of the primary elections and these officers, who were of different parties, endeavored to prove by the greatness of their offers that the opposite party was guilty of the act. In some cases of incendiarism or poisoning, a reward of $1,000 has been offered. It should be observed, however, that in England, outside of London, and here in the United States there is no organized police like ours and it therefore becomes necessary that the citizens themselves act as a police.

The maxim here is that everything is to be paid for. Here museums and institutions for higher instruction which are free are unknown. And unknown here are those unpaid offices which take a citizen from his business and would make it impossible for him to provide for the support of his family if he discharged them faithfully. The municipal offices in the country have no pay attached to them because they take up little time and require little attention, and because a man in the country has more leisure than the busy inhabitant of the city. But in the cities all officers are paid as soon as their functions come to occupy much of their time. The custom of paying by the day which prevails in England is quite general here. Members of Congress are paid at the rate of eight dollars a day and if a legislative committee prolongs its sessions beyond those of the legislative body the pay is continued on the same footing. All the State legislatures are paid by the day. Canal commissioners, who are generally men of some distinction, that is, rich men, are generally paid in the same way, an account being kept of the number of days they are employed in the public service; for them the pay amounts merely to the payment of their expenses. Those, however, who are permanently occupied receive an annual salary. In some offices, the incumbents are paid by fees for each affair in which they become engaged; this is generally the case with the States' Attorneys and the Justices of the Peace and with the aldermen in some of the cities. The public officers who are regularly employed, such as the governors of the States and the mayors of the principal cities, have a fixed annual salary. It is a settled principle here that all work should stand on the same footing with industrial labor and be paid in the same manner. Intellectual merchandise and material merchandise, capital and talent, dollars and science, are here placed on the same level; this practice puts everyone at his ease and facilitates, abridges, and simplifies all operations. No one feels the least embarrassment in asking for a service for which he knows he will pay. Everything is settled plainly and easily because in an industrious and prosperous society everyone has the power to be liberal.

Money is made an instrument of punishment as well as of reward. It is well known that in England a conviction for adultery enriches the wronged husband at the expense of the guilty paramour. The same practice would prevail here if the crime were not extremely rare. The American law is very sparing of bodily punishments for simple misdemeanors, but it makes very free use of fines. On most bridges there are notices forbidding crossing with horses at any other pace than a walk, under penalty of a fine of two, three, or five dollars. When a man is suspected or even accused of a crime, such as forgery, arson, or murder, it is not his person but his purse that is secured; that is, instead of being arrested, he is obliged to give bail in a sum which is left to the discretion of the judicial authority. Last year, while a convention for revising the constitution of Tennessee was in session in Nashville, one of the members, a militia general, of whom there are thousands in the country, a man of large property and therefore very respectable, got into a quarrel with an editor of a newspaper and uttered violent threats against him. Some days afterward, in company with another violent fellow, he actually discharged a pistol at his adversary in the barroom of a hotel and wounded him dangerously. The affair was brought before the proper authorities and the assailant was admitted to bail, being thus left at full liberty on depositing some thousand dollars, continuing to sit in the convention and to assist in the formation of the new constitution of the State. So much tenderness toward an assassin, and similar proceedings which I have witnessed relative to incendiaries and persons guilty of forgery, recall to mind those barbarous times when criminals were redeemed at a price. But, on the other hand, is it not barbarous to deal severely with simple misdemeanors, or special offenses like those of the press, by the brutal method of jail sentences? Is not preventive arrest, in most cases, an odious and useless show of force? In an age when milder customs restrain all those who feel the urge toward violence, when work has become the common law, is it not more human and more moral to punish those who break the law by a fine, that is to say by a levy on their work, past or future? It will readily be imagined, after what has been said, that imprisonment for debt is repugnant to Americans. In fact, a general clamor has been raised against it; most of the States have already abolished it and others will soon follow.

Money is, therefore, the sanction of the laws and of the most simple police regulations. If a magistrate has good reason for believing that an individual has intentions to break the peace, instead of taking him into preventive custody he requires him to give bail for his good behavior. It is by money, also, that chartered companies are obliged to conform to the provisions of their charters. It is by money that even the magistrates are punished for neglect of duty. To remedy the inconveniences arising from the minute subdivision and dispersion of administrative authority in the New England States, resort is also had to money. In that part of the Union the repair of roads is left to the care of the towns. One can see that under this system one refractory town could obstruct travel through an entire State. It is, therefore, provided by law that every town shall be responsible to travelers within its limits for any accidents which may be due to the bad state of the roads; it is not uncommon to read accounts in the newspapers of a town being forced by the courts to pay a traveler, who has been overturned on its roads or bridges, $500 or $1,000 damages. The city of Lowell was recently made to pay $6,000 to two travelers who had broken their legs by such an accident. The judge charged that the plaintiffs should not only be reimbursed for the expenses of the cure, but also for the estimated probable earnings of their industry during the length of the treatment.

Among us, it is not money, but honor, that occupies the most conspicuous place. If it be admitted that the sentiment of honor lies at the foundation of monarchies, and if everything turn upon this ideal principle, well enough. The principle of honor is quite as good in every view, logically, morally, or practically, as the principle of money. It is, indeed, more congenial to the generosity of the French character; but then it is necessary that honor should be real, that the proof it gives should be incontestable. The authority which is the source of honor must itself be respected. If the supreme authority is insulted and despised, public office has a title, not to respect, but to insult. If jealousy and suspicion of power are admitted and consecrated by the modern spirit of legislation and administration, is it not true that your pretended recompense of public service by the consideration and dignity they confer is a mockery, and that your whole system is founded upon a contradiction? If royalty still sat all-powerful on the magnificent throne of Versailles, amid its guards glittering with steel and gold, surrounded by the most brilliant court which history records and by the fascinations with which the homage of the arts invested it; or if the prince, savior of his country, surrounded by the banners of victory, still gave his orders to the world from the palace of vassal kings, or from the Schoenbrunn of conquered Kaisers; if he crowned and uncrowned kings as our ministers now make and unmake subprefects; if at a breath of his mouth victorious veterans calmly met death; if the world did him homage; if he were the anointed of the Lord, the choice and idol of the people; if you had yet the monarchy of **Louis XIV**, or of **Napoleon**, you would be welcome to speak of consideration and honor! It was then distinction enough to be noticed by a royal look. The favor of the sovereign then secured the confidence or at least the outward homage of the people. The point of precedence was worthy of being a subject of envy in the days of the splendor of Versailles, or when one might lose oneself in the crowd of kings in the Tuileries. But what does it signify nowadays, when royalty has lost its poetical attributes, when public ceremonies are abolished, when there is no longer a court or court dress? Titles have been profaned and degraded by the ignorance and stupidity of those who ought to have supported their dignity, or sullied by the jealousy of the commons. As for your ribands, you have been obliged to scatter them under the hoofs of horses. The system of honor is, therefore, gone by; to restore it a revolution would be necessary; not a revolution like that of July, but a revolution like that which was going on during the three centuries between Luther and Mirabeau and which, ripe at last, has been shaking both worlds during the last fifty years; a revolution in the name of authority, like that which our fathers accomplished in the name of liberty.

Among the sayings attributed to M. de Talleyrand, the following is often quoted: "I do not know an American that has not sold his horse or his dog." It is certain that the Americans are an exaggeration of the English, whom Napoleon called a nation of shopkeepers. The American is always bargaining; he always has one bargain afoot, another just finished, and two or three he's thinking of. All that he has, all that he sees, is merchandise in his eyes. The poetical associations which invest particular spots or objects with a character of sanctity have no place in his mind. The spire of his village church is no more than any other spire to him, and the finest, in his view, is the newest, the most freshly painted. To him a waterfall is simply water power for his machinery; an old building is a quarry of bricks and stones which he works without the least remorse. The Yankee will sell his father's house, like old clothes, old rags. As pioneer, it is his duty to attach himself to nothing, to no place, edifice, object, or person—except his wife, to whom he is indissolubly bound night and day from the moment of marriage till death parts them.

At the bottom, then, of all that an American does is money; behind every word, money. But it would be a mistake to suppose that he is not capable of making pecuniary sacrifices. He is in the habit of subscribing to all useful objects and he does so without reluctance or regret, more than we are accustomed to do and more liberally also; but his munificence and his donations are systematic and calculated. It is neither enthusiasm nor passion that unties his purse strings, but motives of policy or considerations of propriety, views of utility and regard for the public good in which he feels his own private interests to be involved. The American, therefore, admits some exceptions to his general commercial rule of conduct. He gives money, he attends committee meetings, he draws up in haste a report or an opinion. He even goes in person, in great haste, to Washington to present a set of resolutions to the President, or he hurries to a neighboring city to attend a public dinner and returns as quickly; but he requires in this case that the exception to the general rule should be sharply defined and the cause strongly marked, that the public interest should be at stake. And he particularly insists that the sacrifice should be of money only, once and for all, and that his time should be respected. To everything of a private nature, to everything that takes up his time and demands his attention, he applies the mercantile principle, nothing for nothing. He pays the services of others with dollars and he expects others to do the same by him because he looks upon compliments as too hollow and light to be put in the scale against labor, and because distinctions, as for instance precedence, are unknown and incomprehensible to him. With him it is an indisputable maxim that the laborer is worthy of his hire. The ideas of service and salary are so inseparably connected in his mind that in American almanacs it is common to see the rate of pay annexed to the lists of public officers. He is of opinion that nobody can live on a dry crust and glory; he thinks of the welfare of his wife and children, of provision for his old age, and if he were told that there is a country in which these considerations are disregarded for the purpose of obliging a neighbor or paying courtesy to a magistrate, such a thing would appear absurd to him.

In France, our customs are those of a society of idlers where minutes have no value and one can do nothing better with his time than to oblige his neighbor. Apart from the prejudices of a narrow liberalism by which we have shown ourselves too often to be dominated but which cannot prevent our true nature from breaking through, we are carried away by the attention of a superior, we are elated by social distinctions. Twenty years ago the French risked their lives for a scrap of ribbon. Such we have been, such we continue to be. We will never be Americanized; I might even suppose that the time is not far off when the Americans will make themselves over in some degree in our style; but can we not, should we not, change our ideas up to a certain point in the light of their experience?

Our system of free public service assumes that France has a sufficiently considerable number of men of great wealth and liberal education to allow the government or the electors a certain latitude in their choices. Such is not the case. France is a poor country. The growth of wealth in some commercial centers, scattered here and there in the world and in nearly all of England, and the refinements of civilization as a consequence of this rise in the standard of living, have remarkably extended the list of basic necessities for all classes. You are pinched today on an income that would have made you fabulously wealthy a hundred years ago and well off thirty years ago. Transport, then, Madame de Sévigné, with her ten thousands in rents, to the midst of our great balls or even into our Parisian salons! The best-provided class in three fourths of France has meanwhile the ten thousands of Madame de Sévigné. I do not speak here of the mass which swirls around this aristocracy; the very idea of so much misery makes my blood run cold. Take away Paris and four or five large cities and you can count the number of wealthy people on your fingers. They do not form a class. Actually, as for classes which are spread over our entire country, we have none which has raised itself above a modest level of competence. It is true that among those who are well off gentlemen of leisure abound and it would seem that the government could hardly choose among them. Unhappily, these men of leisure, by the very fact that they are and always have been men of leisure, because they have been raised amid the ideas and the atmosphere of the leisure class, are unable to administer and direct the affairs which are dominant today, the affairs of industry and labor. A literary education is common among them, but a broad liberal training is very rare. Men of this class have seen very little; they know Rome and Greece, but they ignore Europe as it now stands and, with good reason, the world as it is; they are strangers to the real and actual condition of France herself.

One could understand the advocates of a system of voluntary services if they were partisans of the aristocracy, if they wished to weed out men of little talent from the administration of the country, and if they wished to gather all influence to the increase of wealth; but, on the contrary, they are the apostles of liberalism, the defenders of equality. Sincere friends of the poor, I am sure, they have it in their heads that the best way to lessen the burden of the people is to reduce public expenditures; for them, every reduction in public office is a victory, every abolition of a public office a great conquest. That is why they have been so proud when framing municipal laws to insert an article forbidding mayors to receive anything from the town, whatever title they bear. The major cities used to allow their mayors indemnities to defray the costs of their office and other expenses. It was just, not only because the functions of mayor in a large city are difficult to fulfill, taking all the energy of a man, leaving him no time to pursue his own affairs, but also because the task of being mayor commits the office-holder to a thousand expenses which our parliamentary economists in their metaphysical empyrean have never dreamed of. It was deplorable to take away these indemnities the morning after a Revolution which was accomplished despite the great property-holders of France, who, as a consequence, necessarily separated themselves from public service. It was then, at a time of terrible crisis, that the municipal offices in our great cities such as Lyons, Marseilles, Rouen, and Bordeaux needed men of mind and spirit at any price. Meanwhile our rigorous paring of the budget carried everything away, and if no one could be found in our great cities to take charge of municipal affairs, if our leaders had to hawk these offices in the street to any takers, it is to them that the major share of the blame belongs.

High pay is, however, repugnant to democracy because it is incapable of discerning its propriety. The worker who makes $500 a year thinks himself generous toward a public officer to whom he gives $1,500 or $2,000; just as our citizens of the middling class in Paris who have an income of 10,000 francs cannot see why a public functionary should not be content with 12,000. The Americans thought that among them, as elsewhere, there would be two kinds of coin: money and public consideration. They were persuaded, on the authority of Franklin, that it would be easy to find able public officers whose salary should chiefly consist in the honor of public station. They were mistaken. Office is here no title to respect, but quite the contrary; as public services are neither paid by dollars nor consideration, only a Hobson's choice is left to the people. With the exception of a small number of places which the delights of power still cause to be sought after, notwithstanding the cost of the pleasure of commanding and having dependents or subordinates, office is generally sought for only by the floating part of the population which has been unsuccessful in business and tried one occupation after another in vain. It is not even, strictly speaking, a profession, but rather the temporary resort of persons who have no settled pursuit, who, as soon as they find better employment in industry or speculation, take leave of the state. The West Point Academy sends out about forty lieutenants for the army annually; about one third of these resign their commissions before two or three years of service because the pay of the officers, although much higher than with us, is quite inconsiderable compared with the profits of a merchant or the salary of an engineer.

The duties of a public officer are generally less difficult in the United States than in France. Among us every question that arises embraces a great complication of interests and requires more knowledge. The powers and duties of the government in France are much more extensive and more various, and more care is required of persons in the public employ among us, than in this country. Yet the average of salaries here is much greater than with us. When the Congress and the States shall stand in need of able men for functionaries, they will do as the American merchants do to their clerks, they will pay them. Congress, having lately become sensible of the importance of securing the services of good naval officers, has just raised the pay of that corps. It may even be said that the number of office-holders who are treated with illiberality is very small. They are the governors of most of the States and the heads of the executive departments at Washington. The latter receive only $6,000, and they are obliged to keep up a certain style of living. Out of 158 persons employed in the service of the Treasury Department at Washington, there are only six who receive less than $1,000; it is true that there are only two who receive more than $2,000; this is the application of the principle of equality to salary. As the price of common objects of consumption, that is, bread, meat, coffee, tea, sugar, and fuel, is generally lower in the United States than in France and especially in Paris, a salary of $1,500 or $2,000 is sufficient in most cases to support a family in comfort and abundance. An officer of the government who receives from $400 to $600 in Paris lives only by practicing the strictest economy if he is a bachelor, and suffers great privations if he is a married man. At Washington he would receive from $1,000 to $1,200 and would live in abundance and comfort, if not in style and luxury. Nor would he here, as with us, be condemned to the punishment of Tantalus, for the pomp and splendor of the privileged classes in the European capitals is unknown in the United States. In Paris, the wage-earner is spattered with mud by the equipage of a man who spends his $20,000 a year; in the streets of Philadelphia, he would elbow a rich capitalist who kept no coach because he would not know what to do with it and who, with a revenue of $30,000 or $60,000, cannot spend more than $8,000 or $10,000 at the most. The ratio of conditions which in Paris is as 1 to 40 is here not more than 1 to 8.

Here the condition of the richest merchant and that of a mechanic and a farmer are not essentially different; the difference is merely in degree and not in kind. All have similar houses, built on a similar plan; only one has a front five or six feet wider and is one or two stories higher; the arrangement of the rooms and the furniture are the same. All have carpets from the cellar to the garret, all sleep in large high-post bedsteads very much like each other, projecting out into a chamber without closets, alcoves, or double door, and with bare walls; only the carpets of the one are coarse and those of the other are fine, the bedstead of the rich is of mahogany and that of the mechanic of cherry or walnut. In general the table is served much alike; there is the same number of meals and there is nearly the same number of dishes. This is so much the case that if my French palate had to decide between the dinner of a great city hotel (excepting those of Boston, New York, Philadelphia, and Baltimore) and a country inn where I should sit by the side of the blacksmith of the place, with sooty visage and with sleeves rolled up, I think that I should really choose the latter. This is especially the case in the North, particularly in New England, the land of the Yankees. In the South, the condition of the planter on his estate gains all that is taken from the mass of the population, the slaves. And lately in the North, the commerce which has collected men into large cities has also accumulated capital in single hands and created great fortunes. The inequality of condition is, therefore, beginning to manifest itself; the style of the new houses in Chestnut Street, Philadelphia, with their first story of white marble, is a blow at equality. The same innovation is creeping in in New York; the antidemocratic tendency of commerce is revealing itself.

I am often humiliated here by what I hear said about the mean spirit in which part of our commercial dealings are carried on and which loses for us the esteem of people quite readily disposed to admire and to like us, like the people of the southern part of the United States. I console myself always with the thought that, if abroad we give some region reason to believe that we are a faithless and lawless people, at home there is abundant proof that there are no people richer in selflessness and virtue. In what country of the world have there ever been magistrates more pure? Even in this century of universal hostility not a breath of suspicion can be aired against them. With what impartiality is justice not done among us by judges paid at the rate of 1,200 francs, by presidents at 1,800 francs and senators at 3,000 francs! If from the courts we turn to the army, we have officers who have gold and silver only on their epaulets and who still remain honest and devoted; I say nothing of their courage, which the world knows well enough. Consider again this navy of ours, which in foreign ports affirms the honor of our flag, not by the sumptuous parties it gives, but by its order and discipline; and our civil and military engineers who handle enormous sums and are content with their modest pittance, without even the honor of resisting temptation because they could never conceive of it; and, even in the civil administration, that crowd of modest employees who have not, like others, the inexpensive charm of study to sweeten their poverty or the deep benefits of high education to make them scorn the seduction of shady deals, whose probity never even falters. Throughout a society where luxury and temptation cry out everywhere, all of them stick by their conscience without ever letting themselves drift against the rock of corruption. It is one of the glories of France, a glory of which France is not sufficiently proud.

But the question to answer is not if this state of affairs is honorable, but if it can last if we do not prepare for the future, if we do not change in the midst of a society of new customs and new ideas which, in a short time now, will render old ways impracticable.

The great revolution which has been going on for the last three hundred years and which has changed the religious faith of half the world has finally, in politics and philosophy, laid hold of France, which had escaped it since the time of Luther and Calvin. The Reformation, expanding its influence more and more, has invaded the material basis of society. One fruit of the intellectual revolution is that work, in all its forms, now gives abundantly to all the rewards which formerly went only to a small number, an imperceptible minority. The circle of wealth has expanded tenfold, that of modest competence a hundredfold. One has only to open his eyes to see a new order of things coming in all corners of the world, an order where agriculture, manufactures, and commerce, infinitely more vigorous and better organized than our forefathers could ever imagine, will be infinitely more productive and where a much fairer distribution of goods will call the great majority, if not all mankind, to the delights of sharing in the consumption of things.

But will this industrial and material revolution not react on morality? The day when it is possible for all to find the way to wealth or ease through work, will abstinence and poverty remain to support those high virtues needed for advancement in the world? Can we then continue to make voluntary service to the state a permanent law? Would that be reasonable? Would it be possible? Public servants do not consist of an inferior order of beings, living apart, detached from the interests and feelings of this earth; they are men of the world with mundane desires. They have wives and children they wish to do well by; they have the right to make as much as the merchant, the banker, the notary, the ironmaster, the doctor, the lawyer, the painter, the composer, or the actor.

France, I repeat, is a poor country. Outside of our great cities and in some areas in the North where public wealth has developed and where luxury and consumption have followed the same progressive law, the condition of most of our public servants is still tolerable. With their appointments at 1,500, 2,000, or 3,000 francs, in many of the provinces they are on top of the world. They only sense their poverty when they move outside their usual milieu and especially when, showing their faces abroad, they come in contact with the English. But when the material base of society has developed in France, when, by the establishment of public and private credit, by the creation of new means of communication, by the reform of education, one can direct his energies toward agricultural, commercial, and manufacturing callings; when the springs of wealth have been multiplied and many will be able to draw from them, from what right and under what pretext can one then impose a life of sacrifice on our public servants, on them and their families? Those who today are resigned to straitened circumstances will then demand ease and comfort. Then, to pay them cheaply or to keep them content, it would be necessary to take into public service men who are the cast-offs of all the other professions. The elite of French youth still compete for the modest state appointments of civil and military engineers and spend eight years of apprenticeship in college, polytechnic school, and practical training in order to reach the grade of lieutenant in the artillery or the engineer corps, or assistant engineer in public works or mines, with salaries of 1,500 to 1,800 francs and the prospect of 6,000 to 8,000 francs after twenty-five years of service. But tomorrow when industry is undergoing great advances, the most capable of these young men will desert service to the state once their education is finished, like those thousands of West Point students. They will seek careers in industry, unless the state decides to treat them better in order to hold on to them.

Our parsimonious habits were born in the midst of a reaction against the principle of authority, a reaction which was legitimate, considering the abuse of power. When rulers affected to believe that the people had been created only to be ruled and exploited, the people had reason to treat them in their turn as parasitic excrescences on society. Every salary paid then was tribute paid to an enemy. The present condition of our public servants, with respect to their material condition and their social status, is then one of the effects of a revolutionary crisis which, I believe, is reaching its end. When society has once again taken up its normal course of advance, when rulers have proved that they are worthy to lead the people, the people who are led will give them their support and will put an end to their hostility against them.

It might be expected that among a people so deeply absorbed in material pursuits misers would abound, but it is not so. There is never any niggardliness in a Southerner; it is sometimes found in the Yankee, but nowhere, North or South, do you see specimens of that sordid avarice of which examples are so common among us. The American has too high a notion of the dignity of human nature to be willing to deprive himself and his children of those comforts which soften the asperities of life; he respects his own person too much not to surround it with a certain degree of decency. Harpagon is never to be met with in the United States and yet Harpagon is not by a great deal the most wretchedly degraded miser that European society exhibits. The American is devoured with a passion for money, not because he finds pleasure in hoarding it up, but because wealth is power, because it is the lever by which he governs nature. I ought also to do the Americans justice on another point. I have said that with them everything was an affair of money; yet there is one thing which among us, a people of lively affections, prone to love and generous by nature, takes the mercantile character very decidedly and which among them has nothing of this character; I mean marriage. We buy a woman with our fortune or we sell ourselves to her for her dowry. The American chooses her, or rather offers himself to her, for her beauty, her intelligence, or her amiable qualities and asks no other portion. Thus, while we make a traffic of what is most sacred, these shopkeepers exhibit a delicacy and loftiness of feeling which would have done honor to the most perfect models of chivalry. It is to industry that they are indebted for this superiority. Our idle cits, not being able to increase their patrimony, are obliged in taking a wife to calculate her portion in order to decide if their joint income will be enough to support a family. The American, having the taste and the habits of industry, is sure of being able to provide amply for his household and is, therefore, free from the necessity of making this melancholy calculation. Is it possible to doubt that a race of men which thus combines in a high degree the most contradictory qualities, is reserved for lofty destinies?

XXV

Speculations

Speculations in Land, Railroads, and Banks — Speculation Fills a Need for Americans; They Find Excitement in It — Unsettled Condition of Everything in the United States — Workers' Organizations — Inevitable Progress in the Material Conditions of Civilization — Inconveniences Attending Excessive Innovating Force

Johnstown (Pennsylvania), August 4, 1835. The present aspect of this country is in a high degree calculated to encourage the friends of peace in their hopes and wishes with respect to a rupture with France. The Americans of all parties conduct themselves in their private affairs like men who are convinced that business will experience no interruption from that quarter. A person who landed at New York, Boston, or Philadelphia on the day that news was received of the effect produced in France by the President's message, and had since played Epimenides, would not now recognize the United States; the most unlimited confidence has succeeded the general anxiety. Everybody is speculating and everything has become an object of speculation. The most daring enterprises find encouragement; all projects find subscribers. From Maine to the Red River, the whole country has become an immense *rue Quincampoix*. Thus far everyone has made money, as is always the case when speculation is in the ascendant. Since with money it is easy come, easy go, spending is enormously increased and Lyons feels the effect.

I said that everything has become an object of speculation; I was mistaken. The American, essentially practical in his views, will never speculate in tulips, even at New York although the inhabitants of that city have Dutch blood in their veins. The principal objects of speculation are those subjects which chiefly occupy the calculating minds of the Americans, that is to say, cotton, land, city and town lots, banks, railroads.

The lovers of land in the North contest with each other for valuable timberlands; in the deep South, for Mississippi swamps and Alabama and Red River cotton lands; in the far West, for the cornfields and pastures of Illinois and Michigan. The unparalleled growth of some new towns has turned people's heads and there is a general rush to any location which is fortunately situated; as if, before ten years, three or four Londons, as many Parises, and a dozen Liverpools were about to display their streets, their monuments, their quays crowded with warehouses, and their harbors bristling with masts in the American wilderness. In New York enough building lots (a lot is generally from 22 to 25 feet front, and from 80 to 100 feet deep) have been sold for a population of two million; at New Orleans, for at least a million. Pestilential marshes and naked precipices of rock have been bought and sold as places to build. In Louisiana, the quagmires, the bottomless haunts of alligators, the lakes and cypress swamps, with ten feet of water or slime, and in the North, the bed of the Hudson with twenty, thirty, or fifty feet of water, have found numerous purchasers.

Take the map of the United States; place yourself on the shore of Lake Erie, which twenty years ago was a solitary wilderness; ascend it to its head; pass thence to Lake St. Clair and from that lake push on toward the north, across Lake Huron; go forward still, thread your way through Lake Michigan and advance southward till the water fails you; here you will find a little town by the name of Chicago, one of the outposts of our indefatigable countrymen when they had possession of America. Chicago seems destined at some future period to enjoy an extensive trade; it will occupy the head of a canal which will connect the Mississippi with the Lakes and the St. Lawrence; but at present it hardly numbers two or three thousand inhabitants. Chicago has behind it a country of amazing fertility; but this country is yet an uncultivated wilderness. Nevertheless the land for twenty-five miles around has been sold, resold and sold again in small sections, not, however, at Chicago, but at New York which by the route actually traveled is two thousand miles away. There you may find plans of enough Chicago lots for three hundred thousand inhabitants; this is more than any city of the New World at present contains. Surely, more than one buyer will count himself fortunate if, on examination, he finds no more than six feet of water on his purchase.

Speculations in railroads have been hardly less wild than those in land. The American has a perfect passion for railroads; he loves them, to use Camille Desmoulins' expression in reference to Mirabeau, as a lover loves his mistress. It is not merely because his supreme happiness consists in that speed which annihilates time and space; it is also because he sees, for the American always reasons, that this mode of communication is admirably adapted to the vast extent of his country, to its great maritime plain and to the level surface of the Mississippi valley, and because he sees all around him in the native forest abundant materials for executing these works at a cheap rate. This is the reason why railroads are multiplied in such profusion, competing not only with each other but entering into a rivalry with the rivers and canals. If the works now in process of construction are completed (and I think that they will be), there will be within two years three distinct routes between Philadelphia and Baltimore, exclusive of the old post route; namely, two lines consisting wholly of railroads, and a third consisting in part of steamboats and in part of railroad. The line that has the advantage of half an hour over its rivals will be sure to crush them.

The manner of establishing banks, universally adopted here (it is the same for all enterprises which affect the public welfare, even when they are handed over to private enterprise), is this: a legislative act authorizes the opening of books for public subscription of stock and all persons have the right to subscribe on payment of a certain sum, say five, ten, or twenty per cent on the amount of stock taken by them. The day the books are opened is a matter of great moment. In France, we queue up at the doors of the theaters; but in the United States, this year, lines of deeply anxious people form at the doors of those special places where the books for subscription to bank stocks are deposited. In Baltimore the books were opened for a new bank, the Merchants' Bank, with a capital of 2 million; the amount subscribed was nearly 50 million. At Charleston, for a bank of the same capital, 90 million was subscribed and, as the act in this instance required the advance of 25 per cent, the sum actually paid in, in paper money to be sure, but yet in current bills at par, amounted to 22½ million, or more than 11 times the capital required. This rage for bank stock is easily explained. Most of the banks here are, in fact, irresponsible establishments which have the privilege of coining money from paper. The shareholders, by means of a series of ingenious contrivances, realize 8, 9, 10, and 12 per cent interest on capital which they do not actually hold; and this in a country where the 5 per cents of Pennsylvania and New York and the 6 per cents of Ohio are at 110 to 115. The Ohio sixes! What would the heroes of Fort Duquesne think of that, if they should come back?

Most of these speculations are imprudent, many of them are foolish. The boom today may and must be followed by a crisis tomorrow. Great fortunes, and many of them too, have sprung out of the earth since the spring; others will, perhaps, return to it before the fall. The American does not worry about that. Violent sensations are necessary to stir his vigorous nerves. Public opinion and the pulpit forbid sensual gratifications, wine, women, and the display of a princely luxury; cards and dice are equally prohibited; the American, therefore, has recourse to business for the strong emotions which he requires to make him feel life. He launches with delight into the ever-moving sea of speculation. One day, the wave raises him to the clouds; he enjoys in haste the moment of triumph. The next day he disappears between the crests of the billows; he is little troubled by the reverse; he bides his time coolly and consoles himself with the hope of better fortune. In the midst of all this speculation, while some enrich and some ruin themselves, banks spring up and diffuse credit; railroads and canals extend themselves over the country; steamboats are launched into the rivers, the lakes, and the sea; the career of the speculators is ever enlarging, the field for railroads, canals, steamers, and banks goes on expanding. Some individuals lose, but the country is a gainer; the country is peopled, cleared, cultivated; its resources are unfolded, its wealth increased. *Go ahead!*

If movement and the quick succession of sensations and ideas constitute life, here one lives a hundredfold more than elsewhere; here, all is circulation, motion, and boiling agitation. Experiment follows experiment; enterprise follows enterprise. Riches and poverty follow on each other's traces and each in turn occupies the place of the other. While the great men of one day dethrone those of the past, they are already half overturned themselves by those of the morrow. Fortunes last for a season; reputations for the twinkling of an eye. An irresistible current sweeps everything away, grinds everything to powder and deposits it again under new forms. Men change their houses, their climate, their trade, their condition, their party, their sect; the States change their laws, their officers, their constitutions. The soil itself, or at least the houses, partake in the universal instability. The existence of social order in the bosom of this whirlpool seems a miracle, an inexplicable anomaly. One is tempted to think that such a society, formed of heterogeneous elements, brought together by chance, each following its own orbit according to the impulse of its own caprice or interest—one would think that after rising for one moment to the heavens, like a waterspout, such a society would inevitably fall flat in ruins the next; such is not, however, its destiny. Amid this general change there is one fixed point; it is the domestic fireside, or, to speak more clearly, the conjugal bed. An austere watchman, sometimes harsh even to fanaticism, wards off from this sacred spot everything that can disturb its stability; that guardian is religious sentiment. While that fixed point shall remain untouched, while that sentinel shall persist in his vigilant watch over it, the social system may make new somersaults and undergo new changes without serious risk; it may be pelted by the storm, but while it is made fast to that anchorage, it will neither split nor sink. It may even be broken up into different groups nearly independent of one another, but it will expand across the earth, it will still grow in energy, in resources, in extent.

The influence of the democracy is so universal in this country that it was quite natural for it to raise its head among speculators. There have, therefore, been strikes on the part of workmen who wish to share in the profits of speculation and who have demanded higher wages and less work. The demand for higher pay is just since all provisions, all articles of consumption, have risen in price. These coalitions are by no means timid in this country; the English practice of haranguing in public and getting up processions prevails here and the working class feels its strength, is conscious of its power, and knows how to make use of it. The different trades have held meetings in Philadelphia, New York, and other places, discussed their affairs publicly, and set forth their demands. The women have had their meeting as well as the men. That of the seamstresses of Philadelphia attracted notice; Matthew Carey, known as a political writer, presided, assisted by two clergymen. Among the various demands one might point out is that of the journeymen bakers who, by virtue of the rights of man and the sanctity of the seventh day, would not make bread Sundays. The principal trades have decided that all work shall be suspended until the masters, if this name can be applied here except in derision, have acceded to their ultimatum. That everyone may know this, they have published their resolutions in the newspapers, signed by the president and secretaries of the meeting. These resolutions declare that those workmen who shall refuse to conform to their provisions will have to abide the consequences of their refusal. The consequences have been that those refractory workmen who persisted in working have been driven with stones and clubs from their workshops without any interference on the part of the magistrates. The consequence is that, at this very moment, a handful of boatmen on the Schuylkill Canal prevent the coal boats from descending to the sea, lay an embargo upon them, and thus interrupt one of the most lucrative branches of the Pennsylvania trade, deprive the mariners and shipowners who transport the coal to all parts of the coast of wages and freights and expose the miners to the danger of being dismissed from the mines. Meanwhile the militia looks on; the sheriff stands with folded arms. If this minority of boatmen—for these acts of disorder are the work of a small minority—persists in their plans, a fight between them and the miners is conceivable. In Philadelphia, the consequence has been that the carpenters in order to reduce some contractors to terms have set fire to several houses which were being built. This time the authorities at length interfered, the mayor issued a proclamation reciting that, whereas there is reason to believe these fires to be the work of some evil-minded persons, he offers $1,000 reward to whoever shall disclose the authors of the same. But it is too late. The municipal authorities, for the purpose, it is said, of gaining a few votes on the side of the Opposition, instead of interposing their power between the workmen and the masters, hastened from the first to comply with all the demands of the former, who were employed on the municipal works.

The philosopher, in whose eyes the present is but a point, may find reason to rejoice in considering these facts. Workmen and domestics in Europe live in a state of nearly absolute dependence which is favorable only to him who commands. Monarchists, republicans, the classes in between, all comport themselves toward the worker they employ or the domestic in their service as if he were a being of an inferior nature who owes his master all his zeal and all his efforts, but who has no claim on any return beyond a miserable pittance of wages. One may be permitted to wish for the establishment of a juster scale of rights and duties. In the United States—the absolute principle of the popular sovereignty having been applied to the relations of master and servant, of employer and operative—the manufacturer, the contractor, and the entrepreneur, to whom the workmen give the law, endeavor to dispense with their aid as much as possible by substituting more and more machinery for human force; thus the most painful processes in the arts become less burdensome to the human race. The master, whose domestics obey him when they please and who pays dear for being badly and ungraciously served, favors, to the extent of his power, the introduction of mechanical contrivances for simplifying work in order to spare himself the inconveniences of such a dependence.

It would be worth while to study not only the great manufacturing machinery, but the common hand tools and domestic utensils in this country. These utensils, tools, and machines exert a powerful influence upon the practical liberty of the greatest number; it is by means of them that the most numerous class of society gradually frees itself from the yoke which tends to crush and abase it. In this point of view, what goes on here between employer and employee, between master and servant, tends to hasten the coming of a future which every friend of humanity must hail with joy. But if philosophical satisfaction is amply present, physical comfort is almost absolutely wanting. Whoever is neither operative nor domestic, whoever, especially, has tasted and enjoyed the life of the cultivated classes in Europe will find the actual practical life in America, the mere bone and muscle, as it were, of life, to consist of a series of jars, disappointments, mortifications—I had almost said, of humiliations. The independence of the workers is sometimes the ruin of the employers; the independence of servants involves the dependence of the women, condemns them to household labors little consonant with the finished education which many of them have received, and nails them to the kitchen and the nursery from the day of their marriage to the day of their death.

When the force of innovation, acting without check or balance, operates with an excess of energy, all classes suffer equally from the derangement. Not only what in Europe are called the higher classes (but which here must take another name) are deprived of a thousand little enjoyments which it is a matter of convention to despise in books and set speeches, although everyone sets a high value on them in practice; but the whole social machine gets out of order, discomfort becomes general, and the extravagant claims of the lower classes, to speak as a European, recoil violently on themselves. At this very moment, for example, the Sybarites of Philadelphia whose hearts are set upon having fresh bread on Sunday are not the only persons who suffer or are threatened with suffering. If the exaggerated pretensions of the working classes are persisted in, the market will decline, there will be no demand for labor. Speculations, if not made solid by labor, will burst like soap bubbles and, if a reaction comes, the operative, who is little used to economize, will feel it more forcibly than others.

XXVI

Bedford Springs

Exclusiveness — Religious Festivals Formerly Democratic Festivals — Political Processions — Camp Meetings — Role of Women in Camp Meetings and in Roman Catholic Festivals — Suppression of Popular Festivals in Europe — Influence of the Philosophy of the Eighteenth Century on All Which Touches the Imagination — Inability of the Parliamentary Regime — Struggle Between the Young, the Middle-Aged, and the Old in France — Kinds of Satisfaction the Imagination Finds in England and in the United States

Bedford Springs (Pennsylvania), August 7, 1835. Here I am at Bedford, one of the American watering places; it is hardly three days since I arrived and I am already in haste to quit it. American men and, still more especially, American women must be desperately listless at home to be willing to exchange its quiet comfort for the stupid bustle and dull wretchedness of such a resort.

It would seem that in a truly democratic country, as is the case here in the Northern States, nothing like our watering places could exist; and you will see that in proportion as Europe grows democratic, if such is its destiny, your delightful summer resorts will lose their charm. Man is naturally exclusive; there are few pleasures which do not cease to be such the moment they become accessible to all, and for that reason only. At Saratoga or at Bedford, the American soon grows weary because he sees that there are twenty thousand heads of families in Philadelphia and New York who can, as well as he, if the notion seizes them—and it actually does seize them—have the satisfaction of bringing their wives and daughters to the same place and, once there, of gaping from a chair on the piazza the whole day; of going fully armed (I mean with knife and fork) to secure their share of a wretched dinner; of being stifled in a crowded ballroom during the evening; and of sleeping, if it is possible in the midst of such a hubbub, upon a miserable pallet in a cell echoing one's tread from its floor of pine boards. The American passes through the magnificent landscapes on the Hudson without noticing them because he is one of six hundred or a thousand on board the steamer. And to confess the truth, I have become an American myself in this respect and admired the panorama of West Point and the Highlands only when I found myself alone in my boat on the river.

Democracy is too much a newcomer in the world to have been able as yet to organize its pleasures and its amusements. In Europe, our pleasures are essentially exclusive, they are aristocratic like Europe itself, and cannot, therefore, be at the command and for the use of the multitude. In this matter, then, as in politics, American democracy must create everything anew. The problem is difficult, but it is not insoluble, for it was once solved by us. The religious festivals of the Catholic Church were eminently democratic; all were called to them, all took part in them. To what transports of joy did not all Europe, great and small, nobles, burgesses, and serfs, give itself up in the time of the Crusades, when the victory of Antioch or the capture of Jerusalem was celebrated by processions and *Te Deums*? Even to this day in our southern provinces, where faith is not yet extinct, there are still ceremonies which are truly popular; such are the festival of Easter with the representations of the Passion exhibited in the churches, and the processions with banners and crosses, the brotherhoods of penitents with their quaint frocks and flowing robes, and the long files of women and children; with the effigies of the saints in full dress, and their relics piously carried about; and, finally, with the military and civil pomp which, notwithstanding the atheism of the law, is mingled with the show. This is the poor man's spectacle and one which leaves on his mind better and more vivid recollections than the atrocious street dramas and the fireworks before the king's castle leave on the common people of Paris.

Already democracy, especially in the Western States, is beginning to have its festivals which thrill its fibers and stir it with agreeable emotions. There are religious festivals, the Methodist camp meetings, where the people go with delight, despite the philosophical objections of other more middle-class sects who find fault with their heated zeal and noisy ranting, and despite, or rather in consequence of, the convulsive and hysterical scenes of the *anxious bench*. In the older States of the North there are political processions, pure party demonstrations for the most part, but which are interesting in that the democracy has a share in them; for it is the Democratic party that gets up the most brilliant and animated. Besides the camp meetings, the political processions are the only things in this country which bear any resemblance to festivals. The party dinners with their speeches and deluge of toasts are frigid, if not repulsive; for example, I have never seen a more miserable affair than the dinner given by the Opposition, that is to say, by the middle class, at Powelton, in the neighborhood of Philadelphia. But I stopped involuntarily at the sight of the gigantic hickory poles which made their solemn entry on eight wheels for the purpose of being planted by the democracy on the eve of the election. I remember one of these poles, its top still crowned with green foliage, which came on to the sound of fifes and drums and was preceded by ranks of Democrats, bearing no other badge than a twig of the sacred tree in their hats. It was drawn by eight horses, decorated with ribands and mottoes. Astride the tree itself were a dozen Jackson men of the first water, waving flags with an air of anticipated triumph and shouting, *Hurrah for Jackson!*

But this parade of the hickory tree was but a by-matter compared with the procession I witnessed in New York. It was the night after the closing of the polls when victory had gone to the Democratic party. (See Chapter XV.) The procession was nearly a mile long; the Democrats marched in good order to the glare of torches; the banners were more numerous than I had ever seen in any religious festival; all were transparencies on account of the darkness. On some were inscribed the names of the Democratic societies or sections; *Democratic young men of the ninth* or *eleventh ward;* others bore imprecations against the Bank of the United States; *Nick Biddle* and *Old Nick* were shown, more or less ingeniously, doing business together; it was their form of our banner with the prayer, "Deliver us from evil." Then came portraits of General Jackson afoot and on horseback; there was one in the uniform of a general and another in the person of the Tennessee farmer with the famous hickory cane in his hand. Portraits of Washington and Jefferson, surrounded with Democratic mottoes, were mingled with emblems in all designs and colors. Among these figured an eagle—not a painting, but a real live eagle —tied by the legs, surrounded by a wreath of leaves and hoisted upon a pole, after the manner of the Roman standards. The imperial bird was carried by a stout sailor, more pleased than was ever any city magistrate permitted to hold one of the cords of the canopy in a Catholic ceremony. Farther than the eye could reach the Democrats came marching on. I was struck with the resemblance of their air to the train that escorts the Eucharist in Mexico or Puebla. The American standard-bearers were as grave as the Mexican Indians who bore the sacred candles. The Democratic procession, also like the Catholic procession, had its halting places; it stopped before the houses of Jackson men to fill the air with cheers and before the doors of the leaders of the Opposition to give three, six, or nine groans. If these scenes were to find a painter, they would be admired at some distant day no less than the triumphs and sacrificial pomps which the ancients have left us in marble and brass. For this is something more than the grotesque fashion of scenes immortalized by Rembrandt; this belongs to history, it belongs to the sublime; these are episodes of a wondrous epic which will bequeath a lasting memory to posterity, the memory of the coming of democracy.

Yet, as festivals and spectacles, these processions are much inferior to the revivals which take place in camp meetings. All festivals and ceremonies in which women do not take part are incomplete. Why is it that our constitutional ceremonies are so entirely devoid of interest? It is not because the actors are merely *bourgeois* citizens, respectable surely, but prosaic, and that the pomp of costumes and the fascination of the arts are banished from them; it is rather because women do not and cannot have a place in them. A wit has said that women are not poets, but they are poetry itself.

I remember what made the charm and the attraction of the processions in my provincial city. We opened our eyes with wonder at the red robe of the chief president; we gazed with delight at the epaulets and gold lace of the general, and more than one youth was inspired with military ardor on that day; we stretched forward with impatience to catch a glimpse of the episcopal train; we threw ourselves on our knees instinctively on the approach of the canopy with its escort of priests and the venerable bishop, crowned with the miter, bearing the host in his hands; we envied the glory of those boys who had the privilege of enacting St. Mark or St. Peter for the day; more than one tall stripling would have renounced his fifteen years, in which he prided himself, for the sake of assuming the character of St. John, clad in a sheepskin; but the whole multitude held their breath when, beneath the forest of banners, through the peaked frocks of the penitents and the bayonets of the garrison, amid the surplices and albs of the priests, there appeared in sight one of those young girls in white robes who represented the holy women and the Mother of the seven woes; or she, who in the person of St. Veronica displayed the handkerchief with which the sweat was wiped from the Savior's brow as he ascended Mount Calvary; or she who, loaded with gold chains, ribands, and pearls, represented the empress at the side of the emperor; or those who had just been confirmed by my lord bishop and still bore the traces of the emotions excited by that solemn act. So it is because there are women at the camp meetings and because they are as active as the most rousing preachers, it is on this account only that the American democracy throngs to these assemblages. The camp meetings with their delirious female oracles have made the fortune of the Methodists and attracted to their church in America a more numerous body of adherents than is numbered by any of the English sects in Europe.

Take women from the tournaments and these become nothing more than fencing bouts; take away the *anxious bench* from camp meetings, remove those women who fall into convulsions, shriek, and roll on the ground, who, pale, disheveled, and haggard, cling to the minister from whom they inhale the Holy Spirit; or seize the hardened sinner at the door of the tent, or in the passageway, and strive to melt his stony heart; it will be in vain that a majestic forest overshadows the scene of a beautiful summer's night, under a sky that need not fear comparison with a Grecian heaven; in vain will you be surrounded with tents and numberless chariots that recall to mind the long train of Israel fleeing from Egypt; in vain the distant fires, gleaming among the trees, will reveal the forms of the preachers gesticulating above the crowd; in vain will the echo of the woods fling back the tones of their voice; you will be weary of the spectacle in an hour. But camp meetings, as they are now conducted, have the power of holding the people of the West for whole weeks; some have lasted a month.

I allow that camp meetings and political processions are as yet only exceptions in America. A people has not a complete national character until it has its peculiar and appropriate amusements, national festivals, poetry. In this respect, it will not be easy to create an American nationality; the American has no past from which to draw inspiration. On quitting the old soil of Europe, on breaking off from England, his fathers left behind them the national chronicles, the traditions, the legends, all that constitutes country, that country which is not carried about on the soles of one's feet. The American, then, has become poor in ideality, in proportion as he has become rich in material wealth. But a democracy always has some resource, so far as imagination is concerned. I cannot pretend to decide how the American democracy will supply the want of a past and of old recollections, any more than I can undertake to pronounce in what manner it will bridle itself and curb its own humors. But I am sure that America will have her festivals, her ceremonies and her art, as I am sure that society in America will assume a regular organization; for I believe in the future of American society, or, to speak more correctly, of the beginnings of society, whose growth is visible on the east and still more on the west side of the Alleghenies.

In France for more than a century we have been struggling with ourselves in the attempt to lay aside our national character. We strive to become reasonable according to what we imagine to be the English pattern; after our example, southern Europeans endeavor to torture themselves into a parliamentary and calculating manner. Imagination is treated as lunatic. Noble sentiments, enthusiasm, chivalric loftiness of soul—all that made the glory of France and gave Spain half the world is regarded with contempt and derision. The public festivals and popular ceremonies have become the laughingstock of free thinkers. Love of the fine arts is nothing more than a frivolous passion. We make the most desperate efforts to starve the heart and soul, conformably to the prescriptions of our religious and political radicals. To strip life of the last vestige of taste and art, we have gone so far as to exchange the majestic elegance of costume which we borrowed from the Spaniards when they ruled Europe for the undress of the English, which may be described bluntly as suited only to the climate of Great Britain. This could be borne, if we had merely flung away our tournaments, our games, our jubilees, our religious festivals, our elegance of garb. But unhappily we have gone to the sources of all national and social poetry, to religion itself, and tried to dry them up. Our manners and customs scarcely retain the slightest tincture of their boasted grace. Politics is abandoned to the driest matter of fact. The national genius would have to be given over as past cure, did not now and then some gleams and outbursts prove that it is not dead but sleeps and that the holy fire is yet smoldering beneath the ashes.

France, and the peoples of southern Europe whom she leads, certainly owe much to the philosophy of the eighteenth century; for that was our Protestantism, that is to say that it raised the standard of liberty among us, opened a career for the progress of mind, and established individuality. But it must be confessed that it is inferior to German, English, and American Protestantism because it is irreligious. The writings of the Apostles of that great revolution will survive as literary monuments, but not as lessons of morality; whatever is irreligious can have but a transient social value. Place the remains of Voltaire and Montesquieu, of Rousseau and Diderot in the Pantheon; but on their monuments deposit their works veiled under a shroud. Teach the people to bless their memory; but do not teach them their doctrines and do not permit them to learn them from the servile followers whom those great writers, if they could return to the earth, would disavow; for men like them belong to the present or a future age, but never to the past.

In return for all that has been taken from us, we have received the representative system. This, it has been supposed, would satisfy all our wants, would meet all our wishes in moral and intellectual as well as in physical things. Far be it from me to undervalue the representative system! I believe in its permanence, although I doubt whether we have yet discovered the form under which it is suited to the character of the French and the southern Europeans; but whatever may be its political value, it cannot be denied that it does not, that it never can, of itself alone, make good the place of all that the reformers have robbed us of. It has its ceremonies and its festivals; but these smell too much of the parchment not to disgust our senses. It has, to a certain degree, its dogmas and its mysteries, but it has no hold on the imagination. Art has no sympathy with it; it has not the power to move the heart; and it embraces, therefore, but one fourth of our existence.

I can understand how here in America one could hope to make representative government the keystone of the social arch. An American of fifteen years of age is as reasonable as a Frenchman of forty. Also society here is wholly masculine; woman, who in all countries has little of the spirit of the representative system, here possesses no authority; there are no salons in the United States. But even here the system no longer exists in its primitive purity except on paper. The field of religion, although much narrowed, it is true, still remains open and the imagination still finds food, however meager, within its limits. But among us, it would be sheer fanaticism to set up the representative system as the pivot of social life. All of us, God be thanked, have a period of youth! Among us, women have a real power, although not enumerated in the articles of the Charter; and our national character has many feminine, I will not say effeminate, features. You would have to decimate France and leave only burghers over forty with their senses calmed and well disillusioned, that is to say, unpoetical and dry; even then you would hardly have a community that would be satisfied with merely constitutional emotions.

This is why France is the theater of a perpetual struggle between the old and the middle-aged on one side and the young who find their bounds too narrow on the other. Youth accuses age of narrow views, of timidity, of selfishness; the old complain of the greedy ambition which devours the young and of their ungovernable turbulence. The only good government is that which satisfies the demands for order, regularity, stability, and physical prosperity on the part of those of riper years, and at the same time fills the longings of the young and of that portion of society which always continues youthful for lively sensations, brilliant schemes, and lofty aspirations. By the side of their parliament, the English have their vast colonies by which this spirit finds vent over the remotest seas. The Anglo-Americans have the West and also, like Great Britain, the ocean. This double invasion of the East by the fathers and of the West by emancipated sons is a spectacle of gigantic magnitude and sublime interest. To suppose that we, who stand in need of some vast enterprise in which some may play a part before the eyes of the world and others may enjoy the spectacle of their prowess—to suppose that we shall be content to be forever imprisoned within our own territory with no other occupation than that of watching or turning the wheels of the representative machine, would be to wish that a man of taste, confined to this paltry hamlet of Bedford, should imagine himself in paradise.

XXVII

Authority and Liberty

Situation and Description of Richmond — Slavery — Richmond Flour — Inspection Laws — Liberty in America is the Liberty to Work and Move — Few Restrictions on Internal Commerce — Old Restrictions on French Commerce — Dangers of Extreme Control and Extreme Liberty in Commerce — Decline of French Foreign Trade — Twofold Authority in the United States — Ancient Authority, Caesar — Duties Imposed on All by Self-Government — The Authority of Caesar Could Be Destroyed in the United States, Not in Europe —

AUTHORITY AND LIBERTY

New Authority by the Side of Caesar — Canal, School, and Bank Commissioners; Their Powers — How Industry May Flourish in Europe under Caesarism — Concerning American Liberty — The Liberty of the Yankee Would Be Intolerable to the French — Liberty of the Virginian More Like Our Own — Mixture of the Two Liberties

Richmond, August 16, 1835.

Richmond stands in an admirable situation on the slope of a hill whose base is bathed by the James River. Its Capitol, with its brick columns covered with plaster, with its cornice and architrave of painted wood, produces an effect at a distance which even the Parthenon in the days of Pericles could not have surpassed; for the sky of Virginia, when it is not darkened by a storm or veiled with snow, is as beautiful as that of Attica. Richmond has its port nearer than the Piraeus was to Athens, while, at the same time, it stands at the falls of James River. Richmond enchanted me from the first by its charming situation and the cordiality of its inhabitants. It pleases me further by its ambition, for it aspires to be a metropolis and is making due preparations by the great works which it is executing or aiding, canals, railroads, waterworks, huge mills, workshops, for which the fall in the river affords an almost unlimited motive power. Here I also found some Frenchmen whose love for their country had not been chilled by fifty years of absence and eighty years of age, who have preserved, amid the simplicity of American manners, that fine flower of courtesy of which the seed is daily disappearing among us. I went yesterday for the second time to visit the cannon and mortars given to America during her struggle for independence by Louis XVI. In the Capitol, by the side of the statue of Washington, I found the bust of Lafayette. I heard the names of Rochambeau and d'Estaing pronounced as if they were old friends who had left but yesterday. I seem to myself at times to have been miraculously transported, not into France, but to the frontier.

My admiration of Richmond is not, however, blind; the founders of the new city have laid out streets one hundred feet wide, like highways in the style of Louis XIV; but in our great roads, between the quagmires on the right and left, there is at least a strip of passable pavement or roadway. The streets of new Richmond have neither pavement nor light. In the rainy season, they are dangerous bogs in which, I am told, several cows, who are here allowed by the municipal authorities to go at large, have met with the fate of the master of Ravensworth in the Kelpie. Richmond has, also, something of the aspect of Washington; with the exception of the business part of the town, it is neither city nor country; the houses are scattered about on an imaginary plan and it is almost impossible to find any lines to guide you, or to recognize the street K, F, or D, to which you are referred; for the alphabet has furnished the names here as arithmetic has done at Washington. The layout of Richmond has, however, this advantage over Washington; it is on a smaller scale and will be more speedily filled up; while Washington with its arrangements for a million inhabitants will not, perhaps, have fifty thousand twenty years hence.

There is something in Richmond which offends me more than its bottomless mudholes, and shocks me more than the rudeness of the western Virginians whom I met here during the session of the legislature; it is slavery. Half of the population is black or mulatto. Physically, the Negroes are well used in Virginia, partly from motives of humanity and partly because they are so much livestock raised for exportation to Louisiana; but, if there is no cause for complaint on the material level, morally they are treated as if they did not belong to the human race. Free or slave, the black is here denied all that can give him the dignity of man. The law forbids the instruction of the slave or the free man of color in the simplest rudiments of learning, under the severest penalties. The slave has no family; he has no civil rights; he holds no property. The white man knows that the slave has opened his ear to the word which everything here proclaims aloud, liberty; he knows that in secret the Negro broods over schemes of vengeance and that the exploits and martyrdom of Gabriel, the leader of an old conspiracy, and of Turner, the hero of a more recent insurrection, are still related in the Negro cabins. The precautionary measures which this knowledge has induced the whites to adopt freeze the heart of a stranger with horror.

Richmond is noted for its tobacco and flour market. Richmond flour is prized at Rio de Janeiro as much as at New York, at Lima as well as at Havana. The largest flour mill in the world is at Richmond, running twenty pair of stones, containing a great variety of accessory machinery and capable of manufacturing six hundred barrels of flour a day. The reputation of Richmond flour in foreign markets, like that of American flour in general, depends upon a system of inspection peculiar to the country which contravenes, indeed, the theory of absolute commercial freedom but is essential to the prosperity of American commerce and has never, that I have heard of, been a subject of complaint. The flour is inspected previous to export. The weight of each barrel and the quality of the flour are ascertained by the inspector and branded on the barrelhead. Superior qualities only can be exported; the inspection is real and thorough and is performed at the expense of the holder. The Havana, Brazilian, or Peruvian merchant is thus perfectly sure of the quality of the merchandise he buys; both the buyer and the seller find their advantage in it. Commerce can no more dispense with confidence in the market than with credit in the countinghouse.

Virginia tobacco is subjected to the same system of inspection. In general, all the coast States, all those from which produce is exported to foreign parts, have established this system and applied it to almost all articles in which frauds can be committed. Thus in New York wheat flour and Indian corn meal, beef, pork, salt fish, potash, whale oil, lumber, staves, flaxseed, leather, tobacco, hops, spirits, are all inspected. In regard to flour, the law is more rigorous than in respect to other articles. The inspector brands with the word *light* those barrels which are not of the legal weight (the exportation of these barrels is also prohibited) and with the word *bad* those which are of poor quality. As for Indian corn, it is required that the grain shall have been kiln-dried before grinding. Flour from other States cannot be sold in the city of New York, even for local consumption, unless it has been inspected the same as if for exportation. Every inspector has the right to search vessels in which he suspects that there is flour that has not been inspected and to seize what has been loaded or what is ready for shipping. There are, besides, various other provisions and penalties to prevent fraud.

If the necessity of these inspections were not sufficiently proved by their good effects and by long experience, it would be by the abuses that prevail in those articles of commerce which are not subject to the system. Complaints have already been made in Liverpool that bales of cotton fraudulently consist of an inferior article concealed beneath an outer layer of good quality. From a report addressed to the American Chamber of Commerce from this center of the cotton trade by the principal cotton brokers, it appears that this is not a matter of just two or three bales in large shipments, but of lots of one and two hundred bales.

What! it will be said, is there not, then, freedom of commerce in this classic land of liberty? No! foreign commerce is not free in the United States, because Americans are not willing to expose the industry and commerce of a whole country to ruin by the first rogue that comes along. The people of this country is, above all else, a working people. Everyone is at liberty to work, to choose his profession and to change it twenty times; everyone has the right to go and come on his business, at pleasure, and to transport his person and his occupation from the center to the circumference, and from the circumference to the center. If the country does not enjoy the political advantages of administrative unity, neither is it hampered in the most petty details of industry by excessive centralization. No man is obliged to go six hundred miles to solicit the license and personal signature of a minister, overloaded with business and harassed by legislative oversight. But American liberty is not a mystical, undefined liberty; it is a practical liberty, in harmony with the peculiar genius of the people and its peculiar destiny; it is a liberty of action and motion which the American uses to expand over the vast territory that Providence has given him and to subdue it to his uses. Liberty of movement is nearly absolute with the exception of some restraints imposed by the observance of the Sabbath. Liberty, or rather independence, in matters of industry is also ample; but if it is abused by some individuals the general tendency is to restrain them by law or by dictatorial measures, or by the influence of public opinion, sometimes expressed in mob rule.

The restraints on internal trade are few; there are, however, some restrictions upon hawkers and peddlers who impose on the credulity of country people. If no effective bankrupt law has yet been enacted, severe penalties are provided against false pretense. If stock-jobbing has not been prohibited, it is not from want of will on the part of the legislators, for they are fully alive to the evils of unproductive speculation which diverts needful capital from industry; it is because they do not see how it is to be effectually prevented. Besides, it is not easy to commit fraud in the United States in the domestic market. Here everybody knows everybody else and everyone is on the watch against others, and it is not difficult to trace a fraud to its source. For merchandise sent to a distant market, detection is not so easy. And, finally, there reigns here a sort of patriotism which is bolstered by self-interest rightly understood and by fear of public opinion, which maintains a certain degree of honesty in domestic affairs and a tone of morality which, if not wholly above reproach, is certainly far superior to what prevails among us; while, to many persons, all is fair in dealings with foreigners, whom they look upon as a kind of barbarian.

Before 1789, in France, we had restrictive regulations not only on foreign commerce but on domestic industry. Everyone knows, at least by name, the oaths and regulations of the guilds. There were special rules for each of the corporate bodies of the society. Even agriculture had its own from time immemorial; unquestionably they were, for example, in the cultivation of grapes, the result of customs developed through long experience. It is to these traditional rules no less than to the nature of the land that our famous regional wines have owed their high reputation for unparalleled quality. Tradition determined where grain could be cultivated and where vineyards planted, how vines should be spaced and when new vines should be pruned. Inspection for export was required for goods sent to the Levant and for other kinds of merchandise sent abroad.

The revolution canceled at a stroke all these old regulations. The destruction of most of them was a good thing because they were outdated and had fallen behind current knowledge; they were generally applied by the letter that kills rather than in the spirit which gives life; the corporate bodies of the state and the guilds were rigid and closed and did not take in new aspirants. In a word, the industrial organization of the country had become sick; another was needed, but the established powers were incapable of creating it. The inept government of the unfortunate Louis XVI, instead of sensing that the greatest force was in the third estate and giving that force a program and direction, took pleasure in insulting it and amused itself by restoring the vigor of antique laws by which only nobles were allowed to wear epaulets in the army. It had come to the point when all power seemed but a scourge of God, all organization only tyranny; and when the nation revolted, instead of correcting abuses and reforming the existing state of affairs, it rejected everything, abolished everything, wiped the slate clean in the organization of business as well as in the organization of society. It was put forth as a matter of principle that business transactions should not fall under anyone's surveillance and not only were guild regulations and tests of fitness suppressed, not only were the privileges allowed the corporate bodies annulled, but also the simplest and safest police measures were destroyed, notably the inspection of goods for export. Yet on the whole we have gained in respect to domestic industry by sweeping away those often cumbersome regulations; but in regard to our foreign trade, the evil has certainly outweighed the good, as the decline of our maritime commerce fully proves.

At the peace of 1814, when the sea was again open to us, our foreign commerce fell into the hands of petty traffickers whose cupidity exhausted the vocabulary of fraud. During the first years after the Restoration, the French name became discredited in all the markets of the Old and the New World. The Levant trade, which we had monopolized, passed into the hands of the English and Austrians. The goods with which we formerly supplied the East, being no longer subject to inspection on exportation, fell short in measure and were inferior in quality. Formerly packages of our goods changed hands without distrust and without search; but it became necessary to submit them to a rigorous examination, for their contents often turned out to be quite different from the invoice. South America was the great theater of these frauds; water was actually sold for Burgundy, rolls of wood for rolls of ribands. The Bordelese, who not without reason charge the prohibitive system with the decline of their prosperity, cannot be blind to the fact that their own unscrupulous rapacity contributed pretty largely to this result.

As customers could no longer be found to deal with us, frauds have necessarily diminished. Our foreign trade has gradually fallen into the hands of a few great houses, and this concentration, which has powerfully contributed to the prevalence of honorable dealings in English commerce, has done something toward reviving ours. Small dealers have been driven out of the field. It is to this cause that we have to attribute the good condition of our trade with the United States. But let us not deceive ourselves; some sleights of hand are still played off; Bordeaux is not yet wholly purged of the infection; French commerce abroad is yet cankered by foul sores.

In the face of facts like these, I do not see how one can speak against the immediate adoption in France of inspection for our foodstuffs and especially our wines which are destined for export. One would have to trust absolutely in theories of commercial freedom, certainly a strange faith in an age which prides itself on freethinking, not to see that the absence of all regulation in the matter of commerce is a monstrous fact, that one must police commerce as well as other social relations, and that, if a people like the Americans, so enamored with self-government and so hostile to regulatory legislation, have in this regard imposed such severe regulations on themselves, we shall bring evil upon ourselves by wishing to see ours pass away. It must be confessed that, if our politics has been marked by good faith and a spirit of disinterestedness that give us a right to denounce the treachery of *perfidious Albion,* the English race can proudly oppose the bold and honorable spirit of its commercial dealings to the pusillanimity and unworthy shifts of our own. Let us confess our shame and submit to the necessary diet for the cure of so loathsome a leprosy.

The United States constitute a society which moves by instinct, rather than according to any premeditated plan; it does not know itself. It rejects the tyranny of a past which is exclusively military in character, yet it is deeply imbued with the sentiment of order. It has been nurtured in the hatred of the old political systems of Europe, but a feeling of the need for self-restraint runs through its veins. It is divided between its instinctive perceptions of the future and its aversion to the past, between its thirst after freedom and its hunger for social order, between its religious veneration of experience and its horror of the violence of past ages.

Hence the apparent contradictions which appear in its tastes and its tendencies; but the confusion is only apparent.

In each State there are two authorities, distinct in their composition and their attributes. One corresponds to government in the European social system, to the old Caesar. At its head is a magistrate who bears the old name of Governor, with the pompous title of commander-in-chief of the army and navy. This authority is reduced to a shadow. In the new States of the West which have come into the world since Independence, its attributes have been gradually suppressed, or rather the citizens have reserved the exercise of them to themselves. Thus the people themselves appoint most of the public officers. The management of funds is rarely confided to the governor, but is generally entrusted to a special board of commissioners. The governor has not the control of the forces of the State; strictly speaking, indeed, there are none; but in case of necessity the sheriff has the right to summon the *posse comitatus* and to oblige all bystanders, armed or not, to render him assistance and to act as police officers. There is no regular police, there are no passports; but nobody can stop at an inn without entering his name and residence on the register. This register is open to the examination of all in the barroom, which is a necessary appendage of every public place, and there it remains at all times to be turned over by all. The barkeeper fills, in fact, the post of commissioner of police, and the crowd that assembles in the barroom to read the newspapers, smoke, drink whiskey, and talk politics, that is to say all travelers, would in case of necessity be ready to act the part of constables. This is real self-government; these are the obligations and responsibilities that every citizen takes upon himself when he disarms authority. The power of the governor, who was formerly the representative of royalty, the brilliant reflection of the omnipotence of the proud monarchs of Europe, has turned to dust. Even the appearance of power has not been kept up; he has no guards, no palace, no money. The governors of Indiana and Illinois have a salary of $1,000 a year, without a house or any accessories. There is not a trader in Cincinnati who does not pay his head clerk better; the clerks at Washington have $700 a year.

This fall of power is to be explained by other considerations than those drawn from the principle of self-government. The ancient power was Caesar, was military in its character. American society has denied Caesar. In Europe, it has been necessary that Caesar should be strong for the security of national independence; for in Europe we are always on the eve of war. The United States, on the contrary, are organized on the principle that war between the States is impossible and foreign war improbable. The Americans, therefore, can dispense with Caesar, but we are obliged to cleave to him. Yet it is not to be inferred that they can and will long dispense with authority, or that they are even now free from its control. There is in America religious authority, which never closes its eyes; there is the authority of opinion, which is severe to the point of harshness; there is the authority of the legislatures, which are often omnipotent; sometimes there is the dictatorial authority of the mob.

Still more; by the side of the power of Caesar in political affairs, a second regular authority is beginning to show itself which embraces within its domain modern institutions and new establishments of public utility, such as the means of communication, banks, and elementary schools, that in the United States have acquired an unparalleled magnitude. Thus there are canal commissioners, bank commissioners, school commissioners. Their power is great and real. The canal commissioners establish administrative regulations which they change at will without previous notice. They fix and change the rate of tolls; they are surrounded by a large body of agents, entirely dependent upon them and removable at pleasure; they are charged with the management of large sums of money; the sums that passed through the hands of the Pennsylvania commissioners amounted to nearly $23,000,000. They are certainly subjected to less minute and rigorous control than is extended to the most trifling affairs of our Board of Public Works or our military engineers. If they had had our financial regulations, our system of responsibility, our court of accounts, they would without doubt have spent ten years more in executing the works entrusted to them and they would have executed them no better and no cheaper. The bank commissioners in the State of New York, by the provisions of the Safety Fund Act, are clothed, by right if not in fact, with a sort of dictatorship; they have in certain cases power of life and death over the banks.

It is in the new States especially that one can see how the commissioners exercise their powers. Last summer the Ohio Canal commissioners, perceiving or thinking that they perceived a conspiracy among persons engaged in the transportation of goods on the New York canals to raise the rates of freight, immediately adopted a resolution to this effect; whereas certain persons have shown a disposition to make exorbitant charges, the toll shall be double on all articles that have paid more than a certain rate on the New York canal. This was establishing a *maximum*, not only in their own territory, but in that of a neighboring State. A director-general of our public routes who should take such a liberty would be forthwith denounced as violating the principles of commercial freedom. In the United States everybody agrees that the Ohio commissioners were right, that the profits of the transportation companies would be somewhat less but that the public would be the gainer, and the entrepreneurs accordingly submitted.

In the United States, then, the general interest is the supreme law; it immediately raises its head and vindicates its rights when it feels the encroachments of private interest. The system of government in this country is, therefore, not so much a system of liberty and laissez-faire as a system of equality, or rather it takes the character of a strong rule by the majority. In looking at some of the provisions in the charters of incorporated companies, one is tempted to ask how associations could be formed on such conditions and how they have been able to procure capital. In Massachusetts, the shareholders are individually responsible for the debts of the company. In Pennsylvania, it is expressly provided that if at any time the privileges granted to the corporation shall prove to be contrary to the public good the legislature may revoke them. This is the germ of despotism; but in the United States, Caesar is disarmed; the old feudal lion has neither fangs nor claws. Industry is prompt to take alarm at the exercise of despotism by Caesar; but it is only at the last moment that it will feel any distrust of a society which lives and flourishes by labor and whose every aim, public and private, is self-aggrandizement by means of productive labor.

Must one believe that in Europe, where the supreme authority is in direct descent from Caesar, that industry must languish? I do not think so. Actually, industry has an irresistible force and if the existence of our European military governments prove incompatible with its development I do not hesitate to say that they will be destroyed. One cannot suppose that Europe will for long present the appearance of a great military camp, or rather of several military camps opposed to one another. The sword which is drawn today can be sheathed tomorrow. It will be sheathed as soon as Europe finds the settlement it seeks and as soon as it has established it by solemn treaties. I admit that the sword will surely remain one of the attributes of our absolute or limited monarchies, or of our ephemeral republics, who can still use it on a moment's notice; but war itself is being transformed. To a high degree, the institutions of war have taken on a character of order and wise regularity which approaches that of industry. Everything, to begin with the army, is susceptible of being employed to renew the earth where before it was good only to destroy. Royalty is undergoing a change and is preparing itself to receive or to take new prerogatives in the place of those it has lost or those which it still should lose. It is preoccupied with new needs and conceives new duties. There remains little more to conserve it and keep it on its shaky base. In a word, in the United States, the old form of power which did not take hold in the land has been destroyed and a totally new form of power has grown up naturally beside the debris of the former. In our old countries of Europe, where the old form of power has struck roots so deep that one could root it out only by turning over the entire society, the new society must emerge from the very trunk of the old royalty.

To understand fully the meaning of the word liberty, as it is used in this country, it is necessary to go to the sources of the American population; that is to say, to the origin of the distinction between the Yankee and the Virginian race. They have arrived at their notions of liberty by different avenues, the one by the gate of religion and the other by that of politics, and have therefore understood it very differently.

When the Yankee came to settle in the New World, it was not for the purpose of founding an empire but to establish a church. He fled from a land which had shaken off the yoke of the Babylon of the Pope, only to fall under that of the Babylon of episcopacy. He left behind him Satan, his pomp, and his works; he shook from the soles of his feet the dust of the inhospitable land of the Stuarts and the Anglican bishops; he sought a refuge in which he might practice his own mode of worship and obey what he believed to be the law of God. The Pilgrims, having landed on Plymouth rock, established liberty according to their own notion; it was a liberty for their own use exclusively, within whose embrace they felt perfectly at ease themselves without caring if others were stifled by it. It might have been expected that, proscribed themselves, they would at least have admitted religious toleration; but they did not grant it the narrowest corner and even now it is far from having elbow room among them. Originally, the right of citizenship was extended only to Puritans like themselves;

the state and the Church were confounded; it was not until 1832 that they were definitely and completely separated in Massachusetts. The Jew and the Quaker were forbidden to touch the soil under the severest penalties and in case of return under pain of death. At present, if the law tolerates the Roman Catholic, public opinion does not, as the burning of the Ursuline convent in 1834 and the scandalous scenes exhibited at the trials of the incendiaries testify. Still less mercy is shown to unbelief; witness the trial of Abner Kneeland for blasphemy on account of his pantheistic writings.

The Yankee type exhibits little variety; all Yankees seem to be cast in the same mold; it was, therefore, very easy for them to organize a system of liberty for themselves, that is, to construct a frame within which they should have the necessary freedom of motion. On their arrival they accordingly formed the plan of one, not merely tracing its general outlines and form, but dividing it into numerous compartments controlling all the details of life with as much minuteness as the Mosaic law did that of the Hebrews. Thus organized, it became impossible for any man not cut to the same pattern to establish himself among them. Although most of those laws which thus reduced life to rules have been abrogated, especially since the Revolution, still their spirit survives. The habits which gave them birth, and to which by a natural reaction they gave strength, still exist and to this day it is observable that no foreigner settles in New England.

For us, the French, who resemble each other in nothing except in differing from everybody else, for us, to whom variety is as necessary as the air, to whom a life of rules would be a subject of horror, the Yankee system would be torture. Their liberty is not the liberty to outrage all that is sacred on earth, to set religion at defiance, to laugh morals to scorn, to undermine the foundations of social order, to mock at all traditions and all received opinions; it is neither the liberty of being a monarchist in a republican country, nor that of sacrificing the honor of the poor man's wife or daughter to one's base passions; it is not even the liberty to enjoy one's wealth by a public display, for public opinion has its sumptuary laws to which all must conform under pain of moral outlawry; nor even that of living in private differently from the rest of the world. The liberty of the Yankee is essentially limited and special like the nature of the race. We should consider it as framed after the model of the liberty of Figaro; but the Yankee is satisfied with it because it leaves him all the latitude he desires, and because of all the lessons of the Bible that of the forbidden fruit, which we have not been able to fix in our brain, has made the deepest impression on his.

Since the Yankee does not suffer under these restraints, because he is or, what amounts to the same thing, thinks himself free, preventive authority is unnecessary for him. This is the reason why there is no appearance of authority in New England and why an armed force, a police, are even more unknown there than in the rest of the Union. The absence of a visible authority imposes on us and we think that the American in general, and the Yankee in particular, is more free than we are. I am persuaded, however, that if we measure liberty by the number of actions that are permitted or tolerated in public and private life, the advantage is on our side, not only in comparison with New England but also with the white population of the South.

The Virginian is more disposed to understand liberty in our way. His disposition has a greater resemblance to ours; the options open to him are less particular, much more general, than those of the Yankee; his mind is more ardent, his tastes more varied. But it is the Yankee who now rules the Union; it is his liberty which has given its principal features to the model of American liberty. Yet to extend its empire it has been obliged to borrow some of the characteristic traits of Virginian liberty; or, I might say, of French liberty, for the high priest of American democracy was a Virginian who had imbibed in Paris the doctrines of the philosophy of the eighteenth century. American liberty, as it now is, may be considered the result of a mixture, in unequal proportions, of the theories of Jefferson with New England usage. From these dissimilar tendencies has resulted a series of contradictory measures which have become strangely complicated with each other and which might puzzle and deceive a careless observer. It is in consequence of these opposite influences in the bosom of American society that such conflicting judgments have been passed upon it; it is because the Yankee type is at present the stronger, while the Virginian was superior in the period of the Revolution, that the ideas which the sight of America now suggests are so different from those which she inspired at the epoch of Independence.

XXVIII

Social Improvement

Appearance of Universal Comfort in the American Population — Effect upon the Condition of Women — Material Condition of the Negroes — Tax Reduction as a Means of Public Improvement — Industrial Growth a More Effectual Means — American Prosperity, the Fruit of Labor — Means of Stimulating Industry in France — Industrial Education — False Ideas About Public Education — Use of the Army on Public Works — Credit; Bad State of Credit in France Paralyzes the Spirit of Enterprise — English or American Banks Must be Modified for Use in France — Credit Must be Made Available to Agriculture — Economies That Better Credit Can Produce — Means of Communication — Influence of Credit on the Communication System — Lowering of Prices by the Ease of Transport — Legislative Reform — The Civil Code Too Closely Modeled on Roman Law; Its Defects in

SOCIAL IMPROVEMENT

Regard to Industry — The Laws in the United States — Jury Trial in Civil Cases

Charleston, September 1, 1835. The United States are certainly the land of promise for the worker and the peasant. What a contrast between our Europe and this America! After landing in New York, I thought every day was Sunday, for the whole population that throngs Broadway seemed to be arrayed in their Sunday's best. None of those countenances ghastly with the privations or the foul air of Paris; nothing like our wretched scavengers, our ragmen, and corresponding classes of the other sex. Every man was warmly clad in an outer garment; every woman had her cloak and bonnet of the latest Paris fashion. Rags, filth, and suffering degrade the woman even more than the man, and one of the most striking features in the physiognomy of the United States is, undeniably, the change which has been introduced because of general prosperity into the physical condition of women. Since the man earns enough to support the family, the woman has no other duties than the care of the household, a circumstance still more advantageous for her children than for herself. It is now a universal rule among Anglo-Americans that the woman is exempt from all heavy work and she is never seen, for instance, taking part in the labors of the field, nor in carrying burdens. Thus freed from employments unsuited to her delicate constitution, the sex has also escaped that hideous ugliness and repulsive coarseness of complexion which toil and privation everywhere else bring upon them. Every woman here has the features as well as the dress of a lady; every woman here is called a lady and strives to appear so. You would search in vain among Anglo-Americans from the mouth of the St. Lawrence to that of the Mississippi for one of those wretched objects who abound in our cities who are feminine only to the eye of the physiologist, or for one of those haggish beldams that fill our markets and three fourths of our fields. You will find specimens of the former class only among Indians and Negroes, and of the latter only among the Canadian French and Pennsylvania Germans; their women labor at least as much as the men. It is the glory of the English race that they have ever and everywhere as much as possible interpreted the superiority of the man to the woman as reserving to man the ruder and harder forms of toil. A country in which woman is treated according to this principle presents the aspect of a new and better world.

Imagine an Irish peasant who at home could scarcely earn enough to live on potatoes, who would look upon himself as a rich man if he owned an acre of ground, but who, on stepping ashore at New York, finds himself able to earn a dollar a day by the mere strength of his arm. He feeds and lodges himself for two dollars a week and at the end of a fortnight he may have saved enough to buy ten acres of the most fertile land in the world, of that famous *American bottom land* in the State of Illinois. The distance from New York to the West is great, it is true; but the fare on the great canal is trifling and he can easily pay his way by the work of his hands. It is also true that the poorest Irishman would not think of buying so little as ten acres; the least that one buys in the West is eighty. What of that? The savings of a few months will enable him to compass them; besides, *Uncle Sam* favors emigrants and if in theory he does not sell his land on credit he is, in fact, very indulgent to the pioneer who comes to subdue the savage wilderness; he allows him to occupy the soil temporarily without charge. Thus the Irish, who would fight anybody for denying in their presence that the isle of Erin was a terrestrial paradise and who, under the inspiration of whiskey, sing the glories of that *first pearl of the sea*, quit it by the fifty thousands for the United States. On their arrival they cannot believe their own eyes; they pinch themselves to find out whether they are not under some spell. They do not dare to describe to their friends in Europe the streams of milk and honey that flow through this promised land. (An

Irishman, who had recently arrived, showed his master a letter which he had just written to his family: "But, Patrick," said his master, "why do you say that you have meat three times a week, when you have it three times a day?" "Why?" replied Pat, "because if I told them that, they would never believe me.")

Even here in the South, where the workman in the towns and the laborer in the country, instead of being as in the North the sovereigns of the country, are slaves, there is more plenty, more physical comfort among the laboring class than is found among us. The colored population, therefore, increases in numbers faster than our rural population. Not that our peasant gives birth to fewer children than the blacks of Virginia and Carolina; but death, led by the hand of want, is active in keeping down the excessive multiplication of arms that would soon become formidable competitors of the fathers and in closing forever mouths that would cry for bread which their parents could not supply. The attention of the benevolent in Europe has long been directed toward the reduction of public expenditures and a more equal distribution of the burden of taxation as a means of improving the condition of the poor. But all these plans, supposing them to succeed according to the views of the projectors, would merely amount to taking a few coppers less from the pockets of the poorer class, while a system of measures concerted in such a manner as to diffuse among them a love of order and habits of regularity and industry, to enlarge the field of labor and to render its terms more favorable to them, would fill those pockets. The relief of one class of the community by merely shifting its burden to the back of another has a revolutionary character which ill agrees with the notions of a generation that is weary of revolutions, or with the nature of a government established for the very purpose of staying the revolutionary flood; on the contrary, all that develops the resources of industry is in harmony with the present inclination of all minds. Labor is an admirable instrument of concord, for all interests gain by the prosperity of industry. This is the pure and true source of all wealth, public and private. Labor alone creates; it alone can relieve the wants of the needy without impoverishing him who has enough or even reducing the luxury of the opulent; it can give wealth to some, competency to others, and to all *the chicken in the pot* which since the revolt of Luther has been the great social problem in the material order of things.

The admirable prosperity of the United States is the fruit of labor, much more than of any reform in taxation. The soil has not the luxuriant fertility of the tropical regions; as the expression has it, roasted larks fly into nobody's mouth. But the American is a model of industry. This country is not a second edition of the Greek and Roman republics, it is a gigantic commercial house which owns its wheat fields in the Northwest, its cotton, rice and tobacco plantations in the South; which maintains its sugar works, its establishments for salting provisions, and some good beginnings of manufactures; which has its harbors in the Northeast thronged with fine ships, well built and better manned, by means of which it undertakes to carry for the world and to speculate on the wants of all nations. Every American has a passion for work and the means of gratifying it. If he wishes to cultivate the soil, he finds waste land enough for his farm in the Northwest or the Southwest. If he chooses to be a mechanic that he may finally become a manufacturer, he has no difficulty in getting credit; he finds unemployed waterfalls all along the rivers which he takes possession of and on which he sets up his wheels. If he has a taste for commerce, he puts himself into the hands of a merchant who sends him, after some years of apprenticeship and trial, to take charge of his business in the interior, or to the Antilles, or South America, or Liverpool, or Havre, or Canton. He may labor without apprehension and produce without stint. Without the overhead of rents, his flour and his salt provisions fear no competition in the markets of South America and the sugar islands. As for cotton, the

United States alone almost supply the world and cannot plant enough. The career open to Americans as active, bold, and intelligent merchants is unlimited and is entered with admirable spirit and success; they beat their rivals, even the English, on every field. If the American devotes himself to some branch of domestic industry, he finds ample room for activity, for domestic consumption is indefinite; everybody here enjoys himself, or at least spends. Everyone produces much, because all consume much; each consumes freely, because he gains freely, has no fears for the morrow either for himself or his children, or at least takes no thought of it.

The most efficient measures of public administration for the amelioration of the condition of the people in France would be such as would tend to increase the industrial qualities of the mass and to furnish them with the means of putting these qualities in action. Such are a system of industrial education; the establishment of institutions of credit which would place within the reach of all the instruments of industry, or, in other words, capital, which is now inaccessible not only to the operative and the laborer but to a great proportion of the *bourgeoisie;* the execution of a complete system of routes of communication, from village roads to railroads, for manufactures and commerce are impracticable where facilities of transportation do not exist; the modification of many laws and customs, judicial and administrative, that now embarrass industry without advantage to anyone.

I dare hardly speak of popular education, where I now am. The people in the Southern States are slaves. The maxim here is that they need no instruction, that the sentiment of fear is the only moral nature suitable to their condition. They have, therefore, no other education than that of their own hands and that, of course, must be limited because their intellectual and moral nature is in fetters. In the Northern States, the laboring classes are whites and there the law makes a liberal provision for popular instruction. Almost everywhere in the North all children go to the primary schools. Elementary education is there more practical than with us; it is our primary instruction with less emphasis on literature and ideality and the addition of some instruction in commercial and economic affairs. But there is no practical industrial education here except by apprenticeship. There are no mechanical or agricultural seminaries. It is useless here to shut up the young in such institutions to inspire them with a taste for commerce, agriculture, or the mechanical arts; they suck it in with their mother's milk; they breathe the air of industry under the paternal roof, in public meetings, everywhere, at all times and in every act of life. When an American wishes to learn a trade, he goes into the workshop, the countinghouse, the manufactory, as an apprentice. By seeing others act, he learns how to act himself; he becomes an artisan, a manufacturer, a merchant; all the faculties of his firm and watchful mind, all the energies of his ambitious spirit are centered in his workshop or warehouse. He directs all his powers to making himself master of his business, to learn the lessons of others' experience, and he succeeds, of course, as everyone does who obeys the voice of his destiny. I do not pretend that the Americans are right in not having recourse to a theoretical preparation for a particular branch of business, for which purpose we have instituted such costly establishments. I only record the fact with the observation that they get on very well without it. Our national character has little disposition for business; we work from necessity and not from choice. Our ideas have little of a commercial or mechanical turn. To make a Frenchman a skillful husbandman, an able merchant, a dexterous mechanic, a long and painful training is necessary; he must change his natural bent and metamorphose all his thoughts and habits; in a word, with us a special professional education must precede apprenticeship. The American learns by example merely; we must learn by general principles; we stand more in need of them and we have a greater aptitude for mastering them than they.

Before passing to the institutions best suited to develop industry, I would observe that a political system which should be particularly calculated to create and sustain them cannot be taxed with materialism. Industry influences the moral nature of man; the material prosperity of a people has an important bearing on public liberty. Men cannot practically enjoy the rights secured to them by law when they are manacled and fettered by poverty; the English and their children in America call a decent standard of living *independence*. The Anglo-Americans have reached wealth through their political liberty; other nations, and we, I think, are of the number, must arrive at political franchises by the progress of national wealth. I now come to the consideration of a credit system.

Suppose, on one side, the landholder who has granaries bursting with corn, his stable filled with cattle, his storehouse crowded with barrels of whiskey and salt meat; then, the merchant with his warehouses full of cloth, and the grocer, well supplied with tea, coffee, and sugar; and on the other, the laborer, the mason, the carpenter, the smith, all skilled in their trade and wanting work to supply them with daily food. A canal or a railroad is projected; the country has capital enough to construct it, since it contains the arms to execute the work and what is needed to provide subsistence for the workers. The construction of the work is indispensable in order to enable the workman to turn his muscles to account and gain his daily bread and to give the merchant a market for his goods. Now in this case, among us, there is no other medium of communication between the laborer and the holder of articles of consumption than the engineer, a man of science but not of capital, and the citizens of the towns which are interested in the scheme; these last have a competence and no more, and they have no means of raising, on their lands or their houses, the ready money which must serve as a medium of exchange between the wares of the merchant, the produce of the cultivator, and the labor of the operative. Among us, therefore, the most useful projects remain on paper. In this country, by the side of the engineer and the citizen, you have one or more banks in which all, laborers, landholders, and traders, have confidence, often, indeed, much more than is deserved. The bank guarantees the cultivator and the trader payment for their produce and merchandise and the laborer his wages; to this end, it offers the shareholder of the projected enterprise, in exchange for his personal engagement renewable at a certain date and often on the pledge of the very canal or railroad shares, paper money which the laborer receives in payment of his wages and with which he procures the necessary supplies from the producer or the trader. Thus every reasonable enterprise passes from theory to practical reality.

To arrive at the same result among us, it would be necessary in the first place that we should possess somewhat more of that genius for business which is characteristic of the American and, then, that the banks should be able to accept with confidence the commitments of the investors; unlike the United States, the latter could not be done among us because, except in the manufacturing towns, the *bourgeois* in general does not engage in business; he is a proprietor living on his income and not increasing it. The American *bourgeois,* on the contrary, is actively engaged in business and is constantly employed in increasing his means; besides, the banks have more hold on his real property than they could have in France.

Finally, it would be necessary for the public, proprietors and laborers, traders as well as landholders, to have full confidence in the bills issued by the bank—which is impossible in a country where all paper money suggests the idea of *assignats*. Even if the people had not that disastrous experiment before their eyes, it would be difficult to teach them to look upon a scrap of paper, although redeemable at sight with coin, as equivalent to precious metals. A metallic currency has, in our notions, a superiority to any other representative of value—which to an American or an Englishman is quite incomprehensible; to our peasants, it is the object of a mystical feeling, a veritable cult, and in this respect we are all of us more or less peasants. The Americans, on the other hand, have a firm faith in paper; and it is not a blind faith, for if we have had our *assignats,* they have had their continental money and they need not go far back in their history to find a record of the failure of the banks in a body. Their confidence is founded in reason, their courage is a matter of reflection. Last winter, for example, it was known to the public that certain banks in New York had on hand only five dollars in specie for one hundred paper dollars in circulation, perhaps even less. In France this would have been the signal for a general panic, and the bill-holders would have thrown themselves in crowds upon the bank to exchange their paper for coin. The bank, thus stormed, would have stopped payment; fifty or seventy bills in a hundred would have become mere rags in the hands of the holders and, what would be more fatal, the banks, which lean upon each other and hold each other's notes to a large amount, would have failed one after another, as those of the Federal District did last April. Each bank failure would have been followed by numerous individual failures which would have involved other banks in their fall and the country would have been ruined. The Americans in this fearful crisis did not quail; they stood firm, like veterans under the fire of a battery or encountering a storm of Arabs at the foot of the Pyramids with crossed bayonets and serried files. None of the New York banks stopped payment and scarcely six or seven small banks failed through the country.

Let us not deceive ourselves; it will be a long time before we in France shall be in a condition to enjoy such a system of credit as exists in the United States or England. In this respect we are yet in a state of barbarism from which we cannot pass to a more perfect condition of things except by a complete revolution in our commercial habits and ideas and even to a certain degree of our national way of life.

SOCIAL IMPROVEMENT

I do not pretend to decide beforehand what the precise organization of a system of credit for France should be. I think it may be safely affirmed that the system which prevails here would not do for us. In appropriating to ourselves the improvements of the English and of their successors in America, we must modify them in conformity with the genius of the nation or they will wither on our soil. As the East is the cradle of religion, so England in our day is the mold in which have been cast the political and commercial institutions that seem destined to rule the world; but just as the religious conceptions of the East have had to undergo a radical change in order to gain a footing in the West, so the political and commercial creations of our neighbors must undergo a transformation before they can become established among us. Coming into the world under circumstances of a peculiar nature, amid a people of an original and peculiar character, born under the unhealthy shadow of conquest and civil war, they are not suited to be transferred bodily to another soil. Already they are undergoing modifications in America, although they exist here among English settlers. Among the people of the South of Europe and among us, when they have taken their final shape, it is probable that they will no more resemble their British type than a Benedictine or a Sister of Charity resembles an Indian fakir or dervish. It would be presumptuous to attempt to pronounce at present what precise form the institutions of credit will assume; yet it is reasonable to presume that to be in harmony with our character and disposition they must lean upon the government, combine their operation with its action, become, in a word, public establishments and be ready to extend a large share of their benefits to the agricultural interest.

Public credit, which in France must be the bulwark of private credit, still feels and will continue to feel the effect of our former bankruptcy. It should be our aim to erase the memory of the breaches of public faith under the monarchy and under the republic and to strengthen the foundations and enlarge the sphere of national credit, which will thus become a suitable basis for the banks, for in France we shall not trust in the bankers, nor will the banks have confidence in themselves, any further than they are propped up by the government and become in fact public establishments. Many sound heads consider it indispensable that the system of credit should be, in many respects, amalgamated with the financial system of the State. This is no rash speculation or untried novelty. In the Southern and Western States, which like France are chiefly agricultural, the principal banks are dependent on the State governments, they are employed in collecting taxes and transferring funds for the State treasury. This is the case, in a greater or less degree, in the Carolinas, Georgia, and Alabama, and still more so in Indiana and Illinois.

The greatest change which institutions of credit will have to undergo in their introduction among us will be the adaptation of them to the wants of agriculture. We are more an agricultural than a manufacturing people; three fourths or four fifths of our population live by agriculture. The English are especially devoted to manufactures and commerce; their banks are most easily accessible to the merchant, next to the manufacturer, and but little, or not at all, to the agriculturist. The feudal traits which landed property still retains among them contribute to this result. In this country, banks have been organized on the English model. They have become excessively numerous in the Northern States, which are inhabited by a people eminently possessing the manufacturing and commercial spirit. Those which have been established in the agricultural States of the South and West have failed at different crises, the most disastrous of which was that of 1819. In 1828, local banks had ceased to exist in Kentucky and Missouri; each of the States of Tennessee, Indiana, Illinois, Mississippi, and Alabama had but one, or had not yet established any. At present they are created in the South and West with something of a public character, the State either becoming the principal shareholder or guaranteeing the loan for raising capital. Several of them have a decided tendency to connect themselves with the agricultural interest. Louisiana has adopted the most comprehensive and important measures in this respect.

It is evident that the extension of credit in France would be the means of a greater saving to the people than any reform in the budget. The average rate of interest on all transactions of all kinds is at least 15 or 20, perhaps 25 per cent. Suppose that this could be reduced only 2 per cent, a result which does not seem very difficult to attain, it is plain that as positive a saving would be made to the country as could be made by a reduction in the expenses of government and would apply to as many millions as the latter would to thousands. It is not possible to give an exact estimate of the amount of the annual transactions in France; it must be enormous, for every time an article of property changes hands there is a transaction affected by the rate of interest; now the total annual produce of French industry is estimated at nearly 2 billion dollars; and we must suppose the amount of transactions to be ten or twelve times greater. The annual amount of commercial transactions alone is about 4 billion. Admitting the average credit to be four months and the mass of transactions to amount to 16 billion, a saving of 2 per cent a year would be equal to 100 million. Add to this that the creation of institutions of credit would make a saving once for all of 300 or 400 million by the substitution of paper for a portion of the metallic currency.

It would be superfluous to dwell upon the salutary influence of a judicious system of public works on the prosperity of all classes and more especially the lower classes. On this point everyone is already convinced; it would be an enterprise worthy of a great people to undertake such a system, which would include canals, local roads, and railroads on the great routes; which would drain our bogs and supply water to the districts that need irrigation; which would convert Rouen and Havre, Lille and Calais, Orléans,

Rheims, and Troyes into suburbs of Paris; would consummate the union of Belgium with France; would make Strassburg one of the greatest *entrepôts* in the world; would restore life to Bordeaux, which is now pining away, by giving it easier access to the central and southern departments; would revive Nantes, which is dead, by connecting it with the flourishing interior provinces and particularly with Paris, the heart of France; would bring Lyons into contact with the Rhine and the Danube; would develop our mineral wealth, which now lies useless in the bowels of the earth for want of means of transportation; would not, as is too often the case, overlook our peaceful and laborious country population, but deliver every farm and village from the six months' blockade to which they are now condemned by the mud of every winter. This would be a grand and noble enterprise.

All forms of social improvement affect each other: a good system of public works would exercise a powerful influence on the extension of credit and, reciprocally, a liberal system of public and private credit would communicate activity to public enterprises. I go further; it is impossible that our public works can be carried forward with vigor without the aid of credit. To pretend to execute them wholly by means of taxes would be madness. Without public and private credit Americans would never have had any public works. They have entered upon the construction of their great canals and their innumerable railroads only through the instrumentality of banks and loans. In 1828, the three cities of the Federal District, Washington, Georgetown, and Alexandria, having together a population of 32,000, with little trade, no manufactures or agricultural resources, for the country around is sterile, subscribed $1,500,000 toward the construction of the great canal from the Chesapeake to the Ohio, raising the funds by a loan in Holland. Our large towns, Bordeaux, Marseilles, Rouen, Lyons, will have canals and railroads whenever they see fit to do with moderation what Washington, Georgetown, and Alexandria have attempted on too great a scale.

The improvement of the means of transportation often causes such a fall in the price of articles that the construction of a canal or road relieves the inhabitants to an extent far exceeding the amount of the most oppressive tax. In France, where wine, a light drink which does not make a man a brute, is abundant, it is important to bring it within the reach of the poorer classes and to accustom them to the daily use of it. There are still several districts in central and southern France where wine is transported on the back of mules for a distance of forty miles. Transportation the same distance by a canal would be only one sixth of the price of mule carriage, or a saving of five cents a gallon, which is more than the excise on common wines; so that the construction of a canal, considered in this light, would be a greater relief to certain consumers than the suppression of the excise.

In regard to legislation, we have reason to congratulate ourselves on having a uniform system of laws instead of a jumble of rules and customs derived from all ages and various sources. But with all admiration for our civil code, let me say that it sanctifies a principle which is incompatible with modern society. The spirit of Napoleon pervaded the creation of this noble work. But Napoleon was wholly preoccupied with Roman ideas. He wished to found an empire of adamant on the Roman model. His counselors were possessed with the notion that Roman law was pure, absolute, immutable justice. They have, therefore, given us a code of laws which protects various interests according to the degree of importance they had eighteen hundred years ago rather than what they have in modern times. In the time of the Romans, landed property was almost the only property; agriculture was the only branch of industry held in respect; manufactures were merely a department of domestic labor, carried on by slaves in the house; commerce was given over to foreigners and freedmen. At that time, no one dreamed of the possibility of those huge factories on the English plan, or of that powerful machinery which is the soul of our industry; or those immense docks and storehouses which enable a man in his office to arrange and direct the most extensive operations without touching an article of merchandise or even inspecting samples, merely by setting his signature to a warrant or a receipt. The system of accounts was then unknown; the idea of banks did not occur to the most far-sighted intellect. Governments took little thought for the means of making exchanges sure, easy, and speedy; the great roads opened by the praetors and emperors were military roads. Little care was given to saving time, for time has value only in an industrious community. (Neapolitans are said to have made the following objection to a company which proposed to run a steamboat between their city and Sicily: "Your boat takes us over in one day, and yet you demand the same fare as a sail vessel which is three days. That is absurd; how can you expect that we will pay as much for one day as for three?" This is the reasoning of a people who have no idea of setting an economic value on time.) On the contrary, there was every reason for endeavoring to keep property in the great families. Landed property, with reference to which all the laws were framed, is inconsistent with the idea of constant change. The object of legislation was stability and permanency; the forms which it established were favorable to delay.

Following this example, Napoleon and his counselors gave us a code of laws in which everything is sacrificed to landed property. The law treats the manufacturer and the merchant with suspicion; it looks upon them as the sons of the slave and the freedman, or at least as persons of no consideration, commoners whom it is permitted to treat without ceremony. On the other hand, the presumption is always in favor of the proprietor; he is protected not because he is a cultivator and producer, but simply and abstractly because he is a proprietor, the owner of the soil, the successor of the Roman patrician and the feudal lord. Thus our laws overlook the importance of manufacturing industry and the great destiny which awaits it; they shackle and check it by the complicated formalities to which they subject it and the vexatious details with which they embarrass its movements.

Let me not, however, be too severe on our code; I do not know any other which, all things considered, is more advantageous to industry. Even American legislation has retained the defects of the English laws; it partakes in their vagueness and uncertainty; it is under the almost exclusive dominion of precedents, which it still borrows from English decisions as if North America were still an English colony. In most of the States, the undefined and conflicting pretensions of the common law and equity jurisdiction still remain in force. In some of the old States, as Virginia, the legislation yet bears many of the features of the feudal system. American law, however, has the great advantage of a simpler and less expensive process than ours or the English, and especially of a great economy of time by a reduction of delays attending English and French practice. As for the use of the jury in civil cases, it is of doubtful expediency. I often hear it said that it would be better to leave them to three judicious and irremovable judges than to twelve citizens who often carry their individual prejudices or party passions or class jealousies into the jury box. With a jury, the influence of a skillful advocate often weighs much, the merits of the cause too little. Finally, in this country, the commercial tribunals have no compulsory jurisdiction; the ordinary courts take cognizance of all causes, unless there is a previous agreement between the parties to submit all differences that may arise between them to arbiters or a committee of the Chamber of Commerce, which is merely a voluntary association and is not to be found in all parts of the country.

It is not convenient for a people to change their laws every day, like a shirt. I do not think then that it would be sensible to agitate for a general reformation of our code of laws; there is good reason to wait for only partial and successive changes. From today, without changing a line, one could make our laws far more favorable to the needs of industry. Law is not something absolute and inflexible, like a formula in algebra; it is as elastic as the spirit of the men entrusted with its application. Without insult to our courts, one can recall, time after time, when according to the needs of the time they have given our laws different and contradictory interpretations. The judge, especially in civil cases where he is both judge and jury, has a freedom of action which he can exercise and has in fact always exercised within that limit without which he would cease to be honest and responsible. If our courts would say, in a number of cases, that justice demands that the law be interpreted in an industrial sense, rather than in a feudal or Roman sense, you would erase a thousand minor obstacles which stand in the way of industry without twisting the law in the least.

Unfortunately, the education which our new judges and aspiring lawyers receive in law school puts them in a decidedly contrary attitude. They are wrapped in an absorption with the past and turn their backs on the future; they are saturated with the antique; they are accustomed to weigh social interests in the scales of the jurists of Justinian who received their standard from the first Caesars. The notions of justice and injustice with which they are impregnated are those suited to a society totally different from ours. The result is that they frequently apply laws by a view of society two thousand years behind the times. I make this criticism without any bitterness and with a certain sorrow, because no one more than I respects the noble character of our magistrates. But on the other hand, the interest of France requires them to accept the obligation of projecting thoughts for the future into the code of the emperor, mixing them with the dust of twenty centuries.

The supremacy, then, for the last fifty years that lawyers

have enjoyed in France, except during the imperial period, has made the spirit of the court dominate everywhere. It is the mode today to analyze and be subtle, but to analyze in the spirit of a praetor of the Roman republic and to be subtle in the manner of the feudal castle. Our bureaucracy is infested with this sickness. Anyone high in administration today thinks so much this way that by twisting the spirit of the law he has come to adopt the intellectual habits suited to the clerk of a public prosecutor. The result is that the country is overrun with minute regulations too often conceived in the sense which I have pointed out is always in the manner of our courts. As a result, our central authority, without which we surely could not exist, has become our enemy. We are running over with this retrograde and legalistic attitude. It paralyzes the most useful enterprises or kills them before they are even begun. It would not be difficult to remedy this evil if our legislature would leave our ministers time to attend to the needs of the country. Unfortunately, as things stand, their first care is always for political battle and they abandon all administration to the routine of their bureaus.

Now when the east wind blows, a sharp and sickly wind which comes with torrents of raw rain, I feel a sense of despair for the safety of our old France. What other nation has lasted for a full fourteen centuries? Fourteen hundred years of glory, is that not enough for the life of one people? I am overtaken sometimes with the consideration that these are the signs of approaching death, this preoccupation with the past, like an old man writing his last will and testament, this false ideology resurrected from the old Empire, this universal spread of theories of disorganization. But these black thoughts pass as quickly as the thunderstorm; as soon as the sky is blue again I regain my firm faith that our race is not at the end of its destiny, that we still have great things to do, and that we will soon make up for lost time because we have a tremendous capacity to take advantage of that which is new. As long as we have the will, supported by our enthusiasm and our tradition of unity, we will easily leap over the interval which for others has been a laborious path.

XXIX

Social Reform

Moral Obstacles to the Freedom of the Negroes — Exclusive Spirit of the English Race — The Yankees Are New Jews — Difficulty in the Way of Emancipating the Laboring Class is Also Moral — Insufficiency of Philanthropy and Philosophy — Need for the Religious Sentiment — Lack of Religious Authority — In the United States Religion has Presided Over the Progress of the Lower Classes — Role of Politics in Social Reform; Connection Between a People's Religion and its Polity — Protestantism is Republican; Catholicism Monarchical — The Growth of Liberty Depends on the Development of Local Institutions — The Spirit of Association and the Spirit of Division — The Principles of Association and Unity Must Prevail in France

Augusta (Georgia), September 3, 1835. It is impossible to foresee the time when the blacks in this country shall be set free. Here, an abyss opens between the black and the white. The difficulty is not exactly financial; for, to apply to the two and a half million American Negroes the process which the English have applied to their colonies, only three hundred million dollars would be required, a sum which is not beyond the means of North America. By rendering the process of emancipation more gradual, so as to render it slower and safer than in the English Islands, a much less sum would be sufficient; but there is another obstacle against which money can do nothing. The English nature is exclusive; English society is divided into an endless number of little coteries, each jealous of its superior and despising its inferior. The Englishman is in his own country what his country is in reference to the rest of the world, insular.

This spirit of exclusiveness which prevails in society at home appears again in the relations of the English with other people. The Englishman cannot fraternize with the Indians or the blacks; between him and them there is no sympathy, no mutual confidence. The Anglo-Americans have retained and even exaggerated this trait of their fathers; and to the men of the North as well as to those of the South, to the Yankee as well as to the Virginian, the Negro is a Philistine, a son of Ham. In States without slaves, as well as in those in which slavery is allowed, the elevation of the black seems impossible.

An American of the North or of the South, whether he be rich or poor, ignorant or learned, avoids contact with the Negro as if he were infected with the plague. Free or slave, well or meanly clad, the black or the man of color is always a Pariah; he is denied lodging at the inns; at the theater or in the steamboats he has a distinct place allotted him far from the whites; he is excluded from commerce, for he cannot set his foot on 'Change nor in the banking rooms. Everywhere and always, he is eminently unclean. Thus treated as vile, he almost always becomes so.

In Europe, blacks or colored persons have sometimes filled high stations; there is not an instance of the kind in the United States. The republic of Haiti has its accredited representatives at the court of France; it has none in Washington. An anecdote was told me at New York of the disappointment of a young Haitian who was a near relation of one of Boyer's ministers and who had received a good education in France; having arrived in New York, he could not get into any hotel, his money was refused at the door of the theater, he was ordered out of the cabin of a steamboat and was obliged to quit the country without being able to speak to anybody. At Philadelphia, I heard of a man of color who had acquired wealth, a rare thing among that class, who used to invite whites to dine with him and did not sit at table but waited upon his guests himself. At the dessert, however, upon their pressing him to be seated with them, he would yield to their urgency. At the end of 1833, in one of the New England states, and I think it was in Massachusetts, a man of color on board a steamer with his wife wished to get her admitted to the ladies' room; the captain refused her admission. A suit was, therefore, brought against the captain by the man, who was desirous of having it decided by the courts whether free people of color, conducting themselves with propriety, could enjoy the same privileges with whites in a State in which they were recognized as citizens by the laws. He won at the first hearing, but the court of appeals decided on behalf of the captain.

The different nations of the great Christian family, after having for ages received the doctrines taught by the successors of St. Peter, have selected out of the Christian scheme some one principle most congenial to their nature and made it the basis of their character. The French, a most Christian people, have chosen the principle of universal charity. In our eyes, there are no longer Gentiles. Our kindness toward foreigners increases as the square of the distance that separates their country from ours. The Spanish, a chivalric people, have adopted with enthusiasm the adoration of the Virgin, which is of a more modern origin. The Protestants have taken up the principle of individual conscience and this is nearly all that they have accepted from Christianity; they have renounced the successive additions of the Church to the faith of the Apostles and they have even rejected a part of what Christ himself engrafted on the Jewish theology. Among Protestants, the Yankees have carried this retrograde tendency to the greatest extreme; they have, except in some few points, relapsed into Judaism and returned to the Mosaic law. They appeal to the maxims and doctrines of the Old Testament; they borrow their names from it, and among the peculiarities that strike a Frenchman in New England one of the strongest is the great prevalence of Hebrew names, such as Phineas, Ebenezer, Judah, Hiram, Obadiah, Ezra, etc., on the signs and in advertisements.

As a people's religion exercises a controlling influence over the general tone of its feeling and character, the Yankees, having thus fallen back into Judaism, possess like the Jews that exclusive spirit which was already inherent in their insular origin. The fact is that their religious notions square exactly with this depression of the blacks. The blacks seem to them inferior beings; they revolt against the thought of any assimilation with them, even in the slightest degree; a mixture of the two races or, as they call it, *amalgamation*, is in their eyes an abomination, a sacrilege, which would deserve to be punished, as the sin of the Hebrews with the daughters of Moab was punished. The emancipation of the Negro comprises two things; the one, formal, that is manumission by the master, which would not be difficult to effect if a sufficient indemnity were offered to the planters and the country could pay it; the other, moral, that is, a real acknowledgment of the rights of the black by admitting him to the personal privileges of the white man, which would meet with insurmountable obstacles at the North as well as the South and would, perhaps, be even more repugnant to the former than to the latter.

The principal obstacle to emancipation, so far as regards the slave himself, is also of a moral character. To render him fit for liberty, it is necessary to initiate him in the duties and dignity of man, that he should labor in order to pay his debt to society and maintain his family with decency, that he should learn to obey other motives than the fear of the lash. He must learn the sentiment of self-respect; he must wish and know how to be a father, son, husband. He only can have a perfect right to liberty who is in a condition to enjoy it with profit to himself and to society. Slavery, odious as it is, is one form of social order and must be preserved where no better form can be substituted for it, just as it must disappear when the inferior is ripe for a better state of things.

In regard to the working classes of Europe, the difficulty is the same which stands in the way of the emancipation of the American slaves; it is only different in degree and is already half overcome. In order that the hireling should be raised from his present abject state, the upper classes must be ready to treat him as a being of the same nature as themselves, and he himself must have acquired higher sentiments than such as belong to his present condition. He must not only be inspired with the desire of being happier, but also with the ambition of being better. To establish new relations between the proletariat and the *bourgeoisie,* both sides must desire it with a will strong enough to reshape ideas and habits. The question of the improvement of the condition of the lower classes is essentially a moral question. A moral remodeling of society is the necessary preliminary. Now, whoever pronounces the word *moral* in the wider sense of the term means religion. Philanthropy and philosophy have no hold on the moral nature of man unless they borrow it from religion. Religion only can move the hearts of all classes deeply enough, and enlighten the minds of all strongly enough, to cause the rich and the poor to conceive new ideas of their mutual relations and to realize them in practice.

History shows us that civilization in its successive phases has gradually improved the condition of the lower classes; it testifies also that each of the great changes that have taken place in the condition of the mass has been consummated or prepared by religion and accompanied by a change in religion itself. It was religion that struck off the fetters of the slave, that gradually freed the serf from the glebe. The emancipated principles of the French Revolution were only the precepts of the Christian religion practiced by persons who were no longer Christians, and the revolutionary actors themselves gave to Christ the title of *sans-culotte,* in their eyes a title of honor.

To render the efforts of the upper classes in favor of the people vigorous and sustained, they must, then, be directed by religion. To raise the lower classes effectually from their abasement, religion must fix them steadily on that high moral level to which they have occasionally soared by sublime, but fitful and faltering, flights. But the *bourgeoisie* have little faith. If among the leaders of that class the irreligious philosophy of the eighteenth century has of late lost adherents, it restores and increases its numbers from among the ranks. Skepticism has lowered its aim a peg; its train has lost in quality, but gained in quantity. Irreligion is at work among the populace of the cities, disposes them to revolt, and would make them unfit for the regular enjoyment of liberty. When we have roads, when schools have taught the whole population to read, which will be soon, you will see irreligion infecting the country people if you do not provide against its approaches beforehand.

Christianity, or at least Catholicism, seems to be on the verge of a general collapse among us. And yet how far we are from having drawn out from Christian principles, which some among us affect to consider exhausted, all the elements of popular liberty and happiness which they contain! We are a most Christian people in this sense, that we believe in the unity of the whole human family, and we prove it by our good will to all nations; but it seems as if we diffuse abroad all the warmth that Christianity has developed in our souls. We, the apostles of the brotherhood of nations, we have not yet breathed into our relations to each other the principle of the fraternity of men. We of the middle class, the sons of freedmen, think that laborers, the sons of slaves, are a different nature than we. We have still a remnant of the old pagan leaven at the bottom of our hearts. We do not, indeed, with Aristotle teach the doctrine of two distinct natures, the free nature and the slave nature, but we act in practice as if we were brought up in that faith. We are not yet become the fathers and elder brothers of the peasant and the operative; but in our relations to them we are still their *masters*, and hard masters too.

And unfortunately, while society, driven about by the waves, at the mercy of chance and without a compass, is exposed to disasters which the control of religion alone can prevent, religion makes no effort to resume the helm and recover her authority. In the midst of nations which rush toward every risk, Catholicism stands still, silently shrouded in her mantle, with arms folded and eyes bent on heaven. The Church bore all the shocks of the revolutionary storm with heroic resignation; she meekly submitted to be scourged with rods, like the Just One; like him she has been fixed to the Cross and has opened her mouth only to pray for her executioners. But the sufferings of the Just saved sinners and changed the face of the world; nothing betokens that the recent sufferings of the Catholic Church will have any saving power. From the tomb where it was laid for dead, we see it bring back no scheme for the restoration of suffering, longing humanity.

The Roman Church is what it was four hundred years ago; but within that period the world has become quite another thing; it has made great progress and freed itself from the past with the firm purpose of never turning back. If civilization, then, is about to assume a new form, as everything forebodes, religion, which is at once the beginning and end of society, the keystone and the cornerstone—religion must also recast herself. Would it be the first time that Christianity has modified her forms and rules to adapt herself to the instincts and the tendencies of the nations she has sought to bless?

Here in the United States religion has presided over the progress of the lower classes. Puritanism has been the starting point of the democratic movement. The Puritans came to America, not in quest of gold, nor to conquer provinces, but to found a Church on the principle of primitive equality. They were, as I have said before, new Jews; they wished to govern by the laws of Moses. In the beginning the state was completely swallowed up by the Church; they divided themselves into religious congregations in which all the heads of families were equal, in conformity with the Mosaic law, over which the elders and the saints presided and in which all earthly distinctions were abolished or contemned. Under the influence of their religious views one of the first objects of their care was to establish schools in which all the children should be educated together and in the same manner. Although unequal in respect to property, all adopted the same habits of life. The physical exertions to which all were obliged to devote themselves in common in order to defend themselves from famine and the savages strengthened their habits and feelings of equality. Now, New England, which is inhabited exclusively by the sons of the Puritans and in which their traditions and their faith are still kept unchanged, has ever been, and is yet, the focus of American democracy.

Thus American democracy has been enabled to organize and establish itself. On the contrary, all our efforts to found a democracy in France in 1793 would have been vain, even had we not been unfitted for democratic habits, because we wished to build on irreligion, on the hatred of religion. Manners and feelings must prepare and inspire the means of social improvement; the laws must express and prescribe them. Politics and religion, then, must join hands in this difficult task. Politics, as well as religion, must be transformed for the furtherance of civilization and the safety of the world.

I admire the results which the political system of the United States has produced in America. But it seems to me impossible that the institutions by which the condition of the people has been so much bettered here can be naturalized among us. There must be harmony between the political and religious schemes that are suited to any one people. Protestantism is republican; Puritanism is absolute self-government in religion and begets it in politics. The United Provinces were Protestant; the United States are Protestant. Catholicism is essentially monarchical; in countries which are Catholic, at least by recollections, habits, and education if not by faith, a regular democracy is impracticable. The anarchy of the former Spanish colonies fully proves to what bitter regrets Catholic nations expose themselves when they attempt to apply to themselves the political institutions of Protestant countries.

Under the influence of Protestantism and republicanism, social progress has been achieved by pushing the process of division to its extreme, that is, individualism; for Protestantism, republicanism, and individualism are all one. Individuals have cut themselves off from each other; each has isolated his personality in order to protect it; or if they are associated together, they have formed associations for only limited purposes, with no other tie between them.

The republic of the United States is subdivided indefinitely into independent republics of various classes. The States are republics in the general confederation; the towns are republics within the States; a farm is a republic in a county. Banking, canal, and railroad companies are so many distinct republics. The family is an inviolable republic in the State; each individual is a small republic by himself in the family. The only effective militia consists of volunteer companies which have no connection with each other. The religious organization of the country resembles its civil and political organization. The different sects are independent of each other and most of them tend to split up into completely detached fragments.

Our national genius, on the contrary, requires that in France we should act chiefly under the influence of association and unity, which are characteristic traits of Catholicism and monarchy. France is a specimen of the completest political and administrative unity that there is in the world. Our individual existence must be bound up with others; we love independence, but we do not feel that we live unless we make a part of a whole. Solitude overpowers us; the personality of the Englishman or the American can sustain itself alone; ours must be linked with that of others. For a people eminently social, like the French, how is it possible that the spirit of association should not be the best? But it must retain the distinction of ranks; for with us, a republican association would degenerate into anarchy.

If, then, I should attempt to define the conditions most favorable to the improvement of society in France, I would say it should be undertaken under the influence of religion; that its accomplishment should be, in most cases, confided to the constituted authorities, central and local, and, above all, to royalty; that it should be effected principally by means of institutions bearing the double impress of unity and hierarchical order and reposing immediately on the general association which is the state, or supported by powerful intermediary associations which should be themselves attached to the state. The nearer we approach these conditions, the more complete will be our success, the sooner shall we have the happiness of seeing our beloved France, prosperous within, recover the high station which we ought to occupy in the world.

XXX

The Empire State

Centralized Character of New York State — Centralization of Schools and Instruction in General; of Banks; of Public Works — Results of Public Works — Charters of Railroad and Canal Companies — Influence of New York's Example — Modern Nations Cannot Dispense with Authority — Religion Cannot Completely Take the Place of Political Means of Control — Authority Must Change Its Attributes — Banks,

Means of Communication and Schools Are the Instruments of Government Which Must, in Part, Replace the Old Violent Attributes of Authority — New Degree of the Inviolability of the Human Personality — Favorable Disposition of the Public Spirit

Albany, September 11, 1835.
There are in the United States two strongly marked types, the Yankee and the Virginian, whose mutual balance has up to now been the life of the Union. A third is rising in the West which seems destined to become the link and umpire of the other two if it is able to preserve its own unity —which will not, however, be easy, for the West comprises slaveholding and non-slaveholding States. Provisionally, this high office of moderator is filled by the group of States known as the Middle or Central States, which geographically are intermediate to the two extremes of the Atlantic coast; or rather the position belongs now to New York, which is the most important State not only of this group but of the whole Union. To be a mediator between two types, it is necessary to unite in one person the principal qualities of both; the State of New York, then, should combine the large views of the South with the spirit of detail that marks the North. To be, even imperfectly, the personification of the principle of unity in the great American confederation, it is indispensable that the claimant of that honor should possess in a high degree the spirit of unity. To achieve the work of centralization or consolidation in America, even partially, demands a high degree of the genius of centralization. For some time there has appeared in the administration of the State of New York a character of grandeur, unity, and centralization that has procured it the title of the *Empire State*. Although it is the nearest neighbor of the New England States, and actually borders upon three of them, although a large number of its inhabitants are of New England origin, it has succeeded in freeing itself from the spirit of extreme division that is char-

acteristic of the Yankees, or rather in counterbalancing it by a proportionate development of the spirit of unity.

The Opposition, which is in the minority in the legislature in the State and does not, therefore, feel in good humor, endeavors to create among the people a dislike to this control of the central power. "You are led," it says, "by the Albany Regency; a half dozen of the friends of Mr. Van Buren, taking their cue from Governor Marcy, make you their puppets." The Opposition exaggerates; but it is certain that the organization of the State and the forms of administration which have been established recently under the influence of Mr. Van Buren, and which form a precedent for the future, bear the impress of a centralism at which the friends of unlimited individual independence have a right to take alarm, but which wise men must applaud; for it is precisely by this that the State of New York has become superior to others and it is by this alone that it can maintain its superiority. This combination of expansive force, which prevails everywhere else in the Union, with sufficient cohesive power has given the constitution of New York an elasticity which, for communities as well as for individuals, is the condition of a long and prosperous existence.

The organization of the public schools and of public instruction in general is centralized. Most of the States in the Union have a school fund, the income of which in New England is distributed among the towns, who dispose of it according to their own good pleasure, without the State having the right to exercise any real control over it or impose any conditions in regard to it. New York proceeds more *imperially:* it obliges the different towns to raise a sum equal to that which they are entitled from the State under penalty of not receiving their share of the State fund. This method is preferable to that followed in Connecticut, which distributes annually among the towns about the same sum as New York, but exacts no account of the manner in which it has been employed and cannot even be sure that it has been actually devoted to the purpose of instruction.

In 1834, the primary schools in New York were attended by 541,400 pupils; now the number of children between five and sixteen years of age in the districts from which returns were received, comprising very nearly the whole State, was only 543,085. The whole expenditure for schools was $1,310,000, of which $750,000 was for pay of teachers. The amount expended in France for the same object is only three times as great as that expended by New York, which has one sixteenth of the population of France. The number of children in our schools is 2,450,000, one thirteenth of the population or, proportionately, three times less than in the State of New York.

All the primary schools in New York, more than 10,000, are under the supervision and control of a Board of Commissioners composed principally of several of the chief officers of the government, of which the Secretary of State is the most active member. The commissioners make provision for the instruction of teachers, require an account of the condition of the school and select the textbooks. Virginia, Ohio, and some other States have adopted a similar system, but New York has this peculiarity, that it has also a board, styled the Board of Regents of the University, who are appointed by the legislature and have the control of the higher schools, called academies. There are seven colleges in the State, one of which is styled the University of New York and corresponds, very remotely it is true, to the English and German Universities with their four faculties.

The control of the government over the academies is at present very limited. It consists of little more than an annual visit by one or more of the Regents of the University, but it can easily be extended whenever the State shall think proper by means of the system of pecuniary aid; in 1834, the sum distributed among these seminaries was $12,500. The number of pupils in the academies this year was a little more than 5,000 for a population of 2,100,000, or two and a half pupils for each thousand. In France, out of 33,000,000, there were 80,000 pupils in the colleges, which is the same ratio to the whole population. It would appear from this comparison that in the United States, where the advantages of elementary instruction are universally realized, the desire for a higher degree of instruction is less general than with us, for the number of families that can afford to pay is proportionately much greater in the United States than in France. Thus in regard to higher education we recover in some measure the superiority which the Americans, at least in New York, have over us in respect to elementary education.

The same spirit of unity and centralization has dictated a general regulation for banks, quite remarkable in principle and which may prove to be of great value in practice, to which there is nothing similar either in the other States or in any other country. The Safety Fund Act establishes a bank fund appropriated to making good any losses incurred by the failure of any of the banks. Each bank is required to pay annually to the State treasurer a sum equal to one half of one per cent on its capital, until it shall have so paid in the sum of three per cent on the capital stock. Whenever the bank fund is reduced by paying the debts of an insolvent bank, it must be restored to the proper amount by the same process. The banks, together with the fund, are under the supervision of three commissioners, one of whom is appointed by the Governor and the two others by the banks. The commissioners visit each bank at least once in four months, examine into its operations, and satisfy themselves that it has conformed to the provisions of its charter. They are further required to make a particular examination of any bank on the demand of three other banks and, in case of detecting any violation of the charter, to apply to the court of chancery for an injunction against it.

This law contains several sections designed to aid the commissioners in the execution of their duties and to prevent their being imposed on by the banks; it gives them the right to inspect the books and to examine the officers of the bank under oath. The salary of the commissioners is $2,000, which is paid out of the bank fund. Any bank director or officer who shall make false returns to the legislature, or false entries in the books, or exhibit false papers with intent to deceive the commissioners is subject to imprisonment for not less than three nor more than ten years. The law sets a rate of interest of six per cent for notes of less than sixty-three days; it also sets a limit to the amount of paper money that can be issued as well as loans and discounts; it provides that the issues or circulation of any bank shall not exceed twice its capital stock and that its loans and discounts shall never exceed twice and a half that amount, but this provision has not hitherto been rigidly observed.

The number of banks in the State is 87, of which only 77 are subject to the provisions of the Safety Fund Act, the others having been established before the date of the act. But as all will be obliged to renew their charters within ten years, with the single exception of the Manhattan bank, which has a perpetual charter, they will all, with one exception, be brought under the act. The aggregate of the bank capital in the State is $31,280,000; the bank fund amounts to above $538,000. The annual amount of the loans and discounts of the banks is estimated at about $300,000,000, exclusive of the operations of the three branches of the United States Bank; that of the banks of the city of New York alone is about $180,000,000, or twice as much as that of the Bank of France.

Nothing, however, has contributed so much to give New York its *imperial* reputation as the energy it has displayed in canalling its territory. All the resources of the State were devoted to this object; all the energies of its citizens were bent for eight years on the accomplishment of this great work. In spite of the worst predictions and earnest remonstrances of some of the most respected men in the Union, the confidence of this young State never faltered for a moment. Complete success attended its efforts; the great canal, begun in 1817, was finished in 1825. The State has since executed a great number of canals at an expense of more than $12,000,000, the greater part of which has been raised by loan. Several others are still in progress.

The Erie Canal, the most important of these works, is simple in construction, not very deep nor very wide. But if, as an object of art, it is only moderately interesting, as a commercial artery it is prodigious. You can get no idea from our canals, which are navigated by heavy and clumsy boats slowly and painfully dragged forward by a man, of this great channel with its fleet of light, elegant, covered barks gliding along at a rapid rate, each drawn by a powerful team. Every minute boats are passing each other and the boatman's horn warns the lockmaster to be in readiness. Each moment the landscape varies; now you pass a river by an aqueduct, now you traverse large new towns, as fine as capitals, with all their houses having pillared porticos and looking externally like little palaces; it is an admirable spectacle of life and variety. The amount of various kinds of merchandise annually transported on the Erie Canal is 430,000 tons, on the Champlain Canal, 307,000 tons, at very moderate cost. The annual amount of tolls is $1,500,000; that on French canals and rivers is only $900,000.

In 1817, when it began the great canal, the State of New York contained 1,250,000 inhabitants, scattered over a surface about one fourth as large as France. While in Europe grave publicists were discussing the question of whether a State should undertake the execution of public works and the most powerful governments were listening scrupulously to the debate in order to determine whether they had the right to enrich their subjects by productive enterprises—the same governments who never doubted their right to waste millions of men and treasure in devastating Europe—the modest authorities of this miniature empire solved the question without dreaming that it could embarrass great potentates in other quarters. The State of

New York undertook the execution of public works and has found its advantage in them; after having executed them, it has managed them itself on its own account and found even greater advantages in this. The income from the canals, with the aid of some slight additions, has been sufficient to sink nearly half the debt contracted in their construction. Thus the brilliant success of the Erie Canal became the signal for the greatest undertakings of a similar character by the other States. Pennsylvania, Ohio, Maryland, Virginia, and Indiana have followed the example of New York and have undertaken to open routes of communication of every kind through their territories at their own expense, even at the risk of incurring the reproaches of the timid economists of Europe.

New York has carried her interference in public works still further; in all the charters for railroad companies the State reserves to itself the right of acquiring the property of the railroad after ten years on certain conditions named in the act of incorporation, which are truly liberal on the part of the State; they stipulate repayment of the initial cost plus the sums expended in repairs and the supply of any deficiency in the dividends below ten per cent.

Thus the State of New York, in its imperial humor, has laid hands on public instruction, banks, and the means of communication with the purpose of centralizing them; the design is already effected in respect to public works; it is not yet fully accomplished in regard to the schools and the banks but its fulfilment approaches gradually and surely. As I have already said, the spirit of centralization has penetrated more deeply into the administration of the State than into the acts of the legislature, a guarantee that the laws of unity will not remain paper rules.

The lessons of New York have profited its neighbors; like it, they also begin the work of centralization by embracing schools, banks, and public works within the action of the State. They see, by its example, that the spirit of individual enterprise does not suffer when the government subjects to its control and its authority these three great springs of national prosperity, and even when it sets them in action on its own account; for nowhere is the spirit of enterprise more vigorous and clear-sighted than in New York. In spite of the Safety Fund Act, there are nowhere more numerous applications for the incorporation of banking companies. Notwithstanding the school laws, nowhere do institutions of education increase more rapidly. Nowhere are there more railroads in progress. The State contains 80 miles of canal and 100 of railroads constructed by private companies; from 150 to 200 miles of railroad are now in the process of construction, and a company has been organized for constructing a railroad from the Hudson to Lake Erie through the southern counties, a distance of 350 miles.

It surely would be too much if a country like France, where so much value is set on the principles of unity and centralization, were to be less courageous than these little republics, born under the influence of the individual principle, and if we should any longer delay to take an *imperial* course in regard to institutions of credit, public works, and industrial education. The object to be accomplished is not merely to increase the wealth of the country. There are other and more elevated motives to induce modern governments to take part in such institutions and thus to extend their control over the interests and operations of industry.

With reference to the individual, the progress of civilization is measured by the degree to which each person becomes more and more fit to bear the weight of his individuality. Social order, therefore, having stronger and stronger individual guarantees, seems less and less to require legal and public ones; but in this matter an important distinction must be kept in mind. Civilization gradually strips man of the grosser habits and the brutal propensities of savage life. There are many prohibitions and commands in Deuteronomy which in our day would be perfectly superfluous. Mankind hardly has further need to be taught: *Thou shalt not kill*. The lictor and the headsman are losing their social importance; the constable, the sheriff, and the warden are, it is to be hoped, on the eve of taking their places everywhere. Public order has begun, and will continue more and more, to dispense with the use of the sword; and thus, happily, individual reason substitutes its voluntary sanction for the imperative sanction of political power and the force of arms.

Human understanding is expanded and enlightened by cultivation; the heart is elevated and purified; yet the basic and primitive passions remain the same. They combine in different ways and turn to different objects; but if they are moderated, it is only in outward appearances; if they are polished, it is only on the surface; within all is as rough and fierce as ever. (It was Madame de Staël who said, "Strange destiny of mankind, condemned ever to retrace the same circle by the passions, while ever advancing in the career of thought!") In politics, particularly, jealousy and ambition exist in the same degree among us as among the Greeks and Romans; they no longer wield the dagger or administer poison, they do not even employ an assassin or a Locusta; but they are neither less unjust, nor less insatiable, nor less bitter than in ancient times; they do not stab the body but they wound honor; slander takes the place of the stiletto and serves as well as the juices of some venomous plants; civilization furnishes them a thousand new means of assuaging their thirst. I do not believe that Sylla and Marius, Caesar and Pompey, hated each other more cordially than General Jackson, President of the United States, and Mr. Biddle, president of the United States' Bank. If one were to search out the types of Cain and Abel among modern statesmen, the list would be of frightful length.

To that force of dissolution which increases instead of diminishing, in proportion to the increase in the number of individuals admitted to a share of political influences, it is necessary to oppose cohesive elements of equal activity and intensity. It is for this reason that in the future, as well as in the past, the existence of society involves religion. Even did religion not touch the tenderest cords and stir the liveliest sensibilities of the human heart; if it did not offer to the imagination a vast field in which to wander in safety; even if it were not indispensable to peace of conscience and to domestic tranquillity, it would be impossible to get along without it, for it has also a political necessity. It has been rightly said that if God did not exist, it would be necessary to invent Him.

A single institution, however, would not suffice to regulate and govern the passions at all times and in all places, unless it were to follow men in all their movements, control them in all their acts, bind them hands and feet, or, in a word, unless it were despotic after the image of the old theocracies. It is not, then, possible to hope that in our free countries religion alone can counterbalance human passions and confine them within the limits in which they serve the progress of society; or at least, if it can do this in one of the social hemispheres, the family, it will always be insufficient in the other, the state. For this reason the Middle Ages established a salutary principle when they separated temporal power from spiritual power and gave strength and independence to each. Since then all efforts to confound these two powers or, which amounts to the same thing, to dispense with one of them have been completely unsuccessful; they have generally resulted in establishing a tyranny.

Temporal power, armed with ample prerogatives, is, then, indispensable at the present day in the interest of liberty itself. On the other hand, it is impossible to deny that the tendency of civilization is to strip the throne of its ancient attributes, either in whole or in part. On this our age has taken a decided stand. The resistance of kings to the efforts of those who have assailed the throne has served to exasperate the latter to such a pitch that a party, the republicans, has been formed whose sole object is the complete and radical abolition of monarchy; even the singular doctrine of the inutility and danger of all power has found numerous and warm partisans.

The people are right to desire the kings to lay down or to curtail their old prerogatives; governments, the heirs of conquest, ought to abdicate whatever there is of violence and brutality in their authority. It would be premature to assert that universal peace is about to dawn on the earth or that war will henceforth be only a secondary and accidental matter in the history of nations. Industry, that is to say the art of creating wealth, multiplying the means of happiness, and adorning the globe, the residence of the human family, will henceforth take precedence over the art of slaying and wasting. The sword is ceasing to be the highest emblem of power. But kings are right, in their turn, to prevent their power from being reduced to an empty shadow. Independent of all individual ambition, they see from the lofty height on which they stand that the preservation of the order of society demands the presence of a power worthy of the name. And what proves the justness of their view is the fact that men of all parties who have taken part in the government during our revolutionary crisis have all agreed on this point, whatever their former opinions; it is the only point on which they have been unanimous.

The truth is that while we are taking from governments, we must also be giving to them. War is no longer the principal object of the activity of nations; the employment of brute force becomes less and less necessary to the preservation of society; let us then gradually reduce, with a firm hand, those prerogatives of power which give it an exclusively warlike character and which leave our lives and liberties at the discretion of its armed creatures! Since industry is occupying a wider and wider space in the existence of the individual and the nation, let us see to it that industry falls more and more completely into the sphere of government, and let us class among the attributes of government the three springs of the industrial movement, banks, means of communication, and schools; on condition, be it understood, that government shall use the new powers with which it shall be thus invested for the general good.

Banks, means of communication, and schools are instruments of government which it would be unwise to leave wholly outside the influence of public power, but which there could be no harm in partially incorporating with it in such a manner as not to stifle the spirit of individual enterprise. Public authority would then exercise its functions in conformity with the tendencies of national character and would preside over the most important events of national life; it would then really deserve the name of government; it would possess a new means of coercion and restraint which is the only one compatible with the progress of the spirit of liberty. Instead of having a hold on the body and blood of the subject, it would have a hold on his industry and his purse. A new degree of inviolability would thus be secured to the individual without depriving the social order of its necessary guarantees. By this means, in fine, the political advent of industry would be accomplished. Instead of being a cause of agitation and change, once sure of its rank and secure in its seat, industry would act an important conservative part in society.

Everything is now ripe for this political transformation. Forty years ago, the people wished to march toward progress by the overthrow of the old order of things. Hatred has now ceased to be their chief counselor; the thirst for destruction is cooled; they think less of shaking off the yoke of tyrants, more of freeing themselves from the burdens of ignorance and poverty. The road to liberty which is the better for Europe and which would be preferred today passes through economic well-being, education, and industry. Those who were once the temporal and spiritual heads of the people would soon regain their lost rank if, calming the fears with which the curses uttered against the last of kings and the last of priests had filled them, they knew how to put themselves at the head of such a march; for the people would follow them with joy. By what fatality is it that they still hesitate?

I know not if I deceive myself, but it seems to me that

in this matter the example must come from France. Not that she has greater sums in her treasury, not that she counts more soldiers under her flag, more ships in her ports, more cannon in her fortresses, but that she has the most sagacious intellect and the noblest heart; the world is accustomed to receive the watchword from her. London, with its thousands of ships, might be burned to the ground and the rest of the world would be no otherwise affected by the event than as by a lamentable disaster which has befallen a foreigner; the recoil of a mere riot in Paris is felt to the ends of the world. The revolution of July gave birth to Parliamentary Reform; the Reform Bill would never have brought forth July. It is because France is the heart of the world; the affairs of France interest all; the cause which she espouses is not that of selfish ambition, but that of civilization. When France speaks, she is listened to because she speaks not her own feelings merely, but those of the human race. When she acts, her example is followed because she does what all desire to do.

France was the first on the European continent to enthrone liberty; it is for her to re-seat the principle of authority, for the fullness of its time is come. She protected the people when protection was necessary; it is now for her to protect kings; not by the edge of the sword, although she must not break her own which has done so much for civilization (for that would be sacrilege), but by the wisdom and the moral superiority of her new principles of government, by the creative power of the new attributes with which she invests authority.

XXXI

Symptoms of Revolution

Excesses Committed — Weakening of Respect for the Law — Wrongs of Popular Justice — Riots in Baltimore — Neglect of Great Principles — Decline of Civil Courage — Dependent State of the Press — Lack of Restraining Power — Industrial Superiority and Political Inferiority of the Present Generation — Probability That the Crisis Will Turn Out Well

Baltimore, September 25, 1835.
Two years ago Mr. Clay began a speech in the Senate with these words, which have become celebrated on this side of the Atlantic: "We are in the midst of a revolution." It was at the time when, by an act of authority before unheard of in American history, General Jackson had just settled the bank question which his friends in Congress and even his own ministers had refused to decide. These words have often been repeated by others. More recently, since the scenes of murder, outrage, and destruction which have been exhibited through the United States, both in the slaveholding States and in those in which slavery does not exist, in the country as well as in the towns, at Boston, the republican city *par excellence*, as well as at Baltimore, where the bloody excesses during the War of 1812 with England earned it the title of the *Mob Town*, good citizens have repeated with grief: "We are in the midst of a revolution."

It must be granted to the honor of the English race that it is, more deeply than any other, imbued with a feeling of reverence for the law. Until lately, Americans have shown themselves in this respect, as well as in others, to be doubledistilled Englishmen. There are nations who only conceive of law in a living form, that is, only so far as it is personified in a man. They know how to obey a leader but they cannot learn to respect a lifeless letter. With them the glory and prosperity of a state depend little on the character of the laws, but much on the character of the men who are charged with interpreting them. In their view, the empire rises and falls by turns, according as the sovereign, whatever may be his title, is a superior man or an ordinary personage. Such appears to be, in general, the character of the Asiatics. The Englishman is formed in a different mold; he willingly bows to the authority of a text but he stoops to man with reluctance. He does not require that obedience to law should be inculcated by the voice of man, he obeys it without an effort and by instinct. In a word, the Englishman has in himself the principle of self-government. This fact accounts for the success of his political system in the United States, where the native character of the English race is fully developed.

Unfortunately, reverence for the laws seems to be disappearing among Americans. These people, eminently practical in everything else, have allowed themselves to be pushed into the excess of theory in politics and have here taken up abstract logic in spite of everything; they have shrunk from none of the consequences of popular sovereignty, at least while those consequences were flattering to their pride; as if there were a single principle in the world, not excepting Christian charity itself, which could be carried to its extreme logical consequences without resulting in absolute absurdity. They have, therefore, been driven in the United States to deny that there is any principle true in and by itself and to assert that the will of the people is always and necessarily just; the infallibility of the people in everything and at all times has, in fact, become received doctrine, and thus a door has been opened to the tyranny of a turbulent minority which always calls itself the people.

The appearance of this miscalled *popular justice*, administered by the hands of a few desperate or furious men who call themselves the successors of the Boston Tea Party of

1773, is a great calamity in the bosom of a country where there is no other guarantee of the public peace than a reverence for law and where the legislator, taking for granted the prevalence of order, has made no provisions against disorder. This popular justice has the greater condemnation of being for the most part grossly unjust. Most of the men who have been hanged or flogged or tortured in twenty other atrocious ways in the South as Abolitionists, that is, as guilty of instigating the slaves to rise against their masters, were according to all appearances merely guilty of having expressed their abhorrence of slavery with too little caution. It is even doubtful whether the pretended plots for which whites and blacks have been summarily executed really existed. At least no proof of their reality which would be admitted by a court of justice has yet been brought forward. During the outrages last month at Baltimore which lasted four days, this self-styled justice was most stupidly unjust. The mob gave out that it wished to punish those knaves who had shamefully abused the credulity of the poor in the affair of the Bank of Maryland. It is a matter of public notoriety that the bankruptcy of the bank was fraudulent; that just before it stopped payment it had offered a high rate of interest on deposits of any amount in order to attract to its counter the savings of the laboring classes; but it was also a matter of notoriety that the criminal acts of the bank were wholly the work of one Evan Poultney, who alone was, in fact, the bank. Instead of going to take vengeance for the ruin of the artisan, the widow, and the orphan on the author of it, the mob went to call to account the bankruptcy commissioners appointed by the court. It was not till the third day that it thought to make a visit to Poultney, who, without being at all disconcerted, began to cry out that he was a sinner, that he had been guilty of wronging his neighbor. He beat his breast in sign of repentance and in a puritanical slang accused himself more loudly than the rioters had done. Blinded, like Orgon, by so much sanctity, they excused themselves to Tartuffe, carefully swept the hall and the marble doorsteps which they had soiled, and hastened to sack the house of the mayor because a small detachment of militia, spontaneously assembled, had fired upon them in self-defense after having stood patient for some time under a shower of stones.

These disorders are alarming from their general prevalence and frequent repetition and, more so, because their importance is little realized. They meet with few voices to condemn them, but they find many to excuse them. One of the defects of democracy is that it is forgetful of the past and careless of the future. A riot which in France would put a stop to business prevents no one here from going to the Exchange, speculating, turning over a dollar and making money. On meeting in the morning, each one asks and tells the news; here a Negro has been hanged, there a white man has been flogged; at Philadelphia, ten houses have been demolished; at Buffalo, at Utica, some people of color have been scourged. Then they go on to the price of cotton and coffee, the arrivals of flour, lumber, and tobacco, and become absorbed in calculations the rest of the day. I am surprised to see how dead the word *equality* falls when a good citizen pronounces it; the reign of law seems to be at an end; we have fallen under that of expediency. Farewell to justice, farewell to the great principles of 1776 and 1789! All hail to the interest of the moment, interpreted by nobody knows who, for the success of some petty intrigue of politics or business!

Five men, five white men, have been hanged at Vicksburg in Mississippi without even the form of a trial; they were gamblers, you are told, the scourge of the country. The *most respectable* citizens of Vicksburg assisted in their execution. But, one asks, the law which guarantees to all your fellow citizens trial by a jury of peers; but that old Saxon justice of which you boast! What is become of them? The answer—no court would have been able to rid us of them; morality and religion condemn them, and the moral and religious decree, for want of others, we have executed;

it was necessary. *Expediency!* In Virginia, travelers from Northern States, on the slightest pretense, for some tavern gossip or some conversation in the coach, have been dragged before the self-styled *Committees of Vigilance,* then beaten, tarred, and feathered. Others, whose crime consisted in inadvertently having in their pocket some papers which the slaveholder has been pleased to pronounce Abolitionist writings, have been seized by these fanatics and hanged as emissaries of insurrection. What is become of that article of the Constitution which secures to the citizens of each State the protection of the laws in every other State? If we were to insist on these points, we would endanger our union with the South. *Expediency!* Merchants of New York! The planters of one of the parishes of Louisiana have set a price on the head of one of your number because, as they say, he is an Abolitionist, an amalgamator. Will not your national sensibility, so lively in regard to France, be touched by this act of audacity? Our commerce with the South constitutes half the prosperity of New York. *Expediency!* Men of New England! Citizens of the cradle of American liberty! Sons of the pilgrims, self-exiled first to Holland and then to the sandy shores of Massachusetts rather than bow their opinions to the will of the Stuarts! You, so proud of your liberties, how can you abandon the dearest of all, the liberty of the press, to the hands of a postmaster? Always the same reply: *Expediency!*

It seems as if no political principle existed in the United States but the pleasure of the passions, as if law had no force when it jarred with interest. When a State feels itself injured by a tariff, it declares the law null and void, arms its militia, buys powder, and throws down the glove to Congress. When another State, Ohio, is dissatisfied with the boundary line assigned to it, it declares war against Michigan, its neighbor, in order to extend its frontiers by force. When the fanatics of Massachusetts, in their savage intolerance, feel offended by the presence of a Catholic convent in which the Sisters devote themselves to the work of educating young girls without distinction of sect, they plunder it and set it on fire; and the sacred edifice is burned in sight of a city of 70,000 without a drop of water thrown upon the flames and without it being possible to find a jury that would convict the authors of the cowardly outrage. When a governor of Georgia comes into collision with an upright magistrate who interposes his authority between the rapacity of the whites and the poor Indian whom they are impatient to rob, he denounces the just judge to the legislature and urges the passing of a law that will make him a State criminal. And, I repeat it, the worst and most fatal symptom of the times is that the perpetration of these outrages, however frequent they become, excites no sensation. The destruction of the churches and schoolhouses of the blacks in New York was looked upon as a show, and the passing merchants of the city paused to take a moment's relaxation from the sight; the fall of the building was greeted with loud cheers. In Baltimore, a numerous crowd applauded the work of demolition without inquiring whose house was pulled down, and the women, in the excitement of the moment, waved their handkerchiefs in the air.

Another symptom still more alarming! Civil courage, the virtue of the Hampdens, the glory of the English race, which shone with so pure a luster in the United States while the authors of their independence survived, seems to be for a time extinct; I say for a time, for there is a stock of energy in the American character which cannot fail some time or another to revive and put forth its strength anew. The press, which with a few honorable exceptions does not possess and does not merit in the United States the consideration which it enjoys in France; the press, which is here so outrageously violent and brutal in its treatment of members of Congress belonging to the opposite party, is on the other hand more cautious and reserved in regard to the multitude. The American press is free insofar as it gives no bonds and pays no stamp duty, but it is dependent on a capricious, despotic, and not very enlightened public opinion which requires it to flatter the passion of the hour and does not look to it for lessons of morality. The public opinion of the democracy is a master who is easily offended and who quickly shows his displeasure. The American journalist is well aware that for the slightest display of boldness he will be deserted. Since recent events, this is not his only fear, for he knows that if his enemies should choose to brand him as an Abolitionist, for example, it would be easy to raise a mob of vagabonds who would pillage and pull down his house, tar and feather him, and drive him from home without any interference by the public authorities. He is therefore exceedingly circumspect. In a word, the *reign of terror* has begun in the United States. Men of courage and devotion to the cause of law have no rallying point in the press; even when public authority might be disposed to support them, it proves insufficient, either through fear or concern for party interests or want of physical force. For the small number of good citizens in whom the state of the country excites the liveliest alarm, there appears to be no resource left but that of organizing themselves in patriotic societies, forming themselves into military companies, of creating, in fine, a national guard under the form which the laws and national customs would sanction. They feel that this step is necessary, but they hesitate because they fear to kindle a civil war. The people of Baltimore, however, seem determined to make the trial. It has also been proposed that the towns be responsible by law for the damages committed within their limits. Such a law, if it did not wholly prevent the disorders since the taxes here are mostly paid by the rich, would at least have the merit of repairing the losses suffered by means of them.

The present generation in the United States, brought up in devotion to business, living in an atmosphere of self-interest, if it is superior to the last generation in commercial intelligence and industrial enterprise, is inferior to it in civil courage and love of the public good. Deplorable fact! Recently, when Baltimore was given up to the genius of destruction four whole days, when the protection of the city had been vainly transferred from the mayor to the sheriff and from the sheriff to the commanding officer of the militia, when the prisons had been forced, when the mayor and the militia were attacked—when finally the spirit of order began to revive, not a man was found in this city of 100,000 to put himself at the head of the movement. When the most respectable citizens, those most deeply interested in the restoration of public order, held a meeting in the Exchange, the mountain in labor brought forth only a long series of *whereases* on the advantage of public order and a string of wordy resolutions which resolved nothing. Nothing, shameful to relate, but the presence of a veteran of the Revolution with the weight of eighty-four years on his head, who had retired from Congress to end his long career in repose but who felt his blood boil in his veins and mantle in his cheeks at the spectacle before him—nothing but his presence gave courage to this assembly of men in the vigor of life who were letting their city fall a prey to a handful of drunkards and depraved boys. The indignant old man started up and interrupted the reading of the resolutions; "Damn your resolutions!" he cried. "Give me a sword and thirty men and I will restore order." "What! General Smith," said one of these irresolute makers of resolutions, "would you fire upon your fellow citizens?" "Those who break the laws, drive their neighbor from his house, plunder his property, and reduce his wife and children to beggary," answered General Smith, "such fellows are not my fellow citizens." These words which expressed the thoughts of all, but which no one dared utter, were received with a thunder of applause. The aged Senator was named commander of the military force by acclamation and a few days after was chosen mayor. Since that time Baltimore has been quiet. But when we reflect that order has been restored in a large and flourishing city only because there happened to be present a veteran whom death had spared and who had energy enough with one foot in the grave to come forward and teach his fellow citizens by example the lessons of the golden age of American liberty, are we not forced to exclaim with Mr. Clay, "We are in the midst of a revolution"?

Mr. Clay is no false prophet, for the events that have succeeded each other since he uttered these words announce that a crisis is at hand. The American system no longer works well. In the North, the removal of all restrictions on the right of suffrage without the creation of any counterpoise has destroyed the equilibrium. In the South, the old foundation borrowed from pre-Christian times, on which the South has attempted to raise the superstructure of a new social order in the nineteenth century, shakes and threatens to bury the thoughtless builders under the ruins of their half-finished work. In the West, a population sprung from the soil under the influence of circumstances unparalleled in the history of the world already affects a superiority, or rather lays claim to dominion, over the North and South. Everywhere, the relations established by the old federal compact are unfitted to the new state of things. The dissolution of the Union, the mere thought of which would have caused a shudder of horror ten years ago, which was numbered among those acts of infamy that are not to be named—the dissolution of the Union has been demanded and no thunder fell upon the head of the perpetrator of the sacrilege. At present it is a common topic of conversation. The dissolution of the Union, if it should take place, would be the most complete of all revolutions.

What will be the character of this revolution which one feels approaching? To what institutions will it give birth? Who must perish in the day of account? Who will rise on the storm? Who will resist the action of ages? I have not the gift of prophecy and I shall not try to pierce the mystery of the destinies of the New World. But I have a firm faith that a people with the energy and intelligence which the Americans possess, a people which like it has the genius of industry, which combines perseverance with the resources of ingenuity, which is essentially regular in its habits and orderly in its disposition, which is deeply imbued with religious habits even when a lively faith is wanting, such a people cannot be born yesterday to vanish tomorrow. The American people, in spite of its original defects, in spite of the numerous voids which a hasty growth and a superficial education have left in its ideas, feelings, and customs, is still a great and powerful people. For such nations, the most violent storms are wholesome trials which strengthen, solemn warnings which teach, elevate, and purify.

XXXII

The Middle Classes

Elements of French Society — Remnants of the Aristocracy — The Active Middle Class; the Idle Middle Class — Workers and Peasants — Elements of American Society — The Middle Class and Democracy — Difference Between the North and the South — Disappearance of an Idle Class in America — It Must Also Disappear in Europe — Lack of a Reason for Its Existence — It Can Never Fill the Need an Aristocracy Could — Advantages from Merging It with the Active Part of the Middle Class

Baltimore, October 8, 1835.
American society is composed of elements quite different from European society in general, and French society in particular. On analyzing the latter, we find in the first place the shadow of an aristocracy, made up of the wrecks of the great families of the old order that have been saved from the revolutionary storm and the descendants of the Imperial nobility who seem to be already separated from their fathers by centuries.

Next below this is a numerous middle class (*bourgeoisie*)

in two distinct parts: one, the active class, is engaged in commerce, manufactures, agriculture, and the liberal professions; the other, generally designated among us as idle, the *bourgeoisie oisive*, consists of men without active employment, landholders who derive an income of $500 or $1,500 from their estates by rents or by sharing the produce with the cultivator without attempting to increase it, and the small body of holders of public stock.

These two divisions of the middle class differ essentially from each other, the one laboring, the other only consuming and enjoying what they have. The one increases its means and consequently is able to keep itself above the waves and maintain, if not to raise, its level; the other, as M. Laffitte has said, transported by time into one stage of society after another, in each of which large additions are made to the general wealth, finds itself growing relatively poorer and must decrease in numbers. They differ no less in their origin; one belongs essentially to the commons; the other has some pretensions to nobility, being the offspring, or at least the heir and successor, of the country gentry. During the Restoration they differed also in their political views; one took the left side, the other preferred the right. At present, the former accepts the new dynasty without reluctance; the latter, more difficult to be satisfied in regard to the preservation of order and ready to take alarm at every violation of old established privileges, still preserves a secret preference for the legitimate line. In respect to religious sentiments, one is skeptical and prone to believe that the Voltairean philosophy and the theories broached by the Opposition during fifteen years are the *ne plus ultra* of the human understanding; the other, shaken in its faith, still keeps alive the sacred fire of religious feeling, rejects the disorganizing doctrines of the eighteenth century, and holds in scorn the lucubrations of the liberal publicists of the Restoration. One piques itself on its adherence to the positive, the material; the other concerns itself about the great conservative principles of society, but refuses to recognize the new interests which must be allowed to share in the privileges of those of the past.

These two sections of the middle class are not wholly and sharply separated from each other; they run into and across each other. A large proportion partakes somewhat of both characters and joins one side or the other, according to times and circumstances. Yet, although often confounded in the same individual, the two interests are, nevertheless, substantially distinct from each other. The base of the pyramid is occupied by peasants and workers subdivided into two sections: one which has property, the other which has not yet reached that point but aspires after it with eagerness. On one side, we have mechanics and small proprietors; on the other, laborers. Today it is universally recognized that the middle class rules in France. The aristocracy is driven from power or stands aloof. The mechanics and small proprietors hardly yet begin to raise their heads. The laborers are nothing.

In the Northern States of the American Union, society is much less complex in its composition than in France. Exclusive of the colored caste, there are here only two classes: the middle class and the democracy. Of the two conflicting interests, one only, labor, has a public existence here. The middle class consists of manufacturers, merchants, lawyers, physicians. A small number of cultivators and persons devoted to letters or the fine arts is to be added to these.

The democracy is composed of the farmers and mechanics. In general, the cultivator is the owner of the soil; in the West, this rule is without exception. Great landholders do not exist, at least as a class, in the North and the Northwest. There is strictly speaking no proletariat; although there are day laborers and, both in the cities and country, many workmen without çapital, yet these are in fact apprentices, for the most part foreigners, who in turn become proprietors and master-workmen and not infrequently rich manufacturers, wealthy speculators.

THE MIDDLE CLASSES

Between these two classes there is, however, no line of demarcation, for the attempts of some coteries to establish certain fashionable distinctions do not deserve notice, or at least have only a negative value as timid and often absurd protestations against the abuse of equality. The two classes have the same domestic habits, lead the same life, and differ considerably only in respect of the sect to which they are attached and the pews they occupy. One can get a sufficiently exact notion of the relations between these two classes by comparing them in France with the wealthy *bourgeoisie* and the wrecks of the aristocracy.

Political influence is at present entirely in the hands of the American democracy, just as with us it is monopolized by the middle classes. The latter have no chance of getting possession of power in the United States except temporarily, or by means of accidental divisions in the democratic ranks when they may rally to their standard a portion of the farmers and mechanics, as happened in 1834 after General Jackson's attack on the Bank. So in France it will be impossible for the aristocracy to raise, not its own banner (for it has none), but that of the legitimate line, unless the folly of the government should excite new troubles and inspire the middle class, who now support it heartily, with fears for the public security.

In the Southern States, the existence of slavery produces a state of society quite different from the North; half the population there consists of the proletariat in the strictest sense, that is of slaves. Slavery necessarily requires great landed property, which is aristocracy in fact. Great estates still continue to be held in the South despite the custom of equal partition, which has very much narrowed them.

Between these two extremes in the South, an intermediate class has sprung up consisting, like our middle class, of working men and men of leisure, the new interest and the old interest. Commerce, manufactures, and the liberal professions, on one side; on the other, the landholders, corresponding to our moderate country landholders, living on their estates by the sweat of their slaves, having no taste for work, not prepared for it by education, and even taking little oversight of the daily business of the plantation; men who would be incapable of applying themselves to any occupation if slavery were abolished, just as our proprietors would be unable to get a living if they were to be deprived of their estates.

It is plain that the equal partition of estates must have tended to increase the number of this class of men of leisure; it is numerous in the old Southern States, Virginia, the Carolinas, and Georgia, and also in Louisiana; the check which these States at first experienced in their career, while the North was advancing without a stop, and the contemporaneous increase of this class are two correlative facts which account for each other. But we do not find this class in the new States of the South. The new generation there, devoured as in the North with the passion of making money, has become as industrious as the Yankees. The cultivation of cotton offers a wide field of activity; in Alabama and Mississippi, cotton lands are sold at a very low price. The internal slave trade furnishes hands in abundance which are easily procured on credit when one has friends, but no patrimony. The sons of the old Southern States, instead of vegetating on a fragment of the paternal estate with a handful of Negroes, sell off their property at home, extend their means by aid of a loan which they are sure of being able to repay promptly, and go to the Southwest to establish a cotton plantation, a sort of agricultural factory, in which they are obliged to exercise more or less of the activity and to feel more or less of the hopes and fears of a manufacturer.

Thus the part of the middle class which works little or not at all is disappearing in the United States. In the Western States, which are the true New World, it no longer exists at all, North or South; you meet with no one there who is not engaged in agriculture, commerce, manufactures, the liberal professions, or the Church. The United States, then, differ from us in having no aristocracy, no idle middle class, no class of mere laborers, at the least in the North. But a distinction should be made in regard to the absence of these three classes; for while it may be admitted that the last two are becoming absolutely extinct, it would be more correct to say that the first has not yet begun to exist.

Civilization in its passage from one continent to the other has, then, got rid of two classes. This twofold disappearance is, however, only a single phenomenon or, at most, two phases of a single fact, the industrial progress of mankind. It seems to me inevitable that in this matter the Old World should follow the example of the New; it moves toward the same goal under the influence of causes of its own, irresistibly driven onward by what is commonly called the force of events, that is, by the decree of Providence.

There is a rule superior to all social conventions, codes of legislation, or systems of jurisprudence; it is that when a class has ceased to take part in the workings of society its doom is pronounced; it cannot preserve its privileges unless the march of civilization comes to a halt and is kept stationary, as it was in Rome from Augustus to Constantine; but when the column again sets forward, those who will not serve as soldiers and are unfit to be officers, those who can do duty neither in the ranks nor in command, who can act neither in the tent nor the field—all these are abandoned as stragglers and their names are struck from the roll. The law is inflexible and unsparing; no human power can rescue from their doom those whom it condemns; they only can save themselves by taking part in the general movement.

This explains the annihilation of the aristocracy in France. Between it and royalty, as between royalty and the English aristocracy, there was a long struggle, but the results were as different as the characters of the nations. In France, monarchical unity triumphed; Louis XI struck down the aristocracy; Richelieu muzzled it; Louis XIV obliged it to wear the collar. Thus reduced in a political point of view, it was left in possession of the field of taste and art which it devoted to the promotion of irreligion and corruption of manners. When, therefore, it was weighed in 1789, it was found wanting; the decree of destiny had gone forth and the revolution executed it with a cannibal ferocity. The unhappy aristocracy remembered its lofty nature only at the point of death; it mounted the scaffold with dignity.

For the same reason, the idle portion of the middle class tends toward its fall, for it accomplishes no purpose which cannot be effected without it. It does not enrich society by its labor, although it lays claim to be counted among the producers under the pretext that it holds the soil and exercises a sort of superintendence over its cultivation. The truth is that it is wholly ignorant of agriculture; it has received by tradition a certain routine, but the peasantry is as fully possessed of the tradition and needs no teachers on that matter. The proprietor is sometimes, indeed, paid in kind by the peasant and then sells the grain himself; but the peasant could easily attend to that business and would manage it quite as well as his landlord. Neither does this class serve as the representative of knowledge; in this respect, its acquisitions are limited to a little polite literature, an agreeable accomplishment surely, but not answering to the wants and spirit of the age.

Where a nobility exists and maintains its prerogatives, as in England, it performs a twofold office. In the first place, it devotes itself to the most difficult of all arts, that of governing men, and in this it excels; whether because it cultivates it by the traditions of experience or because it vigilantly recruits its ranks by enlisting in them such men as have already proved their superior knowledge of the different interests of society. This reason cannot be urged by our idle middle class as an argument for its preservation; it is notoriously ignorant of the science of government.

The second office of a nobility, not less essential than the first in our polished age, is to serve as a model and an example in the art of living, to teach the art of consuming, without which producing procures only partial and illusive gratification, and to encourage the fine arts. On this head nothing can be said in favor of the class alluded to. It excels neither in grace, nor elegance, nor address. The importance which it has acquired by the destruction of the aristocracy has been fatal to the old French politeness, to that exquisite courtesy on which our fathers prided themselves. Within the last fifty years, while the English have been improving in this respect much more successfully than their stiff and unpliant humor seemed to promise, we have forgotten much and unlearned much under the controlling influence of our middle class.

As for the art of consuming with grace and living well, as for care of the person the English call comfort—the only fraction of fine living the English are sensible of—our middle class has lessons to learn, but none to give. It is not, however, the fault of native qualities. No people has been gifted by nature with finer and more acute senses than ours. Surely our nerves are more sensitive, our ear and our palate more delicate than those of the English. Our superiority on these points is attested by the fact that from one end of the world to the other we are in possession of most of the trades which relate to the person; the office of cook, headdresser, dancing master, valet, or tailor is everywhere monopolized by the French. But to consume, to live well, to surround oneself with comfort in the English style or that more refined comfort which we the French can conceive, one must be rich. Now our middle class is poor, and politically considered this is one of its greatest faults; it grows poorer daily either by the operation of the law which commands the equal partition of estates or by that idleness which condemns it to a stationary income while public wealth and luxury are increasing all around it. It cannot, therefore, encourage the fine arts, for patronage of the arts is costly; besides, taste is growing rare in France since the fall of the aristocracy.

Nor can it be affirmed that the idle middle class in

France represents the element of order and that if it were to disappear France itself would perish in frightful convulsions. For the laboring class is already ripe for a better state of society and requires only the advantages of instruction, and of more favorable terms and more numerous opportunities for industry, to be in a condition to exercise all the rights of a citizen as usefully as the greater portion of the middle class. And even if the latter represents in whole or in part the element of order, it is only by the aid and the instrumentality of four hundred thousand bayonets, exclusive of those of the middle class itself, and thus it retains its predominance only by opposing the multitude to the multitude, a critical and dangerous position which cannot long be held, for the very bayonets are beginning to become intelligent.

The idle middle class has, then, only one course to take, that is, to pass into the ranks of the working men, to fit themselves to become the leaders of the people in its labors. When this is done, our fields which belong especially to their domain will change their aspect as if by enchantment and our peasants, who, it cannot be too often repeated, at present form the poorest and most numerous class in France, will be raised to a better condition which they deserve. The idle middle class must now, along with the government to which the first step in all great projects of improvement belong, become responsible for the progress of twenty-five million agricultural laborers.

In this change it has everything to gain. By this means it will maintain and reconfirm its own social rank, for it will thus recover the confidence of the mass and will turn its superiority to good account by exercising a beneficent patronage. It will exchange a straitened condition for wellbeing, or even wealth and the tedium of a life of inaction for the satisfaction of having done well, the consciousness of having faithfully performed a great duty. This honorable desertion of the standard of idleness for that of industry is now going forward daily. Let us rejoice at it: let us pray that it may speedily become universal, for there is no time to lose. Let us especially urge government to accelerate it by encouraging the development of industry, by all the means and aids that can improve the condition and resources of agriculture, and inspire the young generation of the middle class with a desire to devote themselves to this, the first of all arts.

XXXIII

Aristocracy

Authority Must Organize Itself in the United States — Authority Depends on Centralization and Hierarchy — Present Character of Authority in America — Representative Government, Become the Government of the Majority, Tends to Tyranny — Difference Between the South and the North — Aristocracies of Birth and of Talent — Both Co-existed in Ancient Societies — Forms of Aristocracy Among the Romans and the Greeks — Strong Organization of Feudal Aristocracy — Violent Reaction Against Nobility — Christianity Contributed to This Reaction — The Feudal System Stopped the Barbarians — Primogeniture Among the English Middle Class — Advantage of an Hereditary Aristocracy — Progress of the Sentiment of Family — Necessity of Balancing Innovating and Conservative Forces in Society — How to Obtain Stability Without Heredity — Difficulty Facing Immediate Abolition of Hereditary Aristocracy in Europe — Absolute Hereditary Privilege Irretrievably Weakened — Heredity in Office — Are Philosophical Objections Against Political Influence of Family Sentiment Undeniable? — Where Can the Elements of an Aristocracy Be Found in France? — How Can an Aristocracy Be Estab-

lished in the United States? — Germs of Aristocracy in the South — Dangers of American Society

Philadelphia, October 13, 1835. No great society can be durable except insofar as authority is established in it. We may easily imagine a case, however, in which authority may be momentarily eclipsed: when a great nation is in search of political and social forms suited to its needs; when it is obliged to pass from trial to trial, to feel its way and turn successively to different points; when, moreover, its separation from the rest of the world guarantees its independence and frees it from the necessity of organizing itself against the threat of attack from abroad; it is then allowed, it is even necessary, to provide for the greatest possible freedom of motion and cast off all unnecessary and unprofitable restraints. But still, a society without a fixed order and political ties is an anomaly, a passing phenomenon. The social bonds of opinion and religion, the only ones which exist here, cannot supply the lack of political ties unless they are tightened to such a degree as to become despotic. Besides, when large towns like New York, Philadelphia, and Baltimore have once grown up and there is a numerous floating population which opinion and religion cannot watch closely, manners and belief will have need of the firm support of the laws.

The serious character and frequent occurrence of disorders in the American Union at the present time prove that the period has come when it will be necessary for authority to be organized. There are interests in the South, for example, which are filled with alarm and which for want of legal protection protect themselves, right or wrong, in a brutal manner and feel the necessity of a power upon which they can rely for safety. In the middle class of the cities of the North, there is a population, enervated or rather refined by wealth, no longer ready to exercise that portion of self-government that consists in the suppression of violence by force; and among the democracy there is a restless and turbulent element which force alone can hold in check. These two classes, which are peculiar to the North and whose numbers daily increase, will soon be unable to live with each other without the intervention of power.

Authority has two bases upon which, to stand firm, it must be supported like man upon two feet; these are unity or centralization and the distinction of ranks. The corresponding bases of liberty are equality and independence. The spirit of unity or centralization is already beginning to appear in several of the United States.

It is not strictly correct to say that Americans have renounced the principle of authority because they have from the beginning adopted the principle of the sovereignty of the people. It is true that they understood it, at first, negatively, that is, as a simple denial of authority in the European sense, or of military power founded on conquest; but once the doctrine of equality had assured the democracy superiority over the middle class, the democracy gradually took upon itself the exercise of that sovereignty for its own interest, well or ill understood, at the dictation of its passions good or bad; here, then, was power in the full sense of the word, here was dictatorship, not indeed permanent and steady but showing itself by fits and starts. For most of the time it may be said to have slumbered and left the field free to individualism. It roused itself occasionally only to strike a decisive blow and to sink back again into its slumbers; but however irregular may have been its action, still here has been power, and power legal in its character and bold in its operations, gradually extending its sphere.

The New England States, which are the incarnation of the spirit of division and individualism, have advanced little in this direction. The old Southern States, although they have more of the spirit of centralization, have also shown themselves timid in this matter. The Middle States, and particularly New York, have made the greatest advance;

those of the West, and particularly of the Northwest, seem disposed to imitate them.

This centripetal power has operated in two ways. Negatively, it has set limits, and sometimes narrow ones, to the independence of personal action whether exercised singly by individuals or collectively by companies. It has, for example, reduced the privileges of incorporated companies in general and the railroad and banking companies in particular, or rather it has assumed to itself to be omnipotent in regard to them; at this moment, the democracy in the North is raising the hue and cry after all companies. It has imposed various restrictions upon commerce—for instance, the inspection laws relative to exported produce. Positively, it has interfered with the private transactions of individuals and suspended or annulled them; thus, in the West, *ex post facto* laws have been passed in favor of debtors; or the courts which refused to yield have been abolished in a body, as in Kentucky; or monopolies have been created and sold for the profit of the State, as in New Jersey. In recent years other measures of a more fundamental and comprehensive nature have been adopted, and the centralization of the schools, the means of communication, and the banks, the three institutions of the most vital importance in a society devoted to industry, has already begun. Thus the germ of a vigorous central authority which will embrace all the ruling interests of the country is already beginning to sprout. In this respect the North and the South, the East and the West, with the exception of New England, which is held back by its spirit of subdivision, seem to be unanimous.

If any danger is to be feared in the Northern States during the coming period it is not the absence, but the excess, of power. While the democracy in these States is jealous of military power, it seems to have become easy over legislative power. It refuses to appeal to arms, even for the suppression of the most brutal violence, but it is willing to use or abuse the omnipotence of popular representation, and it would not hesitate, in case it should be provoked by circumstances, to exercise it in the most tyrannical manner. Representative government loses the character of a compromise between different social interests and degenerates into an instrument of despotism in the hands of a numerical majority. In America, it had its origin in the concessions of the middle class to the democracy. At present the positions are reversed; the middle class now stands in need of concessions and does not seem likely to get them.

Instead of the physical tortures of the Inquisition, this despotism, if it gains strength and stability, would practice the most cruel moral tortures; it would have its Procrustean bed for intellect and wealth, its level for genius. Under pretense of equality it would establish the most fatal uniformity. As it would be exercised in turn by the changing favorites of the multitude, it would be eminently fickle and capricious, ever calling in question and unsettling all that was established; it would end by palsying the spirit of enterprise which has created the prosperity of the country.

In the Southern States, the white democracy has a pedestal, slavery. To realize its own elevation it is not obliged to be continually engaged in lowering the superior classes; it exercises its authority on what is beneath and thinks less of attacking what is over it. In the South, society is divided into masters and slaves; the distinction of higher and lower class is there of secondary importance, particularly at the present time, when the alarming state of their relations with the blacks obliges all whites to act in concert. In the South, moreover, slavery will soon oblige the local governments to maintain an armed police which, while it keeps down the slaves, will also serve to prevent the repetition of excesses by which this section of the Union has recently been sullied and prevent the imitation of those outrages on private property and public order of which the North has of late so frequently been the theater.

Centralization is one half of authority; distinction of ranks, the other half, cannot easily be supplied in the United States, particularly in the North, where, however, some institution must give stability and strength to authority. There are two sorts of aristocracy: aristocracy of birth and aristocracy of talents. I do not now speak of the aristocracy of money, for this has no chance of establishing itself and can acquire influence only by being merged in one of the other two.

All great societies which have existed up to this time have established with more or less solidity one or the other of these aristocracies or, to speak more correctly, both. An aristocracy of talents existed even in the bosom of the Egyptian and Hindoo castes; but Christianity first distinctly established an order of classification founded on intellect, not only in each nation, but throughout the Catholic Church; the Roman Catholic clergy was organized on this principle. It could not be otherwise; the unity of God and of the human race was an article of faith; for the Christian there was only one God, the Father of all men, before whom all distinctions of birth were as nothing.

But by the side of this aristocracy of intellect, all nations which have reached a lofty political elevation and founded durable empires have had an aristocracy of birth, a civil and military nobility. Among some few nations of antiquity, the nobility was composed of all free citizens, who were inferior in numbers to the slaves. Such were the republics of Greece, whose political superiority, however, was of short duration. Such were the Arabs, among whom, below the faithful, there were Christians and Jews. The nations which have had most weight in the balance of European civilization have been differently constituted; above the free citizens, they had a hereditary privileged class. Such was Rome; such is England; in the same way the empire of Islam was not solidly or firmly fixed until a handful of Turks was placed as a privileged class over the Arabs.

It is worthy of notice that the last of the great societies which have passed over the face of the earth, Christian society, or that in which the aristocracy of intellect was first fully developed, is also that in which aristocracy of birth has been most strongly marked. The sons of Japhet who gave the impulse and acted as leaders to this movement of civilization brought with them from the North a strong spirit of family, with which their political systems have been deeply impregnated; thus arose the most strictly hereditary nobility which has ever been seen. Till that time the hereditary system had been applied to caste; the Germans extended hereditary distinctions and functions to family, with the additional restriction of primogeniture. What before had been an exception in favor of royal families, they applied to all noble families. This organization, more or less modified, still prevails in most of the European states. Only yesterday it seemed as vigorous as ever in England. It is true that there it has conformed itself to the spirit of the age, that it has become pliant and elastic, opened its ranks to the aristocracy of intellect and consecrated its wealth and employed its privileges, not in gratifying its own caprices nor in satiating its passions, but in spreading all around it the network of a vast and beneficent patronage.

Today there is a violent reaction against hereditary distinctions and aristocracy of birth. On all points of the territory occupied by the Western civilization, the aristocracy of feudal origin has been battered down, here by the democracy, there by the middle class, and elsewhere by royalty. In the general league against it, the emperor of Russia gives his hand to the American democracy and the French *bourgeoisie,* and British democracy, in the person of O'Connell, is allied with the king of Prussia and the emperor of Austria.

The Christian version of the creation of the earth, which pictures God as pouring souls out of the reservoir of his own self without the father and mother decanting any part of themselves into the body of the infant—this doctrine implies a rebuke to the notion of an aristocracy of birth. Now today, all minds, even those most in rebellion against the Christian faith, exist without a doubt on the foundation of ideas put in circulation by Christianity. When modern philosophy points out to us that the chance of birth cannot be a title to social distinction, it is only drawing a logical deduction from the premises taught by Christ; modern philosophy is the continuation of the teachings of the fathers of the Church, except that what it calls chance Christianity calls Providence.

Whatever opinion we may entertain of the present value of aristocracy of birth, we are obliged to acknowledge that in the past it has rendered great service to the human race. But for the establishment of the feudal system, the barbarian hordes would have continued to drive over the face of Europe, tribe dashing against tribe, nation hurled against nation. The principal distinction between the Germans or Normans and the followers of Attila or Genghis Khan is that the former had the instinct of organization, manifested by their conception of the feudal system, and the latter were destitute of it. England is chiefly indebted to her aristocracy for her brilliant success. I do not regret the past, for our share of glory is still great, although France has been conquered by her rival in the field and in the cabinet and in every part of the world, in Europe, America, and Asia. Yet I may be permitted to say that if the French aristocracy had triumphed in its struggle with Richelieu, the destinies of the world might have been completely changed; and France, perhaps, would then have played the part which has fallen to the lot of England.

The right of primogeniture, extended beyond the limits of the aristocracy, ought not to be looked upon as a senseless imitation of the customs of the nobility by vain commoners. Although it may be difficult to defend this custom on the ground of equity, yet it has been one of the causes of the greatness of England. It is clear that it is favorable to the accumulation of capital in a few hands; now capital is, like man, powerful when united in masses, feeble when divided. England is indebted to the law of primogeniture for an ever-swarming army of younger sons eager to exercise their enterprise in the colonies and contented with their lot, whether because they readily obtain assistance from the head of the family, or because they are full of energy and know that by industry they will obtain wealth, or because they do not think that the world can be arranged on a different system. Meanwhile, the elder sons have formed an opulent metropolis which has given ample aid to its distant possessions in all emergencies and has gradually gained the supremacy in Europe.

But it would be madness to think of repairing the broken walls of feudalism, or to wish to copy in France or the United States English aristocracy, even with its mode of recruiting its ranks by those distinguished for merit and services; these orders of things have had their day. Yet all nations which aim to become or to remain powerful must have an aristocracy; that is to say a body which, whether hereditary or not, may preserve and perpetuate traditions, give system and stability to policy, and devote itself to the most difficult of all arts which everyone at the present day thinks he knows without having learned it, that of governing. A people without an aristocracy may shine in letters and art; but its political glory must be as transitory as a meteor.

I know not if I allow myself to be deceived by my admiration for the past, although I do not conceal from myself how much tyranny has been exercised over the great mass of mankind. But I cannot bring myself to believe that the hereditary principle, or, in more general terms, the sentiment of family, should be entirely excluded from the aristocratic part of the new social order which, although yet wrapped in uncertainty and mystery, is now struggling into existence on both sides of the Atlantic. The sentiment of family is not becoming extinct. Like all other social institutions the constitution of the family has undergone various changes since the beginning of recorded time. In earlier times everything was swallowed up in the father, and the individuality of the wife and children was the growth of successive ages; but through all these changes the family sentiment has gained rather than lost. If this progressive movement is not violently checked, the new institutions with which our civilization is now big must give a place in the political system to the family sentiment, and it is not easy to conceive how this can be done without a certain infusion of the hereditary principle.

It may be objected that in the United States family sentiment is much weaker than it is in Europe. But we must not confound what is merely accidental and temporary with the permanent acquisitions of civilization. The temporary weakness of family sentiment was one of the necessary results of the general dispersion of individuals by which the colonization of America has been accomplished; the effect must cease with the cessation of the temporary cause which produced it, that is, with the interruption of emigration to the West. As soon as they have their growth, the Yankees whose spirit now predominates in the Union quit their parents, never to return, as naturally and with as little emotion as young birds desert forever their native nest as soon as they are fledged; but the predominance of the Yankees, at least as they now are, does not seem to me destined to be perpetual; I do not see in them the ultimate and permanent type of the American.

Even among the Yankees themselves the family sentiment has maintained a strong hold by means of the Bible, the sanctity and strictness of the marriage tie, the ample powers left to the father in disposing of his property.

Within the three last centuries, forces of mobility have increased enormously in Western civilization. Manufactures and the press, the organ of philosophy and profane learning, have destroyed the balance between the opposing forces of innovation and conservation, the equilibrium of which is necessary to constitute order. These two new powers whose tendency is to reform everything have gained the advantage over the old powers of society and trampled down the twofold aristocracy of birth and talent, the nobility and the clergy. Must we, then, conclude that these two aristocracies, or even either of them, are stone dead; or must we not rather admit that order, that is to say the equipoise of the innovating and the conservative powers, cannot subsist unless authority is reconstructed in its ancient strength without, however, retaining the brutal traits of its former character? Is not this a reason that the hierarchy should be established at least as firmly as in past times? Although it need not borrow from the past the unyielding, inelastic, and absolute features of the old aristocracies. And is there any principle of stability and solidity comparable to that of hereditary transmission? One may be permitted, or rather obliged, to doubt it.

Systems of great stability have, doubtless, been organized without hereditary succession. The Catholic hierarchy offers the most complete example of this fact; it has now stood eighteen hundred years. But to produce this result it was necessary to root out the sentiment of family from the bosoms of its members by binding them to celibacy, and to substitute for the natural principle of stability that of hereditary succession, a merely artificial principle, and that of rigorous discipline and passive obedience. In a word, stability has here been obtained at the sacrifice of liberty.

The two powers of commerce and the press are especially disturbing and unsettling only because they are not yet regularly organized. They are susceptible of modification, of being restrained in their innovating tendencies so as to render the restoration of the conservative force in all its vigor less necessary. The industrial interest would certainly be less averse to the privileges of the lay aristocracy if it were permitted to participate in them, or if it had its own peculiar prerogatives. Learning, whose sword is the press, would have showed less antipathy toward the spiritual hierarchy had not the latter repulsed and rejected it. It is not impossible that we may be destined to witness a sort of industrial nobility; it is even possible that we may come by degrees in the course of time to entertain the question of a more or less complete monopoly of learning and the press under some form or another. Instead of throwing down the aristocracy, we might give it additional strength and stability by connecting it with learning and industry, which would then serve as its buttresses instead of becoming the instruments of its ruin. In such a system as this the aristocracy would be less compact and less exclusive; it would soar less loftily over the rest of mankind; but it would cover more ground, it would gain in breadth and length what it lost in height, and it would leave nothing beyond the reach of its influence. Equality would probably gain by this arrangement; but human independence would lose by it.

It would be idle to attempt to guess at the future forms which hierarchy may assume, to foresee the different interests of which society will hereafter be composed, or to name beforehand the institutions in which they will embody themselves. A multitude of combinations which no one can divine are possible. Many will take place, either successively in the same country or simultaneously in different countries. But two things appear to me to be certain: one of these is that we are about to see new social phenomena of great magnitude either in America or in Europe; and the other, that the sentiment of family cannot be ultimately and absolutely erased from politics.

For Europeans, the immediate and complete abolition of a hereditary aristocracy seems to me beset with the greatest difficulties. The nations of western Europe have received their laws and usages from the Germans and Romans, that is, from two stocks strongly impregnated with the sentiment of family; there is not an inch of their soil, a stone of their monuments, a line of their national songs, which does not awaken this sentiment by recalling this twofold origin. It seems, then, impossible that they should be ready to adopt at once a political system in which aristocracy was allowed no place or consideration. We may, however, be sure that the principle of hereditary succession must henceforth be limited within certain bounds. The idea of perpetuity, whether of punishment or of reward, is foreign to our age and will not, certainly, be more acceptable to future ages. We live much more than our fathers in the same space of time; the same number of years, therefore, represents a much greater duration than before. As soon as there are forever no more outcasts, then there will be no more eternal privileges. If aristocratic investiture were to endure for only a few generations, aristocracy would not cease to be the most coveted of privileges and the most stable of institutions; while the jealousy of the non-privileged classes would be less keen in regard to prerogatives if the nobility bore upon its front the inscription, "Dust thou art, and unto dust shalt thou return."

This, however, would not be enough. Aristocracy of birth requires a spur. To exercise the most important functions, it is not enough that one has taken the trouble to be born. There is something monstrous in the privilege of the English peerage, of being legislators by hereditary right. In the Middle Ages it was necessary to have gained one's spurs before one could gird on the sword and raise the banner of a knight. In Rome, birth made Patricians, but not Senators. Similar restrictions would be useful in all countries; they would be indispensable with people like the French and the southern Europeans.

Without doubt, the human spirit, or at least that part of public opinion which for a half century now has been accustomed to act as if it had a monopoly on wisdom, today rejects all distinction founded on the mere accident of birth. The logic of the day condemns it; the philosophy of the day abhors it. But the human spirit is not immutable. Sixty years ago mankind thought that hereditary privileges were legitimate, however loudly today it cries out against them as unjust and absurd. Then, as today, it held to a logic and a metaphysic which conformed to its political faith. Humanity has pursued its destiny oscillating first toward liberty, then toward authority, according to the needs of the moment. In this movement it sometimes loses sight completely of the general direction of its course and confuses it with the wake of what it has just left behind. In this case, and especially as it is about to come about on a new tack, it is impossible to define future tendencies by present ones. Moreover, philosophy cannot pretend to rule the world alone. Logic is only half of wisdom; the other half is experience. Our mind should curb its pride in the face of social necessities. When the mind obstinately denies facts because it cannot at all encompass them, the facts will brutally impose themselves on it. Besides, has it been shown that the objections of philosophers against heredity are sanctioned by positive science and that the abstraction made of education and first impressions, the most materialistic physiology, that is to say the most revolutionary, has given an irrevocable sanction to theories which are opposed to the ancient right of birth?

It is not easy to say where hereditary aristocracy in France is to be had, if we must really have one. A nucleus of old families or of military men around which new elements might group themselves would be lacking. Now, the old French nobility allowed itself to be degraded to the state of menials under Louis XIV and sank into the grossest debauchery under Louis XV. The trials of exile did nothing for those who escaped the revolutionary axe; when they reappeared among us they had forgotten nothing and learned nothing. The infusion of the military aristocracy of the Empire has not regenerated it. Is the withdrawal to which the old nobility has condemned itself since the Revolution of 1830 a retreat in which by meditation and repentance it is to renew its youth, or is it not rather a tomb in which it has buried itself forever? Will the old soil be heaved by earthquakes into new inequalities of surface? Have we among our peasants some unknown scions of the slayers of Caesar, or of the children of Brennus who will be revealed to the world by some mighty convulsions? Or will some Tartar horde from the North, the great hive of nations, put an end to our domestic quarrels, fix themselves in our palaces, seize our most fertile fields, wed our noblest, richest, and loveliest heiresses, and sword in hand proclaim to us: "The reign of lawyers is over, ours is begun."

If the United States must also constitute an aristocracy and provide political existence for the sentiment of family, their future would be yet more cloudy and uncertain than our own. The hereditary element of aristocracy has always come from conquest or, at least, has supported itself by alliance or compromise with the sword of the conqueror. How can there be a conquest in the United States? It is possible that they may conquer Mexico, but they cannot be conquered by it. It cannot be supposed that some red Alexander or Charlemagne from the distant steppes of the West, heading the fierce tribes of the Pawnee braves and dragging in his victorious train swarms of rebellious Negroes, can ever become the founder of a military dynasty and aristocracy. If the Union should ever be dissolved and the hardy sons of the West, pouring down from the Alleghenies, should ever conquer the people of the North, enervated by luxury and enfeebled by anarchy, and those of the South, weakened by servile wars, still no germ of a hereditary aristocracy would exist in such a conquest; for the victors and vanquished would be all of the same family.

The Southern States, however, are already organized on the principle of hereditary aristocracy. It is true that the privileged class is so numerous that, unless privilege is established within privilege, they do not form an aristocracy properly speaking; but the fear of a rising of the blacks keeps the whites closely united and forces them to submit at every sacrifice to a vigorous organization of authority. The relative situation of the whites and blacks admits of no hesitation.

It is evident that the establishment of a hierarchy possessing any stability would be most difficult in the States without slaves and that the elevation of the sentiment of family to political power in some form would there encounter the most vigorous resistance. In the maritime

States north of the Potomac, the difficulty would seem to be insurmountable. These States contain large towns with an extensive commerce carried on by great houses, great factories in the English style, powerful trading, financial, and manufacturing companies, that is to say the germs of an extreme inequality; yet their laws consecrate a system of absolute equality, and the sovereign democracy shows itself resolved to maintain it at all costs. Between these two struggling forces a battle is going on and cases might be imagined in which the contest may assume a terrible character. If any cause were to interrupt the prosperity of these States; if, by means of disunion, which however is daily becoming less and less probable, the markets of the South were to be shut against their merchants and manufacturers; if the sons of the farmers and their hired workmen could no longer have access to the lands and growing cities of the West; if, to crown their misery, a foreign war should blockade their harbors—they would be exposed to the most frightful convulsions. The Northern States, then, must remain indissolubly wedded to the Union of the States and firmly devoted to the policy of peace with the European monarchies.

If, then, it were proved that there was an irresistible necessity for a distinction of ranks in every society, and that the principle of inheritance or sentiment of family must be one of the constituent principles of a privileged class which is needed to form the apex of the social pyramid, it must be acknowledged that the prospect of the North is more dark and alarming than that of the South. By the exercise of unyielding vigilance over the slaves, the South may continue to maintain the outward forms of a regular social system. It would, indeed, be a retrograde system, for morally it would be a copy of the ancient order of society which had its day before the advent of the Christ, patched up with the improved material order of modern times; it would be despotism, but an orderly, organized despotism which after all would be a less terrible scourge than the anarchy which threatens the North.

Nevertheless, whatever may be the destiny of aristocracy and the political fate of family sentiment, I am loath to believe that all that energy and intelligence which I have witnessed in the Northern States of the Anglo-American Union can be swallowed up and lost. No deductions of logic can force me to conclude that a society superior to any that has yet flourished in our ancient continent will not one day, and that soon, exist in the fine regions on the east and the west of the Alleghenies, around the wide basin of the Great Lakes and along the far-stretching banks of these mighty rivers. It cannot be that a superior race has transported its children to these shores to devour each other. If, on the one side, American civilization seems to be exposed to formidable dangers, it presents itself in other points of view with strongly marked features of permanency and stability. If great perils surround its cradle, is it not the cradle of an infant Hercules?

XXXIV

Democracy

Burden of the Past on Old Societies — Difficulty of Reforms in Old Countries — Ease of Innovation in New Countries — Advantages Possessed by Americans for Making Social Experiments — The American Worker and Farmer Has Been Initiated — Absence of the Vulgar Herd — The Laboring Classes in the United States Are Superior to Those of Other Countries — Defects of American Democracy — Analogy to the Romans — Superiority of the Educated Classes in Europe — The Respective Merits, Present and Future, of America and Europe

DEMOCRACY

New York, October 22, 1835.

Our old European societies have a heavy burden to bear; it is that of the Past. Each age is responsible for those that have gone before it and imposes a similar responsibility on those which follow it. We are paying interest on our fathers' errors; we pay it in the first place in the form of the public debt; we pay it also in the charges for the support of our fine army, for among the causes which oblige all Europe to keep the flower of its population under arms we must reckon the animosities of our fathers. We pay it, and at a higher rate, in all those habits of distrust and suspicion which have been bequeathed to us from times of anarchy and despotism. The accumulated weight of a long Past must, indeed, be an insupportable burden, since the Roman empire, first in Rome and afterward in Constantinople, where it moved to escape the load, crumbled and sank beneath it. All nations which have been the glory of the world have been ground to a lifeless dust, like the ashes of tombs, by the pressure of a Past which hemmed them in on every side. Will the Europe of our age undergo the fate of its predecessors? There is reason to hope that it will be more fortunate; for, having their example before its eyes, it must be wiser than they, and it is at the same time more elastic in its temper and more flexible in its forms.

One of my friends, some time ago, visiting the great ironworks of Crawshay & Company, in Wales, was struck with the fact that the numerous railroads connected with the works were constructed on an old and very imperfect system. He asked why, observing that the saving in traction would pay the expense of a reconstruction with improved rails. "Nothing is more just," he was told, "but we retain our old flat rails and shall for a long time because it would take two or three years to make a change; in the meanwhile, it being impossible to keep the wagons running on both rails at the same time, we should have to stop operations and leave fifty thousand workmen without work and without bread. The difficulty is merely in the transition, but at present it seems to be insurmountable." So it is in regard to society. It is easy to see that one system has decided advantages over another and that if society could be transported from one to the other by a wave of the wand, much would be gained; but between the two there is a great gulf. How can it be passed? How is it possible to convince vested right to cross to the other side, where nothing is guaranteed? How overcome the opposition of the privileged class who resist change? How check the impatience of the multitude, eager to enter into the enjoyment of the benefits which it expects to find on the other shore?

In regard to social reforms the question is wonderfully simplified by merely transplanting it, that is, by going into new countries to resolve it. The old country is then abandoned to old interests and old ideas and one begins over again disengaged and unembarrassed, ready to undertake everything and disposed to try everything. The emigrant has left behind in the mother country a thousand associations and relations which surround existence and give it, if you please, its ornaments and its charm, but which also tend to check its activity and make society slow to answer the demands for reform. The first of all innovations is the change of soil, and this necessarily involves others. Vested rights do not emigrate; they are bound to the old soil; they know no other and no other knows them. Privileges which are respected because they are consecrated by time do not venture upon new soil, or if they hazard the trial they cannot become acclimated there. A colony is like a besieged city; each one must serve with his person; each one passes only for what he is worth personally. In a society which has no Past, the Past counts for nothing.

It is to be remarked, therefore, that projects of social reform, conceived in the bosom of established societies in which opportunity is afforded for the calm exercise of thought, have generally been obliged to cross to other shores and take root in barbarous lands in order to be carried into execution and to be embodied under the form of a new society. Civilization has advanced from the East toward the West, increasing in vigor at every remove, although the founders of new colonies have generally quitted a more civilized country for a barbarous one. Thus Italy and Greece, daughters of Asia and Egypt, have gone beyond their mothers; thus western Europe has eclipsed the glories of Greece and Rome. Soon after having given birth to new nations, the old ones have perished violently, or have fallen into an obscurity worse than death merely from a want of will or energy to apply to their own needs the principles which gave vigor to their offspring, principles of a new social order, founded on the wider extension of liberty and the greater diffusion of privileges.

Providence had done much to prepare the European races, transported across the Atlantic, for becoming the founders of great and powerful nations. The Anglo-Americans, who were the last comers and did not arrive until after the Spaniards had established their dominion over equinoctial and southern America, left the Old World only after it had been aroused and agitated by the intellectual revolution of which Luther was the Mirabeau and of which in England Henry VIII was the Robespierre and the Napoleon. This great event had already sown those seeds in the human breast which were to swell and expand through succeeding ages. England was already big with those habits of industry and order which were destined to make her the first nation of the Old World in the sphere of industry and in political greatness. Her children, therefore, carried with them the germ of those principles and institutions which were to secure to them the same supremacy in the New. They embarked—at least this was the case with those New England pilgrims, the fathers of the Yankees—after having undergone the ordeal of fire and water, after having been seven times tried between the sledge and the anvil, between persecution and exile. They arrived wearied of political quarrels and bent on devoting their energies to pacific and useful purposes.

They settled in a climate which differed little from that of their native skies. Thus they escaped the danger of becoming enervated by the influence of a warm and balmy atmosphere, like that in which the fiery spirits of the Castilian race were tamed; they landed on an almost uninhabited shore and had only a few poor tribes of Redskins for enemies and neighbors, while the Spaniards had to contend with the numerous armies of the brave Aztecs in Mexico and their successors, the Creoles, then had to keep in check on one side the Comanches and Indians of the North, on the other the Araucans of the southern Cordilleras. If the English had encountered a numerous population like that which resisted Cortez, they would have had to conquer it, and doubtless they would have succeeded in doing so; but after the victory they would have been obliged to keep it in subjection, and the yoke of the English race is harder than that of the Spaniards. Their social organization would then have been founded on the servitude of inferior castes, red and mixed; the new society would have been tainted with a deep-seated disease which would have reduced it to a much lower state than European society, to the level of ancient communities which were founded on personal slavery. It is not, indeed, completely free from this taint at present, since Negroes have been brought into the country and twelve States out of twenty-four are defiled with the pollution of slavery. The portion of the country which has been left for the pure white race is, however, ample enough to receive a large community composed of materials the same as Europe and affording great facilities for combining them in a better order.

If they had found powerful enemies to combat, if war had been constantly hanging over their heads, they would have been obliged to submit themselves to a military aristocracy, despite the instinct for self-government and independence which runs in British veins and of which they had a double share. In that case, Anglo-American society would have been only a copy, and an inferior copy of the

English; as the Canadians, for example, were merely an imitation of the French under the old order of things. The English colonists sometimes had to repel the attacks of the French, who had possession of the West and of the basin of the St. Lawrence; but after the capture of Quebec they found themselves completely delivered from the most momentous public charge, that of defending their territory and their independence. They were, therefore, able to dispense with a military establishment, to turn all their thoughts and energies to their domestic concerns, and to devote themselves exclusively to the work of colonization. They ceased to stand in need of English guardianship, and they freed themselves from it that they might expand and take their own course without let or hindrance. Finally, yielding to their natural impulse, they tried their great democratic experiment, which is already shedding such a brilliant light upon the prospect of improvement in the condition of the lower classes in all countries. From these circumstances and influences has resulted a new political and physiological phenomenon, a hitherto unknown variety of the human race, inferior to the English and French types in many respects, particularly in taste and philosophy, but superior to the rest of the human family by its extraordinary combination of sagacity, energy of will, and hardy enterprise, by its admirable aptitude for business, by its untiring devotion to work, and above all by its recognition and protection of the rights of the laboring classes, hitherto treated as the offscourings of society.

It seems, then, that the Americans are called to continue the series of that succession of progressive movements which have characterized our civilization ever since it quitted its cradle in the East. This people will become the founders of a new family, although perhaps the features which now predominate will hereafter cease to be its foremost traits; while the Spanish-Americans seem to be an impotent race which will leave no posterity behind it unless, by means of one of those inundations which are called conquests, a current of richer blood from the North or the East shall fill its exhausted veins.

An eminent philosopher, M. Ballanche, who is an honor to the French name, defines the progress of the human race in its slow and majestic pilgrimage round our globe by the term *initiation*. Following out this thought, we may pronounce North America, at least the non-slaveholding States, to be already in advance of us, for in many respects what among us is accessible only to a small number of the elect has become common property in the United States and is familiar to the vulgar. The conquests of the human mind to which the Reformation gave the signal, and the impulse and the great discoveries of science and art which in Europe are yet concealed from the general eye by the bandage of ignorance and the mists of theory, are in America exposed to the vulgar gaze and placed within the reach of all. There the multitude touches and handles them at will. Examine the population of our rural districts, sound the brains of our peasants, and you will find that the spring of all their actions is a confused medley of biblical parables with the legends of gross superstition. Try the same operation on an American farmer and you will find that the great scriptural traditions are harmoniously combined in his mind with the principles of modern science as taught by Bacon and Descartes, with the doctrine of moral and religious independence proclaimed by Luther, and with the still more recent notions of political freedom. He is one of the initiated.

Among us the powerful instruments and machinery of science and art, the steam engine, the balloon, the voltaic pile, the lightning rod, inspire the multitude with a religious dread. In France, out of a hundred peasants in the back areas of our provinces you will not find one who, having witnessed their effects, would dare to lay his hand upon them; they would fear to be struck dead like the sacrilegious wretch who touched the ark of the Lord. But to the American, on the contrary, these are all familiar objects; he knows them all by name, at least, and he feels that they are his.

To the French peasant they are mysterious and terrible beings, like the Negro's fetish or the Indian's manitou, but to the cultivator of the western wilds they are what they are to a member of the Institute, tools, instruments of labor or science; again, therefore, he is one of the initiated.

There is no *profanum vulgus* in the United States, at least among the whites. This is true not only in regard to steam engines and electrical phenomena, but the American multitude is also much more completely initiated than the European mass in all that concerns domestic relations and the household. The marriage tie is held more sacred among the lowest classes of American society than among the middle class of Europe. Although the marriage ceremony has fewer forms than among us and the connection is more easily dissolved, cases of adultery are extremely rare. The unfaithful wife would be a lost woman; the man who should seduce a woman or be known to have an illicit connection would be excommunicated by the popular clamor. In the United States, even the man of the laboring class is more completely initiated in the obligations of the stronger sex toward the weaker than most men of the middle class in France. Not only does the American mechanic and farmer spare his wife as much as possible all the hard work and employment unsuitable to the sex, but he exhibits toward her and every other woman a degree of attention and respect which is unknown to many persons among us who pride themselves on their education and refinement. In public places and in public conveyances in the United States, no man, whatever may be his talents and his services, is treated with any particular attention; no precedence or privilege is allowed him; for all men are equal. But a woman, whatever may be the condition and fortune of her husband, is sure of commanding universal respect and attention.

In political affairs, the American mass has reached a much higher degree of initiation than the European mass, for it does not need to be governed; every man here has in himself the principle of self-government in a much higher degree and is more fit to take a part in public affairs. It is also more fully initiated in another order of things which is closely connected with politics and morals, that is, in all that relates to labor. The American mechanic is a better workman; he loves his work more than the European. He is initiated not merely in the hardships but also in the rewards of industry; he dresses like a member of Congress; his wife and daughters are dressed like the wife and daughters of a rich New York merchant and like them follow the Paris fashions. His house is warm, neat, and comfortable; his table is almost as plentifully provided as that of the wealthiest of his fellow citizens. In this country, articles of *the first necessity* for whites embrace several objects which among us are articles of luxury, not merely among the lower but among some of the middle classes.

The American mass is more deeply initiated in what belongs to the dignity of man, or at least to its own dignity, than the corresponding classes in Europe. The American worker is full of self-respect; and he shows it not only by an extreme sensibility, by pretensions which to the European *bourgeoisie* would appear extraordinary, and by his reluctance to make use of the term *master* for which he substitutes that of *employer,* but also by good faith and scrupulous exactness in his engagements; he is above those vices of slavery, such as theft and lying, which are so prevalent among hirelings with us, particularly among those of the towns and their factories. The French worker is more respectful and submissive in his manners, but, hard-pressed by poverty and surrounded by temptations, he rarely neglects a chance of cheating his *bourgeois* when he can do it with impunity. The worker of Lyons secretly steals silk, that of Rheims, gold lace. There are, doubtless, frauds committed in America; more than one smart fellow has his conscience oppressed with numerous peccadilloes. How many strolling Yankee peddlers have sold charcoal for indigo and soapstone for soap to the rural housewives! But in the

United States these petty frauds are rare exceptions. The character of the American workman is to a high degree honorable and excites the envy of the European when the latter compares the prospect here with the aspect of things in his own country.

What I have said about the worker applies still more strongly to the farmer; not being obliged like the worker to argue every day with an employer over the price of his labor, surrounded by equals, and a stranger to the seductions of the city, the American farmer possesses the good qualities of the worker in at least an equal degree and has his faults in a much less degree. He is less unjust toward, and less jealous of, the richer or more cultivated classes.

If, then, we examine the condition of the American multitude, we find it on the whole much superior to that of the mass in Europe. It is true that it appears to be almost completely destitute of certain faculties which are possessed by the European populace. There are, for instance, at times a hundredfold more gleams of taste and poetical genius in the brain of the most beggarly *lazzarone* of Naples than in that of the republican mechanic or farmer of the New World. The houseless young vagabonds of Paris have transient flashes of chivalric feeling and greatness of soul which the American worker never equals. This is because the national character of the Italians is impregnated with a love of art and because generous sentiments are one of the distinguished traits of the French character; the very lowest classes of each nation have some portion of the national spirit. But it does not belong to the multitude to be poets and artists in Italy, or models of chivalry in France. Their perfection, above all and in every country, consists in knowing and fulfilling their duties to God, to their country, to their families, to themselves, in assiduous and honest industry; in being good citizens, good husbands, and good fathers; in providing for the welfare and guarding the virtue of those dependent upon them. In order to make a fair comparison between the multitude in Europe and the multitude in America, we should consider them in reference to these qualities; for these belong to all varieties of the human race and all forms of civilization, and upon their development and stability among the mass depends the strength of empires.

To render the parallel between the two hemispheres perfect, it would be necessary to set against the mechanic and the farmer in the United States the members of a corresponding class among a people of Teutonic origin, language, and religion—that is, the English worker and farmer. European civilization, setting aside the Slavs, who have recently appeared with brilliant success upon the stage, divides itself into two branches, that of the North and that of the South, one Teutonic the other Latin, distinguished by different qualities and tendencies. American society, being a scion of one of these branches, can be more readily compared with it than with any of the offshoots of the other. It is easy, therefore, to determine the superiority of the American mechanic and farmer to those of England, but it is difficult to decide how much inferior or superior any class of American society is to the corresponding Spanish, Italian, or French class; it is only necessary, however, to open one's eyes to be convinced that the multitude among these three people are far from having reached, in the direction in which nature points their career, the same degree of progress that the Americans have done in theirs.

American democracy certainly has its faults, and I do not think that I can be accused of having extenuated them. I have not concealed its rude demands upon the higher classes, nor its haughty airs of superiority to other nations. I will even admit that in many respects it is rather as a class and in the lump that it recommends itself to favor; the individuals that compose it are destitute of those hearty and affectionate qualities by which our French peasantry would be distinguished if it were once delivered from the wretchedness which now brutalizes it; but it is in the mass and as a whole that I now judge the American multitude.

DEMOCRACY

The American democracy is imperious and overbearing toward foreign people; but is not a keen sensibility a good quality rather than a defect in a young nation, as in a young man, provided that it is backed by an energetic devotion to a great work? Pride is ridiculous in an enervated and inert people, but in an enterprising, active, vigorous nation, it is consciousness of power and confidence in its high destiny. The foreign policy of the American democracy is profoundly egoistic because national ambition is the characteristic of a growing nation. Cosmopolitanism is generally a symptom of decline, as religious tolerance is a sign of the decay of faith. The pretensions of the United States are unbounded: they aspire to sovereignty over South America; they covet one by one the provinces of Mexico; but in spite of the rules of morality, it is might which makes right in the relations between people and people. If the United States should wrest the Mexican provinces from the Spanish race, partly by craft and partly by force, they would be responsible to God and to man for the consequences of the robbery; but they would not be alone in their guilt. If the country which they had seized flourished in their hands, posterity would pardon the act; but, on the other hand, it would condemn the Mexicans if, with such neighbors at their doors, they should continue as at present to stagnate in stupid security and in a miserable lethargy; and it would condemn also the powers of Europe if they neglected to warn them and to rouse them from their torpor.

The Romans were intolerably arrogant toward other people; they spoke to the all-powerful sovereigns of the monarchical East and to the heirs of Alexander the Great that brutal and imperious language which General Jackson has flung into the face of a monarchy of fourteen centuries. They treated all who stood in the way of the gratification of their insatiable thirst for conquest as slaves who had revolted against the divine will. That Punic faith which they charged against the memory of their rivals was often the only faith they practiced. Posterity, however, has proclaimed them the greatest people of history because they were successful; that is, because they formed a durable empire out of conquered nations by the wisdom of their laws. The Anglo-Americans have much resemblance to the Romans, whether for good or for evil. I do not say that they are destined to become the masters of the world; I merely mean to affirm that, by the side of faults which shock and offend foreign nations, they have great powers and precious qualities which should rather attract our attention. It is by these that posterity will judge them; by these they have become formidable to other people. Let us aim to get the advantage of them, not by denouncing their defects to the world, but by endeavoring to make ourselves masters of their good qualities and their valuable faculties and by cultivating and developing our own. These are the surest means of maintaining our rank in the world in spite of them and in spite of all.

At the same time that the American democracy conducts itself more and more haughtily abroad, it is jealous of all who fall under the suspicion of seeking to encroach upon its sovereignty at home. In this, it only imitates the most boasted of aristocracies. The system which it has pursued toward the higher classes is dictated by the instinct of self-preservation, just as the European aristocracy and middle class has acted instinctively toward the classes below them. The democracy is determined to lose none of its conquests which have been gained, not by plundering its neighbors, not by pillaging provinces, not by robbing travelers, but by the sweat of its brow, by its own resolute industry. Who, then, among us will cast the first stone? I can readily conceive that, at first sight, we of the middle class in Europe should be offended by its pretensions and that we should feel our sympathy excited by the spectacle of our American fellows conquered and bound. But let us, nevertheless, confess that this democracy has managed the affairs of the New World in such a manner as to justify the supremacy it has won and to excuse its jealousy toward everything that might have a tendency to spoil it of its conquest. This is the first time since the origin of society that the people have fairly enjoyed the fruits of their labor and have shown themselves worthy of the prerogatives of manhood. Glorious result! Even though it has been obtained by the temporary humiliation of the classes with which our education and habits lead us to sympathize, it is the duty of every good man to rejoice at it and to thank God for it!

Woe to tyranny by whomsoever exercised! Far be it from me to apologize for the brutal and savage and sometimes bloody excesses which have lately been so often repeated in most of the large towns in the United States! Should they continue, the American democracy will be degraded and will lose forever the high position it now occupies. But criminal as these acts are, it would be unjust to impute them to the American people and to condemn to ignominy the whole body of these incomparable laborers. Popular excesses in all countries are the work of an imperceptible minority, which the existing system in the United States is powerless to restrain. That system needs, then, some amendment which shall enable it to preserve the good qualities of the nation in their purity and which, indeed, seems already on the point of being introduced, for theories of absolute liberty are evidently losing favor in the United States.

It would be a mistake to infer from what has been said that American civilization is superior to our own. The multitude in the United States is superior to the multitude in Europe; but the higher classes in the New World are inferior to those of the Old, although the merits of the latter are more virtual than real and belong rather to the past or the future than to the present; for the higher classes in Europe, both aristocracy and *bourgeoisie*, turn their good qualities to little account either on behalf of themselves or the people. The higher classes in the United States, taken as a whole and with only some exceptions, have the air and attitude of the vanquished; they bear the mark of defeat on their front. As they have been always and in almost all circumstances much mingled with the crowd, both parties have naturally borrowed many habits and feelings from each other. This exchange has been advantageous to the multitude but less so to the higher classes. The golden buckler of the Trojan has been exchanged for the leather shield of the gallant Diomed. Each of the two is, therefore, superior in one of the two great elements of society and inferior in the other. This is the system of compensation.

If, then, from the superiority of the laboring classes in the United States, it were necessary to draw a conclusion as to the relative rank of European and American civilization in the future, the following would be the only necessary inference: for American society to have the advantage of ours, it would be necessary for it to establish classes which, without being a copy of our aristocracy and middle class, would be in essence and appearance as much elevated above the people, properly so called, as our higher classes are above the great mass of our population; or, in opposite terms, it depends upon us to give our social order the advantage over the United States by raising our rural and urban lower class from the ignorance and brutal degradation in which they are plunged and by developing their powers and qualities in conformity with our national disposition and the character of our race.